The
AMA
Handbook for Developing Employee Assistance and Counseling Programs

The AMA Handbook for Developing Employee Assistance and Counseling Programs

Dale A. Masi, Editor

amacom

American Management Association

This publication is designed to provide accurate and authoritative
information in regard to the subject matter covered. It is sold with
the understanding that the publisher is not engaged in rendering
legal, accounting, or other professional service. If legal advice or
other expert assistance is required, the services of a competent
professional person should be sought.

Library of Congress Cataloging-in-Publication Data

The AMA handbook for developing employee assistance and counseling
programs / Dale A. Masi, editor.
    p.   cm.
  Includes bibliographical references and index.
  ISBN 0-8144-0107-4
  1. Employee assistance programs—United States.   I. Masi, Dale A.
II. American Management Association.
HF5549.5.E42A53   1992
658.3'82—dc20   91-40067
                                                          CIP

Printing number

10   9   8   7   6   5   4   3   2   1

With love to **Tyler** and **Janice Masi.** Tyler, the most recent addition to the family, born January 15, 1991, will spend his entire work life as part of Workforce 2000. Janice represents the modern American woman: wife, mother, professional, and—best of all to the editor—magnificent daughter-in-law.

Contents

Acknowledgments

I thank all of the contributing authors to this book, who kept to the deadlines and cooperated so willingly. Some of them I have never met, but I look forward to doing so; I already feel that I know each of them. Peverly Reyes, in my office, was always patient in maintaining the paperwork for the manuscript. Finally, my research associate, Robin Masi, was my alter ego. She monitored the progress, held us all in line, and was most thoughtful in critiquing the material. It was a joy working with her.

Introduction

In 1989, the Department of Labor issued *Investing in People Workforce 2000,* a document that detailed the emerging crisis in the American workplace. It stated that as a result of decreasing demographic trends, changes in technology, and the growing of international competition, the competitive economic position of the United States could greatly shrink in the coming century. In fact, according to the Department of Labor, the problem has already begun; it is manifested in an unparalleled demand for highly skilled workers that cannot be met because of a diminishing pool of qualified workers from which to draw; moreover, these shortages are likely to increase over the years. Simultaneously, and ironically, many low-skilled workers are having great difficulty finding employment.[1]

Whether the United States will be a force in determining the course of the twenty-first century largely depends on how it responds to the economic challenges set out in *Workforce 2000*. For the first time in centuries, the United States has formidable economic competitors: the European economic community and the Far East. The United States now stands at the crossroads: one way leads to a strong voice in the international world, higher standards of living, and increased productivity; the other leads to economic decline.

As *Workforce 2000* states:

> Eliminating the skills gap and enhancing our nation's competitive position will require a substantial, ongoing national commitment to investment in human resources. To be effective, such a commitment must be based on a shared vision of our nation's potential.
>
> This country has always been willing to commit enormous energy and resources in times of short-run emergencies such as those posed by wars or domestic financial crisis. When danger is imminent, the urgency is obvious. It is always more difficult to make long-run commitments in response to long-run threats. Today, we require a vision to inspire a national strategy of sustained investment in human resources over the next decade. Such a strategy will shape both our economic future and our position in the community of nations for many decades to come.[2]

In order for American companies to grow while meeting these challenges, they must consider the factors changing the work force and adapt their human resources approach accordingly. Among the factors are that in the 1990s there will be 6 million fewer teenagers to draw into the labor pool than in the 1980s, that almost all women will be in the work force (with the exception of a few months or years when they are raising children), and that illiteracy rates are rising. (Figure I-1 indicates the expected composition of the work force by the year 2000.) In addition, the U.S. economy has moved from one built primarily around manufacturing to one of service, a change that requires workers to have a certain level of basic skills. This puts other pressures on human resources managers to develop alternative programs such as career counseling and literary training. These events are forcing corporations to reexamine and make dramatic changes in the human resources area.

James E. Killey, chief executive officer of Towers Perrin, a nationally known benefits consulting firm, recently warned business executives that:

> Developing their company's "human capital" in the future will become at least as important as developing new technologies or mergers and acquisition strategies in terms of competing in world markets. Perhaps for the first time in the history of American business, "human capital" is becoming an asset as vital to corporate survival as physical capital and financial assets.[3]

Companies can no longer afford to ignore their employee resource packages while their competitors outdo them in terms of benefits, perks,

Figure I-1. The new work force: what's ahead in the year 2000.

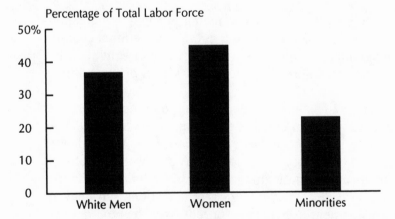

Source: Bureau of Labor Statistics, Office of Projections.

and incentives. They must now show concern for employees' family and individual needs, as well as provide competitive salaries.

This book is a practical handbook designed for human resources professionals to assist them in implementing various human resources programs to meet the needs of Workforce 2000. It covers the full range of relevant workplace programs, including performance evaluation, relocation counseling, health promotion, and elder care services.

Human resources managers should be expected to counsel in human resources matters. Thus, in many cases they should be able to run the programs described here themselves, providing counseling on and training in such areas as performance reviews, career development, health promotion, and retirement. However, many HR programs require specialists with expertise and skills specific to their subject area. It is essential that HR managers know where to find such specialists—not necessarily to take the job on themselves. Employee assistance programs, AIDS-related programs, and child care are examples of such programs that may require an "outsider." In some cases, outsiders may help the HR professionals set up programs they can then run themselves.

This book is a contributed work. To offer readers the most concise, accurate, and practical information, all of the authors are well-known specialists in their fields. This is the first major work encompassing all such programs provided in the workplace. Although individual books have been written on each subject, HR specialists need one resource that is inclusive and comprehensive yet realistic in its presentation of key development strategies.

This book is intended for CEOs (including those of small companies), benefits managers and other key department managers, and HR professionals in both the public and private sectors. Additional audiences include labor union negotiators, university professors (especially in schools of business), health care managers, and professionals who offer counseling. The chapters provide practical steps in designing, implementing, and evaluating programs.

Chapter 1, **Employee Assistance Programs,** describes how employers can adapt their company's EAP to its changing work force. It is estimated that 20 percent of any work force is affected by personal problems that can have an impact on job performance and productivity. This chapter shows that a company that implements and consistently evaluates an EAP can greatly reduce its financial costs, costs associated with liabilities to the company. Essential ingredients of an EAP are given, and relevant forms and sample material are included.

Chapter 2, **Performance Review,** introduces the concept of training supervisors and managers to communicate effectively to employees about their performance. Performance counseling, an excellent tool for realizing all employees' full potential, can be used in conjunction with or in addition to the employee's annual review.

Chapter 3, **Career Development and Growth**, explores the issues surrounding counseling employers to attain personal career goals while remaining within the company. It has been found that over two-thirds of all corporate managers and executives go through the processes of career exploration and change at least once in their career, with the assistance of private individual counselors, career counseling firms (which also provide placement services), or their own corporations. Companies that provide career development counseling hope that they will benefit from employees who stay with them and grow professionally. A wide range of career counseling and skill retraining programs are examined in the chapter.

Chapter 4, **Health Promotion,** looks at a variety of health promotion and illness prevention campaigns, including health counseling, medical programs, smoking cessation, exercise and fitness, substance abuse prevention and treatment, and nutritional education for employees and their families. It describes how corporations can design their own programs or purchase packaged programs from vendors with successful track records. Defining health broadly as encompassing sound physical and mental functioning, the chapter points out how management decisions and corporate policy can have a profound impact on employees' lives. Current trends in health promotion programs are presented, with a special focus on AT&T's worksite health promotion program.

Chapter 5, **Alcohol and Substance Abuse Counseling,** offers employers information on how to intervene when an employee has a substance abuse problem. In 1984, according to a study by the Research Triangle Institute, the U.S. economy lost $57.9 billion due to alcohol and drug abuse.[4] Both large and small corporations are becoming increasingly aware of the insidious effects of this problem on their daily and long-range operations. This chapter provides a comprehensive overview of alcohol and substance abuse counseling in corporate America. Attention is focused on the cost-benefits analysis of implementing such a program. Case study material, with special emphasis on cocaine and alcohol addiction, is used to illustrate the most up-to-date treatment strategies.

Chapter 6, **Child Care,** goes far beyond day care centers and discusses a wide range of organizational efforts to help employee-parents: networking and referral services, dependent care benefits, stipends, and personal counseling seminars. Such services are now provided by about 2,000 corporations in the United States, and this number is expected to increase dramatically during the 1990s. This anticipated increase follows a series of studies that indicate that time taken off for child care is a major disruptive force in American business, especially as the number of families with both parents working has increased. The chapter offers an overview of trends in this area and contains case illustrations of successful corporate child care assistance programs, with attention directed toward using such programs as a way to expand the pool of potential employees by attracting those with needed skills.

Chapter 7, **Elder Care,** looks at corporations that have implemented elder care assistance programs for the elderly parents and grandparents of their employees. Elder care assistance programs provide a myriad of services to relatives, including education, health assistance, adult day care centers, government benefits information, and personal counseling, as well as offering seminars that deal with the issues of aging.

Chapter 8, **Retirement Counseling,** introduces the counseling component for retiring employees. According to most sources, approximately 90 percent of workers, managers, and executives retiring from the work force are fully capable, physically and mentally, of continuing their present jobs or of developing skills to hold a job of equal importance. Retirement assistance can deal with the psychological ramifications of retirement, financial planning, family issues, and second-career training. An increasing number of American businesses are providing (or co-supporting) retirement counseling services for their employees, especially in situations where early retirement is encouraged.

Chapter 9, **Relocation Counseling,** focuses on employees who are remaining within the company but are changing their work location, perhaps to areas once thought remote. This involves a multifaceted approach for assisting personnel who are relocating to new geographic areas—domestic or international—and who are returning home from foreign lands. Policy, administration, implementation, and the counseling aspects of a relocation program are presented. Home sale assistance, spouse career counseling, and transfer assistance are areas that must be addressed when counseling employees in the relocation process.

Chapter 10, **Literacy and Other Essential Skills,** addresses one of the dilemmas facing many organizations: the technological and human relations skills required in the changing workplace depend on more extensive foundations than a very large proportion of the present work force developed during their school years. Therefore, employees must be trained on site so that they have the expertise that their jobs require. The development of an essential skills program is presented as a viable alternative for employers to provide cost-effective, comprehensive training for their employees. In addition, presenting, marketing, and evaluating the program are discussed.

Chapter 11, **Outplacement,** introduces the component of counseling the terminated employee. Because of the increasing number of corporate mergers and budgetary-induced personnel cuts, American corporations are terminating a larger number of mid- to high-level executives than ever before. Outplacement assistance can be crucial to these executives, traumatized by their unexpected separation. This chapter outlines the main concepts of outplacement counseling and surveys the practices and trends in the field today.

Chapter 12, **Cultural Diversity Counseling,** addresses the necessity for the workplace to be receptive to the need to understand and work with people of different backgrounds, cultures, and values in the face of a changing work force. In addition, because of legal issues surrounding employing women and minorities, companies should consider offering counseling that addresses discrimination and harassment issues in relation to these groups.

Chapter 13, **AIDS Counseling,** looks at one of the most profound issues in the workplace today. With the number of AIDS cases in the United States among adults between the ages of 20 to 64 at 188,962 (or 96 percent of the total cases of AIDS) as of October 31, 1991, and with future projections of 1.5 million cases, American business must accept that due to the age group in which the disease is diagnosed, most of the 1.5 million will be in the work force. In addition to covering AIDS in their EAPs, companies should introduce an AIDS education and counseling program. The elements necessary will vary depending on the size and other aspects of the corporations. How to develop and implement an AIDS counseling program is presented in this chapter. Existing AIDS policies from the public and private sector are also examined.

The appendixes following the chapters provide actual policies from the public and private sectors, forms and evaluation material currently used by human resources personnel, organizations to contact for further information, and suggested reading.

NOTES

1. U.S. Department of Labor, Commission on Workforce Quality and Labor Market Efficiency, *Investing in People* (Washington D.C.: Government Printing Office, 1989).
2. Ibid., pp. 1–3.
3. Cindy Skrzychi, "Business Is Slow to Adapt to Changes in Nation's Workforce, Study Shows," *Washington Post,* April 2, 1990, p. A5.
4. H. J. Harwood, D. M. Napolitano, P. L. Kristiansen, and J. J. Collins, *Economic Costs to Society of Drug and Alcohol Abuse and Mental Illness: 1980* (Research Triangle Park, NC: Research Triangle Institute, 1984).

The
AMA
Handbook for
Developing Employee
Assistance and
Counseling Programs

1

Employee Assistance Programs

Dale A. Masi, School of Social Work, University of Maryland

Consider the following:

▴ Drowsiness and confusion are reported in a worker.

▴ The job performance of an otherwise excellent worker has deteriorated rapidly. In addition, he arrives late at the office and calls in sick more frequently.

▴ Concerns are mentioned about a vice-president who is preoccupied with her teenager's erratic behavior.

▴ A generally well-liked supervisor has become unusually irritable and angry.

As recently as the early 1980s, many of these employees would have been reprimanded or even fired. Traditionally employers felt that employee problems were just that and should be dealt with privately, at a distance. Employees, for their part, felt that their employers were disinterested in personal concerns and difficulties. However, recently, major changes in these kinds of attitudes and perceptions have occurred with the development of employee assistance programs (EAPs), designed to deal with employee problems that may affect workplace performance. Their major impact has been to change the view of the workplace from that of a producer of problems to a source of help.[1]

EAPs are a professional assessment and referral and/or short-term counseling service offered to employees with alcohol, drug, or mental health problems that may be affecting their work. They also include managerial-supervisory consultations and training and employee education. Employees are either self-referred to the company's EAP or are referred by supervisors.

EAPs help employees who are dealing with substance abuse, mental health problems, or other emotional issues—either their own or that of a loved one—by showing them how to cope with the anxiety, fear, and other emotions that emerge in response to these problems. EAP staff can work as team members with the personnel and medical staff of the organization, and they can also provide support services to unions for members who are dealing with personal problems.

A company's EAP can serve as a valuable resource in developing employee policies, and it can help allay employee anxieties and fears as the company develops its philosophy and policy surrounding new issues. As society evolves, the workplace must be flexible and open in its commitment to help its employees. And as society becomes more complex, the workplace must be prepared to offer employees help in coping with such issues as drugs, AIDS, sexual harassment, and prejudice. EAP personnel are in a unique position to offer this kind of support, since they are trained in mental health counseling, policy implementation, and education.

EAPs can also help companies to interpret and implement legislation pertinent to employees. For example, the Rehabilitation Act of 1973 and the Americans With Disabilities Act of 1989, which declared persons with certain illnesses to be handicapped, have been interpreted as extending to persons with AIDS. The EAP staff is already familiar with these laws as they pertain to persons with other handicapping conditions. That knowledge is an invaluable aid in understanding ramifications for employees who have AIDS, as issues arise concerning disability benefits and termination on medical grounds.

Need for EAPs

EAP experts often estimate that 20 percent of any work force is affected by personal problems that can have an impact on job performance. Of the affected employees, statistics from the 1989 NIDA *National Household Survey* indicate that 12 percent have alcohol- and drug-related problems, and 6–8 percent have emotionally related problems. These problems can result in a 25 percent decrease in productivity and increased costs for the company. The annual costs to productivity for companies in the United States are $50.6 billion for alcohol and $26 billion for drugs. Figure 1-1 lists the measurable, hidden, and legal costs to the organization arising from job performance problems. Proper utilization of the EAP concept can greatly reduce the financial costs—the costs associated with liabilities to the company.

Just as personal problems can have a negative effect on individuals, work can have a positive influence because self-esteem is tied to job and occupational concepts. An employee may deny a personal problem only until threatened with the loss of a job. Many alcoholics, for example, are motivated to seek help and address their problems only after their jobs and livelihood are in jeopardy.

The percentage of employees seen face to face by EAP staff usually ranges from 4 to 6 percent per year. The proportion of drug- and alcohol-related problems might range from a low of 20 percent of the client population to a high of 60 percent. In general, the demographic propor-

Figure 1-1. Organizational losses resulting from job performance problems.

Measurable Losses	*Hidden Losses*	*Losses Related to Legal Claims*
• Absenteeism	• Diverted supervisory managerial time	• Workers compensation
• Overtime pay	• Friction among workers	• Equal Employment Opportunity Complaints
• Tardiness	• Waste	• Disciplinary actions
• Sick leave abuse	• Damage to equipment	• Grievance procedures/ Other legal actions
• Health insurance claims	• Poor decisions	• Threat to public safety
• Disability payments	• Damage to public image	• Illegal drug trafficking on the job
	• Personnel turnover	• Security issues
	• Premature death	

tions existing within the company population should be reflected in the demographics of the program's clientele. Addictions and mental health problems are found equally in employees regardless of race, sex, or job classification. For example, if the male-to-female ratio of the company is 60–40, the EAP clientele male-female ratio should also be approximately 60–40. However, in a given program, certain groups might tend to be either over- or underrepresented. Executives, minorities, and women are often underrepresented in these statistics. If an EAP is not representative of the employee population at large, charges of singling out employee groups may be made, which greatly undermines a program. Currently, there are few statistics available on utilization of EAPs by minorities.

History of EAPs

Employee assistance programs developed out of the concept of occupational alcoholism programs (OAPs), which began in the 1940s. OAPs were developed through the efforts of recovering alcoholics. They were based on the premise that the troubled employee should be confronted while still on the job; the employer should not try to cover up the problem. In this way the addiction could be treated and the job could be saved.

In the 1940s, Kemper Insurance, Eastman Kodak, and Du Pont Corporation, among others, started OAPs, headed primarily by staff who were themselves recovering alcoholics. With the passage of the Hughes Act (Public Law 91-616) in 1970, these programs received an important boost.[2] The Act established the National Institute for Alcoholism and Alcohol Abuse (NIAAA) as distinct from the National Institute of Mental Health (NIMH) and mandated the establishment of an occupational branch for the NIAAA that granted funds to each state to hire two occupational program consultants (OPCs) charged with developing programs in both the private and public sectors.[3] The Hughes Act also mandated the development of programs for the prevention, treatment, and rehabilitation of federal employees with alcohol and drug problems.[4]

The next year, a group of individuals in the OAP field met in Los Angeles to found the Association of Labor-Management Administrators and Consultants on Alcoholism (ALMACA). ALMACA began as a nonprofit international organization of practitioners involved in occupational alcoholism and employee assistance programming. This organization continues to serve as the professional body for OA/EAP practitioners.[5] Recently, it was renamed EAPA (Employee Assistance Professionals Association) to signify a broader representation than alcohol.

Passage of the Rehabilitation Act in 1973 served to promote awareness of the need for OA/EAPs.[6] Section 504 of the act guarantees the rights of handicapped people; in other words, employers must offer reasonable accommodation to employees with handicapping conditions. In 1978, the U.S. attorney general defined *handicapped* to include alcoholism and drug addiction.

As OAPs developed, practitioners changed their focus from alcohol to job performance and found that programs dealing with a broader base of employee problems were more effective. This evolution into a broader model was the birth of the modern employee assistance program, which now includes such areas as parent-child relationships, emotional and life crisis, drugs, gambling, and eating disorders.

In the evolving EAP, supervisors were trained to focus on and confront employees whose job performance was falling, but they were cautioned not to try to diagnose the problem. This form of assistance focuses on supervisory referral to the EAP, based on observation of poor job performance. This shift in diagnosis from untrained staff to professionals developed as rising health care costs became of such concern to employers. It was found that furnishing counseling within the EAP was a way to limit mental health costs.

The EAP field expanded again in the 1980s as large numbers of employees—from Wall Street to factories, from hospitals to small companies—became exposed to drugs at the worksite. CEOs became aware of and alarmed at having pushers on their payroll. Moreover, the National Transportation Board found that an increasing number of transportation accidents were related to drugs. As a result, the Drug Free Workplace Act of 1988 was passed, encouraging companies to implement EAPs. Ronald Reagan's executive order referenced EAPs as a solution to combat this growing workplace issue.

By developing and maintaining a strong EAP, an organization significantly reduces the many costs, financial and otherwise, that it would have incurred because of employees' personal problems. When considering the more abstract costs, there is no way to measure the savings in relief from anxieties, fears, and distress; however, this savings clearly has a positive effect on overall morale, team spirit, loyalty to the organization, and public image. Figure 1-2 explains the conceptual framework of an EAP.

Numerous companies have measured the effectiveness of their EAPs:

‣ General Motors reduced lost time by 40 percent, sickness and accident benefits payments by 60 percent, grievance proceedings by 50 percent, and on-the-job accidents by 50 percent as a result of implementing its EAP.

‣ A study of the Oldsmobile program involved 117 hourly workers; at a cost of $11,114, it achieved a 49 percent decrease in lost hours, a 29 percent decrease in disability benefits payments, and a 56 percent decrease in leaves of absence.

Figure 1-2. EAP conceptual framework.

---

1. EAPs are based on the premise that work is very important to people (it is ego reinforcing); the work itself is not the cause of the employee's problem. Consequently, the workplace can be a means to get people help.

2. The supervisor plays a key role in getting help for the employee. Often, however, the supervisor denies the problem and even enables the troubled employee to continue the problem behavior. The supervisor is critical in the confrontational process with the troubled employee. Therefore, education is necessary to eliminate the supervisor's tendency to enable the employee by denying the problem.

3. Information about the employee's job performance is extremely important in diagnosis and treatment. It can be used to measure and track whether treatment is successful.

4. Workplace peers and union stewards are very important; however, they too can deny the problem and enable the employee to continue the behavior. Teaching them to confront and consequently break the denial barrier is an important element.

5. Job leverage is the key ingredient. The counselor must be able to use this with the supervisor.

6. EAPs concentrate on personnel issues and job performance. They are not a medical program.

7. Cost-effectiveness is an important consideration and must be addressed with upper management.

8. The EAP practitioner's knowledge about addiction is paramount. Every EAP should be staffed by clinically licensed professionals from the mental health field who are familiar with addictions.

▴ Equitable Life Assurance Society indicated a 5.52-to-1 return on dollars invested in its program.

▴ Kennecott Copper indicated a slightly higher return, at 6 to 1.[7]

Program Models

There are many different EAP models specifically designed to meet the needs of a wide variety of companies, but all of them fall into one or a combination of the following categories:

▴ *In-house model.* The entire assistance staff is employed by the company. A company manager directly supervises the program's personnel, sets policies, and designs all procedures. The program can be housed physically in the company or located in offices away from the worksite. A recent study suggests that top management believes that these programs provide service at a lower cost, with increased control, greater identification of alcoholic employees, increased supervisory and medical referrals, and more positive acceptance by unions.[8]

▴ *Out-of-house model.* The company contracts with a vendor to provide an employee assistance staff and services. The vendor might provide services in its own offices, the company's offices, or both. This model is viewed as providing better accountability, lower legal liability, and ease of start-up and implementation.

▴ *Consortium model.* Several companies pool their resources to develop a collaborative program and thus maximize individual resources. Generally this model works best for companies with fewer than 2,000 employees. Services may be provided on-site or in separate offices. Running these programs may be more complex and may require a difficult decision-making process.

▴ *Affiliate model.* A vendor subcontracts with a local professional rather than use salaried staff. This enables the vendor to reach employees in a company location in which the vendor might not have an office. Usually this model is used in conjunction with a model that involves paid staff. With this model, the vendor may have less control over a subcontracted professional, however; this has become the vehicle whereby employees in various locations can be reached by one responsible vendor. Such programs may offer less accountability and decreased responsiveness.

In determining the best approach, each organization must ascertain how complex a program must be to fit its needs and the level of its commitment to it. Many companies prefer the contractual approach because the commitment need not be long term. If evaluation deems the

EAP is ineffective, it is easier to terminate a contract than to terminate members of the company's staff. Company size, geographic location and diversity, employee population, and values and goals are also important considerations. In many instances, a consultant is useful to help match company characteristics to a particular model.

Recent estimates reveal that there are now approximately 13,000 EAPs in American work organizations, as compared to 5,000 in 1981.[9]

Essential Ingredients

The success of an EAP rests on the following essential ingredients. These elements are all equally important and are not listed in order of priority.

Policy Statement

The written policy statement clearly defines the purpose of the program, organizational and legal mandates, employee eligibility, the roles and responsibility of various personnel in the organization, and procedures. This statement should be endorsed by the highest level of management and should have the formal support of unions (if applicable).

The statement sets important parameters for the entire operation of the employee assistance program. It will indicate, for example:

- Who can use the services
- How confidential information is handled
- Credentials of the staff
- Methods for program evaluation
- Whether an employee should receive free time from work for appointments
- How client records should be kept and for how long

Services

The basic services an EAP can provide are information, assessment and referral, and/or short-term counseling with twenty-four-hour access to an 800 line. It is important for the counselor not only to listen to the employee but also to evaluate the nature and seriousness of the employee's problem before the employee is assisted and a focus for help defined.

Once the problem is defined, the service plan should include a range of options. In some cases, the employee may be helped by simply receiving written information explaining and defining certain difficulties and coping alternatives or resources such as listings of smoking cessation workshops or nursing homes.

For more complex problems, program staff supply a referral to an agency or care giver and help the employee contact and use the services offered by the outside agency or provider. For this reason, the plan must have a system for identifying appropriate community resources and a method of evaluating credentials and skills.

Finally, it has become increasingly common for EAPs to offer short-term counseling. Early short-term counseling can prevent postponement of seeking help, decrease later treatment costs, and reduce confusion about locating services.

Professional Staffing

Staff should be required to have at least two years' experience working with alcoholism and other addictions. The staff should also have education and work experience in the recognized mental health professions—psychology, social work, psychiatry, or psychiatric nursing—and should have the appropriate credentials and/or license. In addition, these professionals have demonstrated the ability and flexibility to work with managers, supervisors, employees, and unions. Because of the combination of the counseling and administrative components, many EAPs separate the EAP's administrative role from counseling. The growth of EAPs has made it difficult to find qualified professionals.

Universities are only beginning to offer EAP-related programs. The University of Maryland School of Social Work is unique in offering an EAP specialization whereby M.S.W. graduates receive a certificate in EAP studies. In addition, the School of Social Work, in conjunction with the School of Business and Management, offers an annual EAP residential institute each spring.

The use of trained, licensed professionals protects the EAP and, ultimately, the company from the legal problems surrounding malpractice because unlicensed persons make an employer vulnerable to legal suit.

If the company has fewer than 2,500 employees at one location, the EAP may use a qualified affiliate or subcontractor from within the community. Subcontractors are used typically when an internal EAP program is too complex for small companies or for smaller branches of larger companies located in distant cities and states. It is important that the subcontractor have the same qualifications as would a regular EAP staff in a larger company.

Confidential Record-Keeping System

Most employees will not participate in the program unless they feel assured their case will remain confidential. Therefore, secure records and training for professional and support staff are essential. Everyone—secretaries, interns, and volunteers—must understand the importance of confidentiality and how easily it can be violated. Files should be locked, access should be limited and monitored, and identifying information kept to a minimum. The staff should be aware of federal and state regulations governing confidentiality and client-professional privilege. Proper release forms should be used at all times.

A Community Resource Referral Network

One of the EAP's responsibilities is to evaluate community resources for appropriate employee referrals and keep the list up to date. For example, in the case of an employee with AIDS, support groups for the employee and family are appropriate.

Attention to community resources has been neglected and even misused. Too often, company officials and supervisors suggest that an employee go to an organization on a resource list without researching and monitoring the qualifications of the organization. This must be done through the expertise of an EAP practitioner. Often companies have considered the compilation of a list of referral agencies to be a sufficient company EAP. It clearly is not. Worse, a company that makes an unqualified referral opens itself up to liability problems.

Appropriate EAP Location

An EAP located within the organization should be under the auspices of the company's human resources or personnel department or occasionally the medical department. It should be situated so that it is accessible to the handicapped and inconspicuous enough to increase confidentiality with well-furnished and -maintained surroundings to demonstrate the company's commitment to the EAP. If the EAP is located off-site, there should be an office on the premises where supervisors and clients can meet with the EAP counselor if requested.

Funding

There are two options: the company maintains an in-house staff, or it contracts out all functions on a per capita basis. The fees, regardless of the option used by the company, range from $22 to $35 per employee per year, depending on the location of the company. This fee is based on the total number of employees in the company regardless of how many use the program and how much they use it. This fee structure runs contrary to the traditional fee-for-service mental health medical model. It is more cost-effective because fee for service provides no motivation to move treatment toward a goal and eventual completion and therefore often results in unnecessarily longer treatment.

Union Support

Historically, unions have been concerned that employee counseling programs might be a management method for circumventing collective bargaining agreements. Companies can gain union support by including them in program planning.

Supervisory Training

Supervisors, especially if they make referrals to the assistance program, must be properly trained. They should understand the program policies, procedures, and services and be clear about their role in relation to the plan. That is, they should identify performance problems, not make clinical diagnoses, and should encourage employees to use the EAP services.

Supervisors must understand that the use of these services is voluntary but that it could be used as a step before a disciplinary process. An assistance program can provide an opportunity for the employee to get help before dismissal. Therefore, it is important that the supervisor is trained to view the referral as a service that helps rather than one that will embarrass or humiliate the employee.

Supervisors should know that referring an employee is a sign of supervisory skill rather than failure. Because of the chronic denial of the addictive person, the role of the supervisor is key in reaching such employees through the possibility of job loss.

Employee Outreach and Education

If the EAP is to be effective, employees must be informed of its availability and services. Memos, posters, and programs, including slide shows or films, can all be used to inform employees about the EAP's existence. They are usually more effective and well received if they are presented on company time, such as lunch hour or coffee break. These should be offered regularly, perhaps several times a year.

In addition, the EAP should provide separate educational sessions and material on substance abuse as well as updated relevant medical research. Many employees, for example, might be only minimally aware of what is troubling them. In the case of substance abuse, denial prevents them from recognizing their problem. Therefore, they must have some basic education regarding when recreational use of alcohol and drugs is really dependence, when fatigue is depression, and when edginess is stress. Employee education programs could use written materials, short talks, workshops, or films and should have a good fit with the company's other communication dissemenation methods characteristics.

Plans that encourage family members' participation should send information to each employee's home.

Sensitivity to Special Populations

Counselors need to pay particular attention to the needs and problems of women, gays and lesbians, the physically challenged and developmentally disabled, and minorities in order to deal with group-specific issues such as sexual harassment, family violence, and role conflicts. Female and minority counselors may be more sensitive to the gender and cultural nuances of a particular behavior or problem area.

▴ *Women.* In their book *Re-Inventing the Corporation,* Naisbitt and Aburdene state: "Women are flooding into the job market, boosting economic growth and helping to reshape the economy dramatically."[10] By the mid-1990s, 75 percent of all women between the ages of 18–64 are expected to be in the work force. This increase of women in the work force brings infinite possibilities, but it also carries with it certain problems: For example, a woman may feel torn between family and career; she may sense the animosity of the bureaucracy as she threatens a male employee's position; and she may be the victim of sex biases and sexual harassment. A woman is almost always the victim of pay inequality; one report states that "in 1985 full-time American women workers earned sixty four cents as compared to the one dollar earned by men."[11]

Because EAP caseloads originally reflected low numbers of women, the need for alternative components became apparent. The following approaches are now being implemented by many EAPs:

1. Women counselors
2. Women's support groups
3. Outreach programs directed at women
4. Special polydrug education about tranquilizers
5. Special training for supervisors in assisting women
6. Support for treatment facilities aimed at women's needs

▴ *The Physically Challenged and Developmentally Disabled.* One of our most underserved populations has been the physically challenged and developmentally disabled. With the advent of the Americans with Disabilities Act, the 1990s are heralding some major changes in this area. EAPs need to give immediate attention to this special population group.

▴ *Diverse Populations.* Although outreach material should be designed so it reaches these groups, it is crucial that such groups are not singled out on the basis of cultural or sexual stereotypes.

It is unclear what motivates different groups to use a particular service; however, there has been some indication that minorities may use EAPs more readily than traditional mental health services. EAPs could be a powerful method for helping groups that have used similar services only minimally in the past.

Legal Issues

The design and implementation of the EAP must be done in accordance with current laws, regulations, and rulings, both state and federal. Issues concerning confidentiality of client records and drug testing legislation are important for EAP professionals to know.

State statutes mandate the disclosure of suspected child abuse to the appropriate state agency. The threat of harm to another made by a participant of the assistance program could require warning the potential victim.

Program policies and procedures should clearly and explicitly reflect all relevant laws and regulations, and all program staff in-house, as well as vendor personnel, should be covered by professional liability insurance.

Program Evaluation

All EAPs should be evaluated to justify their existence and demonstrate their effectiveness. (It is estimated, however, that less than 1 percent of the 13,000 existing EAPs are evaluated, a major weakness in the field.) An evaluation allows the company to assess the extent to which its objectives are being reached and to find ways to improve the effectiveness of the plan's performance. In addition, an evaluation can help ensure that the company EAP is legally protected. Because of the confidentiality issues intrinsic to such programs, a third party evaluator, an individual or corporation without connection to the company, may be necessary to preserve confidentiality and to make an adequate evaluation.

Although a variety of evaluation methods can be used, a truly comprehensive EAP evaluation should include the following two components: (1) the monitoring of the implementation of the program, a "process evaluation," and (2) a study of the effectiveness of the program, "an outcome evaluation."

A *process evaluation* encompasses the review and analysis of monthly EAP statistics, including the number of cases, categories of diagnosis, and supervisory referrals. The purpose of this evaluation component is to ensure that the EAP reaches the appropriate number of employees, including those with alcohol and drug problems; that the client population reflects the work force composition in relation to age, sex, race, job level, and so on; and that there is a baseline date in job performance for comparing performance after going to the EAP.

Diagnosis and referral decisions made by the EAP counselors can be monitored in many ways. One recommendation is that an alcohol/drug history be conducted for each client, regardless of the presenting problem, in order to assist the counselor in detecting employees with symptoms of alcohol/drug abuse and to determine whether the counselor's decision has been appropriate. A sample form used for alcohol/drug intake is in the Appendix to this chapter.

An *outcome evaluation* includes both quantitative and qualitative analysis. The quantitative evaluation determines whether the EAP is cost-effective. Specific elements are measured and compared with information on costs incurred before the company EAP was in place; subsequent quarterly and annual comparisons are used as well. Areas to be evaluated may include:

- Absenteeism
- Advanced leave
- Leave without pay
- Performance appraisal records
- Disability insurance claims
- Sick leave
- Industrial accidents
- Health insurance claims
- Workers compensation claims

These data are matched to control groups, which are refined by age, sex, and managerial level. Data collection procedures vary for each contract, so the evaluation should be designed with data accessibility, the agency's interest, and cost in mind.

A quantitative evaluation is also made of supervisory referrals. They are accomplished by evaluating performance criteria furnished by supervisors at the point of the employee's referral and after three months and one year. Matched to a salary figure, these evaluations have consistently resulted in a $13.00 to $1.00 return on the EAP investment.

EAPs can be evaluated qualitatively through a peer panel approach conducted by recognized experts in the fields of psychiatry, psychology, and social work who provide a professional, comprehensive, and constructive review of individual case records. Concern for the employee as well as possible liability considerations make this an essential part of any program evaluation. The panel should review a number of randomly selected EAP records and provide a written and oral report to management.

Under the Alcohol and Drug Regulation, evaluations are allowed by bona fide evaluators. The author has consulted with U.S. Department of Health and Human Services attorneys; all such procedures for the safeguarding of records, as well as the evaluation process, have been approved.

Peer review, as developed by the author, has precedents in the medical profession and has four major components: (1) a general orientation session, (2) a review of case records, (3) direct dialogue with company vendors (optional), and (4) a company debriefing with a final written report. The individual review of case reports includes a protocol instrument that reviews cases for questions about assessment of problem outside referrals, quality of counseling, and a full discussion of the employee's options.

This method has been used successfully with such companies as IBM, the American Management Association, Bristol Myers, the Internal Revenue Service, and others to address the following factors:

- ▴ Accuracy of diagnosis
- ▴ Treatment planning
- ▴ Referrals to community resources for treatment
- ▴ Employee follow-up after referral for treatment
- ▴ Client and/or supervisor satisfaction with the program

The EAP and Case Management

AIDS and other catastrophic illnesses have been responsible for the acceleration of a relatively new and atypical approach to health care known as *case management,* a system of assessing and monitoring client needs throughout treatment. It is a process specifically designed to customize care for individual patients with catastrophic illnesses. Its elements include assessment of the patient's needs, referral to the appropriate resources, follow-up, and consultation. Extended follow-up is necessary because of the chronic nature of the disease and the potential for varying stages of psychological and physical stresses.

The patient is assigned a coordinator, an experienced health care professional, to provide psychological and sociological support for the patient and the patient's family. The EAP counselor can perform this role effectively. The coordinator acts as a liaison among the patient, the physician, and the family and helps plan details of medical care and finances. Case managers also strive for a timely discharge from hospitals and utilize atypical health care venues, such as hospices or home care settings. The estimated average daily cost for home health care or hospice is estimated to be $100 to $300 per day, in contrast to the average daily cost of hospitalization, which stands at $880 to $1,000 per day. Ironically, only 50 percent of the nation's insurers cover home health care, and only 30 percent cover hospices. In the alternative long-term care situation, the case manager would explore the appropriate options given the insurance plan or perhaps investigate other insurance options. The case management approach has two obvious advantages: it allows clients to achieve their optimum recovery faster, and it greatly reduces the number of unnecessary hospital days.

In their roles as case managers for the employee, EAP practitioners should reach out to the following groups to make their status known:

family members, managers and supervisors, employees, medical department personnel, and senior management. The EAP practitioner coordinates with the insurance company, physicians, and psychological experts and acts as an advocate for the employee.

Future Directions of EAPs

Certain major trends in the organization of EAPs and in the larger social and economic picture have implications for the future of EAPs. Three factors in particular will affect the development of EAPs in the workplace: (1) the role of EAPs in managed mental health, (2) the focus on drug abuse in the workplace, and (3) the increasing number of persons with or affected by AIDS.

Managed Mental Health

At one end of the managed mental health continuum, EAPs are becoming the health maintenance organizations of mental health services. Increasingly, companies request that the EAP provide up to eight counseling sessions for employees who need this service. As a result, the EAP is able to facilitate problem resolution without referring the client to outside resources. Thus, the client avoids the use of costly health care benefits while receiving qualified professional assistance. However, given that the EAP emphasizes short-term self-referral mental health services, it is in danger of losing its original mandate of aggressive outreach to addicted employees.

Increasing health insurance costs have sparked a greater interest in developing methods for monitoring and managing the use of covered services, and concurrently, EAPs are beginning to serve as controls for mental health benefits utilization. Some companies have begun to request that troubled employees be seen by the EAP staff for a second opinion prior to approval of a lengthy inpatient hospitalization or long-term outpatient therapy sessions. EAPs therefore can be both an alternative to the use of outside professional services and a gatekeeper for the use of outpatient and inpatient services. In the future, EAP staff may have the ultimate responsibility for planning and monitoring the entire mental health package.

Alcohol and Drug Abuse

Both public and private companies are seeking to combat alcohol and drug abuse in the workplace. Drug testing is considered one of the most viable solutions to this growing workplace issue, and EAPs will be called on to assist employers in developing policies surrounding employee drug testing and related issues.

Companies have tried to control the problem by using drug screening in preemployment physical examinations and "for cause" and random urinalysis. EAP practitioners need to be skilled in the areas of security questions, employee and public safety, and legal issues surrounding drug screening. EAPs should not be the enforcers of anti–drug use policies and procedures but instead need to work in conjunction with personnel, medical, and security departments for the elimination of legal and illegal drug abuse in the workplace.

One of the most important pieces of legislation that directly relates to the role of the EAP practitioner in the workplace is the Drug Free Workplace Act of 1988. It states that "agencies shall initiate action to discipline any employee who is found to use illegal drugs, provided that such action is not required for an employee who . . . obtains counseling or rehabilitation through an employee assistance program." Organizations are required to publish and provide a copy of the required statement to all employees, establish a drug-free awareness program for all employees, and sanction or require any employee convicted of a drug violation in the workplace to participate in a rehabilitation program. In addition to drug testing, drug screening instruments for assessments should be utilized by EAP counselors. (See the appendix section, "Drug Abuse Curriculum for Employee Assistance Program Professionals.")

AIDS in the Workplace

Increasingly employers are having to address the issue of AIDS in the workplace. The EAP could take the lead in assisting companies with this highly sensitive issue by providing a number of services. EAP intervention in the workplace can include ongoing AIDS education, supportive counseling to co-workers and supervisors of employees with AIDS and facilitating the implementation and maintenance of the company's policy and educational program on AIDS.

Education about AIDS will be the key means of intervention and should not wait to begin after AIDS is identified within a company. Short-term EAP counseling should be made to family, friends, and co-workers on how to cope with the problems presented by the disease on a day-to-day basis.

Additional Issues for EAP Practitioners

Professional Changes

As employee assistance programs have grown, the field has been infused with a variety of professionals and paraprofessional practitioners who vary in their educational level and their amount of experience. One reflection of this change is in the emergence of university-based course work for EAPs. This move toward professionalization is positive. However, care must be taken to ensure that these professionals have the necessary experience and knowledge of addiction problems to identify and refer troubled employees.

Cost-Effectiveness

Industry will not continue to pay for EAPs unless they believe that the programs are cost-effective. Hard evidence of their benefits will be needed in the face of increased budget cuts. At this point, there is a dearth of evaluation and research available to support the contention that EAPs are cost-effective. The very survival of EAPs will depend on the development and implementation of audits.

The world of work and the world of human services have finally combined through the common ground of employee assistance programs. Employers who have brought EAPs into the workplace have demonstrated that they care for their employees, as well as for the bottom line.

To be successful, an EAP cannot stand alone. Even established programs depend on the support and allegiance of other key departments in the organization. One example is the relationship between the EAP and the medical department. The occupational nurse or doctor is a significant source of referrals to the EAP, and many employees will seek them out for assistance. Employees may be sent to the medical department with vague physical complaints when the source of their discomfort is emotional. Other key departments that need to work with the EAP include the personnel department and the security department.

It is not enough simply to have an EAP in a company. All personnel must be devoted to the concept and be willing to participate with the EAP in order for it to achieve maximum effectiveness. A comprehensive approach ensures the best treatment for employees.

Because the EAP field is a new one, there is no accrediting of programs and, as a result, a wide diversity in delivery of services. Some programs have clinically licensed personnel, and others have employee relations people wearing an EAP hat without any human resources training. Because of this, it is difficult to generalize on the appropriate role of the EAP. There is no doubt, however, that as an emerging profession, it has a responsibility to assume a major role in the workplace. Corporate management must ensure that their EAP staffs are trained appropriately to deal with the company's most valuable asset: its employees.

NOTES

1. D. Masi and S. Friedland, "EAP Actions and Options," *Personnel Journal* (June 1988).

2. U.S. Congress, "Comprehensive Alcohol Abuse and Alcoholism Prevention, Treatment and Rehabilitation Act of 1970," December 31, 1970, Public Law 91-616 (42 USC 4582).
3. Ibid.
4. D. Masi and M. Goff, "The Evaluation of Employee Assistance Programs" *Public Personnel Management,* 16:4 (Winter 1987): 324–325.
5. D. Masi, *Designing Employee Assistance Programs* (New York: American Management Association, 1984), p. 14.
6. Office of Personnel Management, *Handbook of Selected Placement of Persons with Physical and Mental Handicaps in Federal and Civil Service Employment,* Document 125-11-3 (Washington, D.C.: Government Printing Office, March 1979).
7. C. Berry, *Good Health for Employees and Reduced Health Care Costs for Industry* (Washington, D.C.: Health Insurance Association of America, Health Insurance Institute, 1981), pp. 28–29.
8. S. Straussner, "Comparison of In-House and Contracted-Out Employee Assistance Programs," *Social Work* (January–February 1988), pp. 53–55.
9. Conversation with R. Bickerton, ALMACA clearinghouse manager, February 1989.
10. J. Naisbitt and P. Aburdene, *Re-Inventing the Corporation* (New York: Warner Books, 1985), p. 209.
11. "Pay Equity/A Fact Sheet," (Washington D.C.: National Commission on Working Women and Wider Opportunities for Women, 1986), p. 1.

SUGGESTED READING

Berry, C. *Good Health for Employees and Reduced Health Care Costs for Industry.* Washington, D.C.: Health Insurance Association of America, Health Insurance Institute, 1981.

Bryant, M. "Ways to Make EAPs More Cost Effective." *Business & Health* (September 1990).

Bureau of National Affairs. *Employee Assistance Programs: Benefits, Problems, and Prospects.* Washington, D.C.: The Bureau of National Affairs, 1987.

Byers, W., and Quinn, J. "Alcoholism as a Major Focus of EAPs" In *The Human Resource Management Handbook.* New York: Praeger, 1985.

Clark, A., and Covington, S. "Women, Alcohol and the Workplace (Part III)." *ALMACAN* (February 1986).

Development Associates, Inc. *Evaluation of the Department of Health and Human Services Employee Counseling Services Programs* (1 May 1985).

Duda, M. "Banking on EAPs Brings Companies Big Dividends." *Safety & Health* (December 1990).

Masi, D. *Designing Employee Assistance Programs.* New York: AMACOM, 1984.

———. *Drug Free Workplace.* Washington, D.C.: Buraff Publications, 1987.

———. "Employee Assistance Programs." *Occupational Medicine* (October–December 1986).

Masi, D., and Goff, M. "The Evaluation of Employee Assistance Programs." *Public Personnel Management* 16:4 (Winter 1987).

Masi, D., and Masi, R. "Why Ethnicity, Culture Concerns and EAPs." *EAPA Monograph on EAPs*. (Arlington, Va.: EAPA, 1990).

Masi, D., and Stanton, K. "Employee Assistance Programmes (EAPs) and Working Women." *Women in Management Review & Abstracts* 5:2 (1990).

National Institute for Alcoholism and Alcohol Abuse. Occupational Branch. Forum on Occupational Alcoholism, "Rights of Alcoholics under Federal Law." Fall 1976.

National Institute on Drug Abuse. "Guidelines for the Development and Assessment of a Comprehensive Federal Employee Assistance Program" (1988).

National Institute on Drug Abuse. "Helping High-Risk Groups." *Employee Assistance* (December 1990).

Office of Personnel Management. *Handbook of Selected Placement of Persons with Physical and Mental Handicaps in Federal and Civil Service Employment*. Document 125-11-3. Washington, D.C., Government Printing Office, March 1979.

Stern, L. "Why EAPs Are Worth the Investment." *Business & Health* (May 1990).

Straussner, S. "Comparison of In-House and Contracted-Out Employee Assistance Programs." *Social Work* (January-February 1988).

Walker, P. "Evaluating Your EAP." *EmployeeAssistance* (December 1989).

Wrich, J. "Beyond Testing: Coping with Drugs at Work." *Harvard Business Review* (January-February 1988).

(continues)

Sample EAP Client Participation Form

_____is interested in obtaining feedback from _____employees on the services offered by _____'s Employee Assistance Program (EAP). Your responses will help us continue to ensure your needs are being met in a responsive and professional manner.

This questionnaire is voluntary, anonymous, and confidential. Please answer the following questions by placing a check next to the answer that best describes your feelings. If you do not wish to answer a particular question, please leave it blank.

1. How did you learn about the EAP? (circle one)
   a. brochure
   b. poster
   c. co-worker
   d. supervisor
   e. other (please specify) _____
2. How did you contact the EAP? (circle one)
   a. 800 number
   b. local number
3. Did you receive prompt attention?   yes _____no _____
4. Was an appointment provided to you within _____ working days?   yes_____ no _____
5. If you called with an emergency situation, was your call answered within two hours of your initial call?   yes _____no _____
6. Were you treated professionally and courteously?   yes _____no _____
7. Was the counselor's office comfortable and easily accessible?   yes _____no _____
8. Are you satisfied that you were served in a confidential manner?   yes _____no _____
9. Did the counselor help you to resolve your problem?   yes _____no _____
10. Did the counselor offer you short-term counseling?   yes _____no _____
11. Did the counselor refer you to a resource outside the EAP?   yes _____no _____

    If you answered yes to this question,
    a. Was the counselor helpful in connecting you with the referral?   yes _____no _____
    b. Did you follow through with the referral?   yes _____no _____
    c. Were you satisfied with the service you received from the resource?   yes _____no _____
12. I met face-to-face with the EAP counselor _____(number) times.
13. The EAP counselor followed up with a telephone call to me _____ (number) times.
14. Overall, how satisfied are you with the service you received through the EAP?

    _____ Very satisfied
    _____ Satisfied
    _____ Neither satisfied nor dissatisfied
    _____ Dissatisfied
    _____ Very dissatisfied

15. I am: (circle one)
    a. an employee
    b. family member
16. I received EAP services in _____.
                                                   city/state
    and my EAP counselor's name was _____.
17. Do you recommend that _____continue
    providing the Employee Assistance Program?   yes _____no _____

Your comments about the EAP

_____
_____
_____
_____
_____
_____
_____
_____

Fold, staple, and return to:

(continues)

Drug Abuse Curriculum for Employee Assistance Program Professionals

MODEL ASSESSMENT TOOL

The following is a model client intake form. Instructions to the EAP counselor appear in parentheses. The initial client-problem question differs in respect to a voluntary referral or a supervisory referral. All other questions apply to all types of consultations.

Despite the length of the assessment tool, it is usually administered in one or two sessions. Administering the tool over a longer period of time, however, is left to the discretion of the EAP counselor.

In regard to interpreting the data gathered from this Model Assessment Tool: The following code (scoring) indicates the possible degree of seriousness and action to be taken to address the problem.

  *A positive response reflects a problem in an early stage.
  **A positive response reflects a critical problem; if a client has more than two positives in this category, immediate action is required.
  ***A positive response reflects an emergency and need for immediate action.

A full drug use history would be done by the referral source, especially in outpatient and inpatient programs.

General Information

Name: _____

Current Address: _____
_____
_____

  1. Date of Birth: _____/_____/_____

  2. Race (check one):
       _____ White (not of Hispanic origin)
       _____ Black (not of Hispanic origin)
       _____ American Indian
       _____ Alaskan native
       _____ Asian or Pacific Islander
       _____ Hispanic-Mexican
       _____ Hispanic-Puerto Rican
       _____ Hispanic-Cuban
       _____ Other Hispanic

This curriculum was developed by the author for the National Institute on Drug Abuse as part of an overall package to assist EAP professionals in assessing employees abusing drugs. It was written with the assistance of an advisory group of drug-abuse experts.

3. Religious Preference (check one):

_____ Protestant
_____ Catholic
_____ Jewish
_____ Islamic
_____ Other
_____ None

I.D. Number: _____

Date of Interview: _____/_____/_____

Time Begun: ___:___

Time Ended: ___:___
Class:

_____ Intake
_____ Follow up
*_____ Enter session number if appropriate.

Gender:

_____ Female
_____ Male

Employment/Support Status

1. Education Completed (GED = 12 years):
   _____ years   _____ months

2. Do you have a valid driver's license?
   _____ yes   _____ no

3. Do you have an automobile available for your use?
   (answer NO if no valid driver's license)
   _____ yes   _____ no

4. Company Position (specify in detail): _____
   _____

5. Does someone contribute to your support in any way?
   _____ yes   _____ no

6. How many people depend on you for the majority of their food, shelter, etc.? _____

7. Salary Range:

   _____ Under $25,000
   _____ $25,000–$40,000

(continues)

Drug Abuse Curriculum for Employee Assistance Program Professionals (continued)

———— $40,000–$65,000
———— $65,000–$100,000
———— $100,000–$200,000
———— $200,000 +

8. How long have you been working for the company? ————————————
——

9. What was your first position? ————————————————————————
——

10. How long were you in that position? ————————————————————
——

11. How many different positions have you had in the company? ——————
——
——

12. Have you ever been disciplined? ——————————————————————
——

13. How many different employers have you worked for full time since entering the work force? ————————————————————————————————————
——
——

**14. If voluntary referral, "What is it that brings you to the EAP office today?" ————
——
——

**15. If supervisory referral, "What is your understanding as to the circumstance that brought you to the EAP office today?" ————————————————————
——
——

Now, we would like to ask you a few questions about your life-style.

Family Social Relationships

1. Marital Status:
———— Married
———— Remarried

_____ Widowed   _____ How many times?
_____ Separated
_____ Divorced
_____ Never Married
_____ Cohabitated

2. How long have you been in this marital status?
_____ years   _____ months

3. Are you satisfied with this situation?
_____ yes   _____ no   _____ indifferent

4. Usual living arrangements (past 3 years)
_____ With partner and children
_____ With sexual partner alone
_____ With children alone
_____ With parents
_____ With friends
_____ Alone
_____ Controlled environment
_____ No stable arrangements

5. How long have you lived in these arrangements?
_____ years   _____ months

6. Are you satisfied with these living arrangements?
_____ yes   _____ no   _____ indifferent

7. With whom do you spend most of your free time?
_____ family   _____ friends   _____ alone

8. Are you satisfied with spending your free time this way?
_____ yes   _____ no   _____ indifferent

9. How many *close* friends (see at least monthly) do you have?
_____

10. How many days in the past 30 have you had serious conflicts:
    A. with your family?   _____
    B. with other people (excluding family)?   _____

11. Have you had significant periods in which you have experienced serious problems with: (circle YES or NO in both columns)

	Past 30 Days	In Your Life
A. mother	yes no	yes no
B. father	yes no	yes no

(continues)

Drug Abuse Curriculum for Employee Assistance Program Professionals (continued)

	Past 30 Days	In Your Life
C. brothers/sisters	yes no	yes no
D. sexual partner/ spouse	yes no	yes no
E. children	yes no	yes no
F. other significant family _____	yes no	yes no
G. close friends	yes no	yes no
H. neighbors	yes no	yes no
I. co-workers	yes no	yes no

*Do any of the above have an alcohol problem? _____

Specify which group(s) by letters: _____

*Do any of the above have a drug problem? _____

Specify which group(s) by letters: _____

Health History

1. Explain your diet (i.e., supplements? What time do you eat?)
   _____
   _____

2. How do you sleep? _____
   _____

3. Are you troubled by frightening dreams?
   _____ yes   _____ no

   If so, please explain: _____
   _____

4. Are you under a doctor's care for any illness?
   _____ yes   _____ no

   If so, please explain: _____
   _____

5. Do you take any medication?
   _____ yes   _____ no

   If so, please explain: _____
   _____

6. How many times in your life have you been hospitalized for medical problems?

_____

[Include o.d.'s, d.t.'s; exclude detox.]

7. How long ago was your last hospitalization for a physical problem?
   _____ years   _____ months

8. Do you have any chronic medical problems which continue to interfere with your life?
   _____ yes   _____ no

9. How many days have you experienced medical problems in the past 30? _____

10. Do you use caffeine-containing products? How old were you when you started? How much do you use? _____

_____

_____

11. With regard to use of tobacco products:
    a. Have you ever used tobacco products?
       _____ yes   _____ no
    b. Approximate age at which you began to use tobacco products? _____
    c. How much do you use now? _____
    d. Regular (daily) use started at age: _____
    e. Describe briefly the pattern of tobacco use: _____

    _____

    _____

    f. Do you perceive tobacco use as a problem in your life today?
       _____ yes   _____ no
    g. What, if any, have been the consequences of tobacco use in your life? _____

    _____

    _____

*12. Do you sometimes need medication to sleep well, e.g., Sleep-eze, Phenobarbital, Seconal, Doriden, or anything similar to these?
   _____ yes   _____ no

[If the answer to question 12 is NO, move on to question 13.] If YES, please explain:

_____

_____

   If YES, how many times have you taken these?
   a. within the past month? _____
   b. within the past six months? _____
   c. over six months? _____
   **d. How has the use of this drug presented problems at work? _____

   _____

   _____

(continues)

Drug Abuse Curriculum for Employee Assistance Program Professionals (continued)

**e. Do you ever mix any of these with alcohol?

_____ yes   _____ no

If YES, please explain: _____
_____
_____

f. [*Person refuses to answer any of the above questions.*]

_____

13. Do you sometimes need medications to stay calm, e.g., tranquilizers or "downers," such as Valium, Compoz, Quaaludes, Librium, or anything similar to these?

_____ yes   _____ no

[*If answer to question 13 is NO, move on to question 14.*]
If YES, how often have you taken any of these?
a. within the past month? _____
b. within the past 6 months? _____
c. over six months? _____
d. How has the use of this drug presented problems at work? _____
_____

**e. Do you ever take any of these before or during work hours?

_____ yes   _____ no

If YES, please explain: _____
_____

f. Do you ever mix any of these with alcohol or with other drugs?

_____ yes   _____ no

If YES, please explain: _____
_____

g. [*Person refuses to answer any of the above questions.*]

_____

14. Which substance is the major problem?
a. drug   _____
b. alcohol   _____
c. drug and alcohol (dual) addiction   _____
d. polydrug   _____
e. other substance   _____
f. no problem   _____

15. How long was your last period of voluntary abstinence from this major substance?

_____

16. How many months ago did this abstinence end?

_____

**17. How many times have you:

had alcohol d.t.'s? _____
overdosed on drugs? _____

**18. How many times in your life have you been treated for:

alcohol abuse? _____
drug abuse? _____

**19. How many of these were detox only?

alcohol? _____
drug? _____

**20. How many days in the past 30 have you experienced:

alcohol problems? _____
drug problems? _____

*21. Do you use or have you ever used marijuana or hashish?
_____ yes _____ no

[*If answer to question 21 is NO, move on to question 22.*]
If YES, how often?
a. within the past month? _____
b. within the past 6 months? _____
c. over 6 months? _____
d. How has using marijuana or hashish presented problems for you at work? _____
_____
_____

e. Do you ever get high before or during work hours?
_____ yes _____ no

If YES, please explain: _____
_____
_____

*22. Do you use or have you ever used heroin or any other narcotics (morphine, codeine, dilaudid, etc.)?
_____ yes _____ no

[*If answer to question 22 is NO, move on to question 23.*]
If YES, how often?
a. within the past month? _____
b. within the past 6 months? _____
c. over 6 months? _____
d. How has the use of these drugs presented any problems for you at work? _____
_____
_____

(continues)

Drug Abuse Curriculum for Employee Assistance Program Professionals (continued)

**e. Do you ever use any of these before work or during work hours?

_____ yes   _____ no

If YES, please explain: _____
_____
_____

f. Do you ever mix any of these with alcohol or with other drugs?

_____ yes   _____ no

If YES, please explain: _____
_____
_____

**g. Have you ever lost large amounts of money as a direct result of the use of narcotics?

_____ yes   _____ no

If YES, please explain: _____
_____
_____

h. [*Person refuses to answer any of the above questions.*]
_____

*23. Do you use or have you ever used any street (nonprescribed) drugs not already mentioned, such as:
a. hallucinogens (PCP, LSD, mescaline, peyote, psilocybin, etc.)? _____
b. inhalants (glue, paint, gasoline, etc.)? _____
c. amphetamines, speed? _____
d. crack, cocaine? _____
e. other drugs not mentioned? _____

_____ yes   _____ no

[*If answer to question 23 is NO, move on to next question 24.*]
If YES, how often?
a. within the past month? _____
b. within the past 6 months? _____
c. over 6 months? _____
d. How has the use of any of these drugs presented problems for you at work?
_____
_____
_____

***e. Do you ever use any of these before work or during work hours?

_____ yes   _____ no

If YES, please explain: _____
_____

    f. Do you ever mix any of these drugs with alcohol or with other drugs?

        _____ yes   _____ no

        If YES, please explain: _____

        _____

        _____

    g. What do you get out of the drug? _____

        _____

        _____

    h. [*Person refuses to answer any of the above questions.*]

        _____

Let's talk about your work . . .

Work History

24. Are you satisfied with your present work situation?

      _____ yes   _____ no

    a. If not, why not? _____

        _____

        _____

    b. If so, why? _____

        _____

        _____

    c. How does the problem for which you come to the EAP affect your work? _____

        _____

        _____

    d. Have you ever discussed this problem with your supervisor?

        _____ yes   _____ no

**25. Have you missed work, had an accident, or become ill because of drugs?

      _____ yes   _____ no

      If YES, please explain: _____

      _____

      _____

**26. Do you believe your work performance is affected by your drug use?

      _____ yes   _____ no

      If YES, please explain: _____

      _____

      _____

**27. Has your drug use ever resulted in poor performance at work in terms of a suspension, adverse action or performance evaluation, or any similar actions taken against you?

      _____ yes   _____ no

(*continues*)

Drug Abuse Curriculum for
Employee Assistance Program Professionals
(continued)

If YES, please explain: _____
_____
_____

**28. Have you ever been fired from a job because of drug use?
_____ yes   _____ no

If YES, please explain: _____
_____
_____

*29. Have you ever failed to get a job or promotion because of drug use?
_____ yes   _____ no

If YES, please explain: _____
_____
_____

**30. Are you often irritable at work and finding yourself arguing with co-workers?
_____ yes   _____ no

If YES, please explain: _____
_____
_____

**31. Are you using more drugs than you did in the past (could include both prescribed and street drugs)?
_____ yes   _____ no

If YES, please explain: _____
_____
_____

**32. Have you ever had a drug habit?
_____ yes   _____ no

If YES, please explain: _____
_____
_____

**33. If YES, have you ever tried to stop?
_____ yes   _____ no

**34. Have you ever sought help to stop?
_____ yes   _____ no

If YES, please explain: _____
_____
_____

**35. How are you supporting your drug habit/use? _____
_____
_____

**36. How many times in your life have you been charged with the following:
    **a. Disorderly conduct, vagrancy, public intoxication? _____
    **b. Driving while intoxicated? _____
    **c. Major driving violations (reckless driving, speeding, no license, etc.)? _____

***37. Do you ever drive while under the influence of alcohol or drugs?
    _____ yes   _____ no

**38. Have you ever perpetrated the preceding without conviction or detection from others?
    _____ yes   _____ no

    If YES, please specify and explain: _____
_____
_____

**39. Have you ever physically harmed anyone else?
    _____ yes   _____ no

***40. Are you harming anyone at the present time?
    _____ yes   _____ no

**41. Have you ever been physically harmed?
    _____ yes   _____ no

***42. Are you being physically harmed at the present time?
    _____ yes   _____ no

43. What are:
    a. the three best things that ever happened to you in your life? _____
_____
_____

    b. the three worst things that ever happened to you in your life? _____
_____
_____

44. Is there any other information you think is important in your evaluation? _____
_____
_____
_____

(continues)

Drug Abuse Curriculum for Employee Assistance Program Professionals (continued)

Interview Checklist

☐ Obviously depressed/withdrawn

☐ Obviously hostile

☐ Obviously anxious/nervous

☐ Having trouble with reality testing, thought disorders, paranoid thinking

☐ Having trouble comprehending, concentrating, remembering

☐ Having suicidal thoughts

GUIDELINES FOR COUNSELOR BEHAVIOR

During the interview and the whole assessment process, other guidelines for counselor behavior are recommended:

Empathy. Empathy, the cornerstone of good counseling and interviewing, strengthens the connection between the counselor and employee and can help accelerate the process of gathering information about the problems of the employee. Feeding back to the employee what he is saying, both in terms of content and feeling, will help to build this connection.

Acceptance. A distinction should be made between accepting the person and accepting some of his/her behavior. The counselor may look at some unpleasant aspects of this individual who may risk expressing behaviors he is not proud of. The counselor will need to remember, and clearly convey, that he/she makes a distinction between the employee's behavior and the employee as a person.

Respect and nonjudgmental attitude. By separating the behavior from the person, the counselor maintains his/her respect for the individual. At times one's value system will differ from the employee's, and one should not make value judgments regarding these differences. The counselor's responsibility is to understand the employee's motivations regarding drug abuse and other connected problems. One's ability to gather good information will be inhibited if the client feels that the counselor is forming opinions and judgments, and the employee will not trust the counselor. Maintain a distance between one's own attitudes and those of the employee and attempt to understand the employee for who he/she is.

Genuineness, humaneness, and hope. Be clear that the image one projects as an EAP counselor has significant impact on the success of the interview process. Understand the importance of this process to the employee, and be clear that one's "real" connection to that person is the main tool for success. A strictly bureaucratic or professional image may not work in extrapolating the kind of information one needs from this person. Use professional judgment here, and be flexible. Last, but by no means least, provide some hope to the employee. It may be the only thing that gets that person back into the office for the second visit. Counselors should acknowledge that the problem presented is solvable in order to inspire hope in the employee.

ROLE-PLAYING VIGNETTE

Identifying information: 41-year-old, white, married female employed as a secretary/receptionist.

Presenting problem: Expresses concerns about tensions and arguments between husband and teenage sons, wonders if "family counseling would help."

Response to self-administered questionnaire: In a self-administered questionnaire completed prior to the intake interview, the client acknowledges feelings of tension, anxiety, and depression; frequent fatigue and minor illnesses (colds, headaches, flu); and difficulty concentrating, both on the job and at home. She reports "occasional" use of alcohol but denies use of any other prescription, over-the-counter, or illicit drugs other than occasional Tylenol for headaches.

Interview behavior: The client is a self-referral seeking advice about "family problems." She states that her husband, age 45, and two teenage sons, ages 15 and 17, "argue all the time," with conflicts typically precipitated by her husband's disapproval of their son's clothing, hairstyles, musical tastes, and friends.

Upon probing, the client acknowledges that her husband can sometimes "really lose his temper," especially if he has had "a little too much to drink." She tends to minimize this behavior, however, pointing to the fact that he is a steady worker and (like herself) a good provider. She acknowledges having a drink with her husband "once in a while" but states emphatically that she has never used "any drugs like marijuana or cocaine." When asked about specific categories of drugs, she admits that around a year ago she was given a prescription for Valium by her family physician when she told him that she frequently felt upset and was not sleeping well. Upon further probing, she reports that she has recently been taking the Valium "a little more often" than the doctor had prescribed, which she attributes to the increasing marital and family stress in her home and to the "loss" of the Valium's "effect."

Underlying dynamics [example]: The client is a multiple substance abuser (Valium and alcohol). Her husband is an episodic heavy drinker who becomes abusive of his wife and sons when intoxicated. The client began drinking with him early in their marriage due to his encouragement and because he seemed less likely to become abusive if she drank with him. Now she also drinks when alone to reduce feelings of stress related to her marital and family problems, and has approximately doubled her intake of Valium in the past few months.

She is aware that she is taking Valium more frequently than prescribed, but she doesn't think of this as a drug problem or drug "habit" since her doctor prescribed it. She seems unaware of the risks of alcohol/drug interactions. Her physician does not know the extent of her alcohol use and has not warned her about the risks of combining alcohol and other sedative drugs. On direct questioning about the frequency and quantity of her alcohol and Valium use, she becomes vague, minimizes her use, and insists that the problem is primarily the tensions between her husband and sons, about which she is obviously genuinely concerned.

2

Performance Review

Stirling Rasmussen, *The Washington Post*

All managers need the ability to engage in performance counseling, as either the counseled or counselor. Performance counseling provides the opportunity for alignment of the individual and the larger unit, growth, adjustment, and corrective action. Performance appraisals let employees know how they are doing, how they can become even better, and whether they are still seen as valuable members of the work group. Given the complexities and interdependencies of modern organizations and their need to adjust quickly to changes in their environment, this alignment of individual effort and organization objectives is critical.

Performance counseling typically does not happen naturally. Managers frequently experience an aversion to entering into a discussion with another person about what they see as problem behavior. They feel uncomfortable, and even awkward, and they worry about a possible angry reaction from the other person, their own defensive reaction, and rejection by the other person. Their response is to put it off or completely avoid it.

This avoidance even carries over to situations where the subject of the counseling is positive. In one Fortune 500 company, 49 percent of the respondents to an organization-wide attitude survey said they did not receive enough feedback on how well they did their work. Fifty-seven percent said that they were much more likely to be criticized for poor performance than praised for good, yet good work was there to be recognized, since 81 percent of the managers and 74 percent of the nonmanagers said that their co-workers were doing a good job. Interestingly, the results of this survey led to the development of organization-wide performance appraisal.[1]

Many organizations carry out formal, written-for-the-record performance reviews at least annually to ensure that there is, at a minimum, a once-a-year communication about how each employee is doing in contributing toward the common good. The hope is that effective performance counseling will take place and individual performance will be influenced and improved. This hope is often not the reality.

Unfortunately for this well-intentioned tactic, performance reviews and counseling are almost the antithesis of each other. One is being judged; the other is being understood. One is for the official record; the other is off-the-record and confidential. Many of those who have looked at performance review have concluded that one cannot judge an employee and develop that person's potential in the same session.[2]

A formal performance review typically calls to mind a picture of a manager putting to paper conclusions about the performance of a subordinate, followed by a session where they go over the manager's conclusions and that manager's documentation of them. There is a judging dynamic at work in this situation. Further, the words of performance management—*expectations, measures, standards, performance appraisal*—suggest that judgment is being made.

In contrast, performance counseling implies something much less judgmental—probably a two-way discussion and decision making about what is important to be done for someone's performance to grow and agreeing on what needs to happen to accomplish the growth. It is a two-way process because the boss, unlike a counselor, has a personal stake in the outcome and represents the interests of the larger organization. Done effectively, performance counseling can contribute to the organization's success, to employees' development, and to employees' positive attitude toward themselves and the workplace.

There is a basic principle in performance counseling: the counselor must be nonjudgmental and accepting, and the counseled must be involved in identifying problems, coming up with solutions, and taking responsibility for making changes. Those who have tried counseling realize the difficulty in learning to set aside naturally arrived-at conclusions about what is at work in the situation and possible solutions. The tough part is staying in a role of encouraging information gathering and exploring and then helping the counseled move to problem identification and solution. Resisting judgment is critical.

The ideal outcome of a counseling session is coming to grips with a situation and putting together a plan for moving forward. This is the outcome that organizations prize and need from performance counseling—each employee deciding what he or she needs to do to grow, become more effective, and move forward in contributing to the success of the organization.

Achieving this sort of counseling is difficult in hierarchical organizations in situations where one person works for another and therefore is in position to be judged—and indeed is judged. The difficulty is compounded when the organization has asked for a formal review session that is documented for the record. This situation repeatedly signals to managers that it is their responsibility to reach these judgments and record them for the formal record in a performance review.

Rarely is the function of the reviewer in a performance review session considered to be that of helping the reviewed analyze his or her performance and decide what to keep doing and what to improve. Yet this shift from appraisal to analysis is exactly what needs to happen.[3] Instead, everything pushes the reviewing manager (even the term *reviewing manager*) to arrive at conclusions about the job performance, the performer, and, probably, solutions designed to improve the performance. This is not the recipe for effective performance counseling.

We seem to be caught in a catch-22. Without regularly required reviews and the written evidence that they have taken place, much performance counseling will not get done. Yet the performance reviews that are instituted to ensure that performance counseling takes place make it difficult, by their very nature, for a counseling session to happen. To break out of this pattern, the prevailing tactic must be to minimize this judging dynamic as much as possible.

Performance reviews, which are, by necessity, report cards, must be recast so that they become either performance counseling sessions or, at a minimum, the basis for counseling to follow. They can be done in a way that the ability to talk honestly and nondefensively about performance—particularly performance problems—is not damaged.

Unfortunately, a lot of barriers are set up, unknowingly, that make it difficult for performance reviews to become performance counseling. Most appraisal systems often require managers to play a judicial role, which is hardly consistent with the role of a leader who is trying to help.[4] This chapter is about removing the barriers and creating conditions where performance counseling can happen.

The extent to which the judging dynamic is present or is reduced is influenced by a number of factors:

▲ The degree of mutuality in the review process, beginning with the extent of agreement and clarity about what the job expectations were and what the actual performance looked like. Is there a common starting point for a discussion?

▲ The procedures set up by the organization for the review process. Can they be altered?

▲ The format of the review itself. Is it a report card, or does it capture a discussion?

▲ The extent to which the discussion and review can cover old ground rather than spring surprises.

▲ The structure of the discussion about the performance. Is it about the performance, or is it about the review document?

▲ The purpose the organization assigns to performance reviews. Is it primarily to have an alignment and counseling discussion, or is it to assist central administrative decisions?

The Mutual Nature of the Review Process

Alignment between any individual and the job is the objective of the organization. The reviewer has a view of a particular employee's performance that is the result of contrasting what is expected with what actually happened. That review gives a picture of whether there is alignment. Further, the reviewer is probably operating with various levels of satisfaction about the extent of the alignment and the need for undertaking reinforcing or corrective actions. If the reviewer—the manager—and the employee whose performance is being evaluated share exactly the same view of the expectations, the actual performance, and the feelings of satisfaction and conclusions about what needs to happen next, the discussion will run smoothly. Indeed, there are managers who have such effective communication abilities that this is typically the case. Most of us are not so skilled—or so lucky.

The performance review, to be performance counseling, must be a mutually engaged-in progression from (1) agreement about what the performance expectations were to (2) agreement about what the actual performance was to (3) agreement about the gap (positive or negative) between expected and actual to (4) agreement about the reasons for the gaps and about what should be continued and celebrated and what should be changed, and finally to (5) agreement about how to make any changes. The mutual nature of this exploration and discussion is important; the review is something that is done with, not to, the performer, if reactive behavior is to be avoided.[5]

The review and counseling process should be entered into with the basic assumption that both parties probably have somewhat different versions of what the expected performance was, different views of what actually happened, certainly different reasons for why what happened did happen, and, therefore, different solutions—assuming there is a shared view that there is a problem. The manager must decide at the outset what the objective is: to have a discussion that results in a situation being understood and worked on or one that is centered on his or her view of reality as being correct? Clearly, in a managerial role of performance counselor, the latter approach is out. This argues for a very open-ended review process that aims at two people coming to the same conclusions about what was expected, what happened, and what needs to be done now.

Designing an Open-Ended Review Process

The first problem facing this open-ended process is that the review is formal and that it is written. The reason for the written report typically is an organizational requirement for written evidence that the discussion has taken place. It is important to emphasize that in this sense, it is the behavior of the reviewer that is being influenced, not the reviewed.

The act of putting it to paper appears to make it a judgment and immediately lessens the chance for a counseling session. A system of formal performance review therefore must be structured to get around the written barrier. The review document must be, and be seen to be, an accurate reflection of the results of a discussion about an employee's past period's performance and what it means. What must be avoided is a "done to" the person discussion that focuses on the accuracy of the manager's written conclusions rather than on the performance itself.

To the extent the review is seen as judgment passed, it will be resisted by the employee. Not only will the immediate objective of successful performance counseling be missed, but the unhappy experience of countering the defensiveness will be something that the manager will not want to repeat. This, multiplied by the number of managerial peers' experiencing a similar reaction from their own staff members will effectively end the organization's review process. Two factors will help avoid reviews' being seen as "judgment passed": the open-ended quality of the organization's review process and the format of the review itself.

The review is only the best draft; it is open for modification. Managers should write the review as their best draft recollection of what they observed and thought about the performance being reviewed. The review is not to be signed before being discussed with the staff member. It is to be open to modification based on the discussion between the manager and the performer about the performance. Modification means making changes if the facts and conclusions shift during the course of the discussion. Relevant performance that the employee brings to the manager's attention can be added. Thus, the document captures the agreement between the two parties.

The following process leads to the desired outcome:

1. *Prepare a solid foundation for the review.* At least two weeks before the review, the manager and the performer meet to make sure that they are in agreement about what it will be based on. If both have been operating with objectives—a job model or job description—they should agree about which parts of it will be the basis of the review. These job definitions should include measures of successful performance and should have been understood throughout the period to be reviewed. It is helpful to review together what good performance would have looked like—that is, "What would we have seen [heard, smelled, felt, etc.] that would tell us that the job had been done well?" In order to successfully contrast actual with expected performance, there must be initial agreement about the expectations.

This alignment forms the background for the comparison of notes about how both parties saw the job being performed, which will be the basis of the discussion. Thus, the performer should be charged with readying notes in preparation for the review session. This also serves to initiate a self-appraisal that allows the responsibility for analysis to be shared by both the performer and the manager.[6] Since performers who appraise themselves realize that self-serving evaluations will affect their manager's perception of them, performance appraisal systems that have self-appraisal take place before the review discussion result in greater acceptance of the final results by both performer and manager.[7]

The reviewer does the same, comparing expected with actual performance and then using these notes to write the draft review document. (A format for the review appears later in the chapter.)

2. *Discuss the draft with the next level of management.* Once this draft has been written, the manager reviews it with the next level of management for agreement, for two reasons. The first is to ensure that any compensation decisions that will be affected by the review will be in sync with the review itself. Many organizations budget compensation increases well in advance of the actual reviews, and if performance has warranted a greater (or lesser) increase, this should be worked out beforehand. The second is to make sure that the manager and his or her boss see the performance in the same way. It provides a chance for another party familiar with the performance to see if anything, positive or negative, has been missed. This is an essential step for the integrity of the review process and is a protection for the person whose performance is being reviewed.

Additionally, sometimes the next level of management does not have as high a view of the employee. This review thus provides a chance to do some mutual education. If, after discussion, the manager and his or her boss cannot reach agreement on the employee's performance, this discrepancy must become part of the review, since performance counseling must include how someone is seen from the upper levels, particularly if that view is negative. The reasons for this divergent view must be clarified by behavioral examples so that performance counseling can identify ways to turn around higher-level perceptions.

Since the review will represent only a best draft, no signatures are needed—just a verbal OK. This is merely a view of the employee's performance. The review at this stage is open for the discussion with the employee that can convert it to a mutually written review, and signatures at this stage will close this possibility off.

3. *Have the review discussion.* Once verbal upper-level agreement is secure, it is time for the review discussion. (The structure of this discussion will be covered later in the chapter.) The discussion begins with the two parties' talking about how the actual job performance compares to the expected and what that means. It is thus primarily about a mutual review of the performance, not about the "best draft."

4. *Make changes based on the discussion.* The manager's views and recollections will be modified by the views of the employee, and these changes are incorporated into the review document. Often managers with access to a personal computer have the draft review on screen and make

the changes while the employee is present. The more open ended the process is, the more likely the discussion will be about the performance instead of the accuracy of the manager's written recollections and conclusions about the person under review.

The essence of the performance counseling discussion must be captured. If the parties cannot come to agreement in part or in whole, these disagreements must be noted.

5. *Put the review document in final form and sign it.* When the review discussion has been completed, the review document has been read and modifications made and is in its final form, the manager and employee sign it to acknowledge that the discussion has occurred. The next-level manager then signs or initials it.

6. *Distribute copies.* The original goes to the official personnel records, and the staff member receives a copy. What is on record reflects the review discussion.

Written Format of the Review

The format of the review can help or hinder the performance counseling aspect of performance review. The more that a format encourages writing down expectations that are specific to the particular job being reviewed and then contrasting actual performance with them, the more likely it is that a discussion will result. It encourages and supports the job objective approach to performance review, a constant theme in the literature since the 1970s. There are some guidelines to follow.

1. *Address the review to the staff member.* Directing the review to the person whose performance is being evaluated subtly changes the tone. It becomes more conversational and less threatening—more of a companion piece to a conversation—and, by its very preparation, it focuses the manager's thoughts toward a conversation with the employee. The pronouns *I* and *you* and the employee's name should be used liberally in the body of the document.

The review, therefore, should be written to the employee, not to someone else *about* the employee. A review addressed to higher-level management or to the human resources department, in contrast, is a report about someone. It is judgment passed, will have been prepared as such, and will be tough to use as the basis of a performance discussion and performance counseling, since the tone that accompanies reporting will come through and inhibit a joint exploration of the performance. Additionally, the manager will be in the business of defending and justifying his or judgment, which will clearly not come across as an interest in counseling.

There is another reason for this direct approach: the more the review seems to be part of the immediate organization and the normal managerial process, the more likely it will be to be sustained.[8] Writing it from a manager to another member of that organization is more sustainable for the long-term success of the review process than is writing it as a product for, say, the human resources department.

2. *Make the review a narrative.* The review should be written in memo or letter form. As McGregor thought, the best review starts with a blank piece of paper.[9] This keeps it from being influenced by trying to fit the review into the labels and boxes that many performance review forms tend to feature. Many forms that are used as the basis of reviews contain boxes to be checked or filled in, each identified by some sort of adjectival label ("above average," "satisfactory," etc.), put there by those who developed the form and not necessarily relevant to the particular job being reviewed, another of the contextual problems seen by McCall and De-Vries.[10]

Labels have different meanings to different people. The experience of the reviewer is often that of confusion in trying to match his or her own conclusions about the performance being reviewed to the labels provided. What is meant by "excellent" or "satisfactory" or "above average"? And once this labeling is done, the difficulty shifts to trying to explain to the person whose job performance is being reviewed what was meant and, at the same time, having to contend with what the label means to him or her. Clearly, the form itself can set up conditions for defensiveness on the part of both parties when it leads from conclusions, not from expectations.

A compounding problem is that these labels encourage drawing conclusions about the performance without first pulling forth the descriptions of the performance that led to the conclusions. The parties, having been led by the format to pass over a mutual exploration of the observations that led to the conclusions, can then enter into a fight about them.

3. *Constantly compare actual performance to expected.* This is the key to successful performance counseling discussions. If supervisor and employee are in agreement about what the job expectations were and about what actually happened, they can arrive at a satisfactory conclusion. The employee can accept the situation, can define any need for improvement, and can understand the supervisor's conclusions about the performance.

4. *Use accurate descriptions of behavior to define expectations and illustrate actual performance.* This is the most important factor in successful performance discussions. The goal here is to avoid conclusionary labels and, instead, describe accurately and clearly the factors that led to the conclusion. It is the difference between saying, "Here's what I've concluded; what's your reaction?" and "Here's what I'm seeing. Let's

compare it to what you see so we can move forward together to a conclusion."

What is a conclusionary label? When we think of someone else's performance, we assign a word or phrase to it to describe our conclusion: "Great," "OK," "spectacular," "disappointing," "solid," "unacceptable." The problem that arises, whether in writing about the performance or talking about it, is to lead with these conclusions—a natural thing to do but a big mistake because the other person has little idea about what went into arriving at the conclusion and may not even have the same definition about what such a generalized conclusion means. The result is, "What do you mean by that?" a phrase that is generally used as fighting words.

The key to successful counseling discussions as part of performance review is for the two parties to be very clear about the expected performance that is being reviewed and the actual performance that took place. It is the discussion about the actual performance contrasted with the expected that leads to the counseling discussion and to a jointly arrived at conclusion about the performance. Before anyone can discuss a problem with someone else, both parties must be in agreement that there is a problem to discuss, which requires a mutual acceptance of the facts of the situation.

An example will illustrate the importance of this concept. A commonly heard complaint about someone's performance is that he or she has an "attitude" problem. At this point, if the manager leads with that conclusion, it might sound like this: "Your attitude is poor and must be improved." The employee's response is likely to be one of developing an "attitude" about that statement, which is conclusionary and judgmental and conveys no information that can be acted on. The employee will develop a defensive posture, and the ensuing exchange will not be a performance counseling discussion.

A complaint that the employee has an attitude problem needs definition. Its origins are probably foggy even to the manager. Among other things, it could mean any of the following:

> "In situations where I suggest to you another way of getting a job done, what I expect are conversational tones and a discussion about my suggestion and your reaction to it. What happens instead is that you respond by raising your voice, frowning, not looking at me, and answering my questions with only a brief 'yes' or 'no.' "

> "One result that I expect from your interaction with customers is no more than an occasional complaint—certainly no more than one a week. Something in the interaction is resulting in a pattern of complaints about cold, uncaring treatment, and there are at least four or five a week."

"Everyone must be here ready to work at the start of the shift. It's one of the requirements of our manufacturing process. You continue regularly to come in 5 minutes late despite our having talked about the problem."

"In a customer service phone operation where there are always calls waiting and therefore no time for any service reps to handle personal calls, you spend 10 percent of your work time taking personal calls."

These are behavioral descriptions that are linked to critical incidents in the performer's job. All of these are descriptions of either observed behavior or measurements of the way the job is being done, contrasted with behaviorally defined expectations of how it should be done. From any of these the manager could conclude (not necessarily accurately) that the employee does not care about the job and has an attitude problem. To reach that conclusion, he or she has mentally progressed from these observations to the conclusions about motivation that spring from them.

Since the employee hears the conclusions and not the observations, the key to having a fruitful discussion is for the manager to back away from the conclusions—to the extent of not even stating them—and instead bring to the light observations. Rather than speaking about an attitude problem, he or she needs to let the employee know what expected behavior or results would look like and the actual behavior or results and the effect that it is having. Both parties can then explore whether they understood the same expectations and agree that the behavior or results are as seen. From that point they can begin to engage in a discussion about what is going on and what to do about it.

The technique for discovering what underlies one's conclusions is to say to oneself, "OK, that's my conclusion [in this case, that there is an attitude problem]. Now what did I actually see and what specifically did I compare it to in order to come to that conclusion?" This process of tracing back from surfaced conclusions to recalled observations is the basis for the performance discussion and the written review. This holds equally for performance that needs improvement and performance that deserves to be recognized.

These behavioral descriptions are critical to performance counseling. Reviewing the measurable accomplishments and objectives of a job, such as volume of sales made or rate of product produced, is one aspect of performance review, but using only this fails to help performers understand what behavior they must modify or adopt to improve the results.[11]

Beer and Ruh have described an approach that Corning used that identified the incidents critical to good performance and then described the specific actions that led to either significant improvements or drops in the organization's performance. These behavioral descriptions of specific actions then are used to help performers learn and grow by comparing their own observed behavior with that of the models of effective behavior.[12]

Harry Levinson also sees the need to define expected behavior. He argues for a dynamic job description—one that enlarges definitions of job responsibility and measurable outcomes by describing the emotional and behavioral lay of the land associated with the job. By then providing feedback that is behaviorally descriptive and verifiable and contrasting it with the enlarged definition, counseling about the job can take place.[13]

5. *Avoid labeling conclusions about performance.* Organizations compound the problem of a natural human tendency to put conclusions and judgment in front of evidence by attempting to distill conclusions about performance into categories, such as "outstanding," "satisfactory," "unsatisfactory," or their equivalents. Often this is driven by the need of the organization's administrative system for numbers that can be used to rank employees comparatively. For two reasons, it is a trap. To see why it is, try an experiment. Ask any group of employees whether they would like being known as a "satisfactory" performer. Most will answer no. One study showed that at General Electric, the average employee's self-estimate of performance was at the seventy-seventh percentile. Kathleen Morris and Joel DeLuca in 1985 estimated that 80 percent of us believe we are in the upper 30 percent of performers. And Edward Mandt states that attitude surveys consistently show that as many as 80 percent of employees self-rate their performance as above average or higher.[14] Most of us resist being seen as average, even if average or satisfactory means working to the standard that the organization has determined is necessary and perfectly acceptable—which is probably what most of us are doing most of the time.

Thus, there is a natural resistance to the labels, and since 80 percent of a company's employees cannot be "above average," or more than "satisfactory," there is a demotivating effect to being so labeled. The need to maintain self-esteem sets up a resistance to the labels, which gets in the way of the counseling aspect of performance reviews.

Managers, realizing the impact of such labeling on motivation, resisting using them. Including them as one of the requirements of written reviews will have a negative impact on the sustainability of an organization's performance review system.

Additionally, any use of categories encourages the reviewer to work through the data about observed performance privately and reach a conclusion about the performance and about the person that may be difficult to understand and accept. It is this label-driven push for conclusion that moves the review session away from being counseling and instead sets up a situation where the person being reviewed becomes defensive and resistant. Michael Beer has described this well:

A manager can minimize defensiveness and avoidance by narrowly focusing feedback on specific behaviors or specific performance goals. For example, rating a person as unsatisfactory on a characteristic as broad as motivation is likely to be perceived as a broadside attack and as a threat to self-esteem. Feedback about specific incidents or aspects of "how" a person is performing the job is more likely to be heard than broad generalizations, and will be more helpful to the individual who wants to improve performance. Thus an appraisal discussion that relies on a report-card rating of traits or performance is doomed to failure because it leads the supervisor into general evaluative statements that threaten the subordinate.[15]

It is the premature drive to conclusions, suggested by the use of labels, that torpedoes many review discussions and ultimately leads managers to avoid performance reviews because they are painful experiences for both parties. Rather than lead with conclusions, a valuable performance review discussion begins with an exploration of specific observed performance as measured against expectations. The conclusions can be jointly derived from that examination.

6. *Develop a sample review format.* To give the written review some structure, headings should be used. A simple format that works well is the one shown in Figure 2-1.

7. *Do not underplay the positive.* Many people in organizations are successful because they are good at seeing what needs to be done or changed and then acting upon it. Thus, in a sense, a natural selection process is at work that picks a preponderance of critical managers. One of the reasons for the "Things Done Well" section of the review in Figure 2-1 is to counter the tendency to overload a review with what must be fixed. A review is also a time to recognize and thank the employee.

The positive behaviors need to be well illustrated with clear behavioral descriptions in order to restate and reinforce performance expectations in an enjoyable way.

There is another reason for making sure that the review contains acknowledgment of the positive. Roughly 40 percent of the population must feel acknowledged and appreciated for what they have accomplished before they can respond to the need to improve other aspects of their performance. This is not a need personally experienced and therefore understood by most of our naturally selected critical managers.[16] But the depth of disagreements over performance that can result from not taking care of this need can be profound, with the one party feeling unacknowledged, unappreciated, and not having been given any credit and the other feeling that the first is failing to face up to reality and is operating out of

(*text continues on page 50*)

Figure 2-1. Sample format for performance reviews.

MEMORANDUM

TO: [*Staff Member*]

FROM: [*Manager*]

SUBJECT: Performance Review

These are my prediscussion thoughts and observations about your past year's performance. Based on our discussion, we may come up with changes to what I've written here. If we do, I'll make them, and we'll both sign the modified version. You'll also see that the last section, "Discussion Results," hasn't been completed. We'll finish it together. A copy of the final version will be forwarded to your personnel file.

RESULTS: [Specifically describe the major objectives and expected accomplishments of the job. Then contrast these with what was actually accomplished, being behaviorally descriptive in both. Both plusses and minuses are captured in this section.]

CRITICAL   [Most often, these behaviors are linked to the human relationships
BEHAVIORS: that are important in any job performance: between the person in the job and the boss, with co-workers, with people in other units of the company, with subordinates (if a supervisor), with customers, and with task force members. Describe acceptable performance in these areas and then contrast it with actual performance, again being behaviorally descriptive. As with "Results," both plusses and minuses are included.]

[OTHER   [If the important messages about performance have been covered
HEADINGS:]   under "Results" and "Critical Behaviors," no other headings are needed, and the review can move directly to the next section. If not, create headings or apply headings from objectives or job models currently being used. Illustrate the conclusions with examples that compare what was expected with what actually happened.]

THINGS DONE WELL: [This section summarizes the plusses that have emerged. It is an important section because it ensures that both the reviewer and the reviewed do not merely see what is missing in a job. It reinforces what is wanted in performance and is a chance to provide thanks.]

THINGS TO WORK ON: [This section ensures that concerns about current performance and opportunities for growth are highlighted and discussed. It is the basis of performance counseling and is pulled from patterns that emerged from previous sections.]

SUMMARY: [This section has several purposes. It first summarizes the manager's conclusions about the performance. Was it a good year, or are there several major corrections that must be made? Were all of the major requirements of the job met and some even exceeded? Were they all clearly exceeded? Was there growth in the job by someone new to it or recovery from earlier poor performance? Are significant responsibilities not being met, and must improvements be made?

This section also provides a chance to jot down thoughts about this employee's development needs, growth, and career. The intent is to stimulate discussion and to plan what is next.

Finally, this is the place to reinforce the good things that should be continued and to outline any thoughts about improvement and growth. It is also a chance to thank the employee for work done well or to give a serious message about expected changes.

DISCUSSION RESULTS: [This section is left blank since it will not be completed until after the performance review discussion. Since review discussions often involve performance counseling, with its improvement decisions and development agreements, this section is used to record those decisions and agreements. Included should be clear statements of the responsibilities of both parties for carrying them out.]

We have discussed this review:

_____   _____   _____   _____
Staff member   date   Reviewer   date

                                         _____   _____
                                         Second-level   date
                                         reviewer

emotion rather than logic. It is a hole that is easily avoided but difficult to escape from.

8. *Remember that the reputation of the staff member is affected by the review.* The final report for the official record will be read by others, an important consideration to keep in mind while writing the review. Everything in it needs to be explained well enough so that its readers will not arrive at inaccurate conclusions (another argument for the use of accurate behavioral descriptions).

Structuring the Discussion About the Performance

1. *Prepare a solid foundation for the review.* At least two weeks before the review, manager and employee should meet and make sure that they are in agreement about what it will be based on, including mutual agreement about performance expectations and measures of success. Each then prepares for the discussion by making notes, point by point, about the actual performance in comparison with the expected. The employee thus shares some responsibility for the performance review by having to prepare notes and thoughts for the review session.

2. *Get started.* This discussion is going to take a while. Allow 2 uninterrupted hours for it. The manager begins by explaining the purpose (mutual analysis of the performance) and the steps of the meeting:
   a. Compare and discuss, point by point, each party's views of the performance as contrasted with what was expected.
   b. Discuss what went well and why, and what did not and why.
   c. Acknowledge and celebrate accomplishments, and identify and agree on areas for growth and improvement and actions to attain them.
   d. Read the draft review and make relevant changes together.
   e. Add the results of the performance discussion to the review document.
   f. Put the review into final form and sign it.

3. *Compare and contrast prepared notes about the performance.* Both parties have come to the meeting with observations of the performance based on the job expectations. The person whose performance is being reviewed starts with the first expectation, talking about what actually happened and how he or she feels about it. The manager responds by sharing his or her own observations of the results and thoughts on them. If there is a difference in what was observed or disagreement in why something happened, both parties work it through. The objective is to provide a mutual basis for acknowledging the causes of good performance and the means for needed improvement. This pattern of discussion— expectation by expectation, employee first and then manager—continues.

Parts of this discussion will be integrated into the written review document, so notes are important.

4. *Go over the draft review.* When the mutual exploration and analysis have been completed, the employee reads the best draft review, or both parties go over it together, paragraph by paragraph; the employee can choose the approach. It is important to work on the positive aspects of the written draft first; reinforcement and recognition are a major objective of the review process.

5. *Make changes.* Changes need to be made if the discussion merits them. If there are areas where both parties disagree, this should be recorded. This is a mutual process, but that does not mean that the manager has to give in on strongly held observations or beliefs.

6. *Complete the "Discussion Results" section.* Record the results of performance counseling in the "Discussion Results" section, specifying the details of any plans that came out of the discussion and noting who is responsible for what. Both parties work out the wording together before concluding the meeting. If there was not agreement on all items, the wording about the lack of agreement should be worked out and recorded. If the employee had something positive to say about the review or about the manager's abilities, this is a good place to note it.

7. *Sign the final documents.* The signatures mean that the discussion represented by the document took place. After the next-level manager signs it, copies are made and distributed.

Some Cautions

Performance counseling needs to be a regular part of each manager's repertoire. The literature is consistent on this point. But the reality for most organizations is that ongoing performance counseling discussions are spotty. That makes it difficult for the performance review to serve as a counseling session since the tendency is to bring up problems that have not been raised as issues before. The result is a nervous reviewer and an angry employee.

Ideally, a periodic performance review is a formal culmination of all the informal performance counseling discussions that have been going on during the year. As such, it contains no surprises but is a formalization of the agreement between two adults about job performance. This lessens the impact of the judging quality of the performance review.

It is important to avoid surprises. Negative items about performance should not be included in the review if they have not been discussed before the formal review. Consider what your own reaction would be if the first time that you learned about a problem that you had allegedly created was in a document that was then going into your personnel file, with no chance to work on it or turn it around before it became part of your official record. Righteous anger is probably one feeling that comes to mind. At this point, all hope of performance counseling is out the window.

One exception is something that just happened and must be immediately corrected. Otherwise, discussions about the problem should occur before the review, even to the extent of delaying the review until the issue has been addressed.

Performance reviews are not written as the planned first step in a disciplinary process. They are not to be used as an instrument for disciplinary action. Performance problems of such severity should have been addressed long before the formal review session, and if they have, there should be ample documentation about the problem, so that the performance review merely captures what has already been going on.

Discussions about compensation must be separate from the review and counseling discussion. Money triggers too many unpredictable responses. The focus of performance review is the individual job; it is not to stir up the zero-sum game of comparing one performer to others.[17] Discussion of salary can trigger feelings of comparison and fairness, and, if part of the review and counseling discussion, can undermine the mutuality of the process by putting the manager on the defensive by having to justify the amount of increase. A number of writers recommend only loosely linking the performance appraisal and pay.[18]

Often, these writers point out, salary is not representative of performance anyway. A simple example will illustrate why. In most organizations, a major role of compensation is to protect good performers from being attracted to competitors by higher pay. In any organization, each job has a range of pay, and often the goal is to move good performers as quickly as possible to within a certain percentage of the top range. Thus, in any group of jobs, newer employees who may have come in at the lower end of the pay range for the job are being quickly moved to the higher percentage bracket through annual increases. In the same group are performers who have been there a long time and are very, very good but are at the top of what the organization is willing to pay for that job. Their increases will be much smaller than the newer members, whom the compensation system is trying to protect. Thus, exemplary new employees may be receiving 6.5 percent raises (in a situation where the average increase is 4.5 percent) and exemplary older, experienced employees are receiving 4 percent or less. In this situation, the reviewer can have a positive performance discussion with the long-term exemplary employee and then end the discussion by talking about the 4 percent raise that he or she is getting, particularly when that same individual asks what the average raise is. The two discussions do not mix, since one is representative of the manager as the helper and the other the manager as the judge. Even a day's separation is enough to avoid contaminating the good that can come out of a decent performance counseling and review session.

Thompson and Dalton, furthermore, warn that once a formal system is set up to publicize a direct link between performance and specific rewards, the reward chosen becomes the only credible indicator of management's evaluation of individual performance. This impoverishes the value of all the other rewards available to an organization.[19] Since factors that are not related to performance and are outside a manager's control influence compensation, this subject is a poor choice for a manager or organization to make the specific reward for performance.

If the system of performance reviews that is operating in one's organization does not allow the separation of the review discussion from compensation, changes need to be made.

The Organizational Purpose Assigned to Performance Reviews

Since the review is written and becomes part of the record, it is very tempting for human resources personnel to use it for purposes that fly in the face of its counseling role. Many organizations mistakenly make the review a primary justification for personnel decisions. This usually becomes the downfall of large-scale performance review attempts.

For counseling to work, the aspects of reviews as report cards must be minimized. If, however, the reviews are to be used as drivers of administrative decisions, reviews must be compared. The larger the organization is, the greater will be the number of reviews to be compared, and the more necessary it will be to reduce the information on each review to some format that lends itself to easy comparison—numerical equivalents or adjectival descriptions such as "at standard," "above standard," or "below standard." The open format I have advocated cannot be used. This understandable administrative drive for simplicity and cross-indexing requires the reviewing manager to reduce a very complex issue—the performance of another person—to some narrow categorizations. This not only reinforces the judging dynamic within the reviewer but also makes it difficult to obtain agreement between the two parties about the value and worth of the performance. The review process becomes uncomfortable and will not be sustained over time.

Organizations thus assign mixed and contradictory purposes to performance reviews. One purpose is to have each individual have a constructive discussion about how he or she is doing and where that leads to. Another is to rate and rank organizational members so that decisions about pay, promotion, and demotion can be made. These are contradictory because the latter requires that the judging dynamic predominate, driving out the likelihood of effective performance counseling. Many organizations that have tried to use performance review as an administrative system have it subverted and manipulated to the point that it winds up accomplishing neither. Warnings that appraisal systems designed to accomplish all the organization's needs do not work are scattered throughout the literature.[20] What suffers in all cases is the performance counseling aspect.

The major purpose of formal performance reviews should be to ensure that at least once a year, there is an alignment between an individual's efforts and what it is that the organization pays that individual to do. That alignment includes not only what is being done but how well it is being done. The value to the organization and to its members of this taking place in every job is very clear.

The purest form of this approach is the review discussion, which is only between the manager and performer and is not for the record. This is what Beer calls the developmental interview; its sole purpose is helping. Unfortunately, these interviews typically do not occur throughout an organization. Thus, there is a need for the discussion to be documented. The documentation represents a "judgment made" situation, akin to what Beer calls the directed interview, where the objective is to communicate a performance evaluation or pay decision that has already been made. What I have described in this chapter is an approach that Beer calls a mixed model appraisal interview. He writes that it can work only if the primary role and goal is helping, not judging.[21]

Using performance reviews to rate and rank individuals for administrative purposes gets in the way of the primary role and goal: to help. It turns a counseling session into an exercise of building a case for the ratings. Supervisors begin playing games with the system, bringing us back to the judging dynamic that effects two factors that will make it very difficult to sustain an organizational process of annual reviews and alignment discussions.[22] One is that the person being reviewed will feel prejudged and will react defensively to the process. The other is that the reviewer will, in turn, react defensively to this defensiveness by having to justify his or her judgments and will avoid a future repetition of such unpleasantness, either by not doing another performance review or by ducking issues that might trigger an unpleasant review experience.

There is also the temptation to tie the review process to the compensation process. Organizations should be wary of making this tie-in much closer than that of requiring that a current review be on record before any compensation change can be processed and that the content reflects a level of performance that justifies any proposed change.

Here is the problem: compensation systems are in the comparative salary business. Their world is comparing the worth of what one person does to that of another. Performance review compares what an individual is doing to the standard of the job, not against what other people are doing. Its purpose is to enable that individual to optimize his or her performance against those job standards, not against the standard of what others are doing. These are incompatible objectives.

Closely linking compensation and review will suggest setting up the administratively driven system of comparative ratings. If performance reviews are driven by a need to justify and rationalize compensation decisions, with their primary objective an administrative one, a process will be created that will ultimately be subverted by managers who skew the rankings to fit the numerical requirements for a particular salary level they want for an individual. That will destroy honest performance counseling, and also give only an illusion of the objective measures hoped for.

Further, this approach to rating performance leads to identifying salary winners and losers by comparing them, by necessity, to generalized criteria. The use of generalized criteria leads to trouble in performance review discussions. Thus, neither the objectives of a joint process of reviewing performance and performance counseling nor an accurate administrative system of review will be achieved.

My argument is that an organization can have a system that achieves performance counseling and a yearly alignment as its primary objective— or nothing at all.

Getting People to Do Performance Reviews

Even when everything has been set up to ease performance counseling— the proper purpose for performance reviews, the training and coaching resources made available to managers, a system that is open-ended and encourages mutuality, the statements from top executives that it will be done—it still will be resisted and put off by many managers.

McCall and DeVries have an interesting theory about why this happens. As they looked at Mintzburg's studies of managerial work, they saw that most managerial activities last 9 minutes or less (only 10 percent went for more than an hour), that the vast majority of the managers' contacts were ad hoc rather than preplanned, that there was a strong preference for current than for historic or future information, and that managers concentrated their efforts on the nonroutine. They then proposed that appraisal systems, which require large chunks of time, are preplanned, look at past information, and are routinized, are structured in ways that contradict managerial work styles and values.[23]

I think they are right. One of the biggest complaints managers have about reviews is about the amount of time they take to do well. One organization I know of has solved the problem by taking steps to reinforce performance reviews for the purpose of feedback and counseling as being part of the manager's job. There, each staff member must have participated in a review discussion and have signed the completed review document by his or her anniversary date. The vice-president of that organization not only looks at every review in terms of honesty, accuracy, and quality but also tracks the percentage of reviews completed on time. All the managers have been told that if they are not completing their reviews on time, no matter how well they have done the rest of their job, when it is time for their own salary review, they will get no more than the average increase—a powerful incentive for the timely completion of the reviews.

NOTES

1. From an internal survey of a Fortune 500 company by Sirota, Alper and Associates.
2. Douglas McGregor, "An Uneasy Look at Performance Appraisal," *Harvard Business Review* (September-October 1972): 133–138; Michael Beer and Robert Ruh, "Employee Growth through Performance Management," *Harvard Business Review* (July-August 1976): 59–66; Michael Beer, "Performance Appraisal: Dilemmas and Possibilities," *Organizational Dynamics* (Winter 1981): 24–36; Derick Brinkerhoff and Rosabeth Moss Kanter, "Formal Systems of Appraisal of Individual Performance" (unpublished paper prepared for the Program on Non-Profit Organizations, Institution for Social and Policy Studies, Yale University, 1979).
3. McGregor, "Uneasy Look," p. 136.
4. Ibid.
5. George A. Reider, "Performance Review—A Mixed Bag," *Harvard Business Review* (July-August 1973): 63.
6. McGregor, "Uneasy Look."
7. Beer, "Performance Appraisal," p. 31.
8. Morgan McCall, Jr., and David DeVries, "Appraisal in Context: Clashing with Organizational Realities," Technical Report 4 (Greensboro, N.C.: Center for Creative Leadership, 1977).
9. McGregor, "Uneasy Look."
10. McCall and DeVries, "Appraisal in Context."
11. Beer and Ruh, "Employee Growth."
12. Ibid.
13. Harry Levinson, "Appraisal of *What* Performance?" *Harvard Business Review* (July-August 1976): 30–36.
14. Edward Mandt, "Who Is Superior and Who's Merely Very Good?" *Across the Board* (National Conference Board) (April 1984): 16–23.
15. Beer, "Performance Appraisal."
16. Susan Scanlon, "How to Keep F's from Failing to Deal with the 'Tough Stuff,' " *Type Reporter* 3:12 (May 1989).
17. Paul Thompson and Gene Dalton, "Performance Appraisal: Managers Beware," *Harvard Business Review* (January-February 1970): 149–157.
18. Ibid.; Beer and Ruh, "Employee Growth"; Kathleen Morris and Joel De-Luca, "Why Performance Appraisal Can't Work . . . A Fresh Look at What to Do about It" (presented at the National Organizational Development Network Conference, 1985).

19. Thompson and Dalton, "Performance Appraisal," p. 154.
20. Ibid.; Brinkerhoff and Kanter, "Formal Systems of Appraisal"; Levinson, "Appraisal of *What* Performance?" McCall and DeVries, "Appraisal in Context."
21. Beer, "Performance Appraisal," pp. 32, 34.
22. Thompson and Dalton, "Performance Appraisal"; Brinkerhoff and Kanter, "Formal Systems of Appraisal"; Mandt, "Who Is Superior?"
23. McCall and DeVries, "Appraisal in Context," p. 5.

SUGGESTED READING

One of the most helpful and easily understood guidelines to performance appraisal is found in Michael Beer's "Performance Appraisal: Dilemmas and Possibilities," *Organizational Dynamics* (Winter 1981).

For a useful but disquieting view of what performance review is up against, see Morgan McCall, Jr., and David DeVries, "Appraisal in Context: Clashing with Organizational Realities," Technical Report 4 (Greensboro, N.C.: Center for Creative Leadership, 1977).

A thought-provoking approach to defining performance measures for any job can be found in Tom Gilbert's chapter, "Measuring Human Competence," in his book, *Human Competence: Engineering Worthy Performance* (New York: McGraw-Hill, 1978).

Excellent examples of the differences between behaviorally descriptive and evaluative language in a performance counseling session abound in Tom Connellan's book, *How to Grow People into Self Starters* (Ann Arbor, Mich.: Achievement Institute, 1988).

How to understand and modify the environmental aspects that affect human performance are clearly treated in Geary Rummler's and Allan Brache's book, *Improving Performance: How to Manage the White Space on the Organization Chart* (San Francisco: Jossey-Bass Publishers, 1990).

A book that managers have found to be a practical and easy-to-understand guide to performance management and coaching is Ferdinand Fournies, *Coaching for Improved Work Performance* (Blue Ridge Summit, Penn.: Liberty House, 1987).

3

Career Development and Growth

Gerald M. Sturman, The Career Development Team, Inc.

Career development probably covers a wider range of corporate disciplines and programs than almost any other subject. Because definitions of it vary widely, it is important to derive a definition out of the purpose of career development rather than out of how programs look to people.

From the context of a business organization—a large corporation or a smaller entity—the purpose of providing career development to employees is to bring some real benefit to the organization, the individual, and the managers and supervisors. The benefits of a career development system to these three stakeholders include those shown in Figure 3-1. Certainly these alone serve to justify the investment by an organization in a career development system, but it is interesting—and valuable—to dig deeper into the nature of what career development can and should be.

Career development has to do with the fundamental nature of the relationship of people to their work and employees to their organizations. The structure of these relationships needs to be defined to develop a clear definition of career development.

In its deepest and most personal meaning, work is "the expression of self in the contribution of value."[1] People derive satisfaction from their work by making a contribution appropriate to their own abilities and desires and useful to their organizations. The deepest satisfaction comes from doing that work as effectively as possible. Only the individual can be truly responsible for discovering his or her own desires and best abilities to seek ways to use these to make the maximum contribution to the goals of the organization. True work satisfaction lies in the full realization of this responsibility.

Career development is the process by which employees take responsibility for developing their ability to make an expanded contribution to the company, a contribution that links individual work satisfaction and performance to the goals and challenges of the company. Career development is not about "getting ahead." It is, rather, about getting to be the best an individual can be and finding that place in the company where he or she can express excellence in contributing to the goals of the organization. Many people discover that place to be where they are right now and

Figure 3-1. Benefits of a career development system.

Managers and Supervisors	Employees	Organization
• Increased skill in managing own careers • Greater retention of valued employees • Better communication between managers and employees • More realistic staff and development planning • Productive performance appraisals • Increased understanding of the organization • Enhanced reputation as a people developer • Employee motivation for accepting new responsibilities • Building of talent inventory for special projects • Clarification of fit between organization and individual goals	• Helpful assistance with career decisions and changes • Enrichment of present job and increased job satisfaction • Better communication between employee and manager • More realistic goals and expectations • Better feedback on performance • Current information about the organization and future trends • Greater sense of personal responsibility for managing careers	• Better use of employee skills • Increased loyalty • Dissemination of information at all organizational levels • Better communication with organization as a whole • Greater retention of valued employees • Expanded public image as a people-developing organization • Increased effectiveness of personnel systems and procedures • Clarification of organization goals

Source: Z. B. Liebowitz, C. Farren, and B. L. Kaye, *Designing Career Development Systems* (San Francisco: Jossey-Bass, 1986).

find opportunity for expanded contribution by looking at their current job with a renewed perspective.

Why Are Corporations Interested—Particularly Now?

A 1986 nationwide corporate survey found that there had been a significant decline in employee attitudes, which was having a serious negative impact on productivity.[2] The causes of this corporate cultural crisis are related to rapidly changing structures of corporate ownership, the emergence of a new set of corporate cultural standards, evolving management values and techniques, the breathtaking pace of new technologies, the increasingly dramatic shift from an industrial to a service economy, the quickening impact of personal computers, the availability of instant worldwide communication, the coming together of private, national, and international economies into a world economy, and even more.

All across the United States, in companies large and small, the same thing is heard: individuals must prepare themselves for rapid changes by being aware of their abilities and by being flexible and adaptable to different needs in their industries that are yet unforeseen.

Career Development vs. Management or Employee Development

The usual goal of management or employee development is to develop the particular adaptive, functional, or specific work-related skills of managers and other employees. While there are skills involved in implementing a career plan, career development is more properly thought of as an ongoing process driven by an attitude or mode of behavior. In its most powerful form, career development provides the best overall framework for management and employee development programs. A properly designed career development program will include a detailed analysis of the future of both the organization and the individual. To the extent that the individual understands his or her own style, motivation, values, needs, and skills and applies these to the needs and opportunities of the organization, the program of skills development designed by or for the individual will be far more appropriate than the usual random selection of interesting courses. Comprehensive career development planning should be a prerequisite for any effective management or employee development program. In the description of a corporate career development system, management development and other forms of employee development are included as part of the career development system.

Corporate Career Development Systems

Despite the fact that the roots of career development theory and practice go back to 1909, a review of the literature indicates that there were few formal career development programs or systems existing in the American corporate workplace prior to 1975.[3] A study by the American Management Association (AMA) in 1979 concluded that "the results suggest that career planning programs for salaried personnel are not nearly as common or as advanced as might be thought. While there is widespread support for career planning as a concept, there is a wide gap between the ideal and the reality of current practices."[4]

A subsequent study, published in 1983 by the American Society for

Training and Development (ASTD), described a survey of forty major American organizations in manufacturing, communication, wholesale and retail trade, finance, insurance, real estate, services, and government.[5] The study was intended to uncover the answers to the following questions:

- ▲ What do organizations consider to be part of the career development effort?
- ▲ What were the factors that led to the creation of a career development program within the organization?
- ▲ Who in the organizations is responsible for career development systems, and what is included in these systems?
- ▲ What career development tools are used, and which of these tools are considered most promising?
- ▲ How is the effectiveness of the programs measured?
- ▲ What are the future plans for career development systems?
- ▲ What conclusions can be drawn by other organizations about the use of career development in the surveyed organizations?

This study showed significantly more involvement in career development by corporate America than a few years earlier. Figure 3-2 shows the extent

Figure 3-2. Use of career development techniques.

Technique	Reported Number	Use (Percent)	Number Rating	Mean Effectiveness[a]
Career planning seminars or workshops	31	78%	28	4.25
Career counseling by staff counselors	28	70	19	3.71
Job posting	18	45	b	b
Career workbooks	16	40	13	3.50
Skills inventory	14	35	b	b
Career pathing	9	23	b	b
Succession planning	8	20	b	b
Career discussions by supervisors with employees	7	18	b	b
Career resource center	7	18	b	b
Outplacement counseling	4	10	b	b

Source: T. G. Gutteridge and F. L. Otte, *Organizational Career Development: State of the Practice* (Washington, D.C.: American Society for Training and Development, 1983). © 1983 ASTD. Used with permission.
[a]Scale is 1–5, with 5 the highest.
[b]An insufficient number of ratings was received to make computation of a mean rating justifiable.

of use of various career development techniques in the responding organizations. Note that 78 percent of the organizations responding used career development seminars—in sharp contrast to the earlier AMA study in which only 11 percent of the companies reported the use of career development workshops. The ASTD study also reported that only 16 percent of the organizations responding had career development programs prior to 1970; 26 percent initiated programs between 1970 and 1975, and 58 percent started their programs after 1975.

With regard to understanding the level of career development activity in corporations, the ASTD study concluded:

1. Practitioners who were interviewed in this research tend to believe that:

    a. There is a need for more integration of career development program components, both with each other and with other existing human resources processes;

    b. Very little formal evaluation is done. Thus, a more systematic evaluation of career development programs is needed, especially to document benefits;

    c. A small percentage of employees is being reached, and techniques for reaching more employees with the least expenditure of resources are needed;

    d. Ways of getting more employees involved in career planning are needed because docile, or passive, employees can seriously restrict the ability of an organization to adapt to change;

    e. Their career counseling-career planning seminars and career workshops are effective with those employees who are being reached;

    f. The future of career development programs is bright.

2. Career development programs in these forty organizations represent either new services offered to employees or a greater willingness on the part of management to take the risks involved in liberalizing older services along lines which present potential dangers as well as potential benefits to individuals and the organization.

3. Reasons for starting career development programs vary considerably from one organization to another, but the major reasons given include top management interest, a desire to promote from within or personnel shortages, employee interest, and equal opportunity or affirmative action pressure.

4. Career development programs tend to begin small and expand; they begin with one activity, and others are added.

5. There is an emphasis on employees taking responsibility for their own career development, coupled with a recognition that they need help in getting information, evaluating it, and implementing plans.

6. There is no magic formula for success in program implementation; to some extent each organization must "reinvent the wheel" because each organization is different.

7. Creating successful programs requires a team effort of top managers and operating level personnel.

8. Much remains to be learned about the state of the practice of career development in organizations, and a number of conclusions regarding future research can be drawn:

   a. Research based on better sampling is needed to get more accurate estimates of the percentage of organizations using various career development practices.
   b. Career development programs are sufficiently complex and variable from one organization to another to make large-scale survey research on total programs very difficult.
   c. Research on the effectiveness of various career development techniques will be difficult because techniques interact with one another and with other organizational variables.[6]

System Elements

An organizational career development system may be broad and all-inclusive or limited to a few elements, depending on the decisions of executives responsible for human resources management policies. Regardless of the need for career management in the organization, executive perceptions or economics will dictate the extent to which systems are designed, developed, and implemented. Figure 3-3 shows the basic elements of an organizational career management system. The elements have been organized into three major categories and are grouped to show organizational support of the individual in taking responsibility for his or her own career management process. The elements in each category—the organization, the supervisor, and resources—represent those activities managed in those categories. The management of the activities in the resources category usually resides in an organization's human resources or personnel department. Most of the elements defined here are familiar parts of the human resources services provided in many organizations. Procedures, processes, and practices such as outplacement, retirement planning, succession planning, management development, technical training, and performance appraisal are described in other chapters of this

Figure 3-3. Organizational career management system.

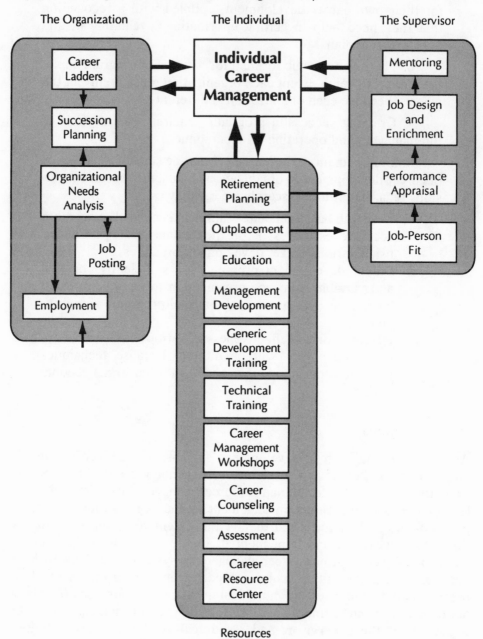

book. Less well known and less frequently documented are the processes associated directly with career development: career assessment, career management workshops, and career counseling (including career coaching).

The Organization

▲ *Organizational needs analysis.* An analysis of the need for specific categories and numbers of people through time. The organization comes first. In order to have the right people in the right places at the right times, it is important to understand where the company is going. Starting with the long-range vision of the chief executive and working down through the staff and line operating organizations, short- and long-range plans based on economic and financial targets and projections, competitive market analyses and strategies, planned developments in technology and products, and demographic changes in the work force market will dictate the organizational needs analysis.

▲ *Employment.* The process of bringing new employees into the organization in response to the overall needs analysis or to specific requests from managers in need of a new position or a replacement. Includes identification, interviewing, assessment, selection among competitors, and negotiation.

▲ *Job posting.* The public listing of specific job openings within the organization, including description of responsibilities, educational or experience prerequisites, pay grade, reporting lines, or other information (varies from company to company).

▲ *Succession planning.* Planning for the development and movement of managers into the top executive positions in the organization to replace executives when they leave.

▲ *Career ladders.* A standard sequence of jobs through which employees usually pass as they move to higher levels of responsibility in the organization. Also called career paths.

The Supervisor

▲ *Job-person fit.* Fitting the right person to the right job by ensuring that the person who will be doing a specific job has the appropriate skills, experience, style, and motivation.

▲ *Performance appraisal.* Critical observation, analysis, rating, and commentary on the work performance of a subordinate. Usually a standard procedure that includes a structured meeting, specific performance elements, rating scales, and suggestions for development.

▲ *Job design and enrichment.* Designing the way a specific job is to be performed to ensure that the required results are achieved. Includes designing the job in such a way that the employee is both challenged and motivated to do the job with excellence and that the employee grows in the job.

▲ *Mentoring.* A relationship between a senior and a junior colleague for the purpose of fostering the career development of the junior colleague. May include sponsorship, coaching, advocacy and protection, brokering and exposure, role modeling, counseling, acceptance and confirmation, and friendship.[7]

Resources

▲ *Career resource center.* A room, group of rooms, or building used to deliver career development services. May include workshop rooms, counseling offices, a library, small-group meeting rooms, and a variety of equipment, such as computers, telephones, and reproduction machines.

▲ *Assessment.* The analysis through inventories, questionnaires, tests, and other instruments of an individual's skills, psychological type, values, needs, interests, career anchors, work style preferences, motivations, and other factors affecting job-person fit, performance, and satisfaction.

▲ *Career counseling.* Person-to-person exploration of an individual's life and career with the goal of clarifying one or more career-related issues of concern. Both short-term and long-term issues related to performance and satisfaction may be involved.

▲ *Career management workshops.* Group exploration with the facilitation of a trainer into life and work issues with the goal of strengthening the participants' abilities to manage their own careers.

▲ *Technical training.* Teaching employees the skills required to master specific jobs or areas of work.

▲ *Generic development training.* Teaching employees adaptive skills (e.g., communication, writing, team building) or behavioral changes with the purpose of expanding their ability to be more effective and satisfied in their jobs and at work in general and to make a greater contribution to the organization.

▲ *Management development.* Teaching managers the skills required to master specific management positions, as well as teaching them adaptive skills (e.g., leadership, mentoring, team building, effective presentation) or behavioral changes in order to expand their ability to be more effective and satisfied as managers and to make a greater contribution to the organization.

▲ *Education.* The use of outside professional resources such as schools, colleges, and universities for courses leading to degrees or to the acquisition of knowledge not usually available within the organization.

▴ *Outplacement*. The training of employees whose jobs have been terminated in the techniques of effective job search outside the organization.

▴ *Retirement planning*. The provision of workshops, counseling, and materials concerning the planning and implementation of a satisfying postorganization life-style.

These elements include much of the human resources planning, training, and development functions in a major organization, as well as some elements that may be included in other functions (retirement planning, for example, may be included in benefits). The extent to which these elements are included in an organization is a good measure of the importance the organization attaches to career development as well as the point of view of senior management about training and its role in enhancing the contribution of people to the enterprise.

Alternative Models

There are probably as many models of career development systems as there are functioning systems in organizations. An examination of the history of the relationship between organizations and the people who work for them reveals three basic models of career development, identified here as nineteenth-century, paternalistic, and third-wave.

The nineteenth-century model of career development is characterized by the attitude that the work world is basically a jungle in which only the most fit survive. The organization owes its employees nothing. They are paid a day's wage for a day's work, and training, development, and career ladders are a waste of time, energy, and money. Those who are shrewd or ruthless (preferably both) will get ahead. The company looks out for itself, and employees had better do the same. The rule is not to communicate and not to complain. Employees who quit are confirming what the organization knew: that the person was not right for the job. Effective career development in this environment requires a deep familiarity with Machiavelli's *The Prince*. There are still many many organizations to which this model applies.

The paternalistic model is represented by the typical corporate or government organization in which employees' careers are managed by a succession of bosses. People are passed from job to job, sometimes up the ladder and often across the organization. Employees are not usually encouraged to seek movement within the company. The organization may provide a substantial set of the system elements—performance appraisal, succession planning, management development, outplacement, retirement planning, technical training, generic development training, education, and assessment—but principally to provide employees with the training needed to do their jobs better (either existing jobs or jobs to which they will soon be assigned). The major missing elements are usually job posting, formal and clearly communicated career ladders, and a career resource center with materials, counseling, and workshops in which employees are encouraged to take responsibility for managing their careers and become active in discovering the best place for them to contribute to the organization. Most large American organizations have progressed from the nineteenth-century model to this paternalistic approach to career development.

The third-wave model, the most advanced of the three, represents a comprehensive approach to career development through the implementation of a system that contains all or most of the elements already described. The organization recognizes that self-determination and self-expression, strengthened through responsible personal career management, are the necessary prerequisites for the creativity and high level of individual contribution that will be required to compete in the 1990s and beyond.

A number of difficulties are raised by considering the move to a third-wave approach to career development. How can a corporation create all of the systems and subsystems without disrupting the flow of work, running up against major cultural barriers, and spending a lot of money? One answer to all of these questions is to start with a minimum system.

Minimum Systems

The simplest form of career development system is the availability of a set of self-administered and self-scoring career assessment and planning materials. The planning materials could include a book or other publication describing the career management process. (A list of such materials is contained in the chapter appendix.) The total cost of these materials to the organization would probably be less than $100 per set.[8]

The first level of expansion to this minimum system is a workshop for managers and supervisors to train them in coaching their employees in career management. (Figure 3-4 illustrates the expanding levels of a minimum career development system.) Responsibility for providing career development to employees interested in managing their own careers is placed with the managers and supervisors. The organization must be prepared to promote this policy vigorously, particularly in the face of managerial resistance to accepting what may be a new, unfamiliar, and (for many managers) undesirable responsibility. The workshop should include a strong section on motivating the managers toward implementing career management discussions with their employees.

The second level of expansion is the addition of career management workshops for employees. These workshops bring responsibility for career management directly to the employees and provide them with the motivation and skills necessary to prepare and implement their own development

Figure 3-4. Minimum career development systems.

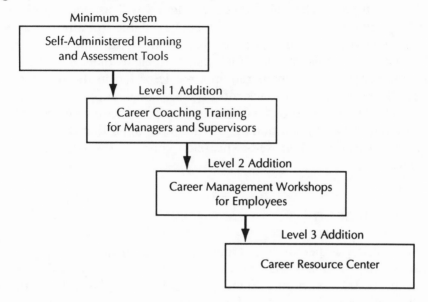

plans—in their current jobs and for the future. The most successful career management workshops integrate employee skills, interests, and developmental needs with the goals and challenges of the organization.

A career resource center is the third level of expansion. The center can start as a minimum facility and contain a small library, assessment instruments, and space for counseling or small group meetings. As budget allows, the center can be expanded to include the larger list of resources suggested in the definitions of system elements.

Typically the following question arises when a minimum system is suggested: "How can we do career development without putting all of the elements in place? We don't have job postings or career ladders or a clear statement from the top about the direction of the organization. Won't we just raise people's expectations and then be unable to fulfill them because the systems aren't in place to respond to the rising demands?" The answer lies in the effectiveness of the way in which employees are trained to take responsibility for managing their careers. Fully responsible employees will take charge of their careers regardless of their circumstances. If the organization provides comprehensive support, it will be easier for employees to be responsible. If little or no support is provided, truly responsible employees will still be willing to do whatever is possible to manage their own careers. The enlightened organization will develop systems that provide levels of support appropriate to current and future needs and financial constraints. The enlightened employee will assume career responsibility regardless of the level of support available from the organization. An effective counselor or career management workshop will stress the importance of this attitude and make it clear that effective and responsible career management requires participation in the process regardless of the barriers or lack of organizational support. The only employees whose expectations will be raised will be those who are willing to operate under these conditions and who understand that they can and are willing to expand their self-expression through responsible career management.

Career Counseling

Career counseling is person-to-person exploration of an individual's life and career with the goal of clarifying one or more career-related issues of concern. It can take place in a single meeting between the counselor and the individual or over a series of meetings. Any one meeting can be structured or informal, and the counselor can assign personality and career-interest self-tests for the individual to complete between sessions. Counseling in organizations is delivered by professional career counselors, by managers and supervisors, and by human resources and personnel professionals.

Five groups of questions define the career management process for an individual in an organization:

Assessment Questions

- Who am I in relation to my worklife?
- What are my talents, skills, and areas of competence?
- What are my strengths, and what are my weaknesses?
- What are my main motives, needs and drives, goals in life?
- What am I after?
- What are my values—the main criteria by which I judge what I am doing?
- What kind of career should I be developing?
- What is the right kind of work for me to be doing?

Investigation Questions

- What does the organization need now and in the future?
- Where is the company going in its markets, technology, and products?
- What skills and experience will be required in the future?
- What kinds of people will be needed?

- Which departments or divisions will be changing?
- Where is the industry going?
- What is the competition doing?
- What is the local, regional, national, and global economy doing?

Matching Questions

- Given the answers to questions in the previous categories, what are the appropriate alternative opportunities in the organization for me?
- Where is it appropriate for me to make an expanded contribution—both on my current job and in the future?

Choice Questions

- Given the need for development on my current job and in the future, which opportunities should I choose?
- Which are better for me?
- Which best serve the organization?

Development Questions

- What development do I need, and what is the plan for this development that will meet the opportunities defined in the Choice Questions?
- What skills do I need to sharpen or acquire?
- What attitudes or behavioral changes need to be made?
- How do I get the training, education, and/or job experience required to acquire the skills or make the changes?
- What kind of support do I need, and where do I get it?
- What is an appropriate schedule for the development?

The initial letters of these five groups of questions form a convenient memory device: Assessment, Investigation, Matching, Choosing, Development—or AIM-CD . . . AIM at Career Development. Career counseling should aim employees at personal career management through the implementation of these five elements of the process, answering the questions posed in each of the five groups.

Because a principal goal of career counseling is to expand the employee's ability to take personal and active responsibility for career management, a good counselor will help the employee move through the process by providing the resources necessary for answering the questions themselves rather than answering the questions directly. The effective counselor questions, listens, suggests a range of alternatives, provides information and other useful resources, and, with great care, is a source of reality testing. The facilitative counselor avoids being directive and judgmental, gives little or no advice, and consciously leads from behind to expand the employee's ability to pursue the career management process independently and with minimum support from the counselor.

Perhaps the most difficult task of the counselor is to take an appropriate stand with regard to handling deeper life and personality issues that affect career questions. The difficulty arises frequently because the choices people make in their lives arise out of the complex interconnections of personality, style, environment, values, needs, and other elements. Career questions arise not simply from the direct experience of work but from deeper considerations that span the full range of human activities, history, and environment. Experienced counselors know when to refer the employee to another professional in an appropriate discipline—such as a psychotherapist, assessment psychologist, attorney, or financial planner.

An organizational career counselor can enhance his or her counseling effectiveness by learning as much as possible about the organization: its history, culture, products, markets, trends, vision and plans, career development systems and resources, formal and informal networking protocol, historical career progressions, job requirements, employment trends, and on-the-job and other training and educational opportunities, along with any other information useful to guiding employees in managing their careers.

Career Assessment

Career assessment, an extremely important part of the career counseling process, deals with the discovery of an array of personal characteristics that deal with an individual's relation to work. There are four basic and broad elements that define who people are in relation to their work lives (Figure 3-5):

Style

- ▲ In what ways do people prefer to relate to the world?
- ▲ How do they like to work?
- ▲ What kind of work environment do they prefer?
- ▲ What are their preferred methods of communication?
- ▲ What is their preferred leadership style?
- ▲ What are the appropriate contributions for them to make to an organization?
- ▲ How do they relate to people, and what kinds of bosses, colleagues, and subordinates do they work best around?

Motivation

- ▲ What needs, interests, values, and beliefs determine what people like to do?

Figure 3-5. Elements of effective career assessment.

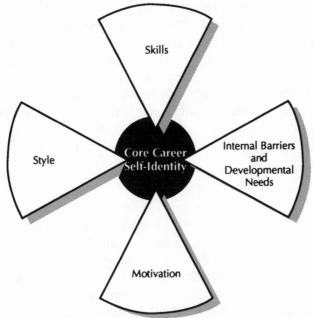

▲ What is most important for them to retain in their work lives?
▲ What kind of work do they really want to do, and what is it that they do not want to do?
▲ What do they want to put into their work, and what do they want to get out of it?

Skills

▲ What are people able to do?
▲ What can they do that they really like to do?
▲ What skills can they take with them wherever they go?
▲ What skills do they most want to use in their work?

Internal Barriers and Developmental Needs

▲ What is it that blocks people from getting what they want out of their work lives?
▲ What attitudes, opinions, beliefs, or behavioral patterns keep them from experiencing success and satisfaction or from performing as effectively as they would need to or want to?
▲ From a clear understanding of the first three elements and their internal barriers, people are better able to derive their developmental needs. That is, what would they like to be able to do or need to do better or differently that will allow them to make full use of their potential?

These four elements are not independent of each other; rather, they are interwoven into the pattern of life and career. Style is one of the determinants of motivation and the skills people choose to develop. Motivation also determines what skills people develop as well as those they choose to use and perfect. Things at which people are naturally skilled contribute to their motivation, and so on. The first three basic elements of style, motivation, and skills, combined with an understanding of internal barriers and developmental needs, tell people a lot about what they need to know to create a more effective and satisfying work life and career. A broad array of instruments are available for assessing these first three elements.

Style

Style is one's natural way of being. It can be described by a set of characteristic preferences that define an individual's psychological type. Each type relates to the world differently, and it is this form of relation that is called style. As author Gerald M. Sturman says, "No type or style is better than any other and each has its own pattern of strengths and weaknesses. Specific types tend to be drawn to certain careers, but research has shown that all types and styles can be found in all careers."[9]

Two important methodologies provide an effective and detailed assessment of style. The notion of preferences and their effect on style was discovered by the psychiatrist Carl Jung and published in 1921.[10] In order to make Jung's work more accessible to people and useful in self-understanding, Isabel Briggs Myers and Katharine C. Briggs devised an assessment of type they called the Myers-Briggs Type Indicator (MBTI). The Indicator yields a four-letter code that identifies an individual's psychological type. Each of the four letters indicates the individual's preference for a specific aspect of relating to the world.

1. *Attitude*. This indicator refers to an individual's preference for extroversion (E) or introversion (I). Extroverts are primarily oriented toward activity and awareness in the external world and look outside themselves more, to interactions with people to derive energy. Introverts look inward to the world of ideas and tend to be most comfortable in the world of ideas and energized by their inner world.

2. *Perception*. The second indicator refers to the two ways people have of perceiving the world: sensing through the five senses (S) or through intuition (N), which is the process of perceiving the world through meanings and relationships that people cannot see, hear, smell, taste, or feel. People who prefer sensing are more interested in what is actually in the environment around them and tend to perceive the world in a more factual, concrete, and specific way. Those who prefer intuition like to read between the lines and look for the possibilities in things rather than

concentrate on the things themselves. They tend to take a more global view.

3. *Judgment*. The third indicator refers to the two ways people have of reaching conclusions about what they have perceived: thinking (T) in which conclusions are reached based on logical processes, or feeling (F) in which conclusions are made on the basis of values. The person who prefers thinking will judge things in the world on whether they are consistent and logical with the individual's ideas tested through reasoning. A preference for judgment does not mean that an individual is judgmental. The person who prefers feeling is more likely to judge things in the world on the basis of whether they are pleasing or appealing or threatening or otherwise consistent with the individual's values. A preference for feeling does not refer to emotions or feelings.

4. *Process*. The final indicator refers to the preferred process that an individual uses in relating to the outside world: judgment (J), in which the outer world is dealt with through one of the two judgment processes, thinking or feeling, or perception (P), in which the outside world is dealt with through one of the two perceiving processes, sensing or intuition. People who prefer the judging process like to bring things to completion in their lives. They prefer to approach life in a more organized and structured way. They prefer to make decisions and shut off the perceiving process to avoid adding confusion. Those who prefer the perceiving process like to keep things open and flowing and tend to delay making decisions to allow time for further evidence. They prefer to approach life in a more open-ended, flexible, less structured manner.

There are sixteen possible combinations of the four preferences, each defining a type. The MBTI uses a series of dual-choice questions to determine which of the sixteen types the individual most resembles. The questions are simple, and each is intended to distinguish the individual's choice for one of the preferences in a pair.

The MBTI is useful in assisting employees in career choice and professional development because psychological type is an important determinant in how people relate to their work, jobs, and careers and to their colleagues, bosses, clients, and the public. One of the most widely published assessment tools in America, the MBTI has been used by small and large and public and private organizations in every conceivable industry, as well as in schools, colleges, and universities and by private practitioners in psychotherapy, career counseling, and a wide variety of other disciplines. The instrument has been exhaustively tested and continues to be the subject of a large amount of research across the country.

The MBTI is available in a number of different formats, including self-scorable versions and versions that include professional scoring and the preparation of a comprehensive computer-generated description of the results. The instrument is available to qualified professionals from Consulting Psychologists Press (Palo Alto, California). Additional information about personality type and the MBTI can be obtained from the Center for Applications of Psychological Type (CAPT) in Gainesville, Florida. CAPT provides education, training, consultation, and research about psychological type and the MBTI.

The second important method for determining work style is the assessment of an individual's Holland Codes (see assumption 1 below). John Holland introduced six personality/occupation types, which are widely accepted and used.[11] He concluded that each individual has a primary resemblance to one of six basic personality types and a secondary and tertiary resemblance to two others of the six types. Holland stated four assumptions for his theory:

1. In our culture, most people can be categorized as one of six types: realistic, investigative, artistic, social, enterprising, or conventional [RIASEC].
2. There are six kinds of environments: realistic, investigative, artistic, social, enterprising, or conventional.
3. People search for environments that will let them exercise their skills and abilities, express their attitudes and values, and take on agreeable problems and roles.
4. A person's behavior is determined by an interaction between his personality and the characteristics of his environment.[12]

Realistic people have athletic or mechanical ability and prefer to work with objects, machines, tools, plants, or animals and also prefer to work outdoors. Machinists, operators, warehouse workers, maintenance staff, and lab technicians, for example, work in realistic occupations.

Investigative people enjoy observing, learning, investigation, analysis, evaluation, and problem solving. They prefer occupations involving methodical analysis and precision—for example, as research scientists, engineers, or market researchers.

Artistic people tend to be expressive, original, innovative, intuitive, and introspective and prefer occupations that allow them to use their artistic abilities, imagination, and creativity—for example, as product designers, advertising artists, or architects.

Social people enjoy working with others in the helping professions—for example, as nurses, counselors, trainers, psychologists—where they can inform, enlighten, train, develop, or cure others.

Enterprising people prefer work that involves managing, leading, or otherwise influencing others to attain organizational goals or financial gain. Typical occupations include managers, salespeople, and attorneys.

Conventional people prefer work in which they can manipulate data, files, records, or other materials and carry out detailed instructions and processes—for example, as financial experts or administrative personnel.

Holland has developed three instruments for determining an individual's vocational preference: the Vocational Preference Inventory, the Self-Directed Search, and the Vocational Exploration and Insight Kit. The Strong-Campbell Interest Inventory also provides Holland codes and is one of the most widely used career assessment tools available. In addition, the entire *Dictionary of Occupational Titles* has been sorted by the Holland codes and forms an excellent reference for career choices. These instruments and books are available from the Consulting Psychologists Press.

Motivation

In addition to defining personality and occupation type, the Holland codes provide an element of motivation—preferred work style.

A second element of motivation was devised by Edgar Schein, who observed that as an individual's career progresses, he or she develops a self-concept that embraces some explicit answers to the following questions:

1. What are my talents, skills, areas of competence? What are my strengths, and what are my weaknesses?
2. What are my main motives, drives, goals in life? What am I after?
3. What are my values, the main criteria by which I judge what I am doing? Am I in the right kind of organization or job? How good do I feel about what I am doing?[13]

As people become more experienced in the world of work, their self-concept becomes more of a constraint on career choices. Schein defines a career anchor as *that element in our self-concept that we will not give up, even if forced to make a difficult choice.*

The career anchor serves to define which needs have the highest priority—which of the factors in our work lives we are not willing to give up because they represent who we truly are. Many people are not clear about what they are unwilling to give up and make career choices that are inappropriate and lead to dissatisfaction at work. The purpose of knowing one's career anchor is to develop sufficient insight to be able to make intelligent and appropriate career choices.

Of the many descriptors of self-concept that can be conceived, eight appear to cover the full range and are identified as career anchors:

1. *Security/stability/organizational identity*. This career anchor is usually subdivided to include two categories of people: (a) those whose

careers are anchored in the stability of employment in an organization—people who are strongly identified with the company and who seek the security of a long-term employment relationship, regular wages, and a modest progression through the ranks—and (b) those who are anchored by geographic location—people who are strongly rooted in the region, often have most of their family resident in the same area, are active in the community, and may sacrifice promotion and their standard of living to avoid moving from one location to another.

2. *Autonomy/independence.* This anchor applies to people who have an overriding need to do things their own way, in their own time, and as independent of others to the greatest extent possible. Being autonomous should not be confused with being an entrepreneur. Building a new business and taking risks are not necessarily components of autonomy. People who value autonomy and independence may find the typical organizational roles constraining and prefer to pursue career paths that are out of the ordinary.

3. *Technical/functional competence.* The person anchored in technical or functional competence is most motivated toward being knowledgeable and producing highly effective work in some field of specialization. Primarily motivated by the content of the work they perform, these people tend to identify strongly with their expertise, and their self-concept is dependent on their ability to succeed and be recognized in their area of specialty.

4. *Managerial competence.* The key motivations for people anchored in managerial competence are advancement up the ladder to higher levels of responsibility, growing opportunities to serve in positions of leadership, increasing contribution to the overall success of the organization, and a long-term opportunity for high income.

5. *Entrepreneurial creativity.* The individual with an entrepreneurial anchor has a strong need to create a new business, the motivation to overcome obstacles, the willingness and the courage to run risks, and the desire for personal gain and recognition for what is accomplished. These individuals seldom stay with an organization that is not their own for long. They are eager to be fully active in an enterprise of their own creation where they can succeed (or fail) on the merits of their personal ideas, abilities, personality, and drive.

6. *Sense of service/dedication to a cause.* People with a service anchor are characterized as being principally motivated by dedicating their work and sometimes their lives in the service of others—perhaps by working in a position in which they can directly serve others in the helping and supportive occupations and professions or by providing comfort, entertainment, leisure activities, athletic training, personal or business support activities, or any other support service that represents a contri-

bution to others. Or they may manifest this dedication through a commitment to the preservation or realization of a set of values that they consider important not only in their own lives but also in the larger world around them.

7. *Pure challenge*. For the challenge-anchored person, the one thing that matters is being challenged at the highest possible level. Success is defined in terms of winning, overcoming obstacles, being the best or first, beating the competition, reaching for their highest, surpassing previous goals, and so on.

8. *Life-style integration*. For these people, work is not the major vehicle of self-expression. They are more interested in ensuring that their life is balanced among various interests, such as family, friends, hobbies, recreational and leisure activities, study and learning other than work-related subjects, and so on. They develop their self-concepts around issues of their total life-style. How they define their life-style is the major guide and constraint on their careers.

The individual taking the career anchor test responds to a series of statements and indicates the level of importance of such indicators as working at the state of the art, having tough problems to solve, or learning new technical skills.

The Career Anchors instrument is available from University Associates in La Jolla, California.

The other elements of motivation are values—the complex set of ideals, beliefs, and standards that characterize an individual's system for relating to the world—and needs—those innate and instinctive factors without which we are unable to function effectively. Some values have such a strong effect on certain needs that they appear indistinguishable from those needs. For example, one of the categories of needs in Maslow's hierarchy is importance, respect, self-esteem, and independence.[14] Autonomy, a value that enhances satisfaction of the need for independence, is difficult to distinguish from that need.

The most widely used formal approach to assessing values and needs is the Career Values Card Sort. The person being assessed is given a set of cards, each containing a value and its description, to sort into groups by order of perceived personal importance. The set of values used includes a sufficient overlap with needs, so it is usually not necessary to assess needs separately. This instrument is available from Career Research and Testing in San Jose, California.

Skills

The assessment of skills may be performed through a wide variety of tools ranging from simple paper-and-pencil exercises to actual physical skill tests (usually limited to various manual skills such as typing or operating machinery). Three basic types of skills should be assessed:

1. *Specific content skills:* Knowledge-based skills used only in a particular job, with little or no transferability to other kinds of work (for example, knowing how to operate a specific mainframe computer, perform open heart surgery, or interpret tax law).

2. *Adaptive skills* (sometimes called self-management skills or personal qualities): Qualities that are temperament-based and that people learn as they grow up in the world and need to, or choose to, use in order to fit (or adapt) themselves into a variety of environments (for example, persistence, confidence, thoroughness, patience, sensitivity, assertiveness, time management, flexibility).

3. *Functional skills:* Skills that describe the competence level at which we deal with people, data (or ideas), and things (for example, organize information logically, lift heavy objects, make decisions, relate effectively to others).

The importance of adaptive and functional skills is that they are transferable; that is, they can be taken from one job or career to almost any other.

A most important element of skills assessment is discovering an individual's motivated skills—those skills that the individual likes to use—rather than just those skills in which the individual experiences competence. The Skills Card Sort is an efficient approach to deriving motivated skills and is also available from Career Research and Testing. Skills are printed on cards and sorted by the person being assessed into different piles based on skill level and the individual's interest in using that skill at work.[15]

Microcomputer-based assessment programs are also coming into use. These programs allow the user to answer questions directly on the computer. The computer then provides scoring and other information about the assessment. CareerPoint, written for IBM-PCs and compatibles, includes Holland's Self-Directed Search, the MBTI, the Work Environment Scale, and the Career Leverage Inventory. The program is available through Conceptual Systems in Silver Spring, Maryland. Another computerized career development tool is Discover, also for IBM-PCs and compatibles, and includes assessments of individual general interests, job-related skills, and work-related values. Discover is available from American College Testing Program Inc. in Iowa City, Iowa.

If You Knew Who You Were . . . You Could Be Who You Are! is a self-paced and self-scorable instrument that takes readers through a step-by-step process that discusses the goals and benefits of self-discovery and provides instruments for determining style, motivation, motivated skills, and developmental needs plus internal barriers. The final element in this instrument is the development of a Personal Career Profile in both a concise form and a detailed description. From this profile, the reader can create career plans and other developmental programs, as well as résumés or other documents useful in career and personal development planning.[16]

Career Management Workshops

The question often arises about the real benefits of taking employees out of their working environment for two or more days and putting them through a workshop rather than relying on the counseling facilities of the organization to handle career development issues. The benefits of using the workshop technique are important in many organizational environments:

▴ Many more employees can be reached for far less money than would be required to provide career counseling as the primary vehicle for career management education.

▴ There is a significant economy of scale in presenting generic information to groups of people rather than to one person at a time. Counselors often have to spend considerable time explaining the fundamentals of career development to employees before they can effectively counsel them. Counseling becomes most effective after an individual has been trained in a workshop.

▴ The energy available in the workshop setting through trainer and individual, small group, and large group interactions provides an important element of motivation otherwise unavailable to many employees.

▴ The interactions in a workshop provide a broad opportunity for peer identification, comparison, reality testing, shared experiences and learning, and networking.

▴ Taking time away from the daily routine can be revitalizing for the individual.

▴ Being steeped in a subject for two or three days along with similarly interested peers greatly enhances learning and provides a greater opportunity for a transformational experience (longer lasting and producing more meaningful changes in skills, attitudes, or behaviors).

▴ The opportunity to learn from outside professionals with specific content knowledge and experience in other organizations is made available to a larger number of employees. (This benefit is reduced when in-house trainers are used.)

Workshop Elements

The purpose of a career management workshop should be to provide the participants with the motivation and technology to take responsibility for managing their own careers. As a minimum, the effective workshop should cover the following subjects:

▴ *Work and life.* An exploration of why people work and what career development means in the organizational context and in the specific environment of this organization.

▴ *Assessment.* May be included in the workshop or done as a pre-assignment.

▴ *Investigation/career research.*

▴ *Visioning.* A bridge between assessment and targeting—looking at the future and creating a desired picture of work and life.

▴ *Targeting.* The matching and choosing process. Should include both short-term targets for development on the current position as well as longer-term targets to meet the needs of the company as it moves into the future.

▴ *Planning.* Creating a development plan.

▴ *Implementation.* How the plan is carried through to action, expected barriers and strategies for handling them, and feedback mechanisms that can be used to make reasonable modifications.

▴ *Effective career communication.* Writing an in-house résumé, communicating individual values and contributions, and improving communication on the job.

▴ *Enhancing the relationship between the individual and his or her supervisor or manager.*

▴ *Understanding the organization's career development systems.* How people move from one job to another, the systems available (job posting, mentoring, succession planning, training), how they are accessed, and how networking works, both formally and informally.

These topics can be covered in a one-day overview, but a minimum of two full days is required to give them justice, and three days is better.

Workshop Structure

An effective career management workshop should have no more than twenty participants and no fewer than ten. With more than twenty participants, the element of individual learning is diminished and certain powerful processes such as video feedback become impractical. With fewer than ten participants, the energy of the group interaction is often too low to maintain the drive needed to motivate people through the more difficult stretches of the workshop.

The workshop room should be large enough for the size of the group (approximately 20 feet by 25 feet for a group of twenty participants), well ventilated, well lit, and without such distractions as telephones, traffic noise, music, the intrusion of messages, or other factors that pull the participants from a full absorption in the topic.

Classroom style with pairs of participants behind tables is most effective for working in workbooks and using other materials, as well as for paired exercises. All furniture should be movable so that group exercises can be accommodated.

Participants should not be required to sit in the workshop room for more than two hours at a stretch, and fifteen-minute breaks should be provided periodically. A one-hour lunch break is sufficient. Long business breaks should be strongly discouraged. If a participant misses a considerable part of a workshop, he or she should repeat the entire workshop for maximum effectiveness. Continuity of process can often be more important than content in effecting meaningful training.

Program Development

Organizations that have training departments with program development capabilities must usually decide whether to create a new program in-house or buy an existing program from a vendor and use it off-the-shelf or in a customized form. To make this decision, they need to consider their own expertise and experience in the subject, whether they have appropriate staff and time to do an excellent job, and the costs. A high-quality, two-day career development workshop, delivered by a professional and experienced trainer from a reputable vendor, will cost between $5,000 and $7,000 for a workshop of up to twenty participants, including use of the vendor's materials.

Workshop materials should be highly professional, well tested in a variety of environments, complete, and linked directly to the workshop. Typical workshop materials include a workbook of 100 or more pages, and assorted one- or two-page handouts of special materials used in exercises or providing information peculiar to the organization. These materials can be developed in-house or purchased from a vendor and should be in a format that allows the workshop participant to use them in the workshop and then take them home for personal reference. Typical career development materials required for a comprehensive two-day workshop and purchased from a vendor range in price from $75 to $250 depending on such factors as size and quality, uniqueness, volume purchased, vendor margins, and licensing requirements.

Generally the materials available from reputable vendors are of a significantly higher quality than the materials developed in-house. The years of experience, the volume of materials they handle, the expertise they bring to the subject, and the need to compete in the marketplace drive vendors to produce the highest-quality products available. In-house materials are often hastily designed and assembled by one or two staff members with insufficient time and resources, using material borrowed from many sources; they are also reproduced by lower-quality printing methods and bound as inexpensively as possible. While the purpose of such an effort may be to save money and to attempt to provide customized material for an in-house program, the result may not support program participants who need truly excellent materials to experience the full benefits of a program.

The Future of Career Development

The dramatic changes taking place in the world present a major challenge to the leaders of organizations in both the public and private sectors. The response to these changes in the area of managing people will be at least as important as the response to any other factor. In many companies, managing people in new ways will be more important than anything else they can do. The shift in attitude, policy, and behavior from dealing with employees as an expense to maintaining people as an asset must be made by any organization that hopes to survive and thrive into the next century.

Critical to this shift is creating a new context for bringing employees into an organization and maintaining their participation in the growth and vitality of the organization. This new context arises directly from the definition of career development stated at the beginning of this chapter:

> Career development is the process by which employees take responsibility for developing their ability to make an expanded contribution to the company, a contribution that links individual work satisfaction and performance to the goals and challenges of the company.

Clearly, career development, or individual career management, should become the overall context for managing and developing the human resources in an organization. Third-wave organizations, the most success-ful organizations in the 1990s and on into the next century, will be those that commit serious resources of people, money, and time to the creation of comprehensive career development systems.

Some radical changes will need to be made. A single human resources development policy must be envisioned, created, communicated, imple-mented, and managed with the same energy, attention, and commitment of resources as organizations now give to marketing and manufacturing. The wasteful rivalries among training, organization development, and personnel departments that undermine the delivery of effective services to people and organizations must be ended. All training and development will need to be organized into the career management system.

Succession planning, management development, education, supervisory training, career counseling, career management workshops, employment, job paths, job enrichment, performance appraisal, outplacement, retirement planning, on-the-job training, mentoring, and all of the other elements that have been separated in almost every organization must be brought together. Every course, workshop, seminar, project, educational program, and developmental process will have to be organized into a coherent system in which each element is consistent with and contributive to meeting the demands of the organizational human resources policy. Employees entering the organization will be given career management training almost immediately and will be initiated into a process that continues for them in the organization. Such resources as counselors and mentors, libraries, and computer systems will be widely and easily available.

This is not a vision to be realized overnight, but it is also not a fantasy to be dismissed. The rapidly changing world will force the leadership of major organizations to wake up about what it means and what it takes to release the maximum energy available in employees toward the achievement of organizational goals. Those who want to maintain leadership will have to add a deeper and clearer understanding of what career management is really about and will have to do something meaningful about it in their organizations.

NOTES

1. Author's definition.
2. *Achieving Competitive Advantage Through the Effective Management of People* (Philadelphia: Hay/Yankelovich, Clancy Shulman, 1986).
3. F. Parsons, *Choosing a Vocation* (Boston: Houghton Mifflin, 1909).
4. J. W. Walker and T. G. Gutteridge, *Career Planning Practices,* AMA survey report (New York: AMACOM, 1979).
5. T. G. Gutteridge and F. L. Otte, *Organizational Career Development: State of the Practice* (Washington, D.C.: American Society for Training and Development, 1983).
6. Ibid.
7. Douglas T. Hall, et al., *Career Development in Organizations* (San Francisco: Jossey-Bass, 1986); Z. B. Leibowitz and N. K. Schlossberg, "Training Managers for Their Role in Career Development," *Training and Development Journal* (July 1981): 74.
8. For a more extensive list of resources, see Z. B. Leibowitz, C. Farren, and B. L. Kaye, *Designing Career Development Systems* (San Francisco: Jossey-Bass, 1986).

9. Gerald M. Sturman, *"If You Knew Who You Were . . . You Could Be Who You Are!"* (Greenwich, Conn.: Bierman House, 1989).
10. C. G. Jung, *Psychological Types* (Princeton, N.J.: Princeton University Press, 1971).
11. John L. Holland, *Making Vocational Choices: A Theory of Careers* (Englewood Cliffs, N.J.: Prentice-Hall, 1973).
12. Ibid.
13. E. H. Schein, "The Individual, the Organization, and the Career: A Conceptual Scheme," *Journal of Applied Behavioral Science 7* (1971): 401–426.
14. A. H. Maslow, *Motivation and Personality* (New York: Harper & Row, 1954).
15. Richard N. Bolles, *The Quick Job-Hunting Map* (Berkeley, Calif.: Ten-Speed Press, 1985), provides extensive material on motivated skills assessment. For a more extensive list of assessment resources, see Leibowitz, Farren, and Kaye, *Designing Career Development Systems.*
16. Sturman, *"If You Knew."*

ANNOTATED CAREER DEVELOPMENT RESOURCES

Introduction to Type: A Description of the Theory and Applications of the Myers-Briggs Type Indicator, 4th ed., by Isabel Briggs Myers (Palo Alto, Calif.: Consulting Psychologists Press, 1987). This thirty-two page booklet contains an excellent and readable introduction to the theory of types and a detailed description of each of the types and styles. A short section is included on applications of type and style in relationships, career choices, the effects of each preference in work situations, and the use of type to improve problem solving.

Introduction to Type in Organizational Settings, by Sandra Krebs Hirsh and Jean M. Kummerow (Palo Alto, Calif.: Consulting Psychologists Press, 1987). This thirty-two page booklet contains brief descriptions of the sixteen types, with material on the effects of preferences in work situations, preferred methods of communication for each of the preferences, and, for each four-letter type, information on its contribution to organizations, leadership style, preferred work environment, potential pitfalls, and suggestions for development.

Please Understand Me: Character and Temperament Types, 4th ed., by David Keirsey and Marilyn Bates (Del Mar, Calif.: Prometheus Nemesis Book Company, 1984). A readable, interesting, and informative paperback dealing with a variety of issues concerning psychological type and style. The book includes the Keirsey Temperament Sorter, an assessment tool that also leads to a determination of the sixteen psychological types using the Myers-Briggs extension of Jungian typology. Long and detailed descriptions of each of the types are given, with information on style with regard to life-mates, temperament in children, and temperament in leading; there are also some statements about career and job preferences as well as work style.

Gifts Differing, by Isabel Briggs Myers with Peter B. Myers (Palo Alto, Calif.: Consulting Psychologists Press, 1980). A warm and moving book that describes the history of the work of Katherine Briggs and her daughter, Isabel Briggs

Myers, in the extension of Jungian typology and the development of the MBTI. The sixteen types are described in considerable detail, and the complementary nature of preferences and types is extremely well developed. Some discussion is given to the relationship of each type to work life.

Career Anchors: Discovering Your Real Values, by Edgar H. Schein (San Diego: University Associates, 1985). A fifty-page large-format paperback that contains a career anchor assessment and detailed descriptions of each of the eight anchors. Written by the originator of the career anchor concept, the book is readable and useful for gaining a deeper insight into the meaning of a specific anchor.

Coming Alive from Nine to Five: The Career Search Handbook, 3rd ed., by Betty Neville Michelozzi (Mountain View, Calif.: Mayfield Publishing Company, 1988). A thorough, 300-page large-format paperback that deals in depth with the subject of job motivation. Includes dozens of inventories, exercises, and other materials that help readers to discover their job satisfiers and an outstanding discussion of the Holland types. The book also contains excellent chapters on job finding and the job market.

Taking Charge of Your Career Direction, by Robert D. Lock (Pacific Grove, Calif.: Brooks/Cole Publishing Company, 1988). A 375-page large-format paperback with the depth and detail of a textbook, which is useful for the extent of its assessments and exercises. The book includes tables of educational majors classified by Holland types, as well as other information about jobs, careers, and the Holland types. The author does an excellent job in dealing with work values, including assessment and inventory exercises.

The Three Boxes of Life, and How to Get Out of Them, by Richard N. Bolles (Berkeley, Calif.: Ten-Speed Press, 1981). Written by America's best-known author on careers and jobs. This book provides a stimulating exploration of the art and technology of creating a balanced life. Almost 500 pages, it provides good job search material, as well as an excellent and detailed section on the Holland types and their relationship to work and specific occupations. Other books by the same author and publisher include *What Color Is Your Parachute? Where Do I Go From Here with My Life?* and *The New Quick Job-Hunting Map.* This last book does an outstanding job on the discussion and inventory of skills.

If You Don't Know Where You're Going, You'll Probably End Up Somewhere Else, by David Campbell (Allen, Texas: Argus Communications, 1974). A 144-page, pocket-sized paperback written to be read in one sitting and filled with amusing drawings, sayings, and an effective message about life and work planning. The section on the Holland types is succinct and informative.

The Salaried Professional: How to Make the Most of Your Career, by Joseph A. Raelin (New York: Praeger, 1984). A detail-packed book of almost 300 pages that provides one of the few discussions of the relationship among psychological type, career anchors, career types, values, skills, and the other indicators of people's relationship to their work lives. Fully referenced, with inventories and exercises useful to career exploration and to understanding ways of excelling in a job and effectively developing and managing a career.

The Complete Job-Search Handbook, by Howard Figler (New York: Henry Holt and Company, 1988). Written by one of the most articulate writers in the career field and containing a series of discussions and exercises on motivation, values, and skills in this paperback of almost 400 pages. Figler's work on values is particularly good, and the discussion of skills is outstanding.

Successful Manager's Handbook: Development Suggestions for Today's Manager, 3rd ed., ed. Brian L. Davis, Lowell W. Hellervik, and James L. Sheard (Minneapolis: Personnel Decisions, 1989). Perhaps the outstanding management development book. A large-format paperback of over 450 pages, this volume contains detailed developmental exercises, tips, advice, and other useful information for the personal development of anyone interested in becoming an excellent manager. Administrative, leadership, interpersonal, communication, and cognitive skills are covered in detail, along with personal adaptability, personal motivation, and occupational/technical knowledge.

Guerrilla Tactics in the Job Market, by Tom Jackson (New York: Bantam Books, 1978). One of the best job-finding books ever written. In this small-format and inexpensive paperback, the author captures the essence of the issues and barriers inherent in the whole job-finding process, from self-assessment through targeting, research, résumé writing, getting in the door, and interviewing. Full of practical tips, useful exercises, solid rules of thumb, and more than seventy-five "tactics" that work in almost any job market.

Career Development in Organizations, by Douglas T. Hall et al. (San Francisco: Jossey-Bass, 1986). A joint publication in the Jossey-Bass Management Series and the Jossey-Bass Social and Behavioral Science Series and part of the series on Frontiers of Industrial and Organizational Psychology, this text features a series of articles by academic and corporate professionals covering topics pertaining to organizational career development and serving to illuminate the state of the art rather than serve as a comprehensive guide for the creation of career development systems in organizations.

Career Choice and Development, by Duane Brown et al. (San Francisco: Jossey-Bass, 1984). Another joint publication in the Jossey-Bass Management Series and the Jossey-Bass Social and Behavioral Science Series, this book provides a detailed and thorough description of the relationship of psychology to career choice. Extensively referenced, the sixteen chapters provide career counselors with a deep exploration of the major factors underlying effective and meaningful career development.

4

Health Promotion

Deborah Jaffe Sandroff, Worksite Wellness Council of Greater Chicago

Between 1980 and 1990, the price of medical services and supplies increased 136 percent in the United States, and the cost to employers of providing health care benefits rose 400 percent, a trend that promises to continue.[1] Unchecked, these rising costs threaten to erode corporate profits. Many companies have identified the implementation of health promotion programs as a strategy for combating these costs; in 1985, 66 percent of work sites with fifty or more employees had health promotion activities.[2]

It has been suggested that getting people to adopt the following types of health behaviors would result in the most lives saved and the most misery avoided:

- ▲ Exercise aerobically three to five times a week.
- ▲ Consume a balanced diet that is high in complex carbohydrates and fiber and low in total fat, as recommended by the American Heart Association.
- ▲ Don't smoke.
- ▲ Don't drink, or use alcohol only in moderation.
- ▲ Take medication only as prescribed and abstain from illegal drugs.
- ▲ Use proper body mechanics, regular exercise, and other strategies to minimize risk of back injury.
- ▲ Manage response to stress and maintain a balance in one's life.
- ▲ Minimize the risk of motor vehicle injury by driving within the speed limit, wearing seatbelts in automobiles and helmets on bicycles and motorcycles, and avoiding drinking and driving.
- ▲ Have smoke detectors in the home with charged batteries.
- ▲ Abstain from high-risk sexual behavior.[3]

More often than not, it's not uncontrollable health risks—environmental factors, heredity, or even lack of available medical cures—that are causing health problems but life-style behaviors that individuals have choice over. Research has implicated life-style behaviors as being responsible for more than half the deaths in the United States.[4]

This alarming fact has serious implications for businesses: rising health care costs, premature mortality, morbidity, and lost work time.[5] But it also means that businesses can develop and employ strategies for helping employees modify their unhealthy practices. Businesses with a healthy work force have a distinct advantage over competitors. Even if their products and services are not dramatically superior, their employees, an indisposable resource, will be working at full capacity.

How can a business incorporate the health of its work force as a business strategy? There is no one answer and no simple solutions. The biggest challenge is that most people already know what they are doing right or wrong in terms of their health habits. The media regularly bombard the public with warnings from the surgeon general and research findings on the benefits of healthy life-style practices. But in most cases, people lack the skills and support necessary to give up poor habits and develop and sustain new ones.

A review of the AT&T work site health promotion model can highlight the elements that are essential to a successful program. This approach recognizes that improvements in the health of individuals and the organizations for which they work are possible only if everyone shares responsibility for both work and profitability.[6]

Health Promotion at AT&T

Health services have a long history at AT&T. As early as 1886, the company supported an on-site medical department that provided such occupational health services as treatment for on-the-job injuries, back-to-work exams, preemployment physicals, occupational exams, and, in some cases, primary care medical services. In 1986 the medical department became known as the Health Affairs Organization, more accurately reflecting the broad range of programs it offered.

During the early 1980s, a corporate-wide EAP was established to address a variety of personal problems among employees, ranging from emotional, financial, and marital difficulties to substance abuse. In 1986 the EAP became the only bargained-for service in the union contract provided by Health Affairs.

Health promotion was formally introduced in 1983 when the Total Life Concept (TLC) program was piloted and tested at several AT&T locations. Participants attended orientation sessions, completed health-risk appraisals (HRAs) and biometric measurements (blood pressure, total cholesterol, HDL, height, and weight), and were given the opportunity to participate in up to three life-style–change modules. Eight classes were offered (fitness, blood pressure control, cholesterol control, nutrition, weight management, stress management, back care, and interpersonal communication), from six to twelve weeks in length. HRAs and biometric measurements were repeated at the end of the pilot to assess changes in risk factors. Based on the results of the pilot study, AT&T has since supported the gradual expansion of TLC.[7] The medical department has also had responsibility for disability case management and certain safety programs.

A Multidimensional Framework for Health Promotion

In the late 1980s, the Health Affairs Organization undertook a lengthy examination of its services in an attempt to incorporate evolving trends in occupational health care and emerging business needs. The outcome of this analysis was the implementation of a unified direction for the department, termed health risk management. This approach to the provision of health services focuses on prevention and involves health professionals from each of the core services—clinical services, TLC/health promotion, the EAP, and disability case management—working as interdisciplinary teams.

To understand health risk management, it is useful to review the philosophy and approach of TLC, since it contributed to the foundation for the department's redirection. The TLC program is based on a conceptual framework for health promotion that incorporates three key dimensions of health status:

1. *Individual health factors*. The attitudes, values, beliefs, and health behaviors of employees within the corporation. These factors are shaped by a myriad of influences within each person's experience (Figure 4-1).
2. *Organizational health factors*. The corporate values, cultural norms, policies and procedures, and performance indexes that affect the health of individual employees.
3. *Environmental health factors*. Variables in the physical work environment, such as ergonomics, safety risks, and cafeteria/vending selections, that affect employee health.

These dimensions are closely interrelated and coexist in a dynamic equilibrium. When the health status of one dimension improves or declines, the other two dimensions are affected. Envision health on a continuum from illness to optimal well-being (Figure 4-2). When individuals practice a proactive approach toward health through prevention, early detection, and healthy life-style habits, enormous potential benefits, both personally and to the corporation, ensue. Conversely, individuals who take a reactive approach toward health increase their risks and serve as detriments to a company's performance.

Organizations that take a proactive approach to health provide sup-

Figure 4-1. Determinants of individual health factors.

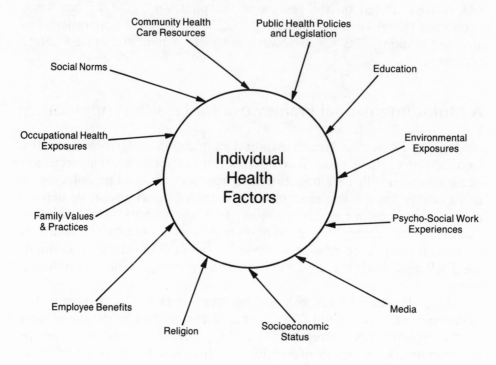

Figure 4-2. Multidimensional health continuum.

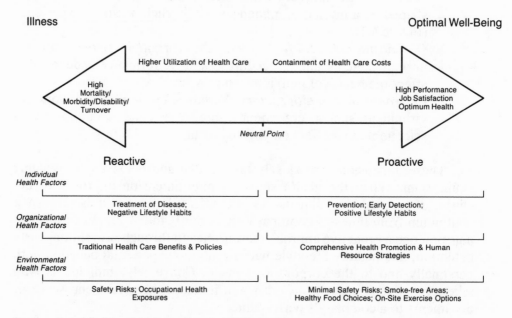

Source: D. Ardell, "Meet John Travis, Doctor of Wellbeing," *Prevention* 4 (1975): 62–69.

port for individuals in achieving their optimal well-being. They implement comprehensive health promotion and human resources strategies that nurture personal development, career growth, and health status.[8] At the same time, they profit from the well-being of their employees. On the other end of the spectrum are organizations whose policies are to fix problems once they occur rather than prevent them. In extreme cases, the organizational norms may even increase employees' health risks through high-stress factors such as 60-hour workweeks, unpredictability, and perpetual reorganizations. The net result is that if employees' health suffers, the company's success is negatively affected as well.

In the environmental dimension, a proactive strategy creates a climate that minimizes safety risks and reinforces individuals' attempts to lead healthy life-styles through such efforts as providing healthy foods at the work site, developing smoking policies, and providing on-site showers or exercise facilities. At the other end of the continuum are work environments that pose safety risks and occupational health exposures and do not reinforce healthy life-style practices. These environments present dangers to individual employees as well as to the company.

A comprehensive approach to health promotion that targets all three dimensions results in positive movement along the health continuum; a fragmented approach that targets only one or two dimensions ultimately fails. The reasons become clear by considering a few examples.

In the late 1980s, AT&T was in the process of implementing health promotion for all long-distance-operator offices. In preparation, focus groups were conducted in selected offices around the country to identify issues that might be barriers to the program's success. During the introduction to one of these focus groups, the TLC manager explained the purpose of the session and the rationale behind work site health promotion. She stressed that the leaders of the department were supporting the program because they cared about the employees; they were not looking for concrete data to validate the success of the program. During the course of the session, individuals raised questions about whether the organization was sincere in its concern for its employees, citing several perceived safety risks in the work environment that had not been addressed to their satisfaction. Essentially their question was, "How can you claim that you're doing this because you care about us? If you were really concerned about our well-being, you would have resolved these risks."

The health promotion staff recognized that until these issues were solved, the credibility and success of the health promotion program would be seriously undermined. A safety risk in the work environment, real or perceived, had already affected employees and moved them closer to the negative end of the health continuum. Lowered morale and negative feelings about the company can result in an "I don't care attitude" about both personal health habits and getting the job done well. A person might say, "Why should I stop smoking if I put myself at risk every time I come to work?'' The result is that the health status of the organization shifts to the left as well when productivity suffers as a result of poor morale.

During the planning phase for health promotion in other departments, the TLC staff faced comparable obstacles as a result of a variety of organizational practices. The following types of complaints, certainly not unique to AT&T, illustrate that everyday business practices can affect employee well-being:

"They never tell us *why* all these changes are taking place."

"Headquarters always makes decisions without consulting those of us in the field who truly understand what works best."

"I only get feedback when I make a mistake, never when I've done a good job."

"How can we continue to be given more responsibility with fewer people to do the work? I enjoy working hard, but I'm exhausted, and I'm ready to kick the dog!"

"My boss makes me sick. I'm having migraines. He yells at me even after I've done exactly what he requested."

Sometimes the way a company, department, or supervisor does business can make people sick. Such organizations may already be closer to the illness side of the health continuum; they move farther to the left when employees are ill or do not show up for work because they are used up or worn out. Even environmental health can decline when individuals become careless in response to the style in which they have been managed. Ironically, people can create their own occupational hazards.

Guidelines for Organizational Values and Practices

The following organizational values and practices, summarized by the acronym PERKS, are associated with healthy companies:[9]

▴ *Participation.* Involving people at all levels of the organization in the decisions that affect them. Employees feel devalued when they are excluded from this process.

▴ *Environment.* Creating a climate that nurtures employees' development, allows them to excel, and encourages them to contribute new and innovative strategies for achieving the common goals of the business.

▴ *Recognition.* Acknowledging and rewarding peoples' everyday efforts along with their larger successes. Remember that it takes four strokes ("great job") to every one poke ("you blew it") for an employee to feel as if his or her efforts have been recognized.

▲ *Knowledge.* Giving employees the information they need to understand why decisions are made and where the company is headed. The more they know, the better they can contribute and adapt to change.

▲ *Style.* Managing and communicating with employees in a style that is right for them. No one style works for everyone. Some people need a lot of structure; others are stifled by it. Some thrive when given the freedom to function independently; others are lost.

The significance of organizational factors suggests that the management team must possess certain qualities.[10] Leaders need to employ supervisors who respect the contributions of others, have the skills to communicate effectively with many kinds of people, know how to coach rather than boss, and will be supportive of their employees' work, family, and health needs.

Supervisors' Impact on Employee Health

AT&T has documented a supervisor's impact on employee health through data provided from the TLC Health Audit, an internally developed survey that assesses personal life-style practices, characteristics of the work environment, perceived organizational norms relative to health, sources of support, areas of interest for making life-style changes, and people's self-efficacy or confidence in their ability to make changes.[11] The Health Audit is administered to members of an organization to gain an overall impression of the needs and interests of that particular group. The results can be used for planning purposes when health promotion is being initiated in a new organization and for program evaluation.

An analysis of over 16,000 responses to the Health Audit indicated that 40 percent of employees reported they experience stress on the job hourly or daily; these respondents were classified as "high stress." The 4.4 percent of the sample who reported experiencing hourly stress were classified as "super stress." The analysis performed on the responses of these two groups identified that the most powerful predictor of stress was a lack of support from one's boss.

Further analysis of high-stress employees who also reported high work morale indicated that the strongest predictor of high morale under high stress was having a supportive boss. It was assumed that these employees are more successful in coping with their stress. These findings suggest that perceptions of stress in the workplace, along with the ability to cope with that stress, may be related as much to employees' interactions with their bosses as on individual coping skills or the job itself. This information provides a convincing argument for strongly emphasizing organizational health promotion strategies that help managers understand the significant impact they can have on the health of their employees.

The analysis of stress-related variables also indicates that high-stress and super-stress employees are less likely to look after their own health. They avoid regular exercise and do not attend to nutrition and weight control. Super-stress employees are also more likely to report high blood pressure, less likely to have it checked, and twice as likely to report frequent back pain (25 percent versus 12 percent). However, the high stress–high morale individuals are more likely to report regular exercise, attention to good nutrition, and success with weight control.

Organizational Health Promotion Strategies

Many supervisors need to be taught how to communicate their support to their employees. This can be accomplished through organizational health promotion strategies such as TLC's Managing for Health and High Performance, a half-day seminar for supervisors that provides an introduction to health promotion as a primary business strategy and illustrates the connection between health and productivity. During the seminar, data from the Health Audit are reviewed to stress the impact supervisors can have on the health of their work group. In addition, participants complete the Insight Inventory to develop an understanding of their personality strengths, how they are perceived by others, and differences among co-workers' communication styles.[12] The inventory is a self-scored instrument that provides participants with a profile of strengths in four categories: getting their way, direct versus indirect; responding to people, reserved versus outgoing; pacing activity, urgent versus steady; dealing with details, unstructured versus precise. Techniques are introduced to help participants use these insights to improve personal effectiveness in the workplace and beyond the job.

A primary goal in organizational health promotion is to establish an active commitment to health by managers. This does not mean that all supervisors are expected to embrace an intensive exercise regime and reform their eating habits (although positive role models will not be discouraged); rather, an active commitment is demonstrated when managers establish goals for creating healthy norms for regular business practices. This can be initiated by defining objectives in each of the areas identified in PERKs, for example. These managers understand that employee productivity is directly linked to physical and emotional well-being, which are heavily influenced by an employee's daily work experiences. They then take responsibility for establishing healthy business practices.

Certainly it is important that the message, "good health is good business," be communicated from all levels of management, but employees will also need to learn how to work well and accept responsibility for their work behaviors. Teaching them how to control their blood pressure is not enough. Team-building sessions for work groups can help employees to understand personality strengths within their ranks and how to capitalize on these to promote the group's effectiveness. These sessions can give employees the opportunity to identify strengths and suggest areas for improvement in organizational policies and practices. Over time, work groups learn to provide mutual support for health behavior changes on individual, organizational, and environmental levels.

Prevention Through Health Risk Management

In addition to incorporating a multidimensional health promotion model, AT&T recognized the need to apply more of its health resources toward preventing illness rather than treating disease. It used a recent review performed by a task force commissioned by the U.S. Department of Health and Human Services to support the initiation of its health risk management focus.[13] AT&T cited several important findings from this study:

▲ Interventions that address personal health practices are among the most effective means available to health professionals for reducing the incidence and severity of the leading causes of disease and disability in the United States.

▲ Primary prevention strategies that address such risk factors as smoking, physical inactivity, poor nutrition, and alcohol abuse can contribute more improvements in overall health than many secondary preventive measures, such as routine screenings for early disease.

▲ Services such as testing for disease and provision of preventive programs should be implemented selectively.

▲ Education and counseling may be of more value than conventional clinical activities such as diagnostic testing. Since these activities were once considered outside the traditional role of health care providers, many health professionals may need to develop new skills.

▲ Individuals must assume greater responsibility for their own health.

▲ Improving access to preventive services for all members of a population is more likely to reduce morbidity and mortality within that population than increasing the frequency of preventive services for those who are already regular recipients of preventive care.

The AT&T Health Risk Management Process

The AT&T health risk management process (begun in 1990) is performed by interdisciplinary teams, called local area health teams (LAHTs), of health professionals who have primary expertise in clinical services (nurses and physicians), TLC/health promotion, the EAP, or disability case management. An LAHT is assigned to each of sixteen discrete geographical regions, called local areas, in an effort to give all employees closer and more equal access to health services.

Corporate Direction/Goals

The health risk management (HRM) process (Figure 4-3) begins by defining the corporate direction and goals as "a philosophy and approach to Health Care that helps identify individual and group risks so that appropriate interventions, referrals and follow-up activities can be offered."

LAHT Strategic Plan

The next step in the process is to develop a strategic plan for each LAHT. This is completed by a planning and coordinating (P&C) committee in each local area comprised of a representative from each of the core service areas. Each P&C committee is charged with developing a work plan that targets 20 percent of its population to be offered health risk management each year for five years, until all employees have been involved. Information from all LAHT members is obtained before the work plan is completed.

Initiation of Strategic Plan

The work plan is initiated at targeted sites through meetings with key decision makers. Staff representatives explain the HRM process and detail the benefits of a preventive approach to health services. For many managers, the new plan may involve a major change in expectations. Under HRM, services are extended equitably to all employees; employees who historically received more extensive services may perceive the change as a loss of coverage.

Upon gaining management approval to introduce HRM at a targeted site, the staff representative proposes that baseline data be obtained through administration of the Health Audit to provide local management and program planners with information on the needs and interests of employees at the site prior to initiating the HRM process. These data can be used for program planning purposes as well as comparisons to other locations where the Health Audit has been performed. An organization may learn, for example, that it has a relatively low incidence of employees who smoke and does not need to concentrate resources in this area. On the other hand, it may report higher levels of stress and lower morale, suggesting the need for strategies in these areas.

Additional data sources can be obtained from medical claims and disability and absence records. For large locations, with over 5,000 em-

Figure 4-3. The health risk management process.

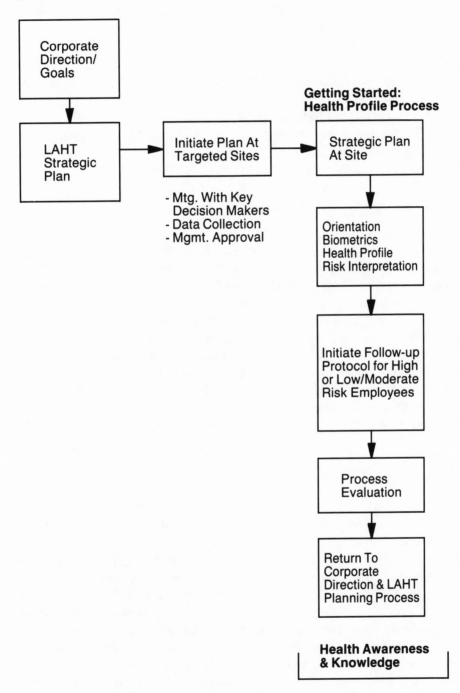

ployees, data will be available for that particular population. With smaller groups, company-wide data are used. Staff may also suggest that focus groups be conducted to gain information on such questions as:

> "What is a typical work day like for you?"
> "What types of classes or activities have been successful in your work group?"
> "What contributed to their success?"
> "What are potential obstacles to successful health promotion efforts in your location?"
> "Can you suggest strategies for overcoming them?"'

Strategic Planning at Targeted Sites

After data collection is completed, Health Affairs staff and key decision makers from the site establish a strategic plan. During this process, local management must decide whether they are interested in committing themselves to a comprehensive health promotion process through the TLC program or whether they are interested only in offering the Health Profile Process, a form of health risk appraisal used to assess the presence or absence of life-style or behavioral factors that contribute to the incidence of particular diseases. This decision is based on how much the organization is willing and able to allocate resources and on the organization's desired outcomes. The Health Profile Process can lead to improvements in health awareness and knowledge among employees; TLC is more successful in effecting sustained life-style behavior changes by participants (Figure 4-4).

Implementing the Health Profile Process

At locations that opt for the Health Profile Process only, the Health Affairs staff bears primary responsibility for implementing the process. Local management commit only space, two hours of each employee's time, and a representative to assist with administrative details. (Introductory letters to employees and managers explaining the program are reproduced in the chapter appendix.)

Initiation of the process at the employee level begins with group orientation sessions facilitated by Health Affairs staff who explain the concept of health risk management and the company's reasons for supporting the program. Employees are given the opportunity to participate in biometric testing to obtain baseline measures of their height, weight, blood pressure, and total cholesterol. They are also given a health profile to complete, which serves as the primary instrument for assessing individual health behaviors, history, and risk factors to identify employees at high risk. Additionally, the health profile is used to educate and motivate

Figure 4-4. The health risk management process and health promotion options.

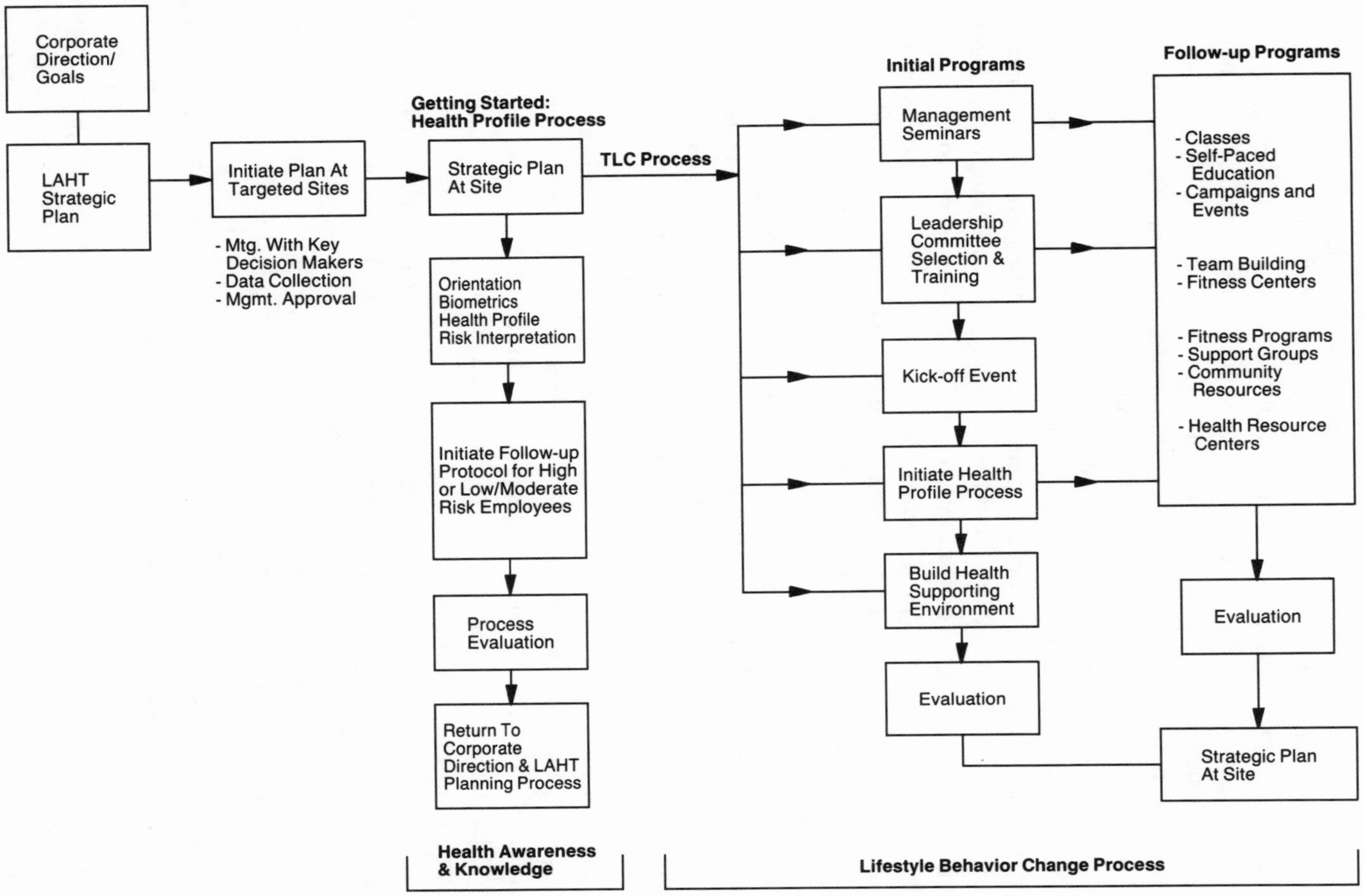

employees toward positive health behavior change and provide a format for communication between employees and Health Affairs professionals.

Several weeks after employees complete the Health Profile, they attend a group risk interpretation session where they receive a copy of their confidential personal report detailing the results of their risk analysis. This summary highlights positive health behaviors that employees are encouraged to maintain and makes suggestions for areas in need of improvement. The risk interpretation session is a critical step in the HRM process; it serves as the main opportunity for most employees to receive education and counseling on health behavior concerns.

During the first part of the session, a member of the Health Affairs staff reviews each risk variable, item by item, to help employees understand risk factors and differentiate between noncontrollable ones and those over which they have control. Participants are taught the meaning of commonly discussed but often misunderstood terms such as *blood pressure, cholesterol, heart attack, stroke,* and *body composition.* Questions are encouraged, and employees have an opportunity to clarify their understanding of the profile results, as well as any other health-related concerns.

During the second part of the session, employees are given a workbook to help them target health behavior changes to improve their overall well-being and reduce their health risks. A strong emphasis is placed on the importance of personal control and self-responsibility in life-style behaviors.[14] Participants are guided to consider factors such as their personal motivation to make changes and the level of support they can expect from family and others who are close to them. They are encouraged to create a vision by picturing success in areas they have the confidence to change. In addition, they are counseled to set a specific and realistic goal in order to ensure success.

Many employees who attend the risk interpretation session have attempted health behavior changes in the past. Those who have been successful have confidence in their ability to make changes and know how to create a plan that will help them realize their goals. Those who have failed need guidance to anticipate barriers and develop coping strategies for overcoming obstacles. They also need reminders that a setback is not a failure; temporary lapses do not imply that someone is helpless, hopeless, or out of control unless he or she dwells on mistakes and neglects to develop a plan for refocusing energy in a positive direction. Above all, participants are cautioned that there are no easy answers or quick fixes to long-standing struggles. If they expect someone else to "do it to them," they will sabotage their efforts from the start. But if they invest their own time and energy and deal with setbacks, they can be successful in their efforts to improve their health.

Follow-Up Protocol

During the next step in the process, follow-up protocols are initiated based on each employee's risk level. Low- and moderate-risk employees are provided education materials and assistance as requested and as health campaigns and programs are offered in the workplace. High-risk employees are provided with individual telephone consultations initiated by a member of the Health Affairs staff. All participants are informed from the outset of their involvement in HRM that anyone who is assessed at high risk in one or more of the following categories will receive a telephone call to begin the consultation process: blood pressure, cholesterol, body composition, tobacco use, alcohol abuse, motor vehicle injury, general well-being, stress, vascular disease, cancer, and stroke.

When the follow-up protocols were established, it was estimated that approximately 40 percent of participants would fall in at least one high-risk category. In fact, during the first three months of administering Health Profiles, between 60 and 80 percent of the population was assessed at high risk. This has important implications for the volume of calls required by staff.

The effectiveness of the high-risk follow-up protocol depends on the counseling skills of the health professional and the employee's interest in and readiness for making changes in health habits. In addition, the staff member will have to use careful judgment to limit the scope of the consultation. For people accustomed to serving as primary providers of health services, the tendency might be to maintain their role as primary providers within the context of the telephone consultation. This raises the risk of fostering too much dependence on the company by the employee and decreases the likelihood that the individual will take responsibility for pursuing referrals to providers in the community.

Before contacting the employee for the first time, the case manager assigned to counsel a high-risk employee reviews a summary of the individual's risk assessment and characteristics of the employee's work and work location. In addition, he or she prepares to discuss appropriate referrals for clinical services, treatment, health education, or behavior change classes at the work site or in the community.

Upon establishing contact with an employee identified at high risk, the case manager's first objective is to develop an alliance with the individual, not always an easy process. Employees might be defensive about their health behaviors and deny their level of risk, suspicious about the motives of the company, concerned about the confidentiality of the interaction, or angry about being labeled high risk. In general, a low-key approach at the outset can be the most effective means of reassuring employees that the caller has his or her best interests in mind.

After identifying themselves and establishing their professional expertise, case managers might begin by informing the employee that they are calling to provide follow-up as part of the HRM process. They can then ask the individual whether he or she has any questions about the results of the profile, especially in areas where the person was assessed at above average risk. The caller is trying to ensure that the information provided to the employee is clear and to explain that the follow-up is being conducted to ensure that the Health Affairs Organization fulfills its professional responsibilities now that it has become aware of the employee's specific health risks.

The next step in assisting high-risk employees is to help them make a commitment to their health. A discussion of the employee's history of past attempts to change health behaviors serves to highlight factors that may lead to success or failure in the future. By assessing barriers to change and establishing whether the employee has other health concerns that did not emerge from the Health Profile, the case manager can begin to gain a sense of the individual's readiness for and interest in making changes and of the areas of most importance to the employee. If the employee indicates that he or she does not want to modify any current health behaviors, the case manager might explain that a health professional is available in the future in case the employee has a change of mind.

For employees who want to improve their health behavior(s), the case manager can guide the development of an action plan: prioritizing needs and interests, considering options, and establishing goals and time frames. At this point, the employee should be given information and assistance to support efforts to achieve established goals.

AT&T has defined three levels of interventions that can be matched to the high-risk person's level of motivation, commitment to change, time constraints, and available support:

▴ *Level 1 interventions.* Informational materials such as pamphlets and brochures that can present reliable background information, clarify misconceptions, and motivate people to consider a more active approach. They provide education for individuals who are interested in learning more about a health topic but are not yet interested in more extensive follow-up.

▴ *Level 2 interventions.* Self-help strategies that guide people to set goals, modify behaviors, and build support without professional assistance.

▴ *Level 3 interventions.* Formalized health behavior change programs, medical consultation, ongoing community-based support programs, and professional counseling. (AT&T does not pay for level 3 interventions, although some of these services may be covered by the employee's health care benefits.)

These three levels of interventions have been defined for each of eight core areas addressed in the high-risk follow-up process:

1. Hypertension control
2. Weight management
3. Stress management
4. Back care
5. Fitness
6. Drug and alcohol use
7. Smoking cessation
8. Cholesterol control

Each intervention was chosen based on core criteria established by the department to ensure that the programs and materials use current, scientifically based information and behavior change strategies.

A case manager who suggests a level 3 intervention to an employee forwards a list of consumer guidelines to assist the person in assessing the quality of community programs under consideration. Since one of the HRM goals is to increase employee responsibility for personal health care, the consumer guidelines attempt to inform participants of factors that will reinforce their likelihood of achieving long-term success through accurate, scientifically based, high-quality programs. These guidelines also reassure the health professional that people have the information they need to identify and receive appropriate care.

After an action plan is established, the high-risk employee will continue to receive recommendations and guidance. The suggested protocol includes a call one month after the initial contact, at the end of any intervention, and as a final follow-up to assess the outcome of any referrals that were pursued or changes that were attempted. Ultimately, professional judgment will determine the appropriate frequency for follow-up contacts.

Evaluation

AT&T uses a variety of methods to evaluate the effectiveness of the HRM process: readministration of the Health Audit to track changes among employees at an organizational level, readministration of Health Profiles to assess individual improvements in health behaviors, and analyses of disability and absence data and medical claims to monitor improvements in the employee population. Customer satisfaction surveys can be used to monitor the quality of services as perceived by participants.

After evaluation data are analyzed, the Health Affairs Organization will be reexamining its mission at the corporate level and using what it has learned at the local level for consideration in future planning. While the expected outcome of this process is improved health awareness and knowledge among employees, it is also hoped that with appropriate referrals and use of community resources, employees will make significant improvements in their health practices.

TLC Within the Scope of Health Risk Management

The TLC process (Figure 4-5) begins with the first four steps in the HRM process. The difference begins during the strategic planning phase when local management commits to more active support for health promotion for its employees. This usually involves substantial time commitments for initial programs and both time and budget allocations for follow-up programs.

Initial Programs

One of the most effective ways to solidify health promotion efforts is to provide programs for managers. Seminars that focus on the connection between employee health and a company's performance communicate to managers an expectation that they actively support health promotion as a business strategy. Without management support, programs are often doomed to fail since most employees would rather risk their health for a sense of job security than vice versa. When employees return from a health promotion program and notice their supervisor glancing at the clock, they may infer that the supervisor disapproved of their involvement. Management seminars can sensitize supervisors to these issues and teach them how to support their employees.

Leadership committees are another means of ensuring program success. These committees are established to coordinate the delivery of the health promotion process for a particular location or organization, thereby reducing the need for on-site health professionals and allowing more extensive programs to reach more employees. Within the TLC process, these are representative groups of eight to twelve employees who are selected based on criteria established by the TLC staff. Sometimes they are chosen by local management, though some organizations elect to have the TLC staff choose members through interviews.

Leadership committees should be comprised of individuals who demonstrate positive health behaviors and serve as good role models. Fanatics and zealots are avoided since they tend to intimidate others, as are employees who are still struggling with such health risks as smoking or obesity. Employees generally respond best to individuals who, like themselves, have had some successes and some failures but overall are making positive health changes.

Employees who serve on leadership committees should demonstrate good interpersonal communication skills, positive relations with and the respect of fellow employees, a supportive supervisor, good organizational skills, self-confidence, and optimism. Once the group is established, the members participate in two to three days of training facilitated by TLC staff. The objectives of the training are to solidify a sense of teamwork, clarify the committee's role, provide an orientation to HRM and TLC's

Figure 4-5. TLC/health promotion within the scope of health risk management.

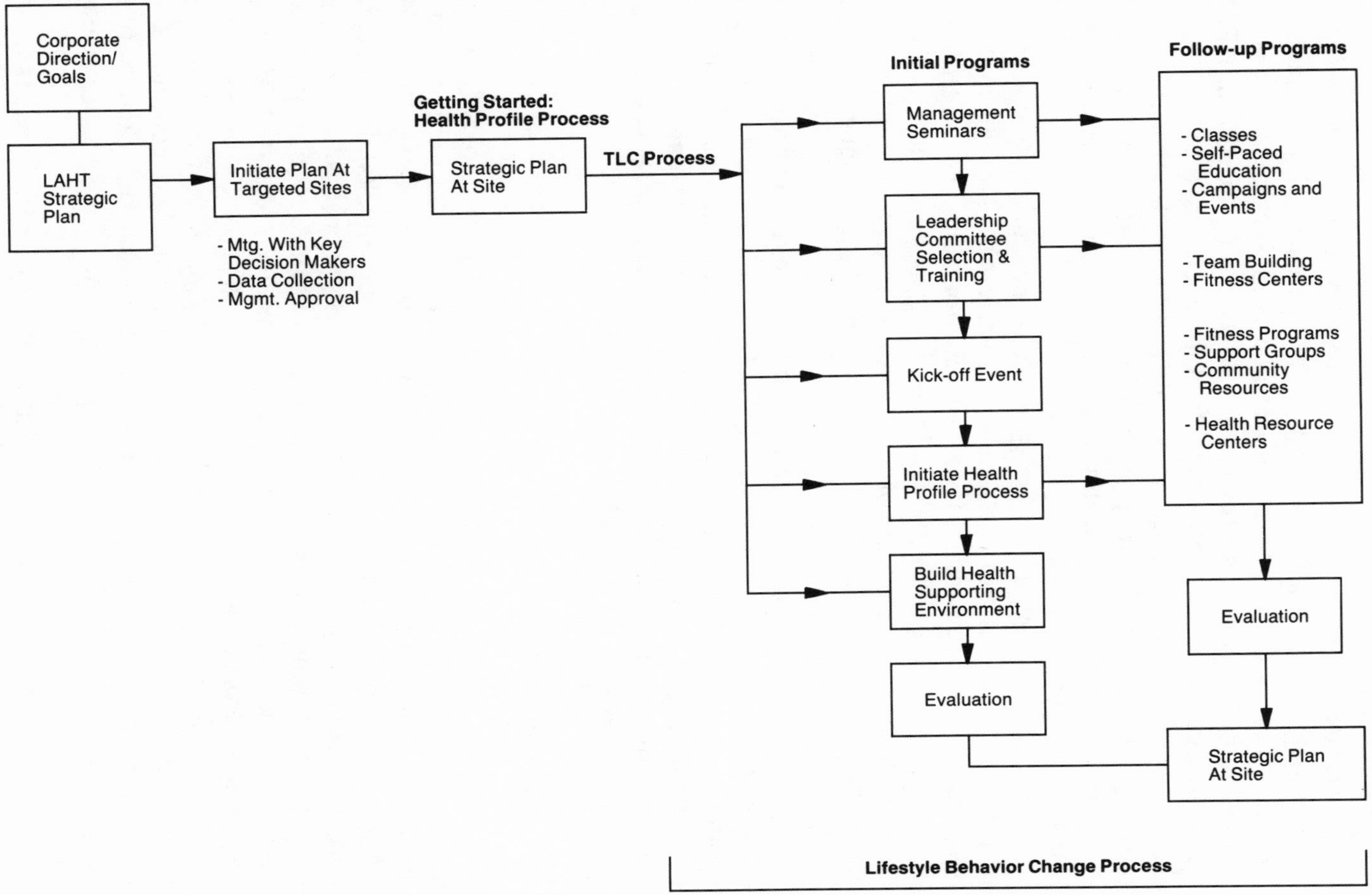

place in the process, teach members the basics of sound, effective approaches to improving health behaviors, and identify programs that the committee can plan for its organization. The final step is the development of an action plan.

Most often leadership committees choose to launch health promotion at their locations with a high-energy kick-off event such as a health fair where local providers and agencies exhibit their services. This is often planned in conjunction with inviting employees to participate in HRM at an orientation session and providing them the opportunity to have biometric testing performed and complete a Health Profile. The health fair provides visibility for the program, reinforces a sense of local ownership in the process, introduces health resources available in the community, and sets the tone for future programming.

A leadership committee's first-year action plan might include a series of programs such as those outlined in Figure 4-6. This illustrates the integration of key elements of HRM with environmental health efforts and other follow-up program options. These programs are chosen after the committee reviews the results of the Health Audit and any other available data. The action plan is thus tailored to meet the unique needs and interests of each organization.

Leadership committees have proved to be invaluable assets for the expansion of health promotion at AT&T. Their commitment, energy, and creativity have led to exciting programs that have gone well beyond what the staff members accomplished on their own. As a committee's action plan is initiated, the TLC staff continues to serve in a consulting or advisory capacity.

Follow-Up Programs

The range of follow-up programs has included many topics frequently addressed in work site health promotion, such as the core risk areas identified on the Health Profile. In addition, programs dealing with parenting, prenatal care, elder care, AIDS education, interpersonal communication, healthy cooking, wellness for women, self-defense, fitness for families, and many others have been planned in response to emerging health care and social issues. Sometimes programs are facilitated by health professionals from community hospitals or health agencies; in other cases, mutual support groups are formed. Periodically, national campaigns such as the American Cancer Society's Great American Smokeout and Low-Fat Pigout, National Employee Health and Fitness Day, and National High Blood Pressure Month provide opportunites for special programming.

The dedication of space for health resource centers provides a powerful means of reinforcing the health promotion message within the work environment. These centers consolidate health education literature, self-

Figure 4-6. Sample action plan.

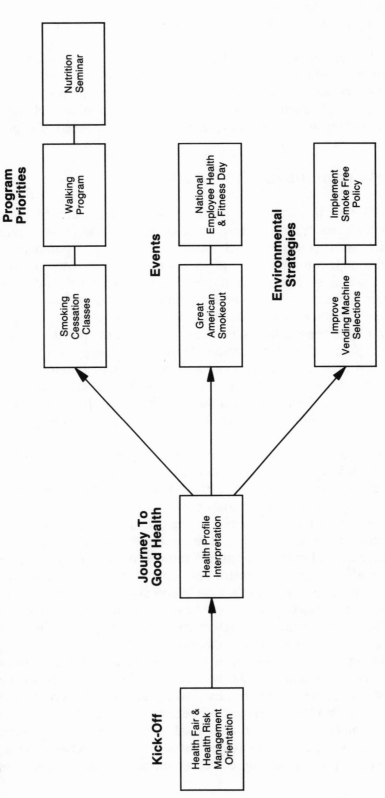

administered blood pressure and weight measurements, videos, and computer programs to communicate corporate support for positive health practices.

The next phase of the TLC process will be evaluation to assess the effectiveness of the program in stimulating employees to make and sustain life-style behavior changes and positive changes in organizational and environmental practices. The final step is reformulation of the strategic plan based on successful strategies and areas still in need of improvement.

Considerations for the Future

AT&T's work in the areas of health promotion and health risk management is probably not typical of most other companies that report having health promotion programs. A much smaller percentage of companies provide broad-based, comprehensive programs and services. More often, companies conduct screenings in targeted areas, provide health information through newsletters, sponsor lunchtime speakers on single topics, and incorporate other low-cost health promotion strategies.

AT&T's approach highlights many important considerations for successful program implementation. More modest approaches can be successful if there is organizational and environmental support for positive health practices, programs are offered based on a plan to meet the needs and interests of the organization and its constituents, employees are involved in planning, and sufficient resources (time, money, people) are allocated.

The costs of implementing health promotion programs vary widely— from $1 to $7 per employee for programs that primarily share information through printed materials, to $100 to $150 per employee for more comprehensive approaches. These costs cover only direct expenses, such as the purchase of educational materials, instructor fees, incentive items, and screening supplies. They do not incorporate staff salaries, capital equipment, construction costs for fitness centers, or rent. Program costs should be considered alongside health care costs for businesses that pay more than a quarter of the nation's $660 billion annual health care bill. Medical expenditure estimates (direct medical costs only) per employee in 1989 were $2,536 according to a Hewitt Associates survey of 976 U.S. companies, and they continue to rise steeply.

Incorporating the health of a work force as a business strategy is a highly complex matter. One way of considering how to maintain and improve employees' health, along with the company's well-being, is to consider a model for stages of behavior change.[15] The first stage is *precontemplation,* when an individual (or an organization) is considering a change and possibly denying that a particular behavior is a serious problem. After change is perceived as necessary and possible, *contempla-*

tion follows. When behavior change is attempted, the *action* stage is reached. The last stage is *maintenance/relapse:* the behavior change has been incorporated permanently or the change has been unsuccessful, and a return is made to *precontemplation.*

The organization's goal is to formulate integrated human resources and health promotion strategies that facilitate movement up one stage at a time for employees and the organization itself. This can be done through repeated, consistent attempts to inform employees of the benefits of improving their health behaviors, providing them motivation to do so through recognition and rewards, and supporting their efforts with a variety of work site initiatives. Newsletters, health breaks, lunchtime seminars, classes, support groups, company challenges, referrals to community providers, resource centers, and health screenings provide opportunities based on employees' level of readiness and interest. As individuals move up one stage and receive reinforcement from working in a safe environment where they are also respected as valuable assets to the organization, a foundation is laid for further movement along the health continuum in all three dimensions. (The chapter appendix contains a list of national resources for work site health promotion.)

Everyone has a role to play if health promotion is to be successful, beginning and ending with the way business is conducted on a daily basis. That is the best bet for a successful outcome in the workplace for employees and their organizations.

NOTES

1. *AT&T Benefits Update,* no. 3 (June 1990).
2. U.S. Department of Health and Human Services, Office of Disease Prevention and Health Promotion, *National Survey of Worksite Health Promotion Activities* (Washington, D.C.: U.S. Government Printing Office, 1987).
3. M. Scofield, "Are We There Yet? Anticipating the Future of Worksite Health Promotion," *Occupational Medicine: State of the Art Reviews* 5, no. 4 (October 1990).
4. Centers for Disease Control, "Premature Mortality in the United States: Public Health Issues in the Use of Years of Potential Life Lost," *Morbidity and Mortality Weekly Report* 35, no. 2S (1986).
5. J. L. Bly, R. C. Jones, and J. E. Richardson, "Impact of Worksite Health Promotion on Health Care Costs and Utilization," *Journal of the American Medical Association* 256 (1986): 3235–3240.
6. R. F. Allen and J. Allen, "A Sense of Community, a Shared Vision and a Positive Culture: Core Enabling Factors in Successful Culture Based Health Promotion," *American Journal of Health Promotion* 1, no. 3 (1987): 40–47.
7. R. Bellingham, D. Johnson and M. McCauley, "The AT&T Communications Total Life Concept," *Corporate Commentary* 1, no. 4 (1985): 1–13; R. Bellingham, D. Johnson, M. McCauley and T. Mendes, "Projected Cost

Savings from AT&T Communications Total Life Concept (TLC) Process," in J. Opatz, ed., *Health Promotion Evaluation* (Stephens Point, Wisc.: National Wellness Institute, 1987), pp. 35–42; M. Spillman, A. Goetz, J. Schultz, R. Bellingham, and D. Johnson, "Effects of a Corporate Health Promotion Program," *Journal of Occupational Medicine* 28, no. 4 (1986): 285–289.

8. R. Bellingham and B. Cohen, *Leadership Myths and Realities* (Amherst, Mass.: Human Resource Development Press, 1989); R. H. Rosen, *Healthy Companies* (New York: American Medical Association Membership Publications Division, 1986); R. P. Sloan, J. C. Gruman, and J. P. Allegrante, *Investing in Employee Health* (San Francisco: Jossey-Bass Publishers, 1987).

9. R. Bellingham, "Debunking the Myth of Individual Health Promotion," *Occupational Medicine: State of the Art Reviews* 5, no. 4 (October 1990); M. Blanchard and M. Tager, *Working Well* (New York: Simon & Schuster, 1985); Rosen, *Healthy Companies*.

10. Bellingham and Cohen, *Leadership Myths and Realities*.

11. M. Scofield and M. Martin, "Development of the AT&T Health Audit for Measuring Organizational Health," *Occupational Medicine: State of the Art Reviews* 5, no. 4 (October 1990); A. Bandura, "Human Agency in Social Cognitive Theory," *American Psychologist* 44, no. 9 (1989): 1175–1184.

12. P. Handley, *Insight Inventory* (Kansas City, Mo.: Insight Institute, 1988).

13. U.S. Preventive Services Task Force, *Guide to Clinical Preventive Services* (Baltimore, Md.: William & Wilkins, 1989).

14. K. L. Green, "Issues of Control and Responsibility in Workers' Health," *Health Education Quarterly* 15, no. 4 (1988): 473–486.

15. J. O. Prochaska and C. C. DiClemente, "Stages and Processes of Self-Change of Smoking: Toward an Integrative Model of Change," *Journal of Consulting and Clinical Psychology* 51 (1983): 390–395.

NATIONAL RESOURCES FOR WORK SITE HEALTH PROMOTION

Wellness Councils of America
(WELCOA)
Historic Library Plaza
1823 Harney
Suite 201
Omaha, NEB 68102
(402) 444-1711

U.S. Department of Health and
Human Services
Office of Disease Prevention and
Health Promotion
P.O. Box 1133
Washington, DC 20013-1133
(800) 336-4797

Washington Business Group on
Health
777 North Capitol, NE
Suite 800
Washington, DC 20002
(202) 408-9320

(continues)

AT&T Sample Letter to Employees

Dear Fellow Employee:

Many of the greatest pleasures in life come from feeling good about ourselves. Our lifestyles determine our emotional and physical well-being as well as the health practices that lead to illness and disability. AT&T's Health Affairs Organization has initiated a new service to all employees called Health Risk Management. This service stresses prevention of diseases and personal responsibility for one's health. You will be hearing more details about this in *Focus* magazine and other forms of employee communication.

We will be sponsoring a TLC Health Fair at your location during which you will have the opportunity to fill out a Health Profile. The Health Profile serves as an entry point to the Health Risk Management process and is an excellent opportunity to assess your health and learn about ways to improve the quality of your life. As a follow-up to this assessment, if there are health concerns that place you at high risk for developing a serious illness, you will be assigned to a health professional who can assist you in reducing that risk. This professional consultation is a highly personalized service that the Health Affairs/Medical Organization is proud to offer. In addition, regardless of your level of health risk, you will have an opportunity to learn more about health, wellness and health enhancing behaviors.

We recognize the hardship and difficulty that illness can bring to you and your family, and want to help you avoid it. We also realize that healthy employees create a healthy work environment for everyone involved.

Participation in the Health Profile process is totally voluntary, and all information is kept confidential. It is our hope that you will choose to participate. If your choice is not to participate at this time, you will not be invited again for *five* years. We believe that this is an excellent opportunity to make your health a priority, utilize our professional health services, and explore ways of enhancing your life.

AT&T Sample Letter to Managers

Dear Manager,

In a short time, all employees at your location will be offered a Health Profile by the Health Affairs/Medical Organization at the TLC Health Fair. The purpose of the Health Profile is to help employees identify health risks that might develop into serious illness in the future. This is the entry point for employees to become involved in Health Risk Management which is Health Affairs' new direction emphasizing prevention of disease and personal responsibility for one's health.

This offering is totally voluntary, and it is the prerogative of each employee to accept or decline this offer. However, this opportunity will not be offered again to employees at your location for five years. All employees who are determined to be at high risk will be personally contacted by a health professional from Health Affairs/Medical soon after the individual receives the results. Suggestions will be made on how to reduce health risks; however, it is the responsibility of the individual to take recommended action. All information concerning the employee results and follow-up activities will be kept completely confidential. A summary of the Health Profile will become part of the employee's medical record.

The future of AT&T will depend on the health and well-being of all our employees. The professional staff of the Health Affairs/Medical Organization are here to help keep our work force healthy and vital. We are interested in particular needs that you have, and would welcome an opportunity to discuss these with you. Additional details, dates and times of this offering will be forthcoming.

Thank you in advance for your cooperation and support in this Health Affairs/Medical service. If you have any questions or concerns, please call me.

5

Alcohol and Substance Abuse Counseling

Lee I. Dogoloff, American Council for Drug Education

Americans have reached a consensus: Drug abuse is the greatest problem facing the United States today.[1] The numbers supporting this belief are startling. More than 70 million Americans over age 12 (37 percent of the population) have used illicit drugs at least once—some 28 million people (14 percent of the population) in the past year and 14.5 million (7 percent) during the month prior to being surveyed. Over three-fourths of illicit drug users are Caucasian, and this problem is increasingly affecting women (41 percent). Moreover, drug use by pregnant women is a continuing problem. Of the 60 million women of childbearing age (ages 15–44), 5 million use illicit drugs, with 4 million using marijuana and 1 million using cocaine. Their drug use has tragic consequences: Of all infants born each year (11 percent of all births), 350,000 have been exposed to drugs in utero.

Substance Abuse in the Workplace

These data on alcohol and other drug abuse have enormous importance to American business. Theft and drug dealing at work to support workers' habits multiply the problems associated with drug use. In fact, the National Household Survey on Drug Abuse found that 70 percent of current drug users are employed.[2] According to a nationwide survey of 1,007 workers in 1989:

▲ Twenty-two percent of respondents said illegal drug use was at least "somewhat widespread" at their place of work. Forty-nine percent acknowledged that illegal drug use occurs in their own workplaces. Moreover, 32 percent acknowledged that illegal drug selling occurs at their work site.

▲ Forty-one percent said drug use by employees in their organization seriously affects the surveyed workers' ability to get the job done.

▲ Twenty-four percent have "personally seen or heard" of illicit drug use by coworkers on the job and 31 percent before or after work.[3]

The implications are serious for businesses, society, and individuals. These behaviors are very expensive to businesses in a variety of ways. According to the U.S. Department of Health and Human Services, the U.S. economy lost $85.5 billion from alcohol abuse and $58.3 billion from drug abuse in 1988 alone.[4] The loss to specific organizations is evident from studies that monitored the effects of employee drug use on employee production and absenteeism. An evaluation of the Utah Power and Light Company made the following conclusions:

▲ Employees who tested positive for drugs were absent 64.6 more hours per year than the corresponding control group.

▲ Costs associated with absenteeism abuses were $75,406 (1986-1987).

▲ Employees who tested positive for drugs were at fault in 80 percent of the automobile accidents they were involved in and were five times more likely to be involved in an accident than those in the control group.

▲ Those who tested positive for drugs took eight more sick days per year and had 45.1 more hours of unexcused absences from work as compared to those who tested negative for drugs.[5]

Another study, this one conducted by the U.S. Postal Service, concluded that employees who tested positive for drugs were 1.75 times more likely to take leave.[6]

These statistics clearly illustrate the loss that businesses suffer as a result of employee drug use. Safety, security, profitability, and illegal activity overlay concerns about wasted human potential and loss of valued employees. Treatment and rehabilitation are not enough to combat the problem; prevention and aggressive intervention are also required. Current knowledge about chemical dependency and the principles derived from treating individual alcohol and other drug abusers establish the basis for a corporate program to combat this serious problem.

Understanding alcohol and other drug abuse requires examining several key principles and the corporate response to each:

Principles of Chemical Dependency and Corporate Response

1. Chemical dependence is a progressive disease. When left alone, it does not get better or just go away; it tends to worsen.

Response: Once alcohol and other drug abuse is accepted as a progressive disease, the critical importance of early identification and intervention becomes clear. The earlier the intervention is, the more positive and less costly the outcome typically is. Like families, businesses cannot wait for the user to hit bottom in the traditional sense; social levers need to be used to raise that bottom.

2. Denial is the critical element that perpetuates and feeds the dis-

ease. Alcohol and other drug abusers rarely see themselves as such. Without this recognition, they cannot self-diagnose their condition, call a halt to their destructive behavior, or present themselves voluntarily for treatment. The chemically dependent individual is not the only one who practices denial. Parents, spouse, friends, and supervisors all tend to overlook the behavior and to avoid the discomfort that attends confrontation. This behavior is called enabling; people close to the user enable the destructive behavior to continue by not intervening.

Response: Accepting denial as the central component of the condition means not expecting, or waiting for, users to seek counseling and treatment voluntarily. Understanding the enabling role of those close to the dependent person sets the stage for an aggressive initiative to break the enabling cycle and to help the enablers become part of solving the problem. In the work force, as in the family, reaching the enablers may be the most important element in beginning a successful intervention.

3. Drug use typically does not stop with one addicted user. Most people are introduced to drug use by a friend or loved one. In this sense, alcohol and drug abuse can be considered "contagious."

Response: Accepting the "contagious" nature of alcohol and drug abuse reinforces the need to identify and help users. If current abusers are ignored, they may lead other employees to illegal drug use.

Clinical understanding of and experience with alcohol and other drug abuse leads inevitably to the conclusion that prevention, intervention, and supportive recovery must be the foundation of any occupationally based program dealing with these problems. The next step is to devise a framework for a company to follow in developing such a program. Although the specific elements of a program differ according to the nature of the business, employee characteristics, size, number of work sites, and managerial style, some generalizations can be made about essential steps:

Basic Plan for Corporate Action

1. Formulate a policy about drug abuse that spells out why it is unacceptable and how it will be addressed. (The appendix to this chapter provides sample drug-free-workplace policies.)
2. Communicate that policy to all employees.
3. Help, encourage, and support supervisors to identify and refer problem workers. This is the bedrock of the program.
4. Locate reasonable treatment and rehabilitation resources.
5. Implement follow-up procedures that consider the nature of the disease being treated and its recovery process.
6. Define at the outset enforceable and appropriate alternative job action for employees who are unwilling or unable to return successfully to full functioning.

For a corporate action plan to work, each of these steps must reflect an understanding of the disease and how it manifests itself in the workplace.

Elements of Substance Abuse Programs

Prevention and Awareness Programs

The first step in developing a company policy is to marshal the facts that specify exactly why drug use is unacceptable and to ensure that the work force understands the impact of drug use on their personal lives, as well as on the company. This drug prevention and awareness component is an important part of the overall effort. The purpose of this educational program is twofold: to provide clear information that establishes the rationale for and benefits to be derived from an alcohol- and drug-free workplace and to educate employees and their families about this issue as part of a case finding or early identification process.

One drug awareness program is *Working Toward a Drug Free Future: A Year Long Program for Managers, Employees and Their Families,* produced by the American Council for Drug Education in Rockville, Maryland. The core of this program consists of twelve drug awareness pamphlets, which ideally are sent to each employee's home. The material describes the costs and consequences of a drug-using workplace, contains information about specific drugs, describes the negative impact of substance abuse on families and the community, teaches parents how to talk to their children about drug abuse, addresses drug abuse and AIDS, and describes how employees can become active in drug prevention.

Another available program, the *Substance Abuse Awareness Program,* has been developed by Drug Prevention Strategies, Inc., of Costa Mesa, California. Comprised of a Facilitator's Guide, Implementation Guide, Employee's Handbook, and 20-minute video entitled "Drugs at Work," this is a comprehensive program designed to educate employees about the impact of drug and alcohol abuse in the workplace. It addresses the physical and psychological dangers to the user, as well as the effects of abuse on job performance and satisfaction, benefits, salary, safety, and the job security of all employees. *The Substance Abuse Awareness Program* targets employees at all levels, including executives and senior- and middle-level managers.

Prevention and awareness programs help establish a workplace ethic that does not tolerate drug use by employees. These programs are directed primarily to nondrug-using or occasional-drug-using employees. The program materials alert them to the health and safety risks, lost productivity, reduced quality control, increased accidents, and lowered morale caused by drug use in the workplace. The more that nonusers become aware of the costs and risks involved, the less use will be tolerated. Such programs also educate management and provide a rationale for a drug-free workplace. When materials are sent home, family members are encouraged to participate in counseling and other employee assistance programs.

Depending on the size of the organization, the cost for a fairly comprehensive year-long program could range from $2 to $5 per employee.

Prevention and education programs can help to advertise counseling services to employees and their families. But because voluntary referral to treatment is rare and enabling is strong, counseling cannot be relied on as the sole source of problem identification.

Urine Testing

As a company begins to confront the problem of employee drug use, the subject of urine testing likely will be broached. A properly performed urine test can detect the presence of a specific drug in a person's system. The time frame for detection will vary by drug; for example, a positive urine test for marijuana means the person used the drug sometime within a period of several weeks, whereas a positive result for cocaine indicates the person used the drug within a much shorter time period, usually 24 to 48 hours prior to the time of the test. Thus, a positive urine test result does not mean that the person is intoxicated or impaired; it indicates only that a person has used a particular drug at some time. A time frame for detection will also vary with the minimal level of drug that must be present before the test is considered positive.

In the work setting, urine testing is generally used in three ways:

1. *For screening as part of the preemployment process.* Most companies announce the screening publicly, notify the applicant about a positive result, and give him or her a resource list for treatment services, if appropriate. Many companies allow applicants who have been detected as drug users to reapply after a certain amount of time has lapsed and after they have entered an appropriate treatment program.

2. *For cause based on a specific incident that might suggest the use of drugs by an employee.* Most commonly, this is done after an accident or other incident where drug use is suspected as a causative factor.

3. *On a random, unannounced basis.* This is generally reserved for jobs where issues of public safety or security are involved (e.g., public transportation) and where it would be irresponsible to wait for a performance decrement prior to taking action.

A company that decides to test must be able to ensure the integrity and reliability of the test results. Several issues are important in this regard:

▴ *Chain of custody.* One must be able to ensure that the sample to be tested did in fact come from the employee tested and that it was not switched or tampered with in any way while in transit to the laboratory or during processing. Good commercial laboratories have devised methods of ensuring the security of samples through chain-of-custody procedures.

▴ *Confirmation of results.* All positive urine tests must be confirmed by a testing methodology that is different from and more sensitive than the original screening method. Generally only when confirmatory results using an alternate technology are achieved can action be taken on a positive test.

▴ *Laboratory selection.* The federal government has established a protocol for certifying that laboratories meet certain standards for testing proficiency. These are generally known as NIDA certified laboratories (standing for the certifying agency of the government, the National Institute on Drug Abuse). By selecting a NIDA-certified laboratory, the company can be assured that the laboratory has met specifications in a number of areas: appropriate experience, adequate methods of screening and confirmation, a quality control program, procedures to ensure adequate chain of custody, provisions for sample retention in case confirmed results are challenged, support by the laboratory if legal action is brought against the employer, and an adequate internal security system.

Urine tests can be an effective tool if they are used properly and if they are a part of a larger, company-wide effort to prevent employee drug use and to respond when drug abuse is detected.

Role of the Supervisor

Getting the supervisor to identify and refer drug-using employees to counseling is a critical and sometimes difficult task. Often supervisors' desire to be liked and reticence to confront poor job performance prevent them from addressing job performance issues. Adding the possibility of employee substance abuse and the normal denial and enabling process to that resistance makes it even more difficult to get a supervisor to identify and refer problem workers.

The first step in addressing this resistance is to teach supervisors the principles of chemical dependence and to help them understand how the worker's denial prevents him or her from coming forth voluntarily and requesting help. Employee assistance program (EAP) personnel can be helpful in providing this supervisory training. (If the company does not have an EAP, then training might be obtained from drug and alcohol treatment providers in the community.) The supervisor must also understand that his or her enabling allows the employee's self-destructive behavior to continue. Identifying and referring a suspected alcohol or other drug abuser should not be viewed negatively—as snitching on someone—but rather as a helpful and caring act for another human being, especially given the progressive nature of this condition and the fact that, left untreated, it almost invariably leads to premature death. But even an appreciation of these facts will be insufficient if the supervisor is not trained in how to identify and refer.

The supervisor is not a diagnostician or clinician and is not expected to make a determination as to the person's alcohol or other drug dependence. Rather, the supervisor is to do that which he or she is trained to do: observe and address job performance. An employee's actual alcohol or drug consumption may not be observed, but signs of trouble may be evident in decreasing work performance and changes in attitudes that are frequently coupled with changes in personal appearance (e.g., weight loss, bloodshot eyes, pallor, inattention to personal hygiene). (Figure 5-1 identifies symptoms of chemical dependency.)

Because these changes may appear gradually, they can be easily overlooked. Moreover, alcohol and other drug use may not be involved at all. But if a pattern seems to be developing—a gradual decrease in performance over time, spotty completion of assignments, absence from or late arrival at work—then a supervisor should intervene. Intervention at this level is based solely on changes in performance or behavior. No diagnosis or accusations should be made or conclusions drawn about alcohol or other drug use. In this context, it is important to recognize that even when substance abuse may be a causative factor and may be ultimately identified as such, it is not the reason for the supervisor's concern. Instead, it is the employee's inconsistent or declining work performance and/or unacceptable behavior that prompts the supervisor to take action and justifies the efforts to assist the employee in resolving the problem.

The exception to this procedure is suspicion that an employee is intoxicated on the job. In this case, the supervisor should handle the situation in accordance with organizational procedures for dealing with an employee unfit for duty (e.g., the employee may be sent to the health office for an explanation of his or her behavior and state of mind).

The process of identifying poor work performance and making a successful referral for counseling is fairly simple and straightforward. The supervisor meets with the employee and shares his or her concern, noting specific, objectively verifiable changes in performance and behavior (e.g., failure to complete assignments on time, tardiness, sloppy work). The supervisor then does the following:

1. Clearly states the consequences of such behavior.
2. Asks for and listens to the employee's explanation.
3. Devises with the employee an appropriate course of action to remedy the performance problems.

Figure 5-1. On-the-job symptoms of chemical dependency.

Absenteeism

- Frequent absences or days off with vague or unlikely excuses
- Excessive use of sick leave
- Tardiness
- Early departures

On-the-Job Absenteeism

- Freqeunt absence from post
- Long lunches
- Withdrawn or preoccupied behavior

Job Efficiency

- Erratic or deteriorating productivity
- Missed deadlines
- Failure to follow instructions
- Errors in judgment
- Pattern of decreased efficiency as compared to past performance

Interpersonal Relations

- Complaints from co-workers
- Complaints from customers
- Avoidance of associates
- Getting other workers to take over job responsibility
- Overreaction to criticism or suggestions

Personal Appearance, Attitude, and Behavior

- Personal appearance becomes sloppy
- Wide mood swings during the day for no apparent reason
- Smell of alcohol or use of breath deodorizers
- Repeated or unreasonable accidents on or off the job

Data Pertinent to Supervisory Level

- Failure to follow through on supervisory details
- Conflicting instructions given to staff members
- Use of other staff members' time and skill to cover own responsibilities
- Submission of incomplete reports and data
- Mismanagement of budgets
- Failure to coordinate schedules

4. Sets a specific date to meet again to review progress.
5. Maintains a written record of the meeting.

At the second scheduled meeting, the supervisor reviews the earlier discussion, including repetition of performance problems, the explanation offered, and the plan agreed upon for improvement, and shares with the employee an assessment of any change that has occurred. Assuming a positive change has occurred, he or she supports that change and sets another meeting for several weeks later to make certain that the improved performance or behavior continues. If performance or behavior has not improved, the supervisor shares concerns in specific terms, again stating the consequences for continued poor performance or behavior, and asks for an explanation.

If no apparently reasonable explanation is offered, the supervisor lets the employee know of his or her concern. If the performance does not improve, the result will be disciplinary action.

At this point, the supervisor can offer to help the employee identify and resolve the problem. The employee should be given the name and telephone number of a counselor to contact and be strongly encouraged to do so. The supervisor might also tell the employee that he or she will call ahead to let the counselor know that a referral has been made. The supervisor then sets another meeting to make sure the employee has followed through with the recommendations and to focus on how to improve job performance.

The discussion in the second meeting has set the stage for counseling to occur. The company presumably has a policy in place, has communicated it to all employees, has initiated a drug awareness and prevention program, and has completed training of its supervisors. Now employees are beginning to request counseling services.

The Counseling Process

Generally there are two ways in which the employee can come to the counseling process: self-referral or management referral. Self-referrals are often initiated by family members when they have access to counseling services. It is unusual for a chemically dependent person to self-refer for treatment since denial usually makes him or her unable to request help voluntarily. Policies that protect the confidentiality of persons who self-refer should be clearly established. Except in extreme circumstances, where violence or safety is clearly at issue, confidentiality must be preserved.

A management referral usually grows out of a series of discussions between supervisor and employee about declining work performance. Here too the policy regarding confidentiality should be established and ground rules set about what information will be communicated between the counselor and the supervisor. Generally this information may be given only with the consent of the employee and is limited to whether the person has kept the appointment. Unless violence or safety is at issue or the employee has authorized disclosure of the information, no communication takes place between the counselor and management.

There are a number of counseling service options available. The company needs to determine which services will be provided by company-employed staff and which will be contracted with an outside vendor. Generally it is appropriate for company-employed staff to perform the intervention, with the assessment performed by either the EAP professional or an outside service provider. Whichever way the company chooses, the counseling component of the program should be able to assess the situation, provide short-term counseling, and make referrals for appropriate longer-term treatment and rehabilitation services.

ASSESSMENT

In the assessment phase, the counselor's goal is to begin with the problem that the client presents and gain a more complete understanding of the client's situation. This information should enable the counselor to make some initial judgments. The counselor should be able to differentiate between the reason the client gives for coming for service, generally known as the "presenting problem," and the problem the counselor determines is the more substantive one, generally known as the "assessed problem." For example, a client may come to counseling for a financial problem that requires budget assistance, but after probing, the counselor might determine the cause of the financial problem to be cocaine use. Substance abuse problems are often associated with other difficulties that are initially presented as, for example, marital difficulties or parent-child relationship problems.

Performing an accurate assessment requires a high degree of skill and forms the basis for the initial treatment plan that follows. Persons doing assessments should have appropriate training and experience, particularly in the areas of substance abuse. It is best if they are credentialed professionals who have completed requisite licensing requirements in the jurisdiction in which they practice. This includes a master's degree in social work with appropriate accreditation from the Academy of Certified Social Workers of the National Association of Social Workers and state licensing where available, a master's degree in psychiatric nursing, or a Ph.D. in psychology and appropriate state licensure or equivalent.

TREATMENT

Once the assessment is completed, which can take from one to three sessions, a treatment plan is developed, communicated, and agreed upon with the employee. If short-term counseling is deemed appropriate to address a relatively minor situational problem, there should be a clear agreement between counselor and employee as to the number of sessions (usually not to exceed six) and a specific treatment contract with areas to be pursued and goals enunciated. In general, short-term counseling is not appropriate for people with alcohol or other drug-dependence problems. Those who are chemically dependent generally require an assessment, which includes identifying appropriate treatment referral options, preparing the client and/or the family to accept the referral, and following up to make certain the client has accepted the referral and is receiving appropriate help. There are generally two types of treatment options available: outpatient and residential.

Structured outpatient treatment usually includes participation in group and individual therapy and a component involving the family. In virtually all cases, the employee can continue to work while involved in outpatient treatment. Such programs should require abstinence from the use of all drugs and alcohol. Abstinence is often monitored by regular laboratory urinalysis checks. These programs typically provide a peer group focus designed to encourage problem solving and taking responsibility for personal behavior, including performance at work and in family relationships and sound decision making. Aftercare and continued participation in group therapy are encouraged to maintain a drug-free life-style.

Outpatient treatment emphasizes the full role of family dynamics in rehabilitation. Family support groups are often included in this approach to help family members deal effectively with their own feelings, to take stock of the health of their family life, and to facilitate their ability to interact effectively with the alcohol- or drug-dependent person. Issues of co-dependency, where the spouse and other family members have taken on roles that are dysfunctional to the family, should be identified and addressed.

For more severely involved employees, a highly structured inpatient residential program should be considered. These programs generally last about four weeks and may be the best source of help for employees with multiple alcohol- or drug-related problems, whose existence centers around compulsive drug use, and who has failed at outpatient treatment. The symptoms manifested by these employees are partially the result of the toxicity of the drugs they are using but may also reflect longer-term psychological problems.

Residential programs emphasize a drug-free existence and learning about the disease. In order to facilitate the ultimate return to the home environment, family participation is encouraged to consolidate the gains of treatment and encourage continued drug abstinence.

A listing of the names and telephone numbers of each state drug and alcohol office appears at the end of this chapter. These government agencies usually have a comprehensive listing of all available treatment and counseling services and can be an excellent resource for such information. In addition, the National Institute on Drug Abuse sponsors a toll-free number for providing individualized technical assistance in determining needs and formulating an appropriate policy.

Most outpatient and residential treatment programs for chemical dependency use some form of a twelve-step Alcoholics Anonymous (AA) or Narcotics Anonymous (NA) program as part of the treatment regimen. The members of these groups are personally familiar with the defenses and barriers to change that are part of the chemical dependence. They are empathetic in their understanding of the basis for compulsive use but confrontational in dealing with each other's rationalizations.

AA's twelve-step program is designed to assist participants in achieving and maintaining abstinence from alcohol and other drugs, as well as changing dysfunctional life-styles. The group provides fellowship and support to individuals in resolving problems associated with continued sobriety. Participants usually have a sponsor selected from the group who is available virtually 24 hours a day to help them as problems emerge. The 90/90 rule, a rule of thumb for people in early recovery, is to attend daily AA meetings during the first ninety days of after-care.

AA sponsors groups for family members too: Alateen for teenagers with an alcoholic parent or other close relative and Al-Anon for assistance in coping with an alcoholic or drug-abusing spouse or other family member. These groups can reduce the sense of isolation and shame experienced by the family members and are useful in helping family members learn more about the disease and in finding constructive ways to deal with their alcoholic relative.

AA and allied groups, available at virtually no cost, are valuable in providing support for recovering users as they continue in alcohol and other drug treatment. However, they are adjuncts to rather than substitutes for treatment. They should not be seen as the primary treatment for chemical dependence, although they may well be necessary for achieving long-term recovery.

The counseling process should create a supportive environment and structure for the patient to abstain from all substance use. This generally requires regular (at least weekly) sessions, the involvement of family members, and supplemental support through involvement with self-help groups such as AA and NA. Initially, counseling focuses almost exclusively on the issues related to maintaining sobriety. Counselors should explain techniques for dealing with feelings of craving for the drug, for avoiding situations where alcohol and other drugs may be present, and for shifting away from alcohol- and drug-using friends.

The second phase of counseling addresses the behavior patterns that often are part of the chemically dependent way of life. These patterns, which include manipulation, dishonesty, and difficulties in personal relationships, must be broken.

Chemical dependence is a chronic lifetime condition. It is not subject to recovery as such; the recovering process is ongoing, and relapse must always be guarded against. For some people, relapse is part of getting well and needs to be recognized as such.

The most important factor in ensuring long-term recovery is supportive counseling over time. Although the intensity and frequency of counseling can be reduced, the counseling service should continue for eighteen to twenty-four months and can be stopped comfortably only when other supportive mechanisms, through family and the fellowship of the twelve-step self-help group, are firmly in place. (Figures 5-2 and 5-3 show the progression and recovery of the alcoholic and his or her family.)

EVALUATION

The counseling process can be evaluated quantitatively and qualitatively. Quantitative evaluation looks at the numbers of people who are referred to counseling, how they were referred (whether voluntarily or through management referrals), the presenting and assessed problems, the number of sessions held, and the course that treatment took.

Ascertaining the quality of service rendered can be more difficult because of the confidentiality protections afforded to employees. Nevertheless, it is important because of the costs of the counseling services and the desire of most employers to make certain that their employees are receiving high-quality care. One mechanism to evaluate the quality of treatment, as developed by Masi Research Consultants, Inc., has an expert team, composed of a psychiatrist, a psychologist, and a social worker, evaluate a selected sample of case records against a predetermined protocol that examines a number of relevant service issues. The client company receives a complete report of the counseling process that evaluates the quality of service rendered, whether the assessment was adequate, whether appropriate referrals were suggested, and how those referrals were followed up to be certain that they were successful. In addition, the experience and qualifications of the counseling staff are evaluated, the ability of counselors to detect and appropriately assess drug and alcohol use is specifically addressed, and recommendations for improvement are offered.

Is counseling cost-effective? A naval military personnel command study released in October 1989 concluded that a savings of $12.90 was realized for each $1.00 invested in the overall rehabilitation program for sailors. This study sampled over 7,000 sailors who were treated in the navy's four alcohol rehabilitation centers and twenty-four alcohol rehabilitation departments associated with navy hospitals from 1982 to 1984. For those sailors successfully rehabilitated and retained, the cost of separation and replacement of trained and highly skilled personnel was avoided and

(*text continues on page 131*)

Figure 5-2. The progression and recovery of the alcoholic in the disease of alcoholism.

To be read from left to right.

Enlightened and Interesting Way of Life Opens Up with Road Ahead to Higher Levels than Ever Before.

Progression

Occasional Relief Drinking
Constant Relief Drinking Commences
Increase in Alcohol Tolerance
Onset of Memory Blackouts
Surreptitious Drinking
Increasing Dependence on Alcohol
Urgency of First Drinks
Feelings of Guilt
Memory Blackouts Increase
Drinking Bolstered with Excuses
Grandiose and Aggressive Behavior
Efforts to Control Fail Repeatedly
Tries Geographical Escapes
Family and Friends Avoided
Loss of Ordinary Willpower
Tremors and Early Morning Drinks
Decrease in Alcohol Tolerance
Onset of Lengthy Intoxications
Moral Deterioration
Impaired Thinking
Drinking With Inferiors
Indefinable Fears
Unable to Initiate Action
Obsession With Drinking
Vague Spiritual Desires
All Alibis Exhausted
Complete Defeat Admitted

Crucial Phase

Inability to Discuss Problem
Decrease of Ability to Stop
Drinking When Others Do So
Persistent Remorse
Promises and Resolutions Fail
Loss of Other Interests
Work and Money Troubles
Unreasonable Resentments
Neglect of Food
Physical Deterioration

Chronic Phase

Obsessive Drinking Continues
in Vicious Circles

Recovery

Group Therapy and Mutual Help Continue
Rationalizations Recognized
Care of Personal Appearance
First Steps Towards Economic Stability
Increase of Emotional Control
Facts Faced With Courage
New Circle of Stable Friends
Family and Friends Appreciate Efforts
Natural Rest and Sleep
Realistic Thinking
Regular Nourishment Taken

Increasing Tolerance
Contentment in Sobriety
Confidence of Employers
Appreciation of Real Values
Rebirth of Ideals
New Interests Develop
Adjustment to Family Needs
Desire to Escape Goes
Return of Self-Esteem
Diminishing Fears of the Unknown Future
Appreciation of Possibilities of New Way of Life

Rehabilitation

Start of Group Therapy
Onset of New Hope
Physical Overhaul by Doctor
Spiritual Needs Examined
Right Thinking Begins
Takes Stock of Self
Meets Normal and Happy Former Addicts
Stops Taking Alcohol
Told Addiction Can Be Arrested
Learns Alcoholism is an Illness
Honest Desire for Help

Smithers

Source: Smithers Alcoholism & Treatment Center.

Figure 5-3. The progression and recovery of the family in the disease of alcoholism.

Enlightened, Future Bright, to Higher Levels than Ever Believed Possible.

Blues
Intolerance
Suspicion
Arguments
Distrust
Problems Multiplying
Unhappiness
Worry
Denial (Fantasy)
Irritability
Threats Made are Not Carried Through
Seeks Answers
Takes Responsibility
Avoiding Reference
Loss of Interest
Extravagance
Illnesses
Self-Defense
Putting Up Good Front
Depression
Uses Patent or Prescribed Medication
Irrational Behavior
Uses Alcohol to Relax
Self-Neglect
Loss of Self-Respect
Alibi
Remorse
Dishonesty
Social Withdrawal
Infidelity
Indefinable Fears
Isolation
More Frequent Use of Drugs/Alcohol
Blames Others
Bankruptcy of Alibis
Escape
Admits Defeat
Jealousy
Chronic Depression
Suicide Attempts

Without Help

Bottom

Awareness
Sincere Desire for Help
Hope
Seeks Help
Recognizes Disease
Recognition of Role
Need to Control Lessens
Honesty
Shares With Others
Trust, Openness
Becomes Willing to Change
Begins to Relax
Release
Develops Optimism
Spiritual Examination
Daily Living Pattern Changes
(Rest, Diet, Sleep)
New Friends
Diminishing Fears
Return of Self-Esteem
Service
Acceptance
Peace of Mind
Guilt Is Gone
Makes Amends
New Interests Develop
Return of Confidence
Love
Appreciates Spiritual Values
Courage
Return of Respect of
Family and Friends
Happiness
Joy
At Ease With Life

With Help

The progression and recovery symptoms listed are based on the *most repeated experiences* of family members in the disease of alcoholism or other chemical dependencies. While every symptom in the chart does not occur in every member of every family, or in the same sequence, it does portray an average chain reaction. The entire process may take years or it may occur in a very short time.

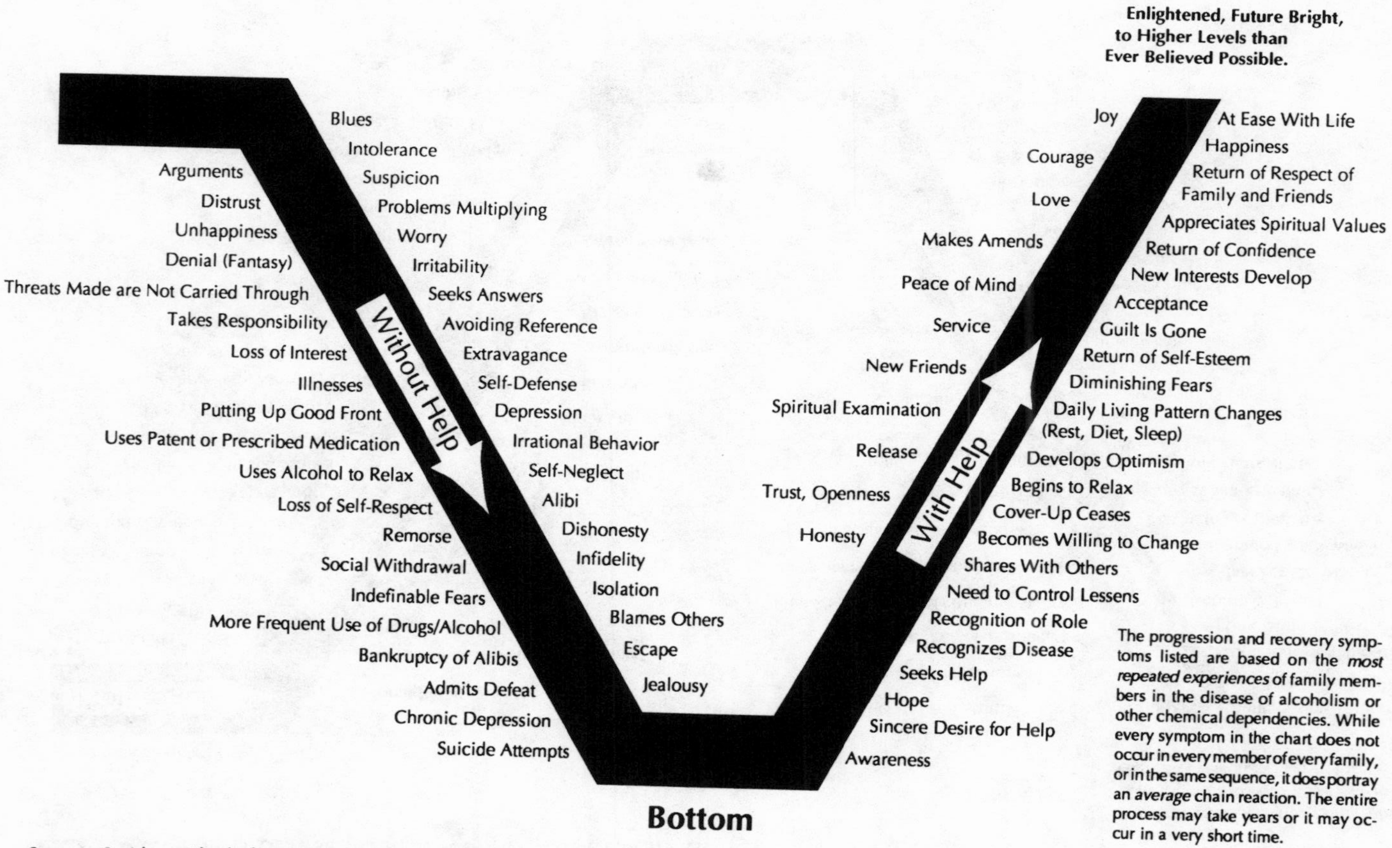

Source: Smithers Alcoholism & Treatment Center.

counted as rehabilitation savings or benefits. The net savings for the program during this time was $435 million.[7]

Similar benefits have been stated by others. General Motors reduced lost time by 40 percent, sickness and accident payments by 60 percent, grievance proceedings by 50 percent, and job accidents by 50 percent after establishing an employee assistance program. (The majority of savings were attributed to substance abuse counseling, which involves about 65 percent of the total array of problems seen by the EAP.) E. I. du Pont's EAP handled 176 alcohol-related cases in its counseling program in one year and had a 70 percent rehabilitation rate, with an estimated cost savings of $419,000.[8]

Conclusion

Alcohol and substance abuse is a national concern and has a serious negative impact on the American workplace. Companies can respond to this issue and substantially reduce its effects. Through a carefully crafted policy based on an understanding of alcohol and substance abuse and with a component for offering education, prevention, and counseling services, the costs associated with this behavior can be substantially reduced. Businesses that institute such policies and programs become important contributors in the quest for a drug-free America.

NOTES

1. *Surveys on the Drug Crisis,* report to the Office of National Drug Control Policy (Princeton, N.J.: George H. Gallup International Foundation, 1989).
2. *National Household Survey on Drug Abuse: 1988 Population Estimates* (Rockville, Md.: National Institute on Drug Abuse, Division of Epidemiology and Prevention Research, U.S. Department of Health and Human Services, 1988).
3. Ibid.
4. H. J. Harwood, D. M. Napolitano, P. L. Kristiansen, and J. J. Collins, *Economic Costs to Society of Drug and Alcohol Abuse and Mental Illness: 1980* (Research Triangle Park, N.C.: Research Triangle Institute, 1984).
5. D. J. Crouch, D. O. Webb, L. V. Peterson, P. F. Buller, and D. E. Rollins, "A Critical Evaluation of the Utah Power and Light Company's Substance Abuse Management Program: Absenteeism, Accidents and Costs," in *Drugs in the Workplace: Research and Evaluation Data* (Rockville, Md.: National Institute on Drug Abuse, 1988), pp. 170–190.
6. J. Normand and S. Salyards, "An Empirical Evaluation of Preemployment Drug Testing in the United States Postal Service: Interim Report of Findings," in *Drugs in the Workplace: Research and Evaluation Data,* p. 128.
7. *Navy Study Finds Rehabilitation of Sailors Is Justified* (Naval Military Personnel Command Alcohol Abuse Prevention and Rehabilitation Program, NMPC-63, October 1989).
8. C. A. Berry, *Good Health for Employees and Reduced Health Care Costs for Industry* (Washington, D.C.: Health Insurance Association of America, 1981).

NATIONAL ASSOCIATIONS OF STATE ALCOHOL AND DRUG ABUSE

Alabama
Division Substance Abuse
    Services
Alabama Department of Mental
    Health and Mental Retardation
200 Interstate Park Drive
P.O. Box 3710
Montgomery, AL 36193
(205) 270-4650
FAX: (205) 240-3195

Alaska
Office of Alcoholism and Drug
    Abuse
Alaska Department of Health and
    Social Services
Pouch H-05-F
Juneau, AK 99811
(907) 586-6201
FAX: (907) 586-1061

Arizona
Arizona Department of Health
    Services
Office of Community Behavior
    and Health
411 North 24th Street
Phoenix, AZ 85008
(602) 220-6478
FAX: (602) 220-6502

Arkansas
Arkansas Office of Alcohol and
    Drug Abuse Prevention
Donaghey Plaza North, Suite 400
P.O. Box 1437
Little Rock, AR 72203-1437
(501) 682-6650
FAX: (501) 682-6571

California
Governor's Policy Council on
    Drug and Alcohol Abuse
1700 K Street
Executive Office
Sacramento, CA 95814
(916) 445-0834
FAX: (916) 323-5873

Colorado
Alcohol and Drug Abuse Division
Colorado Department of Health
4210 East 11th Avenue
Denver, CO 80220
(303) 331-8201
FAX: (303) 320-1529

Connecticut
Connecticut Alcohol and Drug
    Abuse Commission
999 Asylum Avenue, 3d Floor
Hartford, CT 06105
(203) 566-4145
FAX: (203) 566-6055

Delaware
Delaware Division of Alcoholism,
    Drug Abuse and Mental Health
1901 North DuPont Highway
Newcastle, DE 19720
(302) 421-6101
FAX: (302) 421-6086

District of Columbia
District of Columbia Health
    Planning and Development
1660 L Street, N.W.
Washington, DC 20036
(202) 673-7481
FAX: (202) 727-2386

Florida
Alcohol and Drug Abuse Program
Florida Department of Health and
  Rehabilitative Services
1317 Winewood Boulevard
Tallahassee, FL 32301
(904) 488-0900
FAX: (904) 487-2239

Georgia
Georgia Alcohol and Drug
  Services Section
878 Peachtree St., N.E., Suite 318
Atlanta, GA 30309
(404) 894-6352
FAX: (404) 853-9065

Hawaii
Alcohol and Drug Abuse Division
Hawaii Department of Health
P.O. Box 3378
Honolulu, HI 96801
(808) 548-4280
FAX: (808) 548-3263

Idaho
Division of Family and Children
  Services
Idaho Department of Health and
  Welfare
450 West State Street, 7th Floor
Boise, ID 83720
(208) 334-5935
FAX: (208) 334-5694

Illinois
Illinois Department of Alcoholism
  and Substance Abuse
100 West Randolph Street, Suite
  5-600
Chicago, IL 60601
(312) 814-3840
FAX: (312) 814-2419

Indiana
Division of Addiction Services
Indiana Department of Mental
  Health
117 East Washington Street
Indianapolis, IN 46204
(317) 232-7816
FAX: (317) 232-7948

Iowa
Division of Sustance Abuse and
  Health Promotion
Iowa Department of Public Health
Lucas State Office Building, 4th
  Floor
Des Moines, IA 50319
(515) 281-3641
FAX: (515) 281-4958

Kansas
Kansas Alcohol and Drug Abuse
  Services
300 S.W. Oakley
Biddle Building
Topeka, KS 66606-1861
(913) 296-3925
FAX: (913) 296-0511

Kentucky
Division of Substance Abuse
Kentucky Department of Mental
  Health-Mental Retardation
  Services
275 East Main Street
Frankfort, KY 40621
(502) 564-2880
FAX: (502) 564-3844

Louisiana
Division of Alcohol and Drug
    Abuse
Department of Health and
    Hospitals
1201 Capitol Access Road
P.O. Box 3868
Baton Rouge, LA 70821-3868
(504) 342-9354
FAX: (504) 342-4419

Maine
Alcohol and Drug Abuse Planning
71 Hospital Street
State House Station 11
Augusta, ME 04333
(207) 289-2781
FAX: (207) 626-5555

Maryland
Maryland State Alcohol and Drug
    Abuse Administration
201 West Preston Street
Baltimore, MD 21201
(301) 225-6925
FAX: (301) 225-5305

Massachusetts
Massachusetts Division of
    Substance Abuse Services
150 Tremont Street
Boston, MA 02111
(617) 727-8614
FAX: (617) 727-6496

Michigan
Office of Substance Abuse
    Services
Michigan Department of Public
    Health
2150 Apollo Drive
P.O. Box 30206
Lansing, MI 48909
(517) 335-8809
FAX: (517) 335-8837

Minnesota
Chemical Dependency Program
    Division
Minnesota Department of Human
    Services
444 Lafayette Road
St. Paul, MN 55155-3823
(612) 296-4610
FAX: (612) 296-6244

Mississippi
Division of Alcohol and Drug
    Abuse
Mississippi Department of Mental
    Health
Robert E. Lee State Office
    Building, 11th Floor
Jackson, MS 39201
(601) 359-1288

Missouri
Division of Alcohol and Drug
    Abuse
Missouri Department of Mental
    Health
1915 South Ridge Drive
P.O. Box 687
Jefferson City, MO 65102
(314) 751-4942
FAX: (314) 751-7814

Montana
Alcohol and Drug Abuse Division
Montana Department of
    Institutions
Helena, MT 59601
(406) 444-2827
FAX: (406) 444-4920

Nebraska
Division of Alcoholism and Drug
  Abuse
Nebraska Department of Public
  Institutions
P.O. Box 94728
Lincoln, NE 68509-4728
(402) 471-2851, ext. 5583
FAX: (402) 479-5145

Nevada
Bureau of Alcohol and Drug
  Abuse
Nevada Department of Human
  Resources
505 East King Street
Carson City, NV 89710
(702) 687-4790
FAX: (702) 687-4733

New Hampshire
New Hampshire Office of Alcohol
  and Drug Abuse Prevention
Health and Welfare Building
Hazen Drive
Concord, NH 03301
(603) 271-6104
FAX: (603) 271-5051

New Jersey
Division of Alcoholism and Drug
  Abuse
New Jersey Department of Health
129 East Hanover Street
Trenton, NJ 08625
(609) 292-5760
FAX: (609) 292-3816

New Mexico
Behaviorial Health Services
  Division
Runnells Building
Room 3200 North
190 Saint Francis Drive
Santa Fe, NM 87503
(505) 827-2601
FAX: (505) 827-0097

New York
Director
New York Division of Alcoholism
  and Alcohol Abuse
194 Washington Avenue
Albany, NY 12210
(518) 474-5417
FAX: (518) 474-3004

North Carolina
Alcohol and Drug Abuse Section
North Carolina Division of Mental
  Health and Mental Retardation
  Services
325 North Salisbury Street
Raleigh, NC 27611
(919) 733-4670
FAX: (919) 773-9455

North Dakota
Division of Alcoholism and Drug
  Abuse
North Dakota Department of
  Human Services
Professional Building
1839 East Capitol Avenue
Bismarck, ND 58501
(701) 224-2769
FAX: (701) 224-3000

Ohio
Department of Alcohol and Drug
  Addiction Services
170 North High Street, 3d Floor
Columbus, OH 43215
(614) 466-3445
FAX: (614) 644-5169

Oklahoma
Oklahoma Department of Mental
  Health and Substance Abuse
  Services
P.O. Box 53277, Capitol Station
Oklahoma City, OK 73152
(405) 271-8777
FAX: (405) 521-3081

Oregon
Oregon Office of Alcohol and
  Drug Abuse Programs
1178 Chemeketa Street, N.E.,
  No. 102
Salem, OR 97310
(503) 378-2163
FAX: (503) 378-6532

Pennsylvania
Drug and Alcohol Programs
Pennsylvania Department of
  Health
P.O. Box 90
Harrisburg, PA 17108
(717) 787-9857
FAX: (717) 772-6959

Rhode Island
Division of Substance Abuse
Rhode Island Department of
  Mental Health, Retardation and
  Hospitals
P.O. Box 20363
Cranston, RI 02920
(401) 464-2091

South Carolina
South Carolina Commission on
  Alcohol and Drug Abuse
3700 Forest Drive
Columbia, SC 29204
(803) 734-9520
FAX: (803) 734-9663

South Dakota
South Dakota Division of Alcohol
  and Drug Abuse
Kneip Building
700 Governors Drive
Pierre, SD 57501-2291
(605) 773-3123
FAX: (605) 773-4840

Tennessee
Division of Alcohol and Drug
  Abuse Services
Tennessee Department of Mental
  Health and Mental Retardation
706 Church Street, 4th Floor
Nashville, TN 37219
(615) 741-1921
FAX: (615) 741-0770

Texas
Texas Commission on Alcohol
  and Drug Abuse
1705 Guadalupe Street
Austin, TX 78710-1214
(512) 867-8700
FAX: (512) 480-0679

Utah
Department of Social Services
Utah Division of Substance
  Abuse
120 North 200 West, 4th Floor
P.O. Box 45500
Salt Lake City, UT 84145-0500
(801) 538-3939
FAX: (801) 538-4016

Vermont
Vermont Office of Alcohol and
  Drug Abuse Programs
103 South Main Street
Waterbury, VT 05676
(802) 241-2170, 241-2175
FAX: (802) 244-8103

Virginia
Office of Substance Abuse
  Services
Virginia Department of Mental
  Health, Mental Retardation and
  Substance Abuse Services
P.O. Box 1797
109 Governor Street
Richmond, VA 23214
(804) 786-3906
FAX: (804) 786-4146

Washington
Division of Alcoholism and
  Substance Abuse
Washington Department of Social
  and Health Services
Mail Stop OB-21W
Olympia, WA 98504
(206) 753-5866
FAX: (206) 586-7130

West Virginia
West Virginia Division of Alcohol
  and Drug Abuse
State Capitol
1800 Washington Street East,
  Room 451
Charleston, WV 25305
(304) 348-2276

Wisconsin
Wisconsin Office of Alcohol and
  Other Drug Abuse
1 West Wilson Street
P.O. Box 7851
Madison, WI 53707
(608) 266-3442
FAX: (608) 267-2147

Wyoming
Wyoming Alcohol and Drug
  Abuse Programs
Hathaway Building
Cheyenne, WY 82002
(307) 777-7115, Ext. 7118

Puerto Rico
Puerto Rico Department of Anti-
  Addiction Services
Box 21414, Rio Piedras Station
Rio Piedras, PR 00928-1414
(809) 754-3795
FAX: (809) 765-5895

General Dynamics Alcohol and Drug Abuse Program Guide

Letter to Employees

Dear Fellow Employees:

Each of us brings our skills, our beliefs, and our life-styles to our job each day. In that sense, General Dynamics is a reflection of our society and all of its strengths and weaknesses. One of the major problems causing a weakening of our society is the abuse of alcohol and/or drugs. Even though the vast majority of General Dynamics employees do not abuse alcohol or drugs or condone the abuse by others, we as a company are not immune from the problems associated with the abuse in our workplaces.

This guide explains General Dynamics' comprehensive program dealing with alcohol and/or drug abuse. In developing this program, we used your input from the employee survey, consultants, company task forces, and meetings with union leaders and division management. The implementation of this program is consistent with federal, state, and local laws and applicable collective bargaining agreements.

The focus of this program is to help employees and their dependents with these devastating personal problems. Alcohol and/or drug abuse that may impact other employees or the company is not acceptable.

The company's alcohol and drug abuse program is based on two fundamentals:

1. Successful solutions to alcohol or drug abuse require a compassionate and consistent approach using an interaction of education, counseling, assistance, deterrents, and discipline.
2. Confidentiality, consistent with legal, safety, and security regulations, is required if employees or their dependents can be expected to seek help.

Help is available through Employee Assistance Programs that emphasize education, prevention, counseling, and treatment for employees and their eligible dependents who have alcohol or drug abuse problems. Company-trained supervisors and union officials are available to assist in the referral of employees for help.

Alcohol and drug testing is part of this program. The testing program was designed as a deterrent to continued abuse, an encouragement to seek help before personal problems affect job performance, and to help overcome an individual's natural tendency to deny there is a problem. The company has taken the necessary precautions to ensure the accuracy and reliability of all tests.

The company has been testing all applicants being considered for employment for illegal drugs since 1985. Those who tested positive were not hired. Corporate officers, staff vice-presidents, division vice-presidents, employees in safety-sensitive jobs, and those in or seeking security-sensitive jobs are included in "Preventative Testing." In addition, employees who show signs of impairment for alcohol or illegal drugs or who are suspected of having used such substances on company property are included in "For-Cause Testing."

An employee who tests positive receives an opportunity for assistance, not discipline, on the first occasion. Discipline, however, is used for repeat offenders.

The provisions to educate, train, counsel, rehabilitate and deter alcohol or drug abuse reflect our efforts to achieve an alcohol- and drug-free workplace in a fair and compassionate manner. The combined efforts of all employees needed to produce a quality, cost-effective product are also required to rid the workplace of these problems. The result will be not only a better company, but a better society.

Policy

It is General Dynamics' policy to ensure a workplace free of alcohol and drugs for the safety and the well-being of all company employees and the company itself. The problem of alcohol and drug use and abuse is not more or less evident at General Dynamics than in the rest of society. Our business, however, is too important to simply hope the problem will "just go away." As a responsible company, General Dynamics has an obligation to ensure the safety and health of our employees to the fullest extent. Employee alcohol or drug use must not jeopardize employee or public safety or otherwise affect the company, its employees, or its customers.

Why an Alcohol And Drug Abuse Program?

Substance abuse is an unfortunate fact of today's society. Unlike many illnesses, however, such abuse can have far-reaching and negative impacts on the abusers' families, friends, and jobs, not to mention the great destruction to the individual. Alcohol and/or drug abuse erode a person's self-image and sense of value. As such, it is a problem that many people either try to ignore or deny altogether. But that doesn't make the dependency any less real; it just makes it worse.

Alcohol or drug abuse leads to erratic behavior, a lack of compassion and understanding, and enormous financial difficulties. It's expensive in both dollars and personal suffering. Guilt and insecurity by the abuser, resentment by family members, and deep financial problems are just part of the price the abuser pays. Marriages and other family relationships can be damaged beyond repair and also can lead to physical abuse.

(continues)

General Dynamics Alcohol and Drug Abuse Program Guide (continued)

From a business standpoint, employee abuse of alcohol and/or illegel drugs often means excessive absenteeism, tardiness, safety concerns, and decreased productivity and quality of work. As one of America's leading defense contractors, General Dynamics has a responsibility to provide the highest quality products possible in the safest and most productive facilities possible. Employee alcohol and/or drug abuse and the impact it has on other employees and the company cannot be tolerated.

A successful approach to this problem, and one that will benefit all concerned, requires a mixture of education, personal awareness, counseling, assistance, deterrents, and discipline. A program of this nature can be successful if it is administered with compassion and consistency. The implementation of this program involves each employee, the unions, and the company all working together.

Employee Assistance Programs (EAP)

In order to help preserve the physical and mental health of employees, the company has established Employee Assistance Programs that offer services through professional counselors:

- ▲ Referral services for alcohol and/or drug abuse, individual, marital or family difficulties, stress and financial or legal concerns.
- ▲ A 24-hour, seven-day-a-week telephone hotline to professional counselors as needed.

The confidentiality of individuals using EAP services will be maintained as far as safety and security concerns and the law will allow. An employee's decision to seek help voluntarily through EAP will not be used against him or her for disciplinary action.

Your Human Resources Department can provide you with specific information about how to contact your EAP.

Rules of Conduct

Each General Dynamics employee is expected to follow rules of conduct. These rules are very important to the purpose behind our alcohol and drug abuse program. Violation of any of them makes an employee subject to disciplinary action, including discharge.

- ▲ Use, sale, attempted sale, manufacture, purchase, attempted purchase, possession, or transfer of alcohol while on company property or in company vehicles during the individual's business day is a violation of company rules and will result in disciplinary action, up to and including discharge.
- ▲ Use, sale, attempted sale, purchase, attempted purchase, possession, or transfer of an illegal drug on company property or in company vehicles is a violation of company rules and will result in discharge.
- ▲ Being subject to the effects of alcohol or an illegal drug on company property is cause to be referred for alcohol or drug testing. Being subject to the effects of alcohol or an illegal drug does not excuse misconduct when it is a violation of the

law or company rules. For example, an assault committed while subject to the effects of alcohol or an illegal drug will subject the employee to disciplinary action, up to and including discharge, because of the misconduct.

▲ Employees who believe or have been told that their use of a legal medication may present any sort of safety threat are to report such drug use to company medical personnel to ensure the safety of themselves, other employees, company property, and company vehicles.

Inspections

Under this program, all persons who enter General Dynamics properties or facilities, by doing so, consent to an inspection of themselves and their property, including their vehicles. In addition to standard gate inspections, General Dynamics may require individuals to submit to special inspections of personal lockers, purses, briefcases, desks, file cabinets, and other containers while on company property.

Special inspections will normally be made by no fewer than two management officials, including one from Human Resources or Security. If the employee in question is represented by a union, a union representative will be offered the opportunity to be present for the inspection.

Individuals may not be touched during any inspection but may be asked to empty the contents of their clothing. Those who refuse to permit an inspection will be told that allowing such an inspection is a condition of employment. However, in such a case, employees will not be forcibly detained or inspected but will be informed that failure to permit such an inspection will result in immediate suspension without pay and subject them to disciplinary action or discharge. Nonemployees will be subject to the same rules and conditions while on company property.

In addition, trained dogs may be used to detect illegal drugs in personal and company property. These dogs will not, however, be used to detect drugs on individuals.

Alcohol and Drug Testing

Alcohol Testing

Alcohol testing is conducted using a breath alcohol test similar to the tests conducted by the various law enforcement agencies. The test is considered accurate within the testing limits used by the company. If the breath alcohol test is positive, an employee may request to have a blood sample collected and analyzed, but it is not required by the company.

Drug Testing

Drug tests are conducted on urine specimens collected under tightly controlled methods using a strict chain of custody to ensure samples are not mixed up or altered. The company will NOT observe sample collection. All drug samples are submitted to a single nationally recognized testing laboratory.

Drug testing is a multiple analysis process utilizing an initial screen of the sample by immunoassay (or EMIT, as it is generally known) and a confirmation of screened positives by use of gas chromatography/mass spectroscopy (GC/MS). This is the accepted method of drug testing that eliminates errors.

Only those persons administering the alcohol and drug abuse program are allowed access to the alcohol or drug test results.

(continues)

General Dynamics Alcohol and Drug Abuse Program Guide (continued)

Applicants for Employment

All applicants being considered for employment are tested for illegal drugs. An alcohol test is conducted only when there is reason to believe that the applicant is under the influence of alcohol.

Applicants who test positive for either alcohol or illegal drugs or who state that they have used illegal drugs over the preceding 12 months are denied employment.

Current Employees

For Cause: For current employees, alcohol and/or drug testing takes two forms. For-cause testing for alcohol and/or drugs occurs when the company has reason to believe that an employee is being impaired due to alcohol and/or drugs or has used either alcohol and/or drugs on company property. In such a case, the employee is escorted to the Medical Department or the nearest collection site for evaluation and possible testing.

Preventative: The preventative testing program has been designed as a deterrent to the abuse of alcohol and/or illegal drugs by employees in positions of trust and confidence, employees in sensitive positions, and where continued use is evident. Selection for testing within the groups is based on a nonbiased system and is conducted at unscheduled and unannounced times. The following employees are included in this program:

- ▲ Corporate officers, staff vice-presidents, and division vice-presidents.
- ▲ Employees in safety-sensitive jobs.
- ▲ Employees in or seeking security-sensitive jobs.
- ▲ Employees in any segment of the company where this entire program has been implemented but the company has reason to believe that the use of alcohol and/or illegal drugs continues on company property.

Refusal to Consent: An employee's refusal to consent to an alcohol and/or drug test is considered insubordination and will subject the employee to disciplinary action up to and including discharge.

Action Following Positive Test

First Positive

Any employee testing positive will be placed on an immediate leave of absence and provided an option of using the EAP. The leave of absence is without pay, but the employee may use accumulated sick leave and vacation time, and current benefit coverage continues. If the employee chooses to participate in the EAP at this time, it is not considered voluntary participation. The employee may return to work when another alcohol/drug test administered by the company within 30 days, or a maximum of 60 days if the employee is undergoing treatment, is negative.

If the employee returns to work, he or she is subject to unannounced and unscheduled alcohol and/or drug tests for two years following the first positive test.

Second Positive

If an employee tests positive again within two years of the first positive, the employee will face discipline but not discharge. He or she will then be referred to EAP for mandatory participation in a company-approved alcohol and/or drug abuse treatment program and, following the discipline, placed on immediate leave of absence. The leave of absence is without pay, but the employee may use accumulated sick leave and vacation time, and current benefit coverage continues. The employee may return to work when another alcohol/drug test administered by the company within 30 days, or a maximum of 60 days if the employee is undergoing treatment, is negative.

When the employee returns to work, he or she is prohibited from holding or performing any safety-sensitive job for two years and is subject to unannounced and unscheduled testing for two years following the second positive.

Third Positive

If within two years after the second positive, an employee again tests positive for either alcohol or drugs, the employee will be discharged.

Company Social Events

It would be wrong to develop a company program that includes fighting alcohol abuse and misuse if we did not recognize it as a possible problem at company-sponsored social functions. General Dynamics is taking a positive, proactive approach to this issue. Therefore, each division and subsidiary has established procedures that address responsible consumption of alcohol at such events. These include but are not limited to:

- Preventing employees and guests below the legal age from drinking alcoholic beverages.
- Limiting the quantity of alcohol consumed, including the length of time alcohol is served.
- Providing transportation for those whose driving ability is impaired.

Our Responsibilities

The Company

The company will use fair and reasonable methods to ensure a safe and healthful workplace free of the problems associated with alcohol and/or drug abuse. To meet this goal the company will:

- Provide educational material to all employees.
- Train management and union officials.
- Establish and maintain Employee Assistance Programs for employees and their dependents.
- Provide alcohol and/or drug abuse rehabilitation benefits that are consistent with recognized treatment standards.
- Inform all employees of the rules of conduct on alcohol and illegal drugs.
- Establish alcohol and drug-testing programs for employees suspected of being at work under the influence of alcohol and/or drugs or using alcohol and/or illegal drugs on company property.
- Establish alcohol and drug-testing programs for individuals in sensitive positions.
- Ensure alcohol- and drug-testing procedures are accurate, reliable, and confidential.

(*continues*)

General Dynamics Alcohol and Drug Abuse Program Guide (continued)

All Employees

Each employee is responsible for abiding by the company's Alcohol and Drug Abuse Program. In addition, according to the "Anti-Drug Abuse Act of 1988" signed into law on November 18, 1988, each employee of a federal government contractor is required to notify his or her employer of any criminal drug statute conviction for a violation occurring in the workplace no later than five days after the conviction. The company then has a responsibility to inform the government contracting agency within ten days.

EXHIBIT A
Term Descriptions

Being Subject to the Effects of Alcohol or an Illegal Drug: The presence of alcohol, an illegal drug, or a drug metabolite in an individual's system as determined by appropriate testing of a bodily specimen that is equal to or greater than the levels specified below for the confirmation test. This shall be referred to as a "positive test," "positive level," "prohibitive level," or "positive screen."

	Confirmation Test Levels
Alcohol	+0.04%
Marijuana metabolite	20 ng/ml
Cocaine metabolite(s)	150 ng/ml
Morphine and/or codeine	300 ng/ml
Phencyclidine (PCP) (and/or metabolites)	25 ng/ml
Amphetamine and/or methamphetamine	500 ng/ml
Oxazepam and/or other benzodiazepine or metabolite	300 ng/ml
Barbiturates	200 ng/ml
Methadone and/or metabolite	300 ng/ml

Illegal Drug: A controlled substance, as defined by section 802 (6) of Title 21 of the U. S. Code, the possession of which is unlawful under Chapter 13 of that title. The term "illegal drugs" does not mean the use of controlled substance pursuant to a valid prescription or other uses authorized by law.

Safety-Sensitive Job: A job that would expose other employees or the public to the potential of death or serious injury in the event of improper execution of the job.

Security-Sensitive Job: A position for which a Top Secret clearance is required.

EXHIBIT B
Commonly Misused Alcohol and Drugs:
Their Uses, Abuses, Effects, and the Symptoms They Produce

Definitions

drug   A substance that by its chemical nature alters the structure or function of the living organism. (For the purpose of this section, a drug is any chemical substance, including alcohol, that alters mood, perception, or consciousness and is misused to the apparent injury of the individual or society.)

tolerance   A state in which the body's tissue cells adjust to the presence of a drug. The term "tolerance" refers to a state in which the body becomes used to the presence of a drug in given amounts and eventually fails to respond to ordinarily effective dosages. Hence, increasingly larger doses are necessary to produce desired effects.

habituation (psychological dependence)   The result of repeated consumption of a drug that produces psychological but not physical dependence. The psychological dependence produces a desire (not compulsion) to continue taking drugs for the sense of improved well-being.

physical dependence (addiction)   What occurs when a person cannot function normally without the repeated use of a drug. If the drug is withdrawn, the person has severe physical and psychological disturbance.

harmful drugs   Any drug when taken in excess. Even aspirin is a harmful drug, as is, of course, alcohol. Some drugs can also be harmful if taken in dangerous combinations or in ordinary amounts by hypersensitive people.

Identifying the Drug User

A drug user will do everything possible to conceal the habit, so it is important to be able to recognize the outward signs and symptoms of drug misuse. One should be alert to these symptoms, but it is important to realize that the drug problem is so complex that even experts sometimes have difficulty making accurate diagnoses. Therefore, it is important to seek professional advice from experts specializing in drug problems.

It should also be remembered that a person may have a legitimate reason for possessing a syringe and needle (for example, a diabetic) or having tablets and capsules (they may be prescribed by a doctor). The sniffles and running eyes may be symptoms of a head cold or an allergy. Unusual or odd behavior may not be connected in any way with drug use.

Drugs other than narcotics can become addicting. Some people have acquired an addiction to sedatives and certain tranquilizers. Stimulants in very large doses are addictive.

Common Signs of Possible Drug Misuse

- Changes in attendance at work or school.
- Change from normal capabilities (work habits, efficiency, etc.).
- Poor physical appearance, including inattention to dress and personal hygiene.
- Wearing sunglasses constantly at inappropriate times (indoors or at night, for instance) not only to hide dilated or constricted pupils but also to compensate for the eye's inability to adjust to sunlight. Marijuana causes bloodshot eyes.
- Unusual effort made to cover arms in order to hide needle marks.
- Association with known drug users.
- Stealing items that can be readily sold for cash (to support a drug habit).

Indications of Possible Misuse*

- Alcohol: Beer, Wine, Distilled Spirits (Booze, Juice, Sauce, Brew, Vino)
  —Alcohol on breath
  —Staggering, stumbling, or apparent drunkenness
  —Falling asleep at work
  —Slurred speech
  —Aggressive behavior

*Common or slang names appear in parentheses.

(continues)

General Dynamics Alcohol and Drug Abuse Program Guide (continued)

▲ Depressants: Quaalude, Doriden, Barbiturates (Barbs, Bluebirds, Blues, Tooies, Yellowjackets, Ludes, 714s, Sopor)
—Behavior like that of alcohol intoxication but without the odor of alcohol on breath
—Staggering, stumbling, or apparent drunkenness without odor or use of alcohol
—Sleeping on the job
—Slurred speech
—Dilated pupils
—Difficulty concentrating

▲ Stimulants: Amphetamines, RX diet pills, Cocaine (Ups, Uppers, Speed, Crank, Coke, Toot, Blow, Snow, Pearl, Flake, Base, Freebase, Crack, Rock)
—Excessive activity, irritability, argumentativeness, or nervousness
—Excitation, euphoria, and talkativeness
—Dilated pupils
—Long periods without eating or sleeping
—Increased blood pressure or pulse rates

▲ Narcotics (H, Junk, Smack, China White, Black Tar, MPTP, MPPP, PEPAP, White Stuff, M, Morf, Schoolboy, Dolly)
—Scars ("tracks") on the arms or on the backs of hands, caused by injecting drugs.
—Constricted, fixed, or dilated pupils.
—Constant itching.
—Loss of appetite; frequent consumption of candy, cookies, and sweet liquids
—Sniffles, red, watering eyes, and a cough that suddenly disappears after a "fix." During withdrawal, the addict may be nauseated and vomit. Flushed skin, frequent yawning, and muscular twitching are common. These symptoms also disappear when the addict gets a fix.
—Syringes, bent spoons, cotton, needles, metal bottle caps, medicine dropper, and glassine bags in a locker or desk drawer.
—Lethargy, drowsiness, and an alternating cycle of dozing and awakening.

▲ Marijuana (Pot, Grass, Dope, Weed, Homegrown, Sinsemilla, Maui-Wowie, Thai Sticks, Joints, Roaches, Hash, Hashish)
—Rapid, loud talking and bursts of laughter (early stages) or sleepiness (late stages)
—Dilated pupils and bloodshot eyes
—Distortions of perception and hallucinations

▲ Other Hallucinogens (Acid, LSD-25, Blotter Acid, Windowpane, Mesc, Peyote, Peyote Buttons, Love Drug, Ectasy, XTC, Adam, Magic Mushrooms, Shrooms)
—Behavior and mood vary widely. The user may sit or recline quietly in a trancelike state or may appear fearful or even terrified.
—Dilated pupils in some cases.
—Increased blood pressure, heart rate, and blood sugar.
—Nausea, chills, flushes, irregular breathing, sweating, trembling of hands.
—Changes in sense of sight, hearing, touch, smell, and time.

▲ Inhalants: Organic Solvents, Nitrous Oxide, Butyl Nitrite (Solvents, Glue, Transmission Fluid, Typewriter Correction Fluid, Laughing Gas, Whippitts, Nitrous Blue Bottle, Liquid Incense, Room Deodorizer, Rush, Locker Room, Poppers)
—Odor of substance inhaled on breath and clothes
—Excessive nasal secretion and watering of the eyes
—Poor muscular control (staggering) (occurs within minutes of exposure)
—Drowsiness or unconsciousness

—Presence of plastic or paper bags or rags containing dry plastic cement
—Slurred speech
—Bad breath
▲ Phencyclidine: PCP (Crystal, Tea, THC, Angel Dust)
—Feelings of depersonalization and emptiness or "nothingness"
—Perceptual distortions, infrequently evidenced as visual or auditory hallucinations
—Feelings of apathy or estrangement and preoccupation with death
—Drowsiness, inability to verbalize, difficulty in thinking, poor concentration
—Flushing, profuse sweating, involuntary eye movements, muscular incoordination, double vision, dizziness, nausea and vomiting

Exhibit B is based on U.S. Department of Justice, Drug Enforcement Administration (DEA), *Drug Enforcement* 6, no. 2, and DEA, *Controlled Substances: Use, Abuse and Effects.*

Louisiana-Pacific Corporation Western Division Drug and Alcohol Policy

Policy Statement

Louisiana-Pacific Corporation ("L-P" or the "Company") is committed to promoting the safety, health, and productivity of its employees. Consistent with the spirit of this commitment, L-P's goal will continue to be one of establishing and maintaining work environments free from the effects of alcohol and drugs.

While the Company does not wish to intrude into the private lives of its employees, the Company recognizes that employees' off-the-job as well as on-the-job involvement with drugs and alcohol can negatively impact the workplace and the Company's ability to achieve an alcohol- and drug-free work environment.

In accordance with these concerns, L-P prohibits the use, sale, pruchase, possession, transfer, or manufacture of drugs on Company premises or while an employee is on the job. L-P also prohibits its employees from being on the job with a forensically detectable level (i.e., testing positive) of drugs in his or her body. Any violation of these provisions is a dischargeable offense.

Employees are prohibited from being on work time while the employee's ability to perform assigned duties safely and effectively is affected by the use of alcohol or while the employee has a blood-alcohol concentration equivalent of 0.04 or greater. In addition, the consumption, possession, sale, or purchase of alcoholic beverages on work time or on Company premises is prohibited absent prior management approval. Notwithstanding this, the possession of alcohol in a Company or personal vehicle, in compliance with applicable legal requirements, is not prohibited by this policy. Subject to these exceptions, any violation of this policy is a dischargeable offense.

Employees taking prescription medication must ask their physician whether such drugs could adversely affect their ability to perform assigned duties safely and efficiently. If so, the employee shall obtain and provide his or her immediate supervisor with a written note from the physician indicating only the potential adverse effects on safety and performance; the note should not indicate the medication or the condition for which it is being taken. Employees taking over-the-counter medications must report this use to their supervisor when such medication might affect the employee's ability to perform assigned duties safely and/or efficiently. Employees who fail to comply with this paragraph may be subject to discipline up to and including discharge.

Definitions

1. "Company premises" is defined to include any Company property, including job sites and parking lots associated with working area, but shall not include Company-owned living quarters or Company towns.
2. "Drug" is defined to include those drugs defined as illegal under federal, state, or local laws, as well as controlled substances not taken according to a prescription for current personal treatment by an accredited physician.

Louisiana-Pacific's policies vary according to different state laws. In addition, the author of L-P's policy stresses that each organization should seek independent legal advice before formulating policies regarding drug testing.

3. "Possesses" is defined as physically holding the drug and/or alcohol or the drug and/or alcohol being in an area over which the employee has access and control (e.g., inside briefcases, purses, lunch bags, lunch boxes, lockers, personal vehicles).

Procedure

Detecting Policy Violations

L-P may employ various means of detection to enforce this policy, including, but not limited to, searches of Company premises and any property on such premises. The Company may also require urinalysis testing for illegal drugs and/or alcohol under the following circumstances:

1. All applicants must undergo urinalysis as a condition of employment. If the test indicates the presence of prohibited substances, the applicant will be denied employment, and any conditional offer of employment will be rescinded. An employee who tests positive can reapply for a position with the Company after six months.
2. Urinalysis may be required when, based upon specific observations of an employee's appearance, behavior, conduct, speech, and/or body odors, a supervisor or manager has a reasonable suspicion that an employee is in violation of this policy.
3. Urinalysis testing may be required when an employee's act, omission, or order causes or contributes to a serious workplace accident. "Serious workplace accident" is defined to include either: (a) any occurrence or event resulting in an injury that requires medical treatment beyond first aid (treatment of minor cuts, burns, splinters, etc.), or (b) property damage that in the reasonable estimation of a supervisor exceeds $1,000. This provision applies even if the employee who caused or contributed to the accident is not himself or herself injured.
4. Urinalysis tests may also be administered as a part of or as follow-up to counseling or rehabilitation from alcohol or drug abuse.

Consent to Testing

Prior to testing, the applicant or employee will be asked to consent in writing to drug and/or alcohol testing and to the release of medical information. Applicants who refuse to consent may be denied employment. Employees who refuse to consent to testing will be subject to disciplinary action up to and including discharge. Refusal to authorize the release of medical information will not be the basis for disciplinary action. However, a refusal by the employee to consent to the release of medical information will not excuse the employee from the requirement of being tested or prevent the Company from requiring an opinion from its designated physician limited to the employee's fitness for duty. And, in any case, the Company retains the right to take disciplinary action based on any other available evidence.

Collection and Laboratory Procedure

Prior to preemployment testing, applicants will be given the option to report any medications taken within the preceding thirty days. Employees required to participate in reasonable-suspicion, postaccident, or follow-up urinalysis tests may report any medications taken within the preceding thirty calendar days. Such information will be kept confidential and will be reviewed only by the Company's designated physician whose aim will be to ensure that a positive test result is not attributable to a lawful use of medication.

(continues)

Louisiana-Pacific Corporation Western Division
Drug and Alcohol Policy (continued)

Urinalysis testing will be performed by an independent laboratory using accurate scientific testing methods. Procedures will include an initial screen that, if positive, will be confirmed by a different testing method. A physician will review all positive results to rule out the lawful use of medication. Strict procedures will be followed in collecting and transferring specimens to ensure that samples are correctly identified and not tampered with.

Any employee who refuses to participate in required drug and/or alcohol testing will be immediately suspended and will be subject to discipline up to and including discharge based on insubordination and other available information.

Assistance

Employees who acknowledge a drug and/or alcohol problem prior to a suspected policy violation will be afforded assistance by L-P and will not be disciplined based on their admission. Such acknowledgment, however, does not relieve an employee of the obligation to comply with Company policies in the future. As a condition of continued employment and as a further incentive for the employee to remain drug free, the employee may also be required to submit to a maximum of three unannounced urinalysis tests during the year following his or her return to duty.

Confidentiality

L-P will seek to maintain confidentiality of all information pertaining to drug and/or alcohol involvement or testing of applicants and employees and will seek to limit release of such information only to those who have a legitimate, business-related need to know.

Amendments

L-P reserves the right to modify, rescind, delete, or add to the provisions of this policy as it deems appropriate in its sole and absolute discretion. It is not an employment contract.

Midway Airlines Alcohol and Drug Abuse Policy

1.1 Policy Overview

Due to the nature of our business, Midway Airlines, Inc., must ensure its operations are conducted with the highest possible degree of safety to protect the traveling public and our employees. The introduction or use of drugs, including alcohol, capable of threatening the safety of our operations or employees in the workplace cannot be tolerated. We are committed to providing a drug-free work environment for the safety of the traveling public and our employees. This policy applies to all employees of the company and its subsidiaries.

1.2 On-Duty Prohibitions

For purposes of this policy, "on duty" shall mean the time beginning when an employee reports for work until the employee finishes work and leaves company property, including any rest and lunch breaks. It also includes any time an employee is traveling on company business.

a. The possession, use, transfer, or sale of any illegal drug on company property or on duty is strictly prohibited.
b. The possession and/or use of any prescription drugs without the proper medical authorization on company property or on duty is strictly prohibited.
    Employees who are taking or are under the influence* of prescription drugs while on duty will notify their supervisors upon reporting for duty, particularly if these drugs bear warnings not to operate machinery or that drowsiness may occur.
c. Except at company social functions or other authorized company-sponsored activities, the possession, consumption, or dispensing of any intoxicants on company property or on duty is strictly prohibited.
d. Being under the influence of any illegal drug or intoxicant is strictly prohibited.

1.3 Off-Duty Use

a. Use of illicit drugs at any time constitutes grounds for termination.
b. Employees who engage in the excessive use of alcohol that reflects unfavorably on the company or its other employees are subject to discipline.
c. Supervisors and managers must be especially conscious of their off-duty behavior that could impair their proper exercise of managerial responsibilities.

1.4 Air Crew Members: Federal Regulatory Requirements

In addition to Midway Airlines's general policy on drug abuse, all air crew members (flight officers and flight attendants) are subject to federal aviation regulations. Refer to appropriate federal aviation regulations for specific prohibitions.

*"Under the influence" for the purposes of this policy means that the employee is affected by a drug (other than alcohol) in any detectable manner or if the alcohol level in his or her blood is 0.04 percent by weight or more.

(continues)

Midway Airlines Alcohol and Drug Abuse Policy (continued)

1.5 Job Applicant Testing

a. All job applicants will be required to undergo drug screening prior to their employment.

b. Prior to any drug screening, applicants will be informed that such tests are required and that their employment is conditional upon passing such test. The applicant will also be informed of the company's alcohol and drug abuse policy, and a copy of the policy will be made available upon request.

c. If an applicant's initial drug and alcohol test is positive, a confirmatory test will automatically be conducted. No action on the applicant's employment application will be taken until the results of the confirmatory test are available.

d. If an applicant's confirmatory test is positive for either drugs or alcohol, he or she will not be employed.

e. On written request by the applicant, a copy of the test results will be supplied to the applicant.

1.6 Employee Testing for Cause

A supervisor/manager who has reasonable suspicion to believe an employee has violated company policy relating to alcohol or drug abuse may require the employee to undergo drug and/or alcohol testing. Reasonable suspicion may be based on an employee's observed behavior that is indicative of drug or alcohol use, report of suspected drug use or possession, or the employee's admissions of possession or use of drugs.

a. A supervisor/manager who, based on his or her observations of the employee's duty performance, suspects an employee is unfit for duty due to the influence of drugs and/or alcohol while on duty will:

   (1) Solicit an explanation from the employee for his or her apparent physical condition and erratic job performance.

   (2) If the employee cannot satisfactorily explain his or her physical condition and nonsatisfactory work performance, the supervisor may request the employee to undergo a drug (urinalysis) and/or alcohol test (blood alcohol test).

   (a) If the employee concurs, he or she will complete the Midway Airlines Consent Form and be provided transportation to the selected medical clinic for the test. His or her supervisor should accompany the employee to the clinic, if possible.

   (b) If the employee declines to undergo the test or to complete the consent form, he or she will be advised that such behavior constitutes a ground for immediate termination. If the employee still refuses to cooperate, he or she will be relieved of duty pending appropriate disciplinary action.

   (3) In all cases where an employee is referred to a medical clinic for drug screening, the employee will be relieved of his or her duties pending the outcome and confirmation of the drug and/or alcohol tests.

   (4) If the employee tests positive for illicit drugs in his or her system, he or she shall be terminated after confirmatory test results are available. If the employee's blood/alcohol level exceeds 0.04%, he or she will be terminated.

   (5) If the employee is not found to have drugs or alcohol in his or her system but is

still unable or unfit for duty for medical reasons, the employee will be directed to take sick leave until he or she obtains a doctor's release stating he or she is medically qualified to return to work.

(6) If the employee is found not to have drugs or alcohol in his or her system and is otherwise medically fit for duty, the employee will be returned to duty with no loss of pay or seniority.

b. A supervisor/manager who has reasonable suspicion that an employee has violated company work rules relating to on-duty alcohol or drug abuse will:

(1) Advise the employee of his or her belief that the employee has violated company alcohol/drug abuse policy and the basis for such belief.

(2) Request the employee to undergo drug or alcohol testing and sign the consent form.

(3) If the employee declines to undergo such test or to complete the written consent form, he or she will be cautioned that such behavior constitutes insubordination and is a ground for immediate termination. If the employee still refuses to cooperate, he or she will be relieved of duties pending disciplinary action.

(4) If the employee is found not to have drugs or alcohol in his or her system, the employee will be returned to duty without any loss of pay or seniority. If the employee is found to have drugs or alcohol in his or her system, the employee shall be terminated after the confirmatory test results are available.

1.7 Employee Accident-Related Testing

A supervisor/manager may require an employee to undergo drug and/or alcohol testing if the employee has injured himself or herself on the job, caused the injury of a fellow employee on the job, had an accident while operating or assisting in the operation of company machinery, or had an accident while operating a company vehicle or aircraft.

In such cases, subparagraph 1.6b will be followed, except that the employee will be advised that such tests are required as part of the accident investigation.

1.8 Right of Refusal

All applicants/employees have the right to refuse to undergo drug or alcohol screening. Applicants who refuse to undergo such screening will be denied employment. Employees who refuse to undergo such screening, based upon reasonable suspicion or due to accident involvement, will be terminated.

1.9 Test Results

a. Any employee found to have a blood alcohol level of .04 or more shall be considered unfit for duty and shall be terminated.

b. Test results may be provided to employees who request them in writing within five working days of the notification of their confirmatory test results.

c. Both applicants and employees may provide a written explanation for their positive test results and request reconfirmation of their original sample at their own expense.

(continues)

Midway Airlines Alcohol and Drug Abuse Policy (continued)

1.10 Employee Notification

All employees and job applicants will be advised of the company's alcohol and drug abuse policy. Notice of the policy will be posted on employee bulletin boards, and copies of the policy will be conveniently available for job applicants and employees to review.

1.11 Employee Appeal

Any employee may appeal his or her discharge or other disciplinary action taken under this policy through the company's guaranteed fair treatment program or the applicable contract grievance procedure.

1.12 Reporting Requirements

All Midway employees are required to report promptly any known or suspected on-duty drug use to their supervisor/manager. The manager will promptly notify the corporate security director of all such reports.

1.13 Self-Referral Option

Any employee who has an alcohol/drug abuse problem may inform his or her supervisor or manager or Midway's personnel director on a confidential basis. The employee will then be referred by the company to an appropriate drug or alcohol treatment program or facility. The employee may choose to enter a program/facility pursuant to coverage under the company's employee benefit program or pay the treatment cost personally.

a. Such an employee will be promptly reassigned to duties in which his or her personal safety, that of fellow employees, or the traveling public would not be compromised. If no such position is available, the employee will be placed on medical or sick leave until he or she has satisfactorily completed the referral program as evidenced by the written certification of the program director or other qualified professional.
b. Employees who have reportedly violated the company's alcohol/drug abuse policy and know they are under active investigation for such a violation are no longer eligible for the self-referral option.
c. Employees who successfully complete their treatment program are subject to unannounced alcohol/drug testing.
d. Employees who fail to complete their treatment program successfully will be discharged.

6

Child Care

Ethel W. McConaghy
Work/Family Directions, Inc.

Corporate child care assistance is expected to become the norm, not the exception, in the 1990s. Only a decade ago, fewer than 500 companies offered some form of child care support to their employees. Now over 5,000 companies offer child care assistance, and many of them provide a package of multiple child care supports to meet the complex needs of a diverse work force.

Employers are becoming increasingly aware of the business reasons for offering child care and other family-related benefits for their work force: recruitment advantages, increased productivity, and a reduction in turnover, absenteeism, and tardiness. Because of the impending shortage of qualified workers, which is already being felt in some sectors, benefits and human resources departments are designing child care programs and policies to attract employees and to help them balance their work and family responsibilities.

Corporate child care assistance once meant only one option: an on-site day care center for employees. But now a smorgasboard of options has been successfully developed, including parenting seminars, child care resource and referral services, subsidies, temporary backup care, and summer and vacation camps. These programs can be created individually by an employer, in a consortium with other companies, or in partnership with community service agencies. And each year, additional employers, large and small, find new and creative ways to address their employees' child care needs.

The corporate community is also becoming concerned about the availability of high-quality child care and early education programs, whether they are based in schools or in other community agencies. Good educational experiences during early childhood correlate positively with a child's later success in school. As corporations increasingly find they must provide basic education services for employees, they have joined the ranks of those who are committed to improving public schools and making early childhood education programs more widely available.

The Changing Lives of Children and Families

The profile of the American family has changed. Most families no longer have someone at home to care for the children, for an elderly relative, or for another family member who is sick. Fewer than 10 percent of American families fit the traditional mold of a two-parent household with an at-work father who is the breadwinner and an at-home mother caring for the children.

Women have entered the work force at an extraordinary rate since the 1970s. In 1950, only 12 percent of mothers with children under age 6 were in the work force; by 1985, that number had jumped to 54 percent. Now over half of all women with infant children and 70 percent of mothers of school-age children are at work outside the home.

Single mothers and black mothers participate in the labor force at an even higher rate. At the mid-decade census, 64 percent of black mothers with infants were working, and this difference narrowed only once children were in school. The labor force participation of single mothers, although similar to married mothers when the children are preschoolers, widens when the children are in school.[1]

There have also been significant changes in the lives of children, particularly those in inner-city neighborhoods and in minority communities. Children as a group are the poorest segment of our society; one in four children nationwide—and 43 percent of black children and 40 percent of Hispanic children—live in poverty. One in five children is at risk of becoming a teenage parent, and one in seven is at risk of dropping out of school.[2]

During the 1980s, three of five jobs were filled by women, and it is projected that by the year 2000 women will account for 47 percent of the work force. At a time of scarce labor resources, employers increasingly will use dependent care programs as a way to compete for personnel and to retain those in whom they have already invested.

Understanding Employee Needs

Employers who appreciate these trends begin to look at their own work force and to question how employees are balancing their work and family lives. Since child care can be such a pressing issue, it is often where employers start their inquiry. Employers who study the child care needs of their work force find that employees face one or more of the following problems: difficulty in finding care, an inadequate supply of services, the poor quality of some care, high costs, or a need for more flexibility.

▲ *Difficulty in finding child care.* In a *Fortune* magazine study, one of three employed parents of infants and one of four employed parents of preschoolers reported difficulty in their search for child care. The survey also documented that a significant predictor of absenteeism at work is the degree of difficulty in finding child care.[3] Many parents do not know where to start other than the telephone book, and they can become quickly overwhelmed by the choices, the cost, and the lack of openings.

▲ *Inadequate supply of child care*. In most communities, the supply of care does not meet the demand, especially for infants and toddlers and for school-aged children. In 1985, researchers found that California had 50,000 child care spaces for the 209,000 children under age 2 who needed them.[4] A recent Maryland study found only one regulated child care slot for every five preschool children whose mothers were in the work force.[5] When a parent works evening or weekend shifts or when a child is sick, care becomes even harder to arrange.

▲ *Unacceptable quality of some care*. Parents in most communities are having difficulty finding care that meets their standards of quality. Licensing standards vary dramatically from state to state on issues that correlate with quality, such as group size, staff-to-child ratios, and the qualifications and training of staff. In some states, a great deal of child care is exempt from licensure altogether, such as family day care homes that care for only a few children or centers under the auspices of churches or public institutions.

In 1984, the National Association for the Education of Young Children (NAEYC) established accreditation criteria based on child development research and revised by the clinical practice of its 60,000 members. Since 1986, accreditation has been awarded to 1,400 programs, and 3,700 early childhood programs are enrolled in self-study, the first step in the accreditation process. There are currently similar efforts within the National Association for Family Day Care Providers (NAFDC) to develop national standards for family day care providers. Several corporations, concerned about the quality of care available to the children of their employees, have offered financial contributions and other support to these efforts.

As parents become more informed about the components of quality, they are asking for accredited and credentialed providers. Most programs are not accredited, however, and the 1989 National Child Care Staffing Study documented the poor quality of care in five major U.S. cities. This study found that the best programs for children are those where the staff are well educated and well paid, but these are too few in number. The turnover in the field of child care is 41 percent annually, and the study also found the turnover of poorly paid staff is twice that of higher paid staff. In looking at the families enrolled in the programs, the researchers discovered that children of moderate- and middle-income families generally attended the poorer-quality programs, while children of higher-income and lower-income (publicly subsidized) families attended the higher-quality programs.[6]

‣ *Lack of affordable child care.* Cost is probably the most significant child care problem for parents today, although the cost is already being "subsidized" in effect by low staff wages. Child care is the fourth largest expense for families (after housing, taxes, and food). Some have estimated that families can afford to spend approximately 10 percent of their household income for child care. Yet a 1990 report by the Commerce Department's Census Bureau indicated that while wealthy families spend approximately 5 percent of their income on child care, families at the poverty line are spending over 25 percent.[7]

The cost of child care varies by community, age of child, and type of care. The national average cost is $3,000 per year for preschoolers, and the rates are higher for infants and toddlers. Obviously, then, many families have to struggle to purchase any kind of child care, let alone good-quality care for more than one child.

‣ *Need for greater flexibility.* Parents are reporting significant levels of stress as they try to juggle their work and family responsibilities. This is not surprising, given the realities of their lives. In a research study of a large Boston corporation, parent employees, both male and female, reported that they spend from 15 to 25 more hours per week on combined work and family responsibilities than do nonparent employees. The most frequently mentioned sources of job/home conflict were scheduling difficulties, irregular work schedules, or job travel that interfere with personal life and an inability to leave problems at work or at home. Over one-third of parent employees, in fact, reported that they worried "a lot" about their children while at work.[8]

Employer Options

Employees are bringing their child care problems to work. Employers' responses to these child care concerns have been growing rapidly, but much more support is needed. In 1982, only 600 employers were offering a child care benefit for employees. Now the estimate is 5,500 employers, a dramatic increase in absolute terms but still only a small portion of the employers in the United States.

Employers are responding with a variety of programs, usually packaging a number of options together in accordance with the needs of their particular work force. The Families and Work Institute in New York estimates the prevalence of various responses to be as follows:

On- or near-site centers		1,300
by hospitals	800	
by corporations	250	
by government	250	

Other child care programs (family day care, school-aged care, and temporary care)	100
Resource and referral	1,500
Vouchers	100
Dependent care assistance plans	2,500[9]

Small businesses are not as well represented in these efforts as large employers. Although they face the same human resources pressures and select similar options, they do not have the resources or technical expertise to arrange complex benefits. Many of the small businesses that do offer child care assistance had a collaborating partner—a developer, child care provider, or community consultant—who provided the initiative, capital and management.[10]

Types of Care

CHILD CARE CENTERS

Day care centers near- or on-site are a particularly attractive benefit for employees. The peace of mind and the convenience of having their children near to them at work are appealing to parents, especially those with very young children. But because of long commutes, parking problems, and the difficulty of coordination with schools, there are just as many families who prefer child care in their own neighborhoods.

Before seriously considering a child care center, most employers conduct a needs and community resource assessment in order to substantiate the need and to ensure that any center established will be well enrolled if a center is established. If a survey is used, it is important to evaluate employees' needs both for child care now and over the next five years.

It is also important to understand the child care resources in the community. Are services currently available that could be expanded to meet the needs of a company's employees, or is there a vendor with a good-quality program who would be interested in bidding on the project? It is a good idea to engage the services of a consultant to design and interpret the survey results and assess community resources before taking further steps.

One of the first issues to consider in starting a center is the tension between quality and equity. Every employer wants its program to be a high-quality child care center, but child care is very expensive to provide, and unless a program is subsidized, it might serve only the upper-level employees. If a company wants its center to attract entry-level workers or has a culture that would not allow a benefit that is not equally available to everyone, then the task will be more complex and expensive.

Another issue is how to organize and manage the center. Although most employers want to distance themselves from a center because of liability concerns, they should remember that involvement gives them control over critical elements of the program such as quality, location, and hours. Employers with child care programs report that regardless of how a center is managed and however distant they may be from its daily operation, to some extent their employees still hold them accountable for the center.

Child care centers can be legally structured in various ways. Dominion Bankshares in Roanoke, Virginia, retains complete control over its center, managing it as a department within the company, and center employees enjoy the same standing and benefits as other company employees. Merck Pharmaceuticals in Rahway, New Jersey, set up its center as an independent not-for-profit corporation, with company representatives on the board of directors. In many cities, a consortium effort of several companies has created a new child care center. Still other companies have established a partnership with the public sector or a contractual relationship with a for-profit or not-for-profit vendor. In any case, a delicate relationship exists among the employer, the parents using the service, and the management of the center.

There are many other important decisions to consider in starting up a center, such as the age of the children to be served, whether eligibility will be limited to a company's employees or open to the community, and how to capitalize the initial renovation or building costs. In addition, employers would be well advised to design their center to be accredited by the National Association for the Education of Young Children.

There is a growing body of knowledge and resources to help the employer with the process. As a first step, an employer should secure from the state child care licensing department the licensing regulations that centers must meet. The licensing agency should also be able to supply a list of employer-supported centers in the state; personnel at these programs can provide useful advice.

Some states or communities have easily available resources and lists of consultants for employers considering a child care center. Inquire about these resources from other companies, a local child care resource and referral service, or an employer-supported child care office in a state department of commerce or economic development. Resources for Child Care Management, in Berkeley Heights, New Jersey, holds an annual national conference on the start-up of corporate-sponsored child care centers.

FAMILY DAY CARE

Family day care is the most prevalent form of care in the United States, although it is often considered invisible because it takes place in the homes of private providers. Family day care providers are typically women who care for six or fewer children in their own home. (The licensing regulations for family day care vary by state, and some states allow a larger group of children.) It is the form of care that is preferred by most families for infants and toddlers, and it is often used by families needing part-time arrangements or nontraditional hours.

The recruitment and training of family day care homes are usually included in child care resource and referral service contracts. Some employers, such as America West Airlines, have recruited a network of family day care homes to serve their employees. In these instances, the service will recruit, train, and provide ongoing support for the family day care providers.

A significant family day care initiative is underway with foundation support from Mervyns and Target Stores. This Family to Family program has developed training for family day care providers in communities where these corporations have stores, support for the development of national quality standards, and education for parents and the public about good-quality child care.

SCHOOL-AGE CARE

In considering the child care needs of their work force, most employers have devoted their attention to young children, but more and more they are identifying a problem that has come to be called the 3 o'clock syndrome—3 P.M. being the hour when employees call home to find out whether their school-age children have arrived home safely. Today three-quarters of all school-age children live in families in which the parents are working.[11] When these children have no reliable supervision or program after their school day ends, parents can become preoccupied and less productive. Anywhere from 2 million to 10 million school-age children in the United States are now estimated to be latchkey children—essentially on their own in the afternoon hours, at home or in the neighborhood, until a parent returns from work.

According to the Conference Board, about fifty companies have taken action specifically to address the needs of school-age children or have created programs that serve school-age as well as preschool children.[12] Fel-Pro, a Skokie, Illinois, manufacturer, began a summer day camp in 1973 as an employee service and to keep productivity from dropping off during the summer months. The nine-week camp now enrolls about 300 children at a minimal cost to families; Fel-Pro supports 80 percent of the camp's annual budget.

Some companies have concentrated their efforts on self-care and home safety for school-age children, recognizing that the latchkey phenomenon, for better or worse, may be here to stay. The Whirlpool Foundation funds a nationwide effort, Project Home Safe, to train home economists to develop self-care skills for children ages 5 to 13. Since 1986, television station KCTV and Heart of America Family Services in Kansas City, Missouri, have coordinated a PhoneFriend serice, staffed by volunteers to be a contact for children who are home alone.

Fairfax County, Virginia, sponsors the Strong Families/Competent Kids program, which allows children ages 10 to 14 to spend time in a variety of settings agreed upon by their parents: at home, at a friend's or a child care provider's home, or at other locations, such as music classes, sports fields, and libraries. Children are required to check in with the program as to where they will be at all times.

Most initiatives have been collaborative efforts—often with schools and community organizations—to develop programs for school-age children. A particularly successful and comprehensive collaboration was initiated by the Houston Committee for Private Sector Initiatives. The school system donates space and teachers to provide tutoring for the programs, and the private sector underwrites the costs of care for low-income families. The programs are run by community organizations, and some corporations have chosen to adopt a school and to work closely with its after-school program.[13]

EVENING, NIGHT, AND WEEKEND CHILD CARE

An increasing number of parent employees, especially in young, dual-earner families, are shift workers, who do not work during traditional daytime hours. Shift workers now constitute between 13 percent and 17 percent of the work force. Many work in the evenings and on weekends. Others have schedules that rotate from days to evenings to nights or fluctuate from week to week, as with service staff or manufacturing workers. Since most child care programs operate only during the daytime, these parents encounter a great deal of trouble in arranging reliable and flexible care for their children. A recent study found that about 40 percent of part-time workers needed child care during nontraditional hours.[14]

Several companies have developed creative responses to these employees' needs. The Opryland USA complex in Nashville, Tennessee, has an on-site center staffed from 5 A.M. to midnight, and America West Airlines has a center near the Phoenix airport staffed 24 hours a day. America West's family day care network in Phoenix and in Las Vegas also includes some homes that offer 24-hour care.

BACKUP CARE

One of the times when parents need backup arrangements is when their children are sick. Young children experience an average of six to nine mild viral illnesses per year, lasting three to seven days each, and when sickness develops, many child care arrangements break down.[15] A

Boston University study found that 57 percent of women employees and 9 percent of male employees needed to stay home from work when a child was sick.[16] Transamerica Life Companies of Los Angeles found in a survey that it was losing $150,000 to $180,000 a year due to employees' problems in arranging care for mildly ill children.

As a result, some employers are deciding that it is cost-effective to create or support a program to give sick children the individualized, attentive care they need. Most people initially feel resistant to programs that care for children when they are ill, due to a belief that a sick child must have a parent's care. That response is understandable, especially when a child is very ill; on such days, parents should be allowed to use sick leave to care for their child. But there are numerous days of recuperation when a child should be quiet and is not ready to return to day care or school but does not require a parent's presence. These are the times when many parents would be willing to try a program; once they have done so, most parents become repeat users.

The primary models of short-term sick child care are in the child's home, in a provider's home, in a separate facility such as an infirmary, or in a "get well" room at the child's day care center. Designers of these programs are also beginning to plan services for other days when parents need backup care: snow days, periods when existing child care arrangements fall through, overtime workdays, or times when an employee is called out of town for work. A successful model of backup care for all of these emergencies has been established by a consortium of thirteen companies in New York City, including Colgate-Palmolive, Consolidated Edison, Home Box Office, National Westminster Bank, Time, STET, Time Warner, Newsday, Ernst and Young, and Skadden, Arps, Slate, Meagher & Flom, the city's largest law firm. This program is coordinated by Child Care Inc., the local child care resource and referral service, and provides in-home care by two home health care agencies. Five of the participating companies pay the full cost of care (approximately $12.50 an hour) and the others pay for most of it, with employees covering the balance.

Another innovative program, Kids-To-Go, is for school-age children of employees at the John Hancock Life Insurance Company in Boston. During school vacation holidays, a local child care provider organizes activities and field trips for the children. The fee, $25 a day per child, is paid for by parents.

Resource and Referral

Child care resource and referral (R&R) services, a popular benefit for employers, provide a comprehensive referral service for employees, regardless of the age of their children or their preferred type of care, while also working to build up the supply of providers in the employees' community. An R&R service typically provides in-depth consultation to employees about their child care choices, consultation and publications on how to select good-quality care, personalized support during the parent's search for care, parenting seminars, and referrals to providers with openings that meet the parent's specifications.

Child care R&R services are sometimes confused with an information service, which is of limited value to parents when the supply of available care is low. Instead, R&Rs actively recruit and train service providers in the communities where most employees are searching for care. In one community, they may have to work with zoning boards to allow family day care to develop in a neighborhood; for another client, they may recruit providers willing to care for children whose parents work the second shift.

Across the United States, public and private sector employers and both large Fortune 500 companies and small local firms are purchasing these services as a benefit for their employees. Employers with workers in one location often contract with a local R&R agency, which typically provides child care leadership in the community. There are now about 300 child care R&R agencies around the country, as well as a national R&R association. Other companies establish the R&R service in-house. Lincoln National Corporation in Fort Wayne and Steelcase, Inc., in Grand Rapids have developed their own databases and networks of providers. Other companies with an in-house service have arranged to lease the data from the local R&R.

Employers seeking to offer a national R&R program can purchase services through a national vendor, which then subcontracts with a local R&R service in each community where the client has employees.

Financial Assistance

The cost of child care varies according to the age of the child, the form of care, and the location of the program; nevertheless, it is very high for most families. Employers have most often responded to employees' needs for financial assistance by creating a dependent care assistance plan (DCAP), which allows parents to use up to $5,000 of pretax dollars for dependent care services. These plans carry benefits to both the employer and the employee. The savings for the employee come from reduced social security and income tax payments; savings to the employer come from lowered unemployment tax and FICA payments. There are restrictions on these funds. Any money left in an employee's flexible spending account at the end of the year is forfeited. Also, employees can use either a flexible spending account or the IRS dependent care tax credit; for moderate-income families, the tax credit is often more advantageous.

Although the vast majority of financial assistance programs are funded through salary reduction and require no employer contribution, a growing number of companies are contributing to employee DCAP accounts or making other kinds of child care subsidies available to employees. A popular option is for a company to contract with a provider for a discount for its employees. This is most effective when the employer is paying the differential between the public rate and the discounted rate. Otherwise, the discount or lost income may be absorbed by lowering staff salaries—and ultimately the quality of care. In a market where programs are underenrolled, however, it may be fiscally advantageous for the provider to offer discounts to large employers.

Some employers have been exploring models of direct subsidy. Typically the subsidy is offered only to employees with lower incomes or with a total family income under a designated amount, although the Travelers Insurance Family to Family program is open to everyone.

Child Care Plus is the subsidy program that NCNB Corporation, based in Charlotte, North Carolina, offers its employees. The company's goals for the program are twofold: to help attract and retain a capable work force and to promote quality in child care. The NCNB subsidy is available to employees with a household taxable income of less than $24,000 a year, and the subsidy rate varies, depending on whether the care used is licensed. Employees using licensed care are reimbursed for half of their expenses, up to a maximum of $35 a week per child; for those using legally operating but unlicensed care, the reimbursement is up to $15 a week per child.[17]

Some companies have offered a sliding-fee scale subsidy, with the higher reimbursements going to the lower-salaried employees. The Polaroid Corporation initiated the first voucher plan, offering a subsidy based on a graduated scale from 10 percent to 80 percent of the cost of care for employees with family incomes less than $36,500. Travelers Insurance Company also uses a graduated scale of 10 percent to 30 percent of the cost of care, with annual limits of between $400 and $1,200 per employee.

There are many decisions to make in establishing a subsidy plan, including the following:

- Whether to offer subsidies to all families or to set an eligibility cap by employee income or family income
- Whether to make the subsidy payment to the employee or to the child care service provider
- Whether to have a flat reimbursement amount per child or a sliding-fee scale relative to income and/or as a percentage of the cost of care
- Whether to restrict the subsidy to certain types of care (licensed versus unlicensed but legally operating)
- Whether the subsidy will be for all children in care or only for those under age 6 and whether there is a cap on the number of children in one family who can be supported by the program

Flexibility

No matter how carefully families with children plan, no matter how well organized they are on Sunday night, something often happens by Monday morning, and parents need flexibility in order to deal with it. "It" can be anything from a snowstorm and school closing to an early-shift teacher who is late, leaving no one at the center to care for the child. And emergencies are only half the story. Many parents have family duties that typically must be fulfilled during working hours, such as doctors' appointments, school plays, and parent-teacher conferences.

The idea of a fixed work schedule is beginning to give way to the notion that schedules can vary without loss of productivity. A popular response is flextime. About 12 percent of workers in the United States have flextime, and half of all large employers offer this arrangement. The concept began with a set of core hours during which everyone needed to be in the office, with some flexibility around arrival and departure times, although everyone still worked a full 8 hours a day or 40 hours a week. The concept now has multiple versions—for example, a longer lunch break with an early arrival and late departure, and a weekly balancing, which allows the employee some longer and some shorter workdays each week.[18]

Catalyst, a research and advisory organization that supports the career development of women, reported in 1989 the results of an in-depth study of flexible work arrangements for managers and professional staff. Until recently, part-time work and job sharing have been available only in clerical and entry-level positions. Catalyst interviewed human resources personnel and employees who had flexible work arrangements, as well as their colleagues. The study also reported on telecommuting (an employee works from a satellite office). They found that the benefits of these flexible arrangements far outweighed the costs and also produced favorable outcomes in retention, productivity, and morale.[19]

Leave policies are another critical part of flexibility. Although most large corporations are expanding these policies, it is estimated that 60 percent of women workers do not have job protection at the time of childbirth and that most of these women work for small companies. The United States is unique among industrialized nations in not having a leave policy for parents at the time of childbirth. A federal family and medical leave bill was vetoed by President George Bush in 1990 in spite of the bill's wide political support. The bill would have required employers with fifty or more employees to provide up to twelve weeks of unpaid family and medical leave to care for a newborn, a newly adopted child, or a seriously ill family member. Employees on leave would have had continued health benefits, as well as job protection. Versions of this bill had been introduced for three previous years and will likely continue to be introduced. The bill remains controversial; opponents have argued that small employers cannot afford these leaves and that the government should not limit the competitiveness of American business by mandating benefits. About seventeen states have passed some kind of family or medical leave legislation, and both California and Minnesota include leave hours for parents to attend teacher conferences.

Partnerships

Responsibility for child care has been likened to a hot potato: an issue tossed from one sector to another, each considering it too complex and expensive to hold. At last there is an understanding that it will take a partnership of all sectors to make good-quality and affordable child care available to the families who need it.

Partnerships are occurring primarily at a community level. Most of the efforts to date are to increase the supply and quality of child care providers. There have been a number of consortiums of employers coming together to start a day care center, as well as school systems working with business leaders and community groups to develop after-school programs. A comprehensive statewide effort has occurred in California, the California Child Care Initiative Project, which has over 120 funding partners, including both public and private employers at the state and local levels, who have contributed over $4 million since 1985. This project equips the extensive child care R&R network in that state to recruit and train family day care providers and to provide ongoing support to help providers stay in business. This project now has Ford Foundation funding for replication efforts in other states.

Partnerships in a few communities are beginning to take on the complicated issues of the child care delivery system: how to organize and fund high-quality child care services for all families who need them. It will be interesting to see what role employers will play or will be asked to play in this next generation of partnership efforts.

Getting Started

There is so much information available now on child care options for employers that it can feel overwhelming and confusing. Most companies, however, go through stages, starting small and developing additional steps over time. Initial efforts are usually focused on getting support for a specific child care project. It often takes awhile to develop the business case for the project and to overcome resistance. Questions of liability, cost, privacy, and equity usually get raised about any new child care initiative.

Often a company's involvement with child care will grow into an interest in broader work and family issues. There are a host of other programs and supports that employees need, not the least of which is support for their caregiver roles with the elderly. A pattern may emerge from individual programs and policies developed within a company forming the beginnings of a comprehensive strategy on work and family life.

NOTES

1. H. Hayghe, "Rise in Mothers' Labor Force Activity Includes Those with Infants," *Monthly Labor Review* (February 1986).
2. Children's Defense Fund, *A Briefing Book on the Status of American Children in 1988* (Washington, D.C.: CDF, 1988).
3. E. Galinsky and D. Hughes, *The Fortune Magazine Child Care Study* (New York: Bank Street College, 1987).
4. California Child Care Resource and Referral Network, *Infant Facts: State of California* (San Francisco: The Network, 1985).
5. Maryland Employers Advisory Council on Child Care, *Shareholders in the Future: Marylanders Invest in Child Care* (Baltimore: The Council, 1988).
6. M. Whitebook, C. Howes, and D. Phillips, *Who Cares? Child Care Teachers and the Quality of Care in America* (Berkeley, Calif.: Child Care Employee Project, 1989).
7. *National Report on Work and Family,* "Poor Families Pay More Than Do Wealthier For Child Care," August 17, 1990.
8. D. Burden and B. Googins, *Boston University Balancing Job and Homelife Study: Summary of Research Findings* (Boston: Boston University School of Social Work, 1985).
9. D. Friedman, "Update on Employer Supported Child Care," memorandum (New York: Families and Work Institute, 1990).
10. Berkeley Planning Associates, *Small Business Options for Child Care: Final Report,* (Washington, D.C.: U.S. Small Business Administration, 1990).
11. M. Seligson and D. Fink, *No Time to Waste: An Action Agenda for School-Age Child Care.* (Wellesley, Mass.: School-Age Child Care Project, Wellesley College, 1989).
12. Bureau of National Affairs, *Latchkey Children: A Guide for Employers,* Special Report 11, (Washington, D.C.: Buraff Publications, November 1988).
13. D. Euben and B. Reisman, *Making the Connections: Public-Private Partnerships in Child Care* (New York: Child Care Action Campaign, 1990).
14. H. Presser, "Shift Work and Child Care among Dual Earner American Parents," *Journal of Marriage and the Family* (February 1988).
15. "Care for Sick Children: The Newest Support for Working Parents," *Business Link: The Report on Management Initiatives for Working Parents* 2, no. 4 (Winter 1987).
16. Burden and Googins, *Boston University.*
17. "Two Approaches to Child Care Subsidy: NCNB and Travelers," *Business Link: The Report on Management Initiatives for Working Parents* 5, no. 1 (1990).
18. F. S. Rodgers and C. Rodgers, "Business and the Fact of Family Life," *Harvard Business Review* (November–December 1989).

19. *Flexible Work Arrangements: Establishing Options for Managers and Professionals* (New York: Catalyst, 1989).

SUGGESTED READING

Adolf, Barbara, and Karol Rose. *The Employer's Guide to Child Care: Developing Programs for Working Parents*. New York: Praeger Publishers, 1985.

Auerbach, Judith D. *In the Business of Child Care: Employer Initiatives and Working Women*. New York: Praeger Publishers, 1988.

Bureau of National Affairs. *Special Report Series on Work and Family*. Washington, D.C.: The Bureau.

Burud, Sandra L., Pamela Aschbacher, and Jacquelyn McCroskey. *Employer-Supported Child Care: Investing in Human Resources*. Dover, Mass.: Auburn House, 1984.

Child Care Action Campaign. *Child Care: The Bottom Line: An Economic and Child Care Policy Paper*. New York: CCAC, 1988.

Committee for Economic Development. *Children in Need; Investment Strategies for the Educationally Disadvantaged*. New York: CED, 1987.

Emlen, Arthur C., and Paul E. Koren. *Hard to Find and Difficult to Manage: The Effects of Child Care on the Workplace*. Portland, Ore.: Regional Research Institute for Human Services, Portland State University, 1984.

Employer and Child Care: Benefiting Work and Family. Washington, D.C.: U.S. Department of Labor, Office of the Secretary, Women's Bureau, 1989.

Fernandez, John P. *Child Care and Corporate Productivity: Resolving Family-Work Conflicts*. Lexington, Mass.: Lexington Books, 1986.

French-American Foundation. *A Welcome for Every Child: How France Achieves Quality in Child Care: Practical Ideas for the United States*. New York: The Foundation, 1990.

Friedman, Dana E. *Corporate Financial Assistance for Child Care*. Research Bulletin no. 177. New York: Conference Board, 1985.

———. *Productivity Effects of Workplace Child Care Centers*. New York: Families and Work Institute, 1989.

Galinsky, Ellen. *The Impact of Supervisors' Attitudes and Company Culture on Work/Family Adjustment*. New York: Families and Work Institute, 1988.

Growing Together: An Intergenerational Sourcebook. Washington, D.C.: American Association of Retired Persons.

Kamerman, Sheila B., and Alfred J. Kahn. *The Responsive Workplace: Employers and a Changing Labor Force*. New York: Columbia University Press, 1987.

National Academy of Early Childhood Programs. National Association for the Education of Young Children. *Accreditation Criteria and Procedures*. Washington, D.C.: The Association, 1984.

Work/Family Directions. *A Little Bit under the Weather: A Look at Care for Mildly Ill Children*. Boston: Work/Family Directions, 1986.

NEWSLETTERS OF INTEREST

BUSINESSLINK: The Report on Management Initiatives for Working Parents. Resources for Child Care Management, P. O. Box 672, Bernardsville, New Jersey 07924.

ChildCare ActioNews. Child Care Action Campaign, 330 Seventh Avenue, 18th Floor, New York, New York 10001.

National Report on Work and Family. Buraff Publications, Bureau of National Affairs, Inc., 1231 25th Street, N.W., Washington D.C. 20037.

Work and Family Newsbrief. Work and Family Connection, 5197 Beachside Drive, Minnetonka, Minnesota 55343.

ORGANIZATIONS WITH PUBLICATIONS AND OTHER RESOURCES

Association of Child Care
   Consultants International
P. O. Box 77345
Atlanta, GA 30357-1345

Catalyst
250 Park Avenue South
New York, NY 10002-1459

Child Care Action Campaign
330 Seventh Avenue
New York, NY 10001

Child Care Employee Project
6536 Telegraph Avenue, A201
Oakland, CA 94609

Children's Defense Fund
122 C Street, N.W.
Washington, DC 20001

Families and Work Institute
330 Seventh Avenue
New York, NY 10001

National Association of Child
   Care Resource and Referral
   Agencies
2116 Campus Drive Southeast
Rochester, MN 55904

National Association for the
   Education of Young Children
1834 Connecticut Avenue, N.W.
Washington, DC 20009-5786

Resources for Child Care
   Management
261 Springfield Avenue, Suite 201
Berkley, NJ 07922

School-Age Child Care Project
Wellesley College
Center for Research on Women
Wellesley, MA 02181

Women's Bureau, Work and
   Family Clearinghouse
U.S. Department of Labor, Room
   53306
200 Constitution Avenue, N.W.
Washington, DC 20210

Work/Family Directions
930 Commonwealth Avenue South
Boston, MA 02215-1212

7

Elder Care

Diane S. Piktialis
Work/Family Directions, Inc.

Although barely in its infancy as a corporate benefit, elder care is rapidly emerging as a bottom-line concern for leading U.S. corporations. Until a few years ago, the term *elder care* quite simply meant care of the aged. Today, human resources professionals are extending its meaning to a variety of innovative programs designed primarily to help the approximately one out of four employees with caregiving responsibilities for an elder relative. "Elder care is likely to become the new, pioneering benefit of the 1990s," comments the Conference Board's Work and Family Information Center, adding, "It will probably happen faster than the corporate response to child care because it is a more acceptable topic."[1]

What factors explain this sudden and accelerating interest? Is elder care only the latest benefits fad? Or are the new and emerging corporate elder care programs a response to a growing and, so far, only partially recognized need?

Corporate elder care programs are the result of several rapidly converging factors: the aging of America, profound alterations in family structure that have eroded traditional caregiving from the home, changing labor force trends that indicate a growing shortage of skilled workers and the increased employment of women outside the home, and changing societal values affecting the balance between work and family life. Combined, these issues, centering on the employee caregiver, pose a growing challenge to the corporate world at a time of intensifying international competition.

The Avalanche of the Aging

Today, 12 percent of the U.S. population, or approximately 30 million people, are over age 65, compared with only 4 percent in 1900. The percentage is expected to rise gradually to 13 percent, or 35 million, by the year 2000 and to 14 percent, or 39 million, by 2010.[2] The maturing of the baby boom generation will cause a dramatic increase in the numbers of elderly passing through the aging pipeline over the subsequent two decades. Projections for the year 2030 estimate 65 million elderly, a total representing 21 percent of the U.S. population.[3] And the projections continue steeply upward from there.

More pertinent to the elder care issue, the percentage of the very old who need care the most is expanding far faster than the elderly population as a whole. By the year 2000, those over age 75 will number 12 million, or 40 percent of the elderly population. According to 1985–1986 projections by the Senate Special Committee on Aging, persons 85 years of age and over are the fastest growing segment of American society.[4]

Changes in Caregiving Patterns

On its face, the burden of caring for the growing number and percentage of the elderly by the rest of the population is cause enough for concern. But it is exacerbated by the erosion of traditional patterns of caregiving from the home.

Contrary to popular belief, about 80 percent of the care needed by the elderly is, in fact, provided by family members, most commonly female spouses or daughters.[5] Yet the greatly increased participation of women in the work force makes them less available to meet dependent care responsibilities. For the first time, more than half (51 percent) of all adult women are employed outside the home, and 75 percent of these women work full time.[6] Labor force trends indicate that even more women will enter the work force between now and the year 2000, although the rate of increase will taper off.[7] The Bureau of Labor Statistics projects that 69 percent of women between 45 and 54 years of age will be in the work force by the year 2000.[8]

It would be unfair to attribute the erosion of traditional caregiving patterns for the elderly solely to the increasing participation of women in the work force. Other factors are also involved:

  ▲ Since the 1950s, families have become smaller, leaving fewer adult children to take care of elder relatives, who are living longer.

  ▲ There are many more single-parent households in the workplace.

  ▲ The delay in childbearing age by many couples is increasing the number of years that caregivers are torn between their responsibilities to both children and parents—the so-called sandwich generation. For the first time, parents are spending more years caring for parents than for children.[9]

  ▲ Many people who retire are still caring for their parents in a growing number of four-generation families.

  ▲ The increased mobility of both adult children in the work force and their elders during retirement has added a new dimension and complexity to caregiving by creating substantial numbers of "long-distance caregivers."[10] All of these trends increase the strain on those caring for elderly relatives.

Caregiving From Work

How do these overall trends affect the workplace? "Of particular importance," according to *Personnel Journal* is

> the dramatic increase in the ratio of elderly persons to those of working age, from seven elderly per 100 persons age 18 to 64 in 1900 to 19 per 100 today. The U.S. Senate Special Committee on Aging predicts that by the year 2010 there will be 22 elderly persons per 100 working-age persons, a figure that's expected to increase to 38 per 100 by 2050.[11]

A growing number of companies are documenting the substantial caregiving responsibilities of their employees. In its pioneering 1985 study, the Travelers Insurance Companies found that 28 percent of its home office employees over age 30 who responded were providing some kind of care for an elderly relative.[12] A random sampling in 1986–1987 of employees over age 40 at three Connecticut corporations by the University of Bridgeport's Center for the Study of Aging indicated that 25 percent of the respondents were involved in some sort of caregiving.[13] And, in a 1987 random survey of 5,000 employees, IBM reported that 30 percent of its employees over age 30 had some responsibility for an older relative, 8 percent had adult dependents, and 4 percent had adult dependents living with them.[14]

The substantial involvement of both executives and employees in the problems of providing elder care is documented in a 1989 national survey of chief executives and the general population sponsored by *Fortune* magazine and John Hancock Financial Services. Forty-nine percent of executives responding from a mailing to CEOs of the Fortune 1,000 were personally responsible at that time for an elderly person or had been in the previous two years, and 37 percent of employees were likely to be elder caregivers at the time or had been over the last two years. The greater caregiving responsibilities of the executives may be explained by their greater average age: 53.4 years versus 38.5 years for all employees surveyed. Among the employees surveyed with elder caregiving responsibilities, 41 percent reported that they were the ones mainly responsible for taking care of their elderly; on average, employees had been providing care for their elders for four years; and caregiving to the elderly averaged 13 hours per week for the employees surveyed.[15]

In its comprehensive 1987 survey of thirty-three small, medium, and large companies and agencies in the Portland, Oregon, area, the Regional Institute for Human Services and Institute on Aging at Portland State University found that nearly one in four of 9,573 employees participating in the survey reported caring for at least one person 60 years of age or over. Moreover, many of the 2,241 employed caregivers had multiple caregiving responsibilities. And more than one-third of the caregivers cared not only for an elderly person but also had children living in their households.[16]

Such caregiving responsibilities are substantial. The Travelers reported that, overall, caregivers provided an average of 10.2 hours of care per week, with 8 percent reporting more than 35 hours weekly. The National Association of Area Agencies on the Aging reported similar findings in a 1986 study.[17]

Impact on the Workplace

With caregiving responsibilities sometimes amounting to the equivalent of a full-time job, it should come as no surprise that caregiving can take a personal toll on employees and impair their productivity on the job. In a 1984 survey of corporate members of the New York Business Group on Health, absenteeism, lateness, and the use of unscheduled days off were mentioned as problems by two-thirds to three-quarters of the sixty-nine respondents.[18] A 1988 survey of 225 organizations by the Bureau of National Affairs identified similar problems among employees with elder care responsibilities. Based on responses from ninety-nine personnel executives aware of employees with elder care responsibilities, 37 percent singled out absenteeism as a problem; 22 percent, tardiness; 20 percent, visible signs of stress; 18 percent, excessive telephone calls; 17 percent, unavailable for overtime work; 9 percent, requests for reduced hours; 7 percent, turnover; 3 percent, health problems; 2 percent, decrease in quality of work; 1 percent, work accidents; and 2 percent, other.[19]

In a survey of employee caregivers themselves, Transamerica found that 80 percent reported emotional strain; 61 percent, physical strain; and 55 percent, financial strain. In addition, 37 percent reported visiting friends less often, 33 percent said they went out to dinner on fewer occasions, and 50 percent reported having less time for themselves.[20]

Conclusive national studies on the magnitude of caregiving and its effects in the workplace remain to be done.[21] However, a growing number of leading companies have already been responding with new elder care initiatives on the basis of current research. Increasingly, other leading corporations are recognizing that their employees' elder care problems may turn out to be the company's problem. In fact, such employees are typically long-service, experienced employees.[22] About 12 percent of women who care for aging parents must quit their jobs to do so.[23]

Distinctive Requirements of Elder Care

In contrast to child care, where there are clear-cut shortages, many services exist for the aged in most communities throughout the United States. The abundance of such services reflects the growing political power of the elderly over the past several decades, resulting in such landmark legislation as the Older Americans Act of 1965. The act established the U.S. Administration on Aging (AOA) as a federal focal point and advocate for the elderly. AOA set up a network of state units on aging and area agencies on aging. Since that legislation, the AOA, state units, and area agencies on aging have worked to develop many community services for older persons. The availability of Medicare and Medicaid funding has also provided a wide base for consumers to draw on when purchasing certain services for the elderly. Countless entrepreneurs, from developers of retirement communities to operators of nursing home chains, to geriatric counselors and services of virtually innumerable variety, have sprung up in response to a need—and an opportunity.

Despite the recognition of elderly services as a growth industry, however, elder services as a whole are often highly fragmented, overlapping, and with widely varying eligibility requirements. For example, agencies that serve the elderly directly are sometimes not the same as those that serve their family caregivers. Moreover, current and anticipated cutbacks in government funding can be expected to widen the gap between programs primarily for the poor and those available to other segments of the population.

While many services for the elderly are generally plentiful, they are also much more diverse than child care services. They range from Meals-on-Wheels and transportation, to home repairs and nursing home care and financial planning. In many communities, there are shortages of one or more of these services. And while child care is almost always sought near or at home, elder relatives requiring services may live almost anywhere. "People have to negotiate complicated systems of housing, health care and insurance from afar," writes Dana Friedman, co-president of the Families and Work Institute. "And, of course, all these burdens are compounded by the usual ups and downs of a full-time job."[24] Stress is compounded when a caregiver seeking help has never had experience with America's complex and often frustrating system of serving the elderly.

In view of the complicated character of the elder care system, it is not surprising that many employee caregivers express a desire for better information and effective help in finding and making an appropriate choice of services for their elderly relatives. The Travelers 1985 survey study commented:

> When caring for an elder relative or friend, the caregiver may
> have many questions about how to provide this care and what

help may be available. Unfortunately, many caregivers may not know where to turn for answers to their questions. When asked which, if any, of a number of sources had been helpful in providing information about outside resources available, 21 percent indicated that the family physician was most helpful. However, 36 percent did not find any source particularly helpful.[25]

A recent, comprehensive survey of thirty-three employers in the Portland, Oregon, area also stressed a strong employee interest in information and in individual counseling. When asked which services they would "possibly use," 67 percent, the largest percentage of the caregivers responding, chose "information and referral"; 61 percent, the second largest group, selected "individual consultation with a professional." Both services, the report concluded, "could be provided in the work place, either by employers themselves or through subcontractual arrangements with third party service providers."[26]

Elder Care Options for Companies

There are wide variations among company programs in elder care. The main variable appears to be whether one is talking about broad-based initiatives designed specifically for elder care and, typically, employing gerontologic experts, or the extension of current benefits of many types, including sick leave, flexible work schedules, and employee assistance programs (EAPs) to address elder care needs.

In the first category of major initiatives, corporate elder care programs barely rank in the double-digit numbers. Describing major initiatives, such as those by IBM, Hewlett Packard, and Travelers, the *New York Times* reported about "two dozen companies in the United States currently trying to help workers care for their aging relatives."[27] Other companies such as AT&T, Nynex, and Bell Atlantic have negotiated broad benefits in their contracts.

At the other extreme, a Bureau of National Affairs survey of organizations across the United States offers a considerably more inclusive view by considering benefits not specific to elder care but that could assist an employee caregiver as well as elder care programs designed to meet specific elder care needs. "About two-thirds of the firms surveyed in September and October of 1988, offer some type of assistance," the organization reported. Among the 225 firms responding, assistance included "leave benefits, work schedule adjustments, financial benefits, information and referral services, and counseling and support services to employees who attend to senior family members."[28]

Recasting Existing Benefits

In a very recent trend, a few leading-edge companies are recasting their benefits structures—flextime programs, leave benefits, work schedule adjustments, and financial benefits—in a more comprehensive way to focus on a variety of family support programs geared specifically to the dependent care needs of employees. Dependent care—encompassing care for infants, children, adolescents, and the elderly—"is a business issue for the obvious reason that employees cannot come to work unless their dependents are cared for," write Fran Rodgers and Charles Rodgers in the *Harvard Business Review*.[29]

Elder Care Publications

Substantial numbers of companies have published or distributed elder care publications to employees. They include Pepsico, which published *Eldercare* for its work force in 1986, and Champion International, which prepared an information handbook for its employees, *Issues for an Aging America,* in 1987. In addition, some firms such as Travelers have built resource libraries or distributed materials such as the American Association for Retired Persons' (AARP's) *Caregivers in the Workplace* (1987).

Caregiver Fairs and Support Groups

Many of these firms and others are supplementing informational materials with workshops and support groups for employee caregivers. The Travelers has mounted caregiving fairs, lunchtime seminars, employee support groups, and videotaped information about caregiving. Many companies have employed an outside service to conduct seminars on the aging process and elder care services available in the community.

Employee Assistance Programs

Some companies view EAPs as a source of assistance to employee caregivers, especially for individuals dealing with the emotional upheavals inherent in caregiving. Helping to give information about the complex world of elder care resources and information requires specialized training and experiences. Counselors with expertise in drug abuse or alcoholism, it has been observed, are not necessarily experts regarding aging problems. In addition, employees rarely raise the elder care issue with EAP counselors.[30]

Financial Assistance

While direct financial assistance offered to employee caregivers and their elders is still rare, some 1,000 employers nevertheless offer dependent care assistance plans (DCAPs) to employees under the Internal Revenue

Code, which makes care of the elderly a nontaxable benefit. However, because DCAPs are limited to elders who are legal dependents of the employee, the benefit can help only a small proportion of employed caregivers. In a significant departure, the Travelers introduced an insurance program for employees that would cover many elder care costs, including nursing home fees.[31] Many other companies have offered long-term care insurance. In most cases, employees pay the full premium.

Direct Services

Still other forms of direct assistance have been tried or are being planned. Remington Products, for example, offered a respite care program for employee caregivers. The company would pay half the cost of respite care to give the employed caregiver time off. The program did not cover working hours. It ranged from 4 hours to a two-day maximum, with a yearly maximum of 95 hours. Remington worked in conjunction with the Visiting Nurses Association of Greater Bridgeport, which determined the level of care needed by recipients. The program started in December 1987 with a six-month trial, but only a few employees used the respite services. To gain more experience, the trial period has been extended indefinitely.

Intergenerational Day Care

In what may well be a unique approach, the Stride-Rite Corporation, a Cambridge, Massachusetts, manufacturer of shoes, is expanding its Children's Center into an on-site intergenerational day care center to accommodate approximately twenty-four elders and seventy-nine children. A collaborative effort of Stride-Rite, Lesley College, and Somerville-Cambridge Elder Services, the center is intended to foster meaningful relationships between the generations, as well as furnishing high-quality, affordable day care for dependents of the three organizations and the community. It is also hoped that the experimental program will increase public awareness of the need for new partnerships and care options.[32] Stride-Rite conducted a survey of its employees' elder care responsibilities and assessed overall employee interest before proceeding with the development of the center, which became operational in February 1990.

The Stride-Rite Center, located in the firm's corporate headquarters, provides services to elders and children in the same facility. Each group has facilities in separate wings and shares a core central area for group activities, a dining facility, and a resource center with a conference room and library. An outdoor area is under design. The center is expected to serve as a teacher training site for Wheelock College and Somerville-Cambridge Elder Services.

Elder Care Consultation and Referral Services

Taking a broad approach to the range of elder care problems employees face, companies such as IBM, Aetna Life & Casualty, Arthur Andersen/

Andersen Consulting, Johnson & Johnson, the Travelers, U.S. West, and U.S. Sprint are offering their employees elder care consultation and referral services. There are a small number of consulting firms that offer firms nationwide corporate elder care programs.

In one model, the companies pay for employees' use of the service, which streamlines access to an elder care professional wherever an employee's elderly relative may live. The service is delivered through a network of community-based organizations with high-quality standards, materials, and procedures determined centrally by the service. The emphasis is on expert counseling, which includes helping employees identify elder care concerns and reach informed decisions based on detailed knowledge of local community resources. In this regard, the service provides consumer education, through counseling and written materials, to help employees select appropriate care. It also furnishes individually researched referrals on a broad range of providers, including nursing homes, various housing options, in-home health and social services, and community programs. In addition, seminars and resource development activities are provided. Employees and their families remain responsible for selecting and paying for any services that they choose.

Comprehensive Dependent Care Programs

A few companies are developing innovative comprehensive dependent care programs that include elder care. IBM has long been a leader with its comprehensive dependent care benefits. As a pioneer in mounting national child and elder care referral services, the company views family issues in the larger context of its Work and Personal Life Balance Programs. These include flexible and alternative work schedules, a work-at-home plan, work and family seminars, an EAP, and management training. The company expanded these programs in late 1989.

In 1989 Johnson & Johnson announced a broad work and family initiative that includes support for elder care and child care, greater worktime flexibility, management training, and a change in its corporate credo to acknowledge a commitment to help employees balance work and family commitments.[33]

Commenting on its new 1989 labor contract, AT&T chairman Robert E. Allen, wrote, "It [the contract] acknowledges and tries to accommodate a changed workplace. It takes into account that women—as well as men—work; that there's a life both before and after office hours; that there are kids and older people who need help, too."[34] In such comprehensive dependent care programs, elder care is addressed as part of an overall strategy.

The Travelers, which launched national referral services for both elder care and child care on January 1, 1990, is implementing a new financial subsidy program for employees who are caring for their parents or elderly relatives. In addition, the company is permitting employees to take up to one year of unpaid leave to care for a family member, including elder care, and three paid days off a year to care for sick family members under its new Family Care benefits package. "We fully expect the Family Care benefits to aid us in recruiting the best employees, keeping them at Travelers, and making sure they have the opportunities and support to succeed in their jobs," said Thomas E. Helfrich, senior vice-president for corporate human resources and services, in announcing the new benefits package.[35]

Recently companies as diverse as Hewlett Packard, Bell Atlantic, Hoescht Celanese, and Mobil Oil have introduced broad initiatives that contain elder care components. This new view toward progressive family policies appears to be the wave of the future.

New Service Development

In a significant expansion of its comprehensive dependent care benefits, IBM created a $25 million fund in late 1989, available over the succeeding five years, to increase the supply and the quality of child and elder care services in communities where employees, retirees, or their older relatives live. This will be done through a targeted request for proposal (RFP) process. In elder care, the company hopes to develop and expand community projects such as respite care development, recruitment and training of in-home health and social service workers, and intergenerational service programs. In making the announcement, IBM said, "These changes are intended to respond to IBM's business needs, as well as to build on our partnerships with employees and community organizations."[36]

AT&T has also recently announced a broad work and family initiative. AT&T broke new ground in labor relations with its family-centered programs, announced in 1989. A significant component of the company's contract with its two largest unions is a $5 million Family Care Development Fund. That amount was matched for nonunion management employees. The fund will provide seed money and grants to encourage the development of child and elder care facilities and improvement in the quality of services. The contract is expected to push family issues to the forefront of labor management negotiations. (See the appendix to this chapter for examples of some companies' policies and programs for elder care.)

Selecting an Elder Care Program

How does a company get started in elder care? Since many elder care programs are still in their infancy and might therefore be considered experimental, there is ample room for new approaches. Furthermore, once in place, programs can be refined based on a company's experience in serving the evolving needs of its employee caregivers.

There is no one best way to set up an elder care program. For example, Travelers extensively surveyed its population to assess its employees' elder care responsibilities before mounting its programs; Aetna Life and Casualty assumed that it was a microcosm of the nation and established a national consultation and referral service and a family leave policy on that basis. "We knew of and read about other surveys that had been done," says Sherry Herchenroether, manager of family services, in describing the work of a 1987 company task force that addressed the changing demographics of the work force. "We basically said that if we have 43,000 employees, we are affected the way that all other companies are." She observes that elder care is often a silent issue. For a variety of reasons, including guilt and stress, employees often do not voice their concerns, feeling that "they should be able to cope with their elder care responsibilities on their own."[37]

Step 1: Examine Existing Programs

An appropriate first step is to examine existing benefits programs. The most cost-effective approach is to make sure that current policies and programs are working for employees with elder care needs before undertaking any new programs. How well do they serve employees' caregiving needs? Are employees aware that programs such as flextime or leave policies may be utilized for their elder care responsibilities? Organizational flexibility is an essential element underlying dependent care programs.[38] Before tackling elder care, it might be well to consider programs aimed at organizational flexibility in order to build from a sound foundation. If existing programs of this nature are not working, better communication of these programs should be a priority. Finally, any new initiatives should also complement and be consistent with existing programs.

Step 2: Assess Need

USING SURVEYS

Employee surveys are an effective means of quantifying employees' elder care needs and responsibilities. They can indicate the number of employees coping with caregiving responsibilities, the scope and nature of assistance they are providing, and how any resulting stress may be affecting employees' productivity on the job. The AARP Caregivers Survey (included in the appendix) is an example of one elder care survey instrument. Based on the Travelers pioneering survey, the AARP survey has been field-tested by a number of organizations and can be adapted for any company's use. AARP also furnishes useful information on organizing and administering a survey.

A typical survey asks the number of hours an employee devotes to caregiving, the nature of current caregiving responsibilities, the anticipation of additional caregiving responsibilities in the future, what services the employee is using, what additional services might be desired, and the sources of information the caregiving employee has found useful. An occasionally overlooked query that is essential to the planning process concerns where elderly relatives of employees live. Another is the type of stress that the employee is experiencing as a result of his or her elder care tasks. To be effective, surveys should always be designed to ensure the anonymity of respondents.

CONSULTING OUTSIDE EXPERTS

Outside experts are often brought in to develop surveys, analyze survey data, and help formulate a strategy. The advantages of outside experts are their experience in analyzing elder care data or dependent care issues and their ability to compare a particular company's data to those of other corporations. Typically these efforts are broadly focused, examining the full range of dependent care needs.

FOCUS GROUPS, TASK FORCES, AND MANAGEMENT INVOLVEMENT

Focus groups of employees can be used to help clarify survey data. If an internal work group or task force is formed to assess elder care needs and recommend programs, it is helpful to include representatives from top and middle management. Although it chose not to conduct a survey, Aetna Life and Casualty followed the course of using a broad task force before launching its elder care benefits. Management interviews can also serve to gain understanding and commitment among those who must be sensitive and responsive to employees' needs if a program is to succed. Without backing from high levels within a corporation, even the most promising initiatives may have difficulty gaining support and funding. In addition, it is always useful to get first-hand accounts of the experience of other companies with successful programs.

Step 3: Examine Costs

The cost of mounting an elder care program is a major consideration for any company. These costs vary widely, depending on the options a company selects. The choice of options is generally governed by the size of a company's work force and its demographics, as well as budgetary considerations. Because of proprietary issues, exact cost figures are not available for many corporate programs.

There is very little cost in expanding existing benefits programs, such as flextime or leave policy, to cover elder care needs. However, the success of this approach requires targeted communication. Both employees and their managers must be made aware that current support programs have been extended or already apply to cover elder care situations.

Educational materials are another low-cost option. Several elder care handbooks are available at costs ranging from approximately $5 to $10. An in-house resource library can be set up for several hundred to several thousand dollars, depending on its scope. In addition to books on caregiving and community resources, several elder care videotapes are available.

Caregiver fairs can be sponsored for a modest expense. These fairs usually include a wide range of elder care service providers who set up tables from which they furnish information about their services and are available to answer questions. Cost considerations in putting together a caregiver fair include staff time to contact agencies providing elder care services, the handling of logistics in setting up a fair, and developing a communications strategy to get word of the event to employees.

Employee support groups to help employees involved in elder care have been run by companies, like the Travelers, using in-house EAP staff. This option may involve additional training of EAP staff to handle elder care issues. In addition to the time spent by those leading support groups, companies have found that extensive and continuous outreach is necessary to identify and get agreement from employees to participate in these support groups.

Many companies have begun employee workshops or seminars devoted to elder care at either on-site or off-site locations in the community. These seminars are educational in nature and can cover a wide range of topics: how to understand and pay for medical care, legal issues, when and how to select a nursing home, and others. The cost ranges from approximately $150 for a forty-five-minute seminar to about $300 to $400 for a 1½- to 2-hour workshop.

An increasing number of companies offer comprehensive elder care information or consultation and referral programs to their employees. The cost of furnishing counseling and information through these programs amounts to approximately $9 to $12 a year for each active employee in a company's work force. Because older relatives of employees are scattered throughout the country, most of these programs include a national capability for providing information on elder care services in distant communities.

On-site day care centers have recently received wide attention. Stride-Rite's intergenerational day care center cost approximately $500,000 in start-up costs. Ongoing operating expenses are estimated to be about $600,000 a year, or $7,800 for each child or older person who enrolls. Those who use the center pay about $150 a week. However, since Stride-Rite is partially subsidizing the cost of care for its employees, an employee pays a maximum of $100 per week.

In addition to providing elder care programs for their employees, some companies have mounted service or resource development projects to increase the quantity or improve the quality of local elder care services. The cost of such programs varies widely and is at the discretion of the company making the investment. For example, the AT&T Family Care Fund has committed $10 million over three years, and IBM's Fund for Dependent Care Initiatives has committed $25 million over a five-year period to increase the availability or improve the quality of services in some communities.

The Need for Balance

A balanced approach to the needs of all types of employee caregivers is advisable. The consideration of fairness is receiving increased attention as more companies are developing comprehensive family support programs that include elder care as one component. In designing their programs, companies like IBM and Aetna Life and Casualty stressed equity of services to employees in all age categories. Geographic equity is a further consideration. To the extent possible, all employees should receive the same level and quality of services.

Lack of balance caused by addressing a lower-priority need first may actually impede acceptance of an elder care program by creating dissatisfaction among employees with other caregiving needs. For example, a firm with a relatively young employee population may have a greater initial need for child care than for elder care. Successful elder care programs have often followed an initiative in child care as a company's population ages. As a rule, companies are reluctant to disclose specific costs associated with elder care programs. However, many companies observe that "the costs of elder care are more than offset by improved employee morale, recruitment, and retention."[39] This consideration is especially relevant in highly competitive industries where variance in benefits programs can make one employer more desirable to work for than another. Therefore, in planning for elder care, it is desirable to find out what the competition is doing. Overall, however, all companies are faced with the same issue of attracting and keeping good employees in a declining labor market.

Implementing a Program

The desire to initiate an elder care program, and even the demonstrated need for one, does not necessarily ensure that it can be launched successfully. Companies that have followed through effectively in mounting such programs have generally taken a number of successive steps.

The person in the company who is spearheading the elder care initiative is advised to put together a broad-based steering committee or task force, with members drawn from both management and nonmanagement and representing diverse business functions. Members of departments that will be involved in administering the program, such as human resources, benefits and compensation, or employee relations, should be included too.

The working group can help select and refine a proposed elder care option and build consensus around a final decision. The group can be helpful in framing and obtaining support of a budget for the new initiative, and it can assist in the coordination of start-up activities necessary to implement an elder care program.

Early in its work, the group should brief senior management on the initiative. Research has shown that, because of their chronological age, many members of senior management already understand and appreciate elder care issues because they have faced them personally or know someone who has. Failure to enlist support from senior management or taking it for granted until the group completes its work may result in wasted effort and even jeopardize the initiative. Conversely, early commitment from the top can provide leverage for the group's efforts, smooth the implementation process, and increase employee participation.

Finally, the framing of an effective communications program to market the elder care program to employees is essential to its implementation. Because it is virtually impossible to predict which employees will actually make use of the elder care program, the communications program should be multifaceted and reach the largest number of employees. A mailing to employees' homes is the most effective tool initially, since spouses are often involved in elder care. Home mailings can be supplemented by posters, bulletin board announcements, articles in company publications, and other vehicles that a particular company typically uses to communicate to its employees.

Besides informing employees, it is important to communicate to managers and supervisors through a separate vehicle, emphasizing the ways that management can help employees with their elder care needs while maintaining worker productivity.

Managing a Program

How will any new program be managed? Through the company's human resources or benefits and compensation department or by contracting with an expert outside vendor? There are advantages and disadvantages to each approach. Closer control is usually ensured by managing a program in-house. But human resources staffs are often stretched thin, and few have the expertise required to navigate the complex array of services in the elder care field. The geographic scope of a program may also make it difficult to manage a program internally, since elder relatives may live far away from company locations with in-house expertise. Whichever course is chosen, those assisting employees should have professional training in working with older people and their families.

Training of managers and supervisors to be supportive of employees with elder care responsibilities is another essential step in planning and sustaining an elder care program. In 1989, IBM introduced management training on work and family issues for more than 25,000 managers and supervisors. "Middle managers often do not recognize the problems" elder care can cause. "They may be too young to understand," says Barbara Lepis, director of the Partnership for Elder Care, a local partnership of three New York City companies and the New York City Department for the Aging.[40] The partnership trains middle managers and EAP personnel to recognize the symptoms of employees who are experiencing problems providing elder care.

Part of managing the program will be constant communication to employees so they will know about it when they have a need. Making elder care programs visible to employees, not only at announcement but on a continuing basis, should be a priority. This can be accomplished through lunchtime seminars, house organ articles, and executive speeches. Materials used for ongoing communication should stress the many ways that employees are utilizing elder care support. Such materials may be produced in-house or with the help of an outside vendor.

Program Evaluation

Elder care programs are often evaluated solely on their utilization rate— that is, how many employees use the program. Used alone, this measure is inadequate. First, because elder care programs are new, there is little agreement on what a good usage rate is. Second, usage rates do not provide information on employee satisfaction or program performance. And finally, this measure can be influenced by factors extraneous to the programs, such as ineffective communication to employees or the demographic composition of the user population.

An effective evaluation plan starts with thinking about and deciding what information is needed. It should include (1) identification of measurable program objectives such as the employee's success in finding service(s) to resolve an older relative's need, (2) development of instruments or techniques that will give the information necessary to answer those questions, and (3) an analysis plan that will summarize how the information will be used to answer research questions and the criteria for assessing whether key program objectives have been met.

1. *Identification of measurable program objectives and asking the right questions.* A key consideration in asking the right questions is to

think about the information that the evaluation should provide. This process should be tied to the original program objectives, and questions should be framed to reveal specific information to measure whether those objectives have been met. This is usually tied back to the initial needs assessment and the objectives set for the program selected.

2. *Data collection*. There are a variety of data available for evaluation. These can be viewed on a continuum from quantitative measurement to open-ended measurement. They include management information systems data, surveys, focus groups, and individual interviews. Often, several types are useful in capturing quantitative and qualitative information.

3. *Surveys*. Surveys of users are an efficient technique, especially for reaching a large population and when the answers to questions can be put into categories that are complete and mutually exclusive. The survey may pose questions about demographics, how employees heard about the service, whether the service met their expectations, how satisfied they were with the service, whether they found a solution to their problem, and whether they were satisfied with the solution. Surveys are not well suited to collecting detailed, descriptive qualitative or anecdotal information, such as what an employee's elder care situation was and what impact the program had (e.g., how did the service make an employee's life easier, help him or her focus more on work).

Focus Groups

Focus groups of employees are a good way of collecting information about the qualitative issues surrounding elder care. "A focus group can be defined as a carefully planned discussion designed to obtain perception on a defined area of interest in a permissive, non-threatening environment."[41] They allow the major problems and issues to be identified in open-ended discussion among a range of employees. Focus groups are particularly helpful where there is inadequate knowledge of the underlying issues and the difficulties that employees are facing. They can also be used as a first step in designing a survey instrument because they provide a way of defining important issues that can be asked on a survey. However, they are labor intensive and require a trained facilitator, so they are not a cost-effective means of collecting information from a large number of employees. A survey is a more efficient tool for that purpose.

The ideal size of a focus group is six to ten people so that each person can participate fully in the group's discussion. For this interaction to take place, the group should meet for about 2 hours. The goal in selecting participants for each group is to recruit employees who are homogeneous in order to encourage an open and in-depth discussion. Different groups should be put together to represent key work groups—for example, employees who have elder care responsibilities; supervisors, regardless of family responsibilities; hourly employees with parents over age 60; and management and professional employees with parents over age 60.

Recruitment should be done in a manner designed to minimize participant self-selection and to ensure a wide representation of ideas and experience. Recruitment can be handled by identifying and randomly selecting participants from human resources data or by having department supervisors and managers identify a broad selection of employees in each group and then selecting a random sample of that group.

It can be helpful to send letters in advance to both employees and supervisors explaining the purpose of the group and guaranteeing confidentiality.

Sessions should be held in a room that can accommodate the employees. They should be comfortably seated around a table in a room free from distraction.

A focus group should be led by a trained moderator using a previously agreed-to discussion guide. Some areas that should be included are:

- Description of focus groups, objectives, and confidentiality
- Introduction of participants
- Current elder care issues and arrangements
- Impact of caregiving responsibilities on work performance
- Perceived impact of the elder care program (if a program has already been introduced)
- Recommendations for how to address concerns

The consultant, researcher, or vendor selected to conduct focus groups provides a written analysis and report on the groups and meets with company representatives to discuss the results.

Individual Interviews

Another method to supplement other evaluation data are individual interviews with employees who have used the service. Open-ended interviews provide even more in-depth information and additional qualitative data. An outside consultant can be hired to do these, or they can be conducted in-house. In an open-ended interview, the interviewer's function is not to direct the respondent beyond encouraging him or her to talk about a particular topic, in this case, the elder care program. To make these interviews effective, there should be some structure, such as specific issues to probe. Individual interviews should be held in a permissive environment, encouraging the employee to talk freely without fear of disapproval and without too much direction from the interviewer.

Often a program evaluation combines both quantitative and qualitative techniques to elicit a broad picture of how the program is performing and to identify issues or concerns that remain to be addressed. Program evaluation should continue regularly as employee needs and elder care programs evolve.

Building Human Capital

The rapid aging of America is an unprecedented situation that calls for new and innovative solutions at a time when the needs of employees with elder care responsibilities are becoming increasingly clear. The underlying issue is not only a humane concern for those bearing the increasing burdens of elder care; for America's corporations, it is also becoming an issue of lost productivity in the workplace. With severe budgetary constraints cutting back public programs, the private sector can no longer rely on government as the primary source of new programs to aid employee caregivers.

No longer can business concerns be neatly segregated from those of one's personal life. With the work force shortages of the 1990s imminent, activities that were once the sole concern of people in their private lives are now corporate issues as well. As *Business Week* has commented, "Building a new, more diverse work force and making it tick will be one of corporate America's biggest challenges in the decade ahead."[42]

NOTES

1. D. E. Friedman, "Eldercare: The Employee Benefit of the 1990's," *Across the Board* (June 1986).
2. AARP, *A Profile of Older Americans: 1987* (Washington, D.C.: AARP, 1987).
3. Ibid.
4. U.S. Senate, Special Committee on Aging, in conjunction with the AARP, the Federal Council on the Aging, and the Administration on Aging, *Aging America: Trends and Projections, 1985–86*, 99th Cong., 1st and 2nd sess., 1986.
5. N. R. Hooyman and W. Lustbader, *Taking Care: Supporting Older People and Their Families* (New York: Free Press, 1986).
6. U.S. House of Representatives, Subcommittee on Human Services, Select Committee on Aging, *Exploding the Myth: Caregiving in America*, 100th Cong., 1st sess., 1987.
7. Conference Board, Consumer Research Center, *The Changing U.S. Market* (New York: Conference Board, 1988).
8. U.S. Bureau of Labor Statistics, *Projection 2000* (Washington, D.C.: U.S. Government Printing Office, March 1988).
9. U.S. House of Representatives, *Exploding the Myth: Caregiving in America*.
10. N. R. Fritz, "Long Distance Caregiving: Research, Myths and Realities" (paper presented at the National Council on Aging, New Orleans, March 30, 1989).

11. R. S. Azarnoff and A. E. Scharlach, "Can Employees Carry the Eldercare Burden?" *Personnel Journal* (September 1988): 60.
12. Travelers, *The Travelers Employee Caregiver Survey: A Survey on Caregiving Responsibilities of Travelers Employees for Older Americans* (June 1985).
13. M. A. Creedon, ed., *Issues for an Aging America: Employees and Eldercare* (Bridgeport, Conn.: Center for the Study of Aging, University of Bridgeport, 1987).
14. J. D. Carter and D. S. Piktialis, "What to Do about Mother in Milwaukee," *Business and Health* (April 1988): 19–20.
15. *Fortune* Magazine and John Hancock Financial Services, *Corporate and Employee Response to Caring for the Elderly: A National Survey of U.S. Companies and the Workforce* (1989).
16. M. B. Neal, N. J. Chapman, and B. Ingersoll-Dayton, *Eldercare, Employees and the Workplace: Findings from a Survey of Employees* (Portland, Ore.: Research Institute on Aging, Portland State University, 1988).
17. Travelers, *The Travelers Employee Caregiver Survey;* National Association of Area Agencies on Aging, *Breadwinners and Caregivers.*
18. L. J. Warshaw, J. K. Barr, I. Rayman, M. Schachter, and T. G. Lucas, *Employer Support for Employee Caregivers* (New York: New York Business Group on Health, 1986).
19. Bureau of National Affairs, *Bulletin to Management,* BNA Policy and Practice Series (Washington, D.C.: Bureau of National Affairs, February 16, 1989).
20. Azarnoff and Scharlach, "Can Employees Carry the Eldercare Burden?" p. 60.
21. AARP and the Travelers Companies Foundation, *National Survey of Caregivers, Summary of Findings,* (Washington, D.C.: AARP, 1988).
22. AARP, *Caregivers in the Workplace* (Washington, D.C.: Social Outreach and Support Section Program Department, 1987.
23. "Human Capital," *Business Week,* September 19, 1988, pp. 100–120.
24. Friedman, "Eldercare."
25. Travelers, *Travelers Employee Caregiver Survey.*
26. Neal, Chapman, and Ingersoll-Dayton, "Eldercare, Employees and the Workplace."
27. C. Kahn, "Companies Help in Care for Aged," *New York Times,* December 10, 1987, pp. 61–62.
28. Bureau of National Affairs, *Long Distance Eldercare: Spanning the Miles with a New Benefit,* Special Report 22 (Washington, D.C.: Bureau of National Affairs, October 1989).
29. F. Rodgers and C. Rodgers, "Business and the Facts of Family Life," *Harvard Business Review* (November–December 1989).
30. Friedman, "Eldercare."
31. Azarnoff and Scharlach, "Can Employees Carry the Eldercare Burden?" p. 60.
32. K. Liebold, "Employer-Sponsored, On-Site Intergenerational Daycare," *Generations* (special issue on *Business and Aging,* Summer 1989).
33. Rodgers and Rodgers, "Business and the Facts of Family Life."
34. R. E. Allen, "It Pays to Invest in Tomorrow's Work Force," *Wall Street Journal,* November 6, 1989.

35. Bureau of National Affairs, *Long Distance Eldercare*.
36. IBM, *Work and Personal Life Balance Programs*, brochure (November 1989).
37. American Society on Aging, Annual Business Conference, Washington, D.C., October 1989.
38. Rodgers and Rodgers, "Business and the Facts of Family Life."
39. Bureau of National Affairs, *Long Distance Eldercare*.
40. Ibid.
41. Richard Krueger, *Focus Groups* (Newbury Park, Calif.: Sage, 1988).
42. "Human Capital," pp. 100–120.

(continues)

Aetna Life & Casualty Program

In 1988, Aetna's nationwide elder care information and referral service began. It is available to all employees or their spouses who need help for themselves, their parents, or others for whom they are responsible, aged 60 and over. Employees or their spouses can call toll free, from anywhere in the country, and talk with a counselor in the area where their elder relative lives. Elder care services are provided by Work/Family Elder Directions, Inc., a private consulting firm based in Watertown, Massachusetts, with a national network of more than 200 community-based referral organizations familiar with elder care services in their area.

Among Aetna's programs are the following:

Flexible Personnel Policies

▲ Staggered work hours and flextime options
▲ Part-time jobs with full benefits
▲ Job sharing and work-at-home options
▲ Illness-in-the-family paid days
▲ Family leave of absence: Six months unpaid leave with job retained

Benefits

▲ Flexible benefits that encourage choice—for example, a health care spending account, a dependent care spending account, and a long-term-care coverage for employee and spouse
▲ Long-term disability paid by the company

Direct Services

▲ Elder care information, referral, and counseling
▲ Elder care seminars during the workday
▲ Elder care support groups at lunchtime
▲ Family resource lending library of tapes, videos, and books on issues of interest for older workers

Through its elder care program, Aetna has learned a great deal about its employees and their concerns about elder care. Choosing care for an elderly relative is an emotionally charged and sensitive topic. Employees usually feel they should be able to care for an elderly relative on their own. Many exhibit feelings of guilt and denial. Many put off planning for a loved one's care until it's absolutely necessary. And employees find it difficult to talk about their feelings on this subject.

Aetna is among the first companies to hold employee seminars nationwide on elder care. These seminars have been very well received. Of those who have used Aetna's elder care information/referral service:

▲ 95 percent found it helpful.
▲ 98 percent would use the service again.

▲ 71 percent were women, reflecting Aetna's employee population, which is two-thirds female. However, the 29 percent of employees using the service indicate that more men are assuming responsibility for elder care.

▲ 40 percent were long-distance caregivers (living 100 miles or more from the older relative for whom they were seeking help).

Case Histories

The following case histories of those who have used elder care services are illustrative:

▲ An employee called the service for assistance in finding subsidized housing for her father, who is on a limited income. The next day a counselor contacted her with information about an opening at a public housing facility and also told her about several subsidized housing facilities with waiting lists. Jointly, father and daughter could make a decision.

▲ An employee described her father as exhibiting mental deterioration while in the hospital for hip surgery. She needed help with long-term financial planning because her mother, who is more functional, has diabetes. The employee received a referral for estate planning and for respite care to relieve her mother.

▲ A long-distance caregiver needed respite in-home care services to assist her brother with the care of their frail elderly parents. The counselor provided referrals for in-home assistance and discussed the possibility of a hospice program for their mother.

▲ After attending an elder care seminar, an employee requested a handbook. Two weeks later she called to say her 82-year-old father-in-law had recently started showing signs of confusion. She had learned the importance of proper evaluation and requested referrals to geriatricians in the elder's area.

(continues)

Johnson & Johnson Program

As caregivers to ailing spouses or aged parents, the difficulty employees face in finding appropriate elder care can also create great stress. Through Johnson & Johnson's community-based resource and referral network, employees can identify a variety of resources, including care for relatives at distant locations, homemaker services, nursing homes, senior centers, health services, meal services, medical supplies, equipment, and transportation.

The Live for Life program also provides caregivers a variety of educational workshops and materials, support groups, and individual counseling.

Employees with family care responsibilities, whether for children or the elderly, may sign up for the dependent care reimbursement account. Under this program, employees may elect to pay their eligible dependent care expenses on a before-tax basis with money deducted from their salaries before taxes are withheld. The dependent care reimbursement account lowers the employee's taxable salary and allows for reimbursements from the account on a tax-free basis.

From Johnson & Johnson's *Balancing Work and Family* (1989).

The Travelers Program

Let's look at the facts:

▲ One out of every five Travelers employees is responsible for care of an elder.

▲ 67 percent of Travelers workers are women, 65 percent of them in childbearing years.

▲ Our average employee will reach middle age in 1995, sandwiched between elder parents and dependent children.

▲ Almost 40 percent of today's work force are families with both spouses working; another 6 percent are single parents.

▲ One in four parents experience at least one breakdown in their day care arrangement, and employee turnover in day care centers runs at about 35 percent.

The facts speak for themselves: child and elder care are growing issues for today's employee. As we compete for workers in the future, we are going to need new, progressive ways to accommodate these needs.

At the Travelers, we are facing these facts now, with an innovative program of family care benefits. Family care offers meaningful help for the working caretaker: a place to go for information and referrals, time off when you need to care for a dependent and even help in paying the bills.

When it comes to caring for an aging parent or finding high-quality, affordable day care, facts tell only part of the story. These are very personal concerns. The fact that the Travelers recognizes the personal as well as the practical aspects of these issues is what makes our approach unique.

We back our formal family care program with a corporate attitude that recognizes each individual's needs are unique and changing, that acknowledges the stress of balancing professional and personal obligations, and that is willing to explore new options and solutions.

There may not be a single solution. For you, the answer may lie in a combination of services, programs, and benefits. That's why we offer a host of alternatives—from child and elder care referrals to time off and flextime.

Family care also recognizes that your needs are unique and changing. So no matter where you are in life—whether you are a parent, caring for an elder, or approaching retirement—family care offers options that can help.

Caring for Our Elders

Mom gets around so well, I forget she's 73. Still, she worries me, living alone like she does. There's no one nearby to keep an eye on her. We've talked about having her move up here with us, but she hates the city. And it's asking a lot of the family. Besides, I don't think she would come. Still, a day doesn't go by that I don't worry.

Our population is aging. In the past thirty years, the number of senior citizens in this country has doubled, making this the fastest-growing segment of our society. And as baby boomers approach middle age, more and more of us can expect to be caring for an elder.

From *Your Travelers: Passport to Family Care and Your Career* (1990).

(continues)

The Travelers Program (continued)

Now, through family care, you can get help when you are presented with the sensitive and often complex challenges of elder care. Family care offers a national elder care consultation and referral service—a network of specially trained professionals who can give you information, guidance, and help in locating the care that's right for your situation.

Access to the network is easy. A toll-free call puts you in touch with a local specialist who can talk with you about various options, refer you to qualified elder services, or make you aware of other resources that can help.

Whether you are planning for the future or dealing with a crisis, you can get information on a wide range of topics, including medical care, in-home services, housing, community programs, transportation, government subsidies, and case management. Counselors can also guide you to elder care services, ranging from home-delivered meals to nursing home care. Because the network is national, you may also find local assistance for someone who lives elsewhere.

Referral services are intended for those age 60 or older, but this age requirement can be waived for someone with Alzheimer's disease or other illness usually associated with advanced age.

Paying the Bill

The care of a loved one can't be compromised for cost. Yet, the price of quality child and elder care may be outpacing our ability to pay. Child care is now the fourth largest expense working parents have after housing, food and taxes. And just three visits a week by a home health care professional can cost $7,500 a year.

We can't afford to lose qualified employees because they can't afford quality dependent care. Our solution: We help pay the bill.

Family care provides a subsidy for child, elder, or other types of dependent care that allow you to work. It's easy to use. You open a dependent care spending account (DCSA) each year where you deposit part of your pay before tax for dependent care. The company then adds to your account a percentage of what you expect to pay for dependent care, up to an annual maximum based on your income.

Here is a summary of how much you may receive in a Family Care subsidy, based on your income and employment category:

When your annual pay is . . .	The company will pay a percentage of your qualified expenses . . .	Up to an annual maximum subsidy of this amount when you work . . .	
		30 or more hours/week	17½ up to 30 hours/week
Less than $20,000	30%	$1,200	$900
$20,000 to $29,999	20	800	600
$30,000 to $39,999	15	600	450
$40,000 or more	10	400	300

The most that you and the company together may contribute to your account for the year is $5,000.

Time Off to Care

Rhonda is the ideal employee. I don't know what I would do without her. But she's going through a tough time right now. Her husband is really sick, and I know she's torn between home and work. I think she's even thinking about leaving. Maybe there's something we can do. I would hate to lose her.

At the Travelers, we recognize that—in today's world—we can't just manage work. We have to manage people. That means we need to acknowledge the demands and challenges our employees face not only as professionals but as individuals.

To help you manage the personal and professional demands on your time, the Travelers offers a formal policy of paid time off and unpaid family leave.

You can take up to three paid days off each year to care for family members who are ill. For example, you could use this time to take a sick child to the doctor or to help a parent check into the hospital. Family members include your children, spouse, parents, or any other relative that lives with you.

When family commitments require extended time away from work, you may consider an unpaid family care leave. You may request from one week to twelve months off for the birth or adoption of a child, to care for a relative who is very ill, or to deal with another family-related issue. If the leave is six months or less, you can return to your original or a commensurate position, based on what you and your manager decide before you leave. If the leave is more than six months, you may return to the original position if it is open or to a commensurate position if available.

(continues)

Sample Survey Instrument

The questions on this survey ask about your caregiving responsibilities—that is, any activities you do in order to take care of or provide care for an older family member, relative, or friend. These activities could range from shopping for another person who cannot do their own shopping or tending to a bed-bound or home-bound person. Your answers will be kept in the *strictest confidence* and will be used for *statistical purposes only*. So please be open and candid in giving your responses. Please return the survey whether you have caregiving responsibilities or not.

1. **First, please indicate below your general job classification.**
   - (1) ☐ Clerical/Support
   - (2) ☐ Management
   - (3) ☐ Production
   - (4) ☐ Technical
   - (5) ☐ Other

2. **What age group do you fall into?**
   - (1) ☐ Under 30 years
   - (2) ☐ 30–35 years
   - (3) ☐ 36–40 years
   - (4) ☐ 41–45 years
   - (5) ☐ 46–50 years
   - (6) ☐ 51–55 years
   - (7) ☐ 56–60 years
   - (8) ☐ 61 or older

3. **What is your marital status?**
   - (1) ☐ Single
   - (2) ☐ Married
   - (3) ☐ Widowed
   - (4) ☐ Divorced/Separated

4. **And are you . . .**
   - (1) ☐ Female
   - (2) ☐ Male

5. **How long have you been with this organization/corporation?**
   _____ Years

6. **How many children do you have living at home who are . . . (*Please circle the appropriate number or numbers*)**
   - (1) I have no children living at home _____
   - (2) Number of children under age 6 . . . . 1 2 3 4 or more
   - (3) Number of children 6–18 years old . . . . 1 2 3 4 or more
   - (4) Number of children 19 or older . . . . 1 2 3 4 or more

7. **If others, besides children, live with you, please indicate below which people live with you. (*Check all that apply*)**
   - (1) ☐ Spouse
   - (2) ☐ Father or mother

American Association of Retired Persons (AARP) gratefully acknowledges the assistance of The Travelers Companies, which granted AARP permission to adapt for its use The Travelers Companies June 1985 Employee Caregivers Survey. This survey was produced under the auspices of AARP's Women's Initiative which responds to the special concerns and interests of midlife and older women.

(3) ☐ Father-in-law or mother-in-law
(4) ☐ A brother or sister
(5) ☐ Aunt or uncle
(6) ☐ Another relative
(7) ☐ A friend
(8) ☐ Other

8. **Do you have anyone *aged 50 or older* for whom you have caregiving responsibility?**
   (1) ☐ Yes
   (2) ☐ No (If 'No,' that completes the questionnaire—Please return it to person listed on the last page—Thank you)

9. **If "yes," in question 8, how many persons *aged 50 or older* do you have caregiving responsibility for?**
   (1) ☐ One   (2) ☐ Two   (3) ☐ Three or more

   If you care for more than one person, please report on the *one person* for whom you provide the *most* care when answering questions 10–17.

10. **Where does the person for whom you have caregiving responsibility live?**
    (1) In your home .... ☐
    (2) In their own home (near yours) .... ☐
    (3) In their own home (a distance from yours) .... ☐
    (4) In a nursing home (near your home) .... ☐
    (5) In a nursing home (a distance from your home) .... ☐
    (6) Other (specify) _____ .... ☐

11. **If you indicated that a person you are caring for lives in a separate residence, how often do you visit with him or her?**
    (1) Never .... ☐
    (2) Monthly .... ☐
    (3) More than once a month .... ☐
    (4) Weekly .... ☐
    (5) Almost every day .... ☐

12. **Please provide the following information about the person you are caring for.**
    (1) Person's Age _____
    (2) Sex (M = Male   F = Female) _____
    (3) Relation to you (father, mother, in-law, etc.) _____
    (4) How long have you been caring for the person? _____

13. **Who provides most of the care for the person? (*Please check only one*)**
    (1) You .... ☐
    (2) Your spouse .... ☐
    (3) Your father or mother .... ☐
    (4) Your children .... ☐
    (5) Father-in-law or mother-in-law .... ☐
    (6) Your brother or sister .... ☐
    (7) Brother-in-law or sister-in-law .... ☐
    (8) Other relative .... ☐
    (9) Friend .... ☐
    (10) Outside paid help .... ☐
    (11) Other (specify) .... ☐

14. **Currently, how many medical problems are experienced by the person you are caring for (for example, stroke, glaucoma, high blood pressure, heart problems,**

(continues)

Sample Survey Instrument (continued)

cancer, diabetes, memory loss, sleep disorders, Alzheimer's disease, arthritis, incontinence, blindness, depression)?

15. **Did any of the following events happen to the person to cause the need for you to provide care for him or her?** (*Check all that apply*)
    (1) Major illness/injury .... ☐
    (2) Progressive health deterioration .... ☐
    (3) Hospitalization .... ☐
    (4) Death of spouse .... ☐
    (5) Retirement .... ☐
    (6) Laid off or fired from job .... ☐
    (7) Other (specify) _____ .... ☐

16. What kinds of help do you provide to the person? (***Check all that apply***)
    (1) Direct financial support .... ☐
    (2) Manage person's finances .... ☐
    (3) Do household chores for person such as shopping, cooking, laundry, maintenance of living quarters .... ☐
    (4) Assist person with personal care (dressing, bathing, feeding, toileting, etc.) .. ☐
    (5) Provide help moving about in the house or apartment .... ☐
    (6) Provide transportation .... ☐
    (7) Administer medications .... ☐
    (8) Provide companionship by personal visits or by telephone .... ☐
    (9) Make or receive telephone calls for person .... ☐
    (10) Arrange/coordinate outside help for person .... ☐
    (11) Other (specify) _____ .... ☐

17. How many hours **per week** do the following people spend in providing care for the person you are caring for?
    (1) You .... _____ hrs
    (2) Others living within your household .... _____ hrs
    (3) Friends/relatives living outside your household .... _____ hrs
    (4) Paid outside help .... _____ hrs

18. For each of the categories of activities below, please indicate how often your caregiving responsibilities interfere with these activities.

	Most of the time (1)	Often (2)	Sometimes (3)	Seldom (4)	Never (5)
(1) Outside activities (clubs, shopping, etc.)	_____	_____	_____	_____	_____
(2) Work or job	_____	_____	_____	_____	_____
(3) Other family responsibilities (spouse, children, etc.)	_____	_____	_____	_____	_____
(4) Quiet time or rest	_____	_____	_____	_____	_____

19. Other than help provided by you or another family member, does the person receive help from an outside source?

    (1) ☐Yes   (2) ☐No (If 'No,' go to question 21)

20. **If 'Yes' above, which of the following kinds of help does the person receive?** (*Check all that apply*)

    Outside help used for:

    (1) ☐ Homemaking chores (cooking, laundry, etc.)
    (2) ☐ Repairs/maintenance to the household
    (3) ☐ Personal care
    (4) ☐ Companion services
    (5) ☐ Nursing services/therapy
    (6) ☐ Home-delivered meals
    (7) ☐ Counseling
    (8) ☐ Adult day care
    (9) ☐ Transportation
    (10) ☐ Telephone monitoring or reassurance
    (11) ☐ Other (specify) _____

21. Which one of the following has been most helpful in providing information about outside resources available to help in providing care for the person you are caring for? (*Please check only one*)

    (1) ☐ Family physician
    (2) ☐ Visiting nurse or other health care professional
    (3) ☐ Clergy
    (4) ☐ Counselor/social worker
    (5) ☐ Employee assistance or counseling program
    (6) ☐ Friends/family
    (7) ☐ Other (specify) _____
    (8) ☐ Supervisor or co-worker
    (9) ☐ None of the above

22. Do you or do you not need additional assistance in order to continue providing care to the person? (*Please check only one*)

    (1) ☐ I *do not* need assistance, I can continue to provide care.
    (2) ☐ I need *some assistance,* but generally I can do it myself.
    (3) ☐ I need *considerable assistance* in order to continue.
    (4) ☐ Even *with* assistance, I may not be able to continue.

23. When were you last able to take a vacation that allowed you some time away from your caregiving responsibilities? (*Please check only one*)

    (1) ☐ Less than 6 months ago
    (2) ☐ Between 6–12 months ago
    (3) ☐ Between 13 months and 2 years ago
    (4) ☐ More than 2 years ago

24. How helpful would specific information on the following topics be in assisting you with your caregiving responsibilities?

Information on:	Not Very Helpful (1)	Somewhat Helpful (2)	Very Helpful (3)
(1) Specific illnesses	————	————	————
(2) Home care	————	————	————

(continues)

Sample Survey Instrument (continued)

Information on:	Not Very Helpful (1)	Somewhat Helpful (2)	Very Helpful (3)
(3) Community resources	_____	_____	_____
(4) Housing options	_____	_____	_____
(5) How to choose a nursing home	_____	_____	_____
(6) Useful tips for caregivers	_____	_____	_____
(7) Effective communications	_____	_____	_____
(8) Questions to ask your physician	_____	_____	_____
(9) Normal aging process	_____	_____	_____
(10) Stress management	_____	_____	_____
(11) Mental incapacities and aging	_____	_____	_____
(12) Other (specify) _____	_____	_____	_____

25. Which of the following supports would you use if they were available? (*Check all that apply*)
    (1) ☐ Caregivers Fair—an information fair about community resources.
    (2) ☐ Educational Seminars—a series of information sessions.
    (3) ☐ Audio Cassette Tapes—containing useful information for caregivers.
    (4) ☐ Support Groups—scheduled meetings with other caregivers to discuss issues and share helpful information.
    (5) ☐ Respite—temporary relief from caregiving by allowing a trained person to care for relative.

26. How many days (if any) have you lost from work during the past 6 months for the following reasons. (*Enter the number of days for each reason*)
    (1) Illness(es) .... _____ days
    (2) Family emergencies .... _____ days
    (3) Crisis/emergency with person being cared for .... _____ days
    (4) Lack of sleep .... _____ days
    (5) On-the-job accident .... _____ days
    (6) Other (specify) _____ .... _____ days
    (7) _____ Check if *no* days lost in past 6 months

27. Is there someone at work with whom you can discuss your personal problems or family life issues? (*Check all that apply*)
    (1) ☐ No one
    (2) ☐ Co-worker
    (3) ☐ Supervisor
    (4) ☐ Company nurse
    (5) ☐ Employee assistance counselor
    (6) ☐ Other (specify) _____

28. During the past 6 months, have you suffered from any of the following? (*Please check all that apply*)
    (1) ☐ Frequent headaches
    (2) ☐ Weight gain or loss

    (3) ☐ Skin disorders
    (4) ☐ Nervousness
    (5) ☐ Unusual drowsiness
    (6) ☐ Inability to sleep
    (7) ☐ Other (specify) _____

Additonal Comments: _____
_____
_____
_____

That completes the questionnaire. Thank you very much for your time. Please return to:
_____
_____
_____

8

Retirement Counseling

Denise F. Loftus
American Association of Retired Persons (AARP)

Retirement can mean embarking on a new and vital phase of life filled with fresh opportunities, expanded interests, new friends, and deep satisfactions. It can be the most productive and enjoyable time of life, a career like no other—if it is planned for in a constructive and comprehensive way.

For the majority of workers, the idea of retiring from work was unheard of until this century. Most people continued to work until they died or became unable to perform what were often arduous jobs under poor working conditions. With the advent of social security in 1935, Americans ages 65 and older were guaranteed a continuing source of supplemental income. This was followed in the 1940s and 1950s by a rapid increase in the number of private pension plans offered by employers desiring to compete effectively with other employers and to fulfill a commitment to their workers and community.

These two phenomena launched the new era of formal retirement from work. It was not until the 1950s, however, that a few employers began to offer seminars and programs to prepare employees for the financial and emotional adjustments of retirement. Informal estimates of the frequency of ongoing retirement education and counseling programs typically range from 30 to 45 percent for all types and sizes of employers. Even today, the most frequent type of retirement counseling consists solely of providing eligible employees with basic information about their benefits, usually within a few years of anticipated retirement. Given the realities facing today's and tomorrow's retirees, this is a grossly inadequate approach to retirement planning.

In the 1990s, retirement planning is emerging as a vital issue in the life planning of American workers. The aging of the population, the approach of the baby boomers to their half-century mark, world economic trends and countertrends, escalating health care costs, changes in the U.S. workplace—all point to the growing need for individuals to plan for their future earlier and more effectively.

Today, on reaching age 65 an individual can expect to live another nineteen to twenty-two years.[1] At the same time, the average age at which employees retire has declined steadily since World War II. The labor force participation rate for men ages 55–64 fell from 83 percent in 1970 to 67.2 percent in 1989 (Figure 8-1). Nearly half of all male workers and nearly 60 percent of all female workers begin receiving social security benefits at 62, the earliest age possible.[2]

Americans are living longer, healthier lives and have greater expectations for what those added years can offer. At the same time, many people are experiencing increasing fears about how to pay for the retirement lifestyle they want and how to protect their health so that they can fully enjoy their later years.

Retirement counselors now speak of phases of retirement—early, middle, and late retirement—each with its own set of rewards, issues, and challenges. For example, the housing and community that is best suited for a couple in early retirement may be inappropriate for a widowed spouse living alone in later years. Yet financial decisions about housing made in preparation for retirement will largely determine the range of choices available many years down the road. This same complexity holds for other key areas of retirement planning.

Workers are becoming more keenly aware of the need to come to grips with the financial and other aspects of a lengthy retirement. They are discovering that, unlike the preceding generation of retirees, they will need to shoulder a greater part of the financial burden. Costly government

Figure 8-1. Labor force participation rate of older Americans for selected years.

Year	Men			Women		
	45–54	55–64	65 and Older	45–54	55–64	65 and Older
1970	94.3%	83.0%	26.6%	54.4%	43.0%	9.7%
1975	92.1	75.6	21.6	54.6	40.9	8.2
1980	91.2	72.1	19.0	59.9	41.3	8.1
1981	91.4	70.6	18.3	61.1	41.3	8.0
1982	91.2	70.2	17.8	61.6	41.8	7.9
1983	91.2	69.4	17.4	61.9	41.5	7.8
1984	91.2	68.5	16.3	62.9	41.7	7.5
1985	91.0	68.0	15.8	64.4	42.0	7.3
1986	90.1	67.3	16.0	65.9	42.3	7.4
1987	90.7	67.6	16.3	67.1	42.7	7.4
1988	90.9	67.0	16.5	69.0	43.5	7.9
1989	91.1	67.2	16.6	70.5	45.1	8.3
2000	90.5	68.1	14.7	76.5	49.0	7.6

Source: Employee Benefit Research Institute, *Trends and Issues in Early Retirement,* no. 103 (June 1990): 5. Copyright © 1990 Employee Benefit Research Institute. Reprinted by permission.

benefits programs are continually under scrutiny and may change in unpredictable ways. Employers are finding that financing retirement for their employees is very costly, especially given growing international competition in the marketplace. Thus, it appears that increasing numbers of employers will be placing more responsibility for financing retirement onto the worker in the years to come.

Given these new realities, retirement education and counseling can serve as a vital means for employers to provide employees with essential information. More important, it can arm employees with the coping skills and strategies they need to make informed choices about their future life-style and how to achieve the financial means for maintaining that life-style throughout their retirement.

Between 1990 and 2030, more workers will retire than during any other previous thirty-year period in history. These individuals and their families will confront new necessities and new choices in addition to the basic life changes retirees have traditionally faced. Increasing numbers of workers and responsible employers will be looking for innovative and dynamic retirement planning approaches to meet these challenges.[3]

Benefits of Retirement Planning

Retirement planning programs are one of the most positive and cost-effective benefits an organization can provide its employees. A comprehensive, well-thought-out program offers direct and indirect benefits to the employer as well.

Employees who participate in a retirement planning program better understand the company's benefits and the role these benefits play in their long-term financial security. Younger employees in particular benefit from having this information. They will have a longer period over which to accumulate financial assets that can finance retirement along with employer and government benefits.

For more and more people, work of some kind will play an important part in their long-range financial security and their social and psychological well-being too. Retirement planning can explore this issue and provide strategies for identifying interests and abilities, community resources, and various work options.[4] Program participants learn to develop strategies not only to cope with financial realities but also to identify potential health, relationship, legal, and other issues and develop strategies for coping with them.

Retirement planning programs help employees identify the needs being met by work and how they can be replaced in retirement—for example, needs for social interaction, a sense of purpose, and a structure to daily living. Recognizing these needs, program participants can begin to put in place another support system prior to retiring, facilitating the transition to retirement in the process.

Finally, retirement planning programs provide a comfortable and supportive environment in which employees can discuss the reality of retirement with both subject matter experts and their peers.

The employer who offers retirement planning education and counseling also reaps many rewards. Retirement planning:

▴ Increases interest in company benefits and is a vehicle by which employees can ask questions about their benefits. It thus serves as a way to augment the provision in the Employment Retirement Income Security Act (ERISA) requiring employers to provide employees annually with a summary of pension plan provisions and benefits.

▴ Improves the morale and productivity of employees by relieving anxiety about retirement and by giving them a sense of control over their future.

▴ Helps employees determine when to retire or whether to take advantage of voluntary early retirement options by giving them information about their benefits and other retirement planning issues and by arming them with various coping strategies.

▴ Can lessen the requests for individual counseling by addressing key issues in a group setting and by motivating employees to take greater responsibility for their retirement planning. For example, programs provide an ideal setting to review company retirement benefits and their relationship to social security benefits.

▴ Can be a key selling point in recruiting. Such programs are one way employers can be responsive to employee interests and needs, particularly as younger workers see the value in this kind of ongoing education and long-range planning.

▴ Creates a positive image of the employer in the community by generating satisfied retirees who become goodwill ambassadors for the organization.

In the business world, strategic planning is an integral part of operation. Goals and objectives are set, reviewed, and modified. Budgets and activities are planned to meet these goals. Shouldn't individuals do the same with their own lives? Retirement planning education and counseling motivates and helps employees to plan effectively for the rest of their lives. An employer's ability to empower employees to plan for their future may well be the most significantly "human" human resources function an organization can perform.

Selling Retirement Planning to Management

To establish and implement a first-rate retirement planning program demands the commitment of management, adequate budgeted funds and staff time, and dedicated in-house professionals to develop and administer the program. Depending on the organization, management may include the board of directors, chief executive officer, department managers or directors, and supervisors, as well as the staff who will establish and maintain the program. Management commitment to both the concept of retirement planning and the program itself will minimize problems and ensure adequate financial support.

If an organization does not have a retirement planning program, often the first step is preparation of a proposal to management. This requires gathering information on the employee population, determining the cost of implementing a program in terms of dollars and human resources, and presenting a summary of the benefits of a program to both the organization and its employees.

Initial research and data collection for a proposal might include collecting newspaper and magazine articles, reports, and studies on employment and retirement trends for a particular industry and the demographic trends of the organization's work force, relating these to national trends.

A proposal should include a budget for initial setup and ongoing use of retirement planning in terms of dollars and staff time, a statement concerning the company's benefits program, and an overview of the issues that retirement planning education will address. It should provide an analysis of an initial program with a recommendation for growth and an assessment of internal company capabilities and costs. Additional important information concerns what is available in the way of programs and service providers and which ones are likely to meet organizational goals at a realistic cost.

It is also essential to examine the reasons that managers most often give for not having a retirement planning program. Even if management recognizes the value of retirement planning, there are several administrative reasons why programs may not be adopted. Employers responding to the Spencer survey[5] gave the following reasons for not implementing an ongoing retirement education program for their employees:

A younger work force	25%
A lack of perceived needs	24%
Cost	15%
A combination of the three	12%
Other reasons, such as lack of priority and insufficient personnel	24%

Any of the following reasons that apply to the organization should be addressed in the program proposal:

▴ *No employee interest.* Younger workers are beginning to realize that they will bear greater responsibility for their long-term financial well-being than their parents or grandparents. Forward-thinking employers are providing primarily financial planning for those in their twenties and thirties as part of an overall life/work planning approach. More and more employees recognize the need for such programs and are expecting their employers to provide them. Although it is the responsibility of the individual employee to plan his or her own future, the organization can provide the learning environment and information to help facilitate this process.

▴ *Too costly.* Retirement planning is a low-cost benefit given after years of employee service. The public relations value of a good program is incalculable. Retirement planning programs produce more positive and productive employees and retirees, a valuable asset to the organization. Participants return to their work with a greater sense of security, which results in higher productivity and a greater commitment to an organization that has shown a genuine commitment to its employees.

▴ *No qualified personnel available.* Many retirement planning service providers offer the option of professional staff and volunteers to develop and administer the program or to assist in-house personnel in those functions, and many train in-house personnel in presenting their programs.

▴ *Too time-consuming of employees' time.* Programs can be offered during or after work hours. Sessions can be designed to maximize effectiveness while minimizing time: they can be concentrated in two or three days or spaced over a period of weeks; they can run from one to three hours each session, covering one or more related topics. Other options are available to fit the program to the needs of the employer and the employee.

▴ *No desire to bear legal responsibility for advice given to employees on financial and legal issues.* A good retirement planning program does not give a participant advice. Rather, it provides insights into options and alternatives that may not previously have been explored. Participants must define their own solutions.

A well-researched and well-thought-out proposal to win management support presents a walk-through of a typical program, simulating one of the sessions with executives as participants. This exercise will help them relate what they are learning to their own situation and thus see its value from a more personal perspective. A presentation can also feature managers and staff from related organizations that are already offering successful retirement planning programs. Their enthusiasm and experiences will go a long way in convincing one's own management about the value of retirement planning programs.

With at least a tentative green light from management, staff can then launch a pilot program for selected employees. This will give management and staff direct feedback from the work force and a better idea of the organization's resources that will be required to establish and maintain a first-rate program.

Evaluating Potential Programs

After identifying work force needs and researching retirement planning in the area and industry, available programs and services need to be evaluated on program goals and objectives, the teaching-learning style used, the program materials themselves, delivery modes available, ability to tailor the program to the organization's specific needs, ongoing support provided, and cost.

Information about available programs can be obtained from similar organizations with retirement planning programs, by attending sessions as a participant, by interviewing prospective service providers, and by careful review of the program materials. (A list of retirement planning service providers appears at the end of the chapter.)

Program Goals and Objectives

Retirement planning education should inform participants about the basic issues of retirement, motivate them to take action in planning for their future, enable them to proceed independently by providing viable strategies in the key retirement planning areas, and offer ongoing support through identifying resources for more in-depth research.

Responsible retirement education offers alternatives, not solutions. It emphasizes that there is no one right answer for everyone. Each person is unique and must assume personal responsibility for researching, testing, and selecting the best alternative.

Teaching-Learning Style

All precepts of adult learning stress the need for the individual to be an active participant in the learning process, an approach that differs markedly from the way most potential retirees were taught during their school days. Fortunately, with the explosion of continuing education, many adults have been exposed to more appropriate and supportive learning environments.

A good retirement planning program treats participants as responsible, independent adults by involving them in diagnosing their own learning needs and by drawing on their experiences and insights to benefit the group as a whole. It recognizes that participants are looking for practical approaches to retirement issues and want tangible results.

In addition to establishing a warm, receptive, nonjudgmental atmosphere, a good program uses various techniques to facilitate involvement by every participant—for example, discussion of case studies, role playing, buzz sessions, brainstorming, and between-session interviews with retirees, followed by discussion at the next session.

Retirement Education Materials

Printed materials—books or manuals for participants and program leaders—are usually part of retirement planning education. Program materials on the market range from brief overviews of basic retirement topics to workbooks with informational reading, case studies, exercises, and extensive resource lists. Films, videos, and even a few computer software packages are available.

Materials can be obtained on loan and reviewed for accuracy and relevancy. For certain topics such as social security, Medicare, tax laws, and estate planning, an in-house expert or someone knowledgeable in the community should review the materials. Programs being considered should review their materials annually and revise them periodically to reflect the latest information.

Topics Covered

Basic retirement education and counseling provides employees with information about the benefits they can expect to receive from the organization upon retirement. At the next level, programs include primarily financial information such as personal financial planning, estate planning, and how social security relates to company benefits.

Comprehensive retirement education, however, recognizes that there are no purely financial decisions. Rather, it is necessary to analyze the broader issues, problems, and challenges people may face in retirement. For example, without a clear idea of how and where an individual wants to live—that is, preferred retirement life-style—there is no basis for making financial, and even legal, decisions.

A thorough approach to retirement planning includes information and discussion about attitude and role adjustments, changing family relationships, housing needs at various stages of later life, health and health insurance, including long-term care, work in retirement, volunteering, hobbies, and other uses of time. Of growing importance are such issues as health insurance and meeting medical costs, caregiving, long-term-care insurance, changing tax laws affecting pension payouts, changing society security regulations regarding age of eligibility for full benefits and earnings limitations, and developing job search skills for work in retirement.

Delivery Formats

Retirement education can be delivered on a one-to-one counseling basis, in a group program, or through a combination of the two. There are also self-study programs that can be augmented with individual counseling and/

or group sessions. Factors to consider in selecting a format are the number of participants, the ability of the program leader, the budget, and the amount of time and effort the organization, program leader, and participants are able to commit to the program.

SELF-STUDY FORMAT

The simplest format, though often the least effective, is merely to provide printed materials or videos on retirement planning for employees to use on their own time. Some organizations are adding software packages on financial planning that include programs on company pension and benefits. This format is best used to supplement other delivery formats.

The self-study format is useful for organizations with employees in numerous locations such as small regional offices or plants. Program participants in the same area can be encouraged to form study groups and to meet regularly to discuss the issues and to exchange ideas and information.

Computer software programs offer an alternative to traditional self-study methods. Although many focus on financial planning, there is at least one software program available nationally that deals with a broad range of retirement planning issues—finances, investments, budgeting, estate planning, family records, leisure time, and life-style. Working in phases, an employee can create a personal retirement program. The program offers the individual user complete confidentiality, and the system can be customized for employers to reflect benefits packages.[6]

INDIVIDUAL EMPLOYEE COUNSELING SESSIONS

These sessions, offered by growing numbers of employers, typically provide each employee with personal information on pensions and benefits, as well as any other company retirement options requiring decisions or more information. Although this service is usually of the greatest interest to employees, it often is not provided until the employee is within a year or two of retirement. In order to plan effectively, employees of all ages should receive this information annually and be given an opportunity to review it and ask questions.

GROUP PROGRAMS

These programs are often offered by organizations along with individual benefits counseling. If the group sessions are conducted first, less time is needed for individual counseling because the group sessions answer basic questions and give participants a broader perspective on retirement. Therefore, they come to individual counseling better prepared. Group programs can be divided into two basic kinds: (1) lectures and (2) small group discussions or seminars.

The lecture is familiar to anyone who has ever been in a classroom. An expert in a particular field makes a presentation, often followed by a question-and-answer period. In retirement planning, the lecture format is used principally with groups of fifty or more. The chief purpose of a lecture is to provide information. It is considered less effective than the seminar format because it typically provides only minimal opportunity for discussion or interaction among the attendees. Given a small enough group, a good facilitator, and appropriate physical facilities, however, certain techniques of the seminar format—case study discussion, role playing or simulation, games, quizzes, buzz sessions, and brainstorming— can be incorporated into a lecture program to increase group participation.

The small group discussion or seminar format affords the optimum adult learning environment. The seminar is not designed primarily to present a large volume of information but rather to stimulate thought and discussion on the part of the participants, to motivate them to take charge of planning their futures, and to provide basic strategies for doing so. The seminar most effectively incorporates the basic principles of adult learning theory. It is based on the premise that each participant has a wealth of knowledge and experience to share and that participants learn from the mutual exchange of information and ideas.

Typically, the seminar is led by a facilitator, who stimulates discussion and keeps the session on target. There usually is a content expert to help answer technical questions that arise pertaining to the subject under discussion.

Optimal group size for the seminar format is from sixteen to twenty-four people, to allow for a variety of ideas and experiences while giving everyone ample opportunity to contribute.

Elements of the lecture format can be added to the seminar format, and vice versa. For example, when dealing with the more technical topics such as social security and estate planning, the seminar can provide for an overview by an expert followed by questions and answers, as is done in the lecture format. A lecture program can allow time to break into small groups for discussion of a key question addressed in the lecture. Group size and time permitting, each subgroup's solutions can be shared with the entire group. Or the lecturer can incorporate a brainstorming segment, using a chart to record solutions offered by individuals in the group to a particular retirement planning question.

Choice of format may hinge not only on time and budget constraints but also on the number of individuals needing immediate retirement planning assistance. If a large organization has never offered retirement planning and has hundreds of employees eligible for a program, a lecture format is often necessary. As the number decreases, however, a change to a seminar or a modified lecture format is encouraged.

Several small employers or organizations with relatively few middle-aged and older employees may wish to consider cosponsoring a retirement planning program. A consortium of employers, for example, can contract with a retirement planning service provider to develop and present a program to eligible employees.

In one community, an association of retired executives presents a retirement planning program to employees of small businesses in the area. Small businesses in another community send eligible employees to a program provided at the local community college. Such joint programs can be supplemented by individual counseling on each company's own retirement benefits.

Tailoring Retirement Planning Programs

Flexibility and adaptability are crucial factors to consider when evaluating potential off-the-shelf programs. Some materials are inappropriate for different levels of employees and can strike participants as simplistic or otherwise irrelevant to their situation.

A service provider should be able and willing to tailor its program's content and presentation modes to meet a client organization's goals and objectives. Besides meeting time and budget requirements, the program should be adaptable enough to appeal to the ages, income levels, and life-styles of potential participants. For example, for a younger work force, can the service provider offer sequential steps in an overall life planning approach, with greater emphasis on financial planning and career development for people with long-term mortgages and children's educations to consider?

A frequent criticism of off-the-shelf retirement planning materials is that they focus almost exclusively on married couples and do not address the needs of always single and recently single middle-aged preretirees. To respond to these and other special interests and needs of its preretirees, one large employer annually offers a series of optional seminars. Besides covering the basic retirement planning topics such as company benefits, social security, financial planning, and health and fitness, the organization offers seminars on women's issues and on caring for an elderly relative, among others.

Ongoing Program Support

In evaluating potential programs and service, providers ask about ongoing program support, such as training in administering and leading the program, networking available with other program users, and periodic consultation with program specialists to deal with any problems that might arise. Some service providers publish newsletters to keep program users informed about changes in the program and innovations introduced by other users.

Does the service provider offer the option of professionals to develop, administer, and/or present the program? Does the service provider provide guidance in the ethical use of retirement planning in connection with early retirement incentive offers? And are program materials reviewed and updated periodically? How are program changes conveyed to users and at what cost?

Program Cost

Finally, potential retirement planning education programs should be evaluated as to direct and indirect costs to the organization. The cost per employee to offer retirement planning education and counseling can cover a broad range, depending on the services provided and materials used.

Direct costs to present a group program may include:

▴ *Participant workbooks or manuals.* Prices range from free publications to single-subject pamphlets for $3 to $5 to multi-issue workbooks for $15 to $50.

▴ *Program administrator and leader materials.* Prices range from $150 to $750.

▴ *Training programs for program administrators and leaders.* Prices range from $450 to $750 and up. Training generally includes the administrator and leader materials.

▴ *Supplemental video materials.* Prices range from $95 to $350 to purchase; some can be rented.

▴ *Software packages.* Financial planning and other software packages can be designed for a particular organization or bought off the shelf. Prices vary.

Other direct program costs might include the cost of a facility, custodial services, meals or refreshments served, promotional materials (invitation letters, flyers, posters, brochures, and pay envelope inserts), and fees or honoraria for speakers, facilitators, and content experts. (Often content experts donate their time as a public service.)

Available Materials

Local programs conducted through adult education centers, community colleges, and other educational and civic organizations can be found in many communities. There are also a variety of national service providers. Some service providers are nonprofit; others are for-profit ventures. Their programs vary as to format, content, presentation methods, training, and kinds of ongoing support offered. They range from comprehensive multimedia programs to those specializing in a particular area, such as financial planning or benefit analysis. (A brief list of national retirement planning service providers appears at the end of this chapter.)

Program Administration and Leadership

Once commitment from management has been obtained and the budget established, those responsible for implementing the program can proceed. The staff most often responsible for retirement planning education and counseling are in the benefits, training, or human resources department. Usually one or two people are assigned the organization's retirement planning functions.

A distinction needs to be made between administering the program and leading the program. The administrator is responsible for scheduling the sessions, overseeing the program's budget, inviting the participants, making the facility arrangements, ordering materials and equipment, promoting the program, assisting the program leader during the program itself, and performing any necessary program follow-up such as reviewing evaluations and sending thank-you notes. The program leader serves as the moderator for a lecture or the facilitator for a seminar. The leader's major function is to facilitate the learning process during the sessions.

In some organizations, the roles and responsibilities of the administrator and the program leader are filled by one person. In most cases, however, both roles prove too time-consuming for one person to do them well.

Those who administer and lead programs should believe in the value of retirement planning and be able to generate support and enthusiasm for the program in others. Those developing and implementing a program must make a number of key decisions.

Selecting Dates, Time, and Place

Each organization must weigh the pros and cons of programs held on company time versus those held in the evening or on weekends. If held on company time, the program is given more prestige; however, fewer spouses or other guests can usually attend daytime sessions. If the program is held in the evening, issues of transportation, parking, safety, and meals must be resolved. For employers with shift workers, another dimension is added.

Next, consideration must be given to how many sessions to hold and how long each session should run. There are many options: from full-day programs to one-, two-, or three-day duration to a series of sessions running over six to ten weeks. Individual sessions can run from one to three hours, covering one or two subjects a session. Spacing the sessions over a number of weeks allows for more in-depth study of a particular topic; however, it also increases the likelihood that participants will miss one or more sessions because of vacations, illness, or for other reasons.

Holding the program on company premises is less expensive and allows participants to handle important work matters during program breaks. Holding the program somewhere else, on the other hand, gives participants a complete break from work, thus enabling them to give their full attention to the program.

Wherever the program is held, the facilities should be comfortable and conducive to learning. They should convey the message that retirement planning is important to both management and employees.

Decisions about dates, time, and place must be made in the light of budget and time constraints, availability of experts and facilities, and the interest and commitment of the organization and the participants.

Choosing the Participants

How large is the potential pool of employees to include in retirement planning programs? Who should be invited first? An organization launching its first program usually starts with those nearest to retirement and works down to younger employees. Currently, most companies offer programs to employees who are age 55 or older or who are within three to five years of possible retirement. Growing numbers of organizations are offering retirement and life planning programs to those in their forties, and a few larger companies are offering programs to all employees. Certainly it is never too late to begin, but the closer a person is to retirement, the less time he or she has to make changes and choices that could greatly enhance the later years, particularly in financial planning.

The ages and income levels of participants will determine topics and emphasis of the program. Employees in their twenties and thirties typically want to focus on financial and career planning. Starting in the forties, broader issues become more salient to the group: long-term health, housing, use of time, and changes in roles and relationships.

The wisdom of mixing employees of diverse job and economic levels depends largely on how much detail on finances and benefits is to be included in the program. The staff person making these decisions should have a good understanding of the work force and how different areas relate to one another. Where there are unions represented, often union members prefer to have their own programs.

Employers are encouraged to invite spouses and significant others of employees to the program. Many employers find that a letter to the employee's home with an invitation to bring a guest increases the likelihood of attendance. (The chapter Appendix contains a sample invitation letter.)

Selecting Speakers of Content Experts

Lecturers, seminar facilitators, and seminar content experts should be chosen with great care, after much research. Experts used in these roles should be carefully oriented and fully understand that their role is to educate and motivate, not to sell a product or service. An employer should explain to program participants that use of outside experts does not constitute endorsement by the employer of the individual or his or her services.

The program leader, whether a lecturer or a facilitator for a seminar, is crucial to the program's success. That person must establish an atmosphere of trust among the group members and facilitate participation by individuals to the extent allowed by the format being used. This is particularly important in the case of seminars. The seminar facilitator must be able to present essential information clearly, generate group participation, and keep the program on schedule. Organizations often use in-house staff or independent consultants specially trained in small group interaction to fill this key role.

Promoting the Program

One carefully planned and professionally executed program will create a positive attitude and willing participants for future programs. The testimony of program alumni will largely sell the program and decrease the need for extensive promotion of future programs.

The program must be publicized well in advance of the first session. The program can be promoted in the house newsletter, on the bulletin board, and through notices placed in pay envelopes. (The chapter Appendix contains a sample statement for a personnel manual and a sample promotion folder.) Audiovisuals during lunch hours and teaser lectures at brown bag lunches to interest employees in issues of retirement planning work well for many employers. Publicity about the organization's policy statement on retirement planning alleviates fears on the part of some employees that the program might be an attempt to get them to retire early.

Planning for the first program should be extensive, lasting at least three to six months. (The chapter appendix contains a sample planning schedule.) The future of retirement planning within an organization may largely be determined by the success of the first program. Subsequent programs will be easier to implement. Duties will become routine, and those involved will more fully understand their roles. Evaluations by participants indicate ways to improve future programs, thus keeping them responsive to employee needs and interests.

Retirement Planning Issues for the 1990s and Beyond

In *Retirement Planning: Corporate Perspectives for the 1990s,* Helen Dennis summarized the changes that human resources professionals and retirement planning executives she interviewed foresee in the coming decades. Her findings provide valuable insights and guidance to those responsible for the direction of their organization's retirement education and counseling program:

▴ The sequence of education, work, and retirement is likely to change. Individuals may retire, go to school, and then re-enter the workforce. Multiple "retirements" are likely to become the norm with education, leisure, and work as part of the retirement experience in the last third of life. This "distributed" retirement will require more thoughtful planning.

▴ For most companies, bottom-line considerations will drive retirement policies and programs. In the 1960s, many companies were motivated by corporate social responsibility. Today and in the near term, the desire to increase corporate profits, while maintaining or reducing expenses, will continue to dominate corporate activities.

▴ Early retirement programs will continue to be offered as a way to trim expenses of high-salaried, long-term employees. Many employees taking early retirement options will develop new careers and businesses following these offers. A number of these younger retirees will be in a position to take risks since their children are likely to be independent, their homes paid for, and their health intact.

▴ On the other hand, some adult children will return to live with their parents because they need financial support, child care, housing, or further education. This phenomenon will affect decisions of whether or not employees can afford to retire, the amount of income that can be saved, and decisions on housing and use of discretionary time.

▴ Government and corporations will continue to cut back benefits, forcing employees to take greater responsibility for their retirement income and medical costs. In the future, according to several corporations studied, retirees may receive no medical benefits from their employers, and employees who have the opportunity to receive retiree health benefits will have to work for a longer period of time to qualify.

▴ Employees will continue to feel uncertain about their financial stability in retirement. Media attention to the nation's fiscal problems, new laws, and debates on tax reform, social security, and health care will continue to increase employees' awareness of their own financial vulnerability.

▲ The baby boom generation will make extensive use of computer technology for financial planning. This generation, sophisticated in the use of computers, will have less difficulty in developing financial plans than the current generation of retirees who are "technology shy."

▲ More employees will expect retirement planning services as a benefit. According to a recent random survey of 1,400 employees conducted by the Daniel Yankelovich Group for IDS Financial Services, funding a secure retirement is a top financial priority. Only half of the survey respondents believe they are meeting that goal. The majority reported they want and expect more information and help from their employers on saving for retirement. [IDS/Yankelovich Retirement Survey, (New York: The Daniel Yankelovich Group, Inc., 1989).]

▲ Health promotion and wellness will receive greater emphasis from employers because illness under the current health care system is becoming unaffordable. Exercise and nutrition programs, health screening, stop smoking campaigns, and stress management workshops will increase. The relationship between healthy lifestyles and corporate health care expenses will be closely monitored and documented.

▲ Post-retirement employment will emerge as an important subject in retirement planning, as a way to offset shortfalls in retirement income. In addition, retirees will seek employment for job satisfaction, social interaction, and structure. In one example, retirees at the *Los Angeles Times* were informed that ten part-time positions for tour guides were available; 75 out of 300 retirees who were sent notices responded with applications. Other employers have experienced similar enthusiasm from retirees seeking work, and corporations are beginning to fill temporary positions with retired workers. [Helen Axel, *Job Banks for Retirees,* The Conference Board, Report No. 929, 1989.]

▲ As the work force changes, the ethnic, social and cultural diversity of employees will be acknowledged in retirement education. Retirement planning programs will address specific needs of women, singles, Hispanics, Blacks, Asians, and Native Americans. The sheer numbers of these workers will drive program content and emphasis. The National Center for Women and Retirement Research, for one, has already developed subjects for women on social and emotional issues, health and fitness, finances, and employment.

▲ Retirement planning will continue to become part of a larger concept of work-life issues. Programs and strategies will be further developed to prepare employees for the transition to retirement, new careers, and positions in the community.[7]

NOTES

1. *Vital Statistics of the U.S., 1987, Life Tables,* vol. 2, section 6, U.S. Public Health Service, Centers for Disease Control.
2. *Aging America: Trends and Projections,* information paper to U.S. Senate, Special Committee on Aging, serial no. 101-E (November 1989); Employee Benefit Research Institute, "Trends and Issues in Early Retirement," *Issue Brief,* no. 103 (June 1990); U.S. General Accounting Office, *Retirement before Age 65 Is a Growing Trend in the Private Sector,* Report to the Chairman, Subcommittee on Civil Service, Post Office and General Services, Committee on Governmental Affairs, U.S. Senate, GAO/HRD-85-81, July 15, 1985.
3. Malcolm H. Morrison and M. Kathryn Jedrziewski, "Retirement Planning: Everybody Benefits," *Personnel Administrator* (January 1988).
4. Ibid.
5. Polly T. Taplin, "Spencer Survey of Preretirement Counseling: Ongoing, Early Retirement Programs Described," *Employee Benefit Plan Review* (August 1989).
6. FRED (Friendly Retirement Education Database), Employee Benefits System, Inc., P.O. Box 11485, Columbia, South Carolina 29211.
7. Helen Dennis, "Retirement Planning: Corporate Perspectives for the 1990s," New York: The Conference Board (February 1990). Copyright © 1990 The Conference Board. Reprinted by permission.

SUGGESTED READING

Arnone, William. "Preretirement Planning: An Employee Benefit That Has Come of Age." *Personnel Journal* (October 1982).

Dennis, Helen. *Retirement Planning: Corporate Perspectives for the 1990s.* New York: Conference Board, 1990.

Employee Benefit Plan Review (August 1990).

Fullerton, Jr., Howard N. "New Labor Force Projections, Spanning 1988 to 2000." *Monthly Labor Review* 112, no. 11 (November 1989): 3–12.

Gerber, Jerry, Janet Wolff, Walter Klores, and Gene Brown. *Lifetrends: The Future of Baby Boomers and Other Aging Americans.* New York: Macmillan, 1989.

Greenberg, Eric Rolfe. "The Latest AMA Survey on Downsizing." *Personnel* 66, no. 10 (October 1989): 38–44.

Herz, Diane E., and Philip L. Rones. "Institutional Barriers to Employment of Older Workers." *Monthly Labor Review* 112, no. 4 (April 1989): 14–20.

LaRock, Seymour. "Early Retirement Incentives in 1989: Survey Reveals Components of Package." *Employee Benefit Plan Review* (August 1990): 12–15.

"Retirement before Age 62: Growth, Reasons Explored." *Employee Benefit Plan Review* (July 1989): 16–18.

Spencer Survey of Preretirement Counseling. Chicago: Spencer's Research Reports on Employee Benefits, 19xx.

NATIONAL RETIREMENT PLANNING SERVICE PROVIDERS

International Society of
    PreRetirement Planners
11312 Old Club Road
Rockville, MD 20852-4537
1-800-327-ISPP

American Association of Retired
    Persons (AARP)
Worker Equity Department
Work Force Education Section
1909 K Street, N.W.
Washington, DC 20049
202-662-4956
Supplies *Directory of National
    Suppliers of Retirement
    Planning Resources* at no
    charge.

Seibert Associates
3455 Spring Hill Drive
Jamesville, WI 53545
608-755-0300
Sells a compendium of
    preretirement reference
    materials.

Sample Program Invitation Letter

This letter, mailed to the employee's home, can be adapted to send to unmarried employees who may want to bring a close friend or relative. It can also be tailored to include fee information if the organization plans to charge for the program. A registration letter should follow in about one week.

[*Date*]

Dear Mr. and Mrs. Smith:

The SYZ Company is pleased to announce a program on the subject of planning for your retirement that may be of interest to you and your spouse.

This letter is addressed to all employees who are 50 years of age or older, although there is really no "set" age to start thinking about retirement. But one thing is certain—a successful and happy retirement doesn't just happen. It requires planning, and thorough planning takes time.

Planning for retirement involves both husband and wife. That's why we encourage both of you to attend the program. It will be held at [*place*] [*dates*] for [*weeks*], starting [*day, date*].

Professionally trained authorities and specialists will share their knowledge and experience with you. They'll offer ideas you might want to include in your own planning.

Topics will include: [*list subject matter areas.*]

Next week you'll receive a program registration form. Please consider carefully this opportunity to enroll. How you plan now can make a significant difference to your future.

Sincerely,

John Doe
Director, Human Services

Sample Group Program Administration Schedule

Six months prior to program

▲ Confirm availability of facilities.
▲ Select topics.
▲ Set dates and times; check for conflicts with organization, community, national, and religious calendars.
▲ Research expenses.
▲ Prepare budget.
▲ Set fee, if necessary.

Five months prior to program

▲ Develop promotional folder
▲ Develop promotion plan.

Four months prior to program

▲ Have folder printed.
▲ Recruit program leaders and content experts.
▲ Send confirming letter and all relevant materials to program leaders and content experts.

Three months prior to program

▲ Distribute promotional literature.
▲ Distribute invitation letters.
▲ Place articles in company newsletter.

Two months prior to program

▲ Log registrations as received.
▲ Send out registration acknowledgments.
▲ Confirm distribution of brochures.
▲ Confirm newsletter articles.
▲ Order program materials.

One month prior to program

▲ Continue to log registrations as received.
▲ Continue to send out registration acknowledgments.
▲ Continue program publicity.
▲ Orient program leaders and content experts.
▲ Obtain biographies of program leaders and content experts.
▲ Develop appropriate evaluation form for program components.

One week prior to program

▲ Reconfirm dates and place with program leaders and content experts.
▲ Confirm availability of facilities, equipment, and people to assist.
▲ Have all materials on hand and organized.

First program

▲ Check room arrangements for comfort and convenience of program participants.
▲ Check availability of supplies, refreshments, equipment, and materials.
▲ At end of each session, ask participants to complete evaluation form.

After program

▲ Send letters of appreciation to program leaders and content experts.
▲ Analyze each session for ways to improve it; review evaluation forms.
▲ Make preparations for next program while details are still fresh.

(*continues*)

Sample Statement on Retirement Planning Program for a Personnel Manual

Today, more and more people are living longer, healthier, more active lives. And these people have greater expectations for their lives than any other generation before them had. In addition, the definition of retirement is changing. It now can mean a new full-time career, part-time employment, absorbing volunteer work, long-sought leisure pursuits, or any combination of these activities. Each person must define his or her own retirement based on individual needs and aspirations.

Many people are spending thirty or more years in retirement. This vital phase of life is well worth planning for in a thoughtful, careful way before the actual retirement date arrives.

Recognizing these trends and needs [company/organization name] has developed a series of retirement planning sessions for our employees [members]. This voluntary program is intended primarily for those who are age [40 or older] but is available to employees of any age. The human resources department will be happy to provide interested [eligible] employees with details about the program upon request.

Sample Group Program Promotion Folder

Back Panel

Front Panel

Think
of
Your Future

A Retirement Lecture Program on:
- **Dynamic Fitness**
- **Housing Choices**
- **Midlife Roles**
- **Estate Planning**
- **Financial Security**
- **and more**

This back panel is reserved for imprinting the date, time, place, fee, and related information about your local program.

From *Think of Your Future* Administrator's Manual. Copyright © 1989 American Association of Retired Persons. Reprinted by permission.

Sample Group Program Promotion (*continued*)
Inside Panels

PLAN YOUR RETIREMENT— NOW!

Retirement can be the most enjoyable and productive time of your life. But to be successful, retirement must be planned—by you.

You planned for every other important milestone in your life and now is the time to plan for your retirement years! Keep in mind that retirement can be a quarter of your life; you should prepare for it just as carefully as you prepared for your career.

This Lecture Program is designed to help you begin preparing for the adventures that lie ahead. It will *not* tell you the specifics of what to do because charting one's future is a very personal matter. Yet, the lectures, exercises, and reading materials should stimulate you to think about: what your retirement goals will be, how to maintain good health, where to live, what you will do, and how much money you will need. The idea is to figure out what you want from your retirement years and to lay the groundwork now.

Retirement should be your reward for a lifetime of work, a time when you can do what you want to do when you want to do it. You'll be your own boss, gearing your activity to please yourself. You'll have time for adventure—to explore new worlds, both physically and mentally.

This lecture program has been developed to help you explore what alternatives would be best for you and your family. Review the subjects on the next page, then register *now* for this interesting and informative lecture program. Each participant will receive a comprehensive Retirement Planning Workbook to read, to use, and to keep for continuing reference.

PARTICIPANT COMMENTS

A very valuable learning experience
Housewife, Boston, MA

Our company deserves a big hand for this program. I hope others will be able to attend lectures like this!
Maintenance Employee, Cleveland, OH

Every topic had something of value to offer—a new idea, a new point of view, a new twist
Retailer, Anaheim, CA

Enlightening and refreshing—stimulating—positive.
Attorney, Wheaton, IL

YOU'LL HAVE HAPPIER TOMORROWS IF YOU START PLANNING TODAY.

Lecture Program

The subjects for the Retirement Planning Lecture Program have been carefully selected and developed by national authorities. The topics include:

- **Challenge of the Future** Challenges create opportunities. Adding years to your life and new life to those years.
- **Dynamic Fitness** Taking charge of your health. Exercise. Nutrition. Dealing with stress. Wise use of health care.
- **Attitude & Role Adjustments** Optimum happiness in the middle and later years. New goals. New relationships.
- **Housing & Lifestyle** Where to retire. Planning for early and later retirement. Taxes. Home equity conversion. Housing choices.
- **Meaningful Use of Time** Recognizing your psychological needs and how to meet them with leisure pursuits, volunteer activities.
- **Working Options** Practical considerations for working in retirement.
- **Sources of Income** Identifying potential income sources such as pensions, social security, and work.
- **Personal Financial Planning** How to afford the retirement lifestyle you want. Dealing with inflation.
- **Investment Strategies** Basic concepts and procedures for protecting your purchasing power.
- **Legal Affairs & Estate Planning** Contracts. Types of ownership. Making a will. Consumer rights. Selecting advisers. And more.

9

Relocation Counseling

Christine Z. Tafe, Merrill Lynch & Co., Inc.

On the surface, the relocation experience and employee counseling seem to fit hand-in-glove. With considerations such as personal careers in transition, family and home life reorientation, and new languages and cultures to learn, relocation counseling should be widely available. Unfortunately, the reality is that counseling programs are not often available to relocating employees and their families. When assistance is available, it seldom comes packaged as counseling. The main reason that counseling is not an important feature of employee relocation assistance is that most employees resist asking for help, and that help, when available, is quite expensive. But companies that are aware of employees' underlying personal needs and that value a mobile work force are getting help to relocating employees through their greater programs of relocation assistance.

Relocation: The Fast Track to Stress City?

Climbing the corporate ladder still frequently means agreeing to relocate at the request of the company. Refusing a transfer in most corporate cultures takes the employee off the fast track and into a career cul-de-sac:

> A real career means frequent moves on short notice as opportunities arise. Many organizations groom their promising candidates for promotion by giving them short-term experience all over the country. Those who refuse seldom get another chance. Big companies expect a candidate for promotion to be ready to take on the challenge of a new job in another city with little or no time out for the work of moving there. This is hard for women officers, who seldom have a "corporate wife" to do the packing and relocating. It is particularly hard on a single mother being groomed for promotion, because she has no one to house-hunt for her in the new location or even to watch her children while she attempts to do it herself.[1]

To make matters even more pressured, American business is becoming more international. Relocation has become an essential factor in ensuring a company's ability to change, grow, and compete. The deployment of skilled personnel, and the subsequent enrichment of management talent through exposure to national and foreign experience, is no longer an option; it has become a necessity for corporate survival.

Today's social and business worlds work against transferees. Traditional family support systems have eroded, leaving uprooted employees more vulnerable to the difficulties of change. Companies have had to become more demanding of employees in terms of on-the-move performance and flexibility in accepting a move. Two-income families, singles, and single parents are now more the rule than the exception. The support of the transferee wife is steadily vanishing. The at-home partner once helped the employee and children prepare for relocation and then acted as a family ambassador to help the family assimilate into the new community. Today, within the family unit, careers and personal agendas are on a collision course. Even when the trailing spouse moves willingly, he or she cannot devote time to making the relocation work smoothly because of his or her own job concerns. In addition, the sheer physical work and mental effort involved in moving a household is, by itself, a major source of stress.

Career insecurity and personal upheaval make the prospect of a corporate transfer stressful in the extreme. Without a release valve or a person to play the role of burden carrier, relocation stress increases exponentially. Without a personal support system in place, employees who are asked to relocate increasingly find themselves in the situation of making the move adjustment look seamless to the employer, while coping with family and personal adjustment with little or no outside help. (The chapter appendix presents case studies in relocation assistance.)

In spite of these problems, employees rarely step forward in a relocation to ask for the help they need. The key reason is that their career success is often closely linked to a successful corporate record. The transferee must excel in the new job and make the whole transfer look easy to the immediate supervisor, peers, and subordinates. Resilient employees are the ones who succeed:

> Though managers exercise a great deal of control in the areas of decision making and employee management, they may feel less control over their own positions. In order to respond to the changing needs of the organization, managers' positions are often reshuffled. As corporations expand or are restructured, managers may be asked to relocate, a change which can subject the entire family to the stress of moving to a new home, new schools, and a new community. . . . Often [the manager] must fit into a whole new management system, discovering suddenly

that the managerial techniques he has developed over many years are now outmoded and new skills must be learned.[2]

Considering the pressures and the risks, employees are reluctant to voice their insecurities—to expose emotional weakness, family need, or lack of knowledge. For instance, male transferees are often reluctant to ask for help for their working wives or for wives who wish to return to the work force as a result of relocation. In the reverse situation, female transferees resist asking for help for their working husbands, often because the husband's ego cannot withstand it.

Transplanting the fragile support systems families rely on for child care, elder care, and special family needs is the real issue. Unfortunately, these issues often lie dormant—until the move gets underway. In a competitive corporate environment, it is permissible to let off steam but only under certain circumstances. Employees are more likely to point to problems on such issues as home valuation amounts, damaged or lost furniture, the relocation financial package, and the high cost of housing. When the employee is having difficulty coping or feels that he or she might fail in the new location, whatever the latent personal problem, having a scapegoat issue is a convenient way of masking a real concern: the unacknowledged need.

Employees' stonewalling behavior is firmly rooted in the corporate psyche. It manifests itself in different forms: the good soldier, the team player, and sometimes human corporate property. Recognizing this potential time bomb in every relocating employee, companies can offer valuable relocation-related counseling by providing it as a hidden feature of traditional assistance programs, such as home sale, home finding, or household goods transport. (See Suggested Reading and the list of relocation counseling resources at the end of this chapter.)

The Administrator: First Line of Defense

Regardless of the richness of a company's relocation policy, the human resources administrator is usually the primary point of contact responsible for relocation. The administrator is the gateway for any and all assistance to the relocating family. In most situations, this person explains the company's policy, answers initial relocation-related financial questions, reviews relocation expense reporting procedures, and makes the employee aware of available relocation assistance programs, along with an explanation of how to secure that assistance.

Throughout the relocation process, the administrator or relocation coordinator is available to answer questions, handle disputes or problems, and generally troubleshoot the assistance offered by outside relocation service organizations. It is nearly always a tricky proposition for the administrator to become the employee's counselor because the administrator often must represent corporate policy and deny requests for money or restrict access to direct financial assistance. The administrator nevertheless can play a valuable counseling role in many respects.

1. The administrator can set a counseling tone by asking employees to speak up about any concerns they or their family may have. Just as salespeople are admonished to ask for the sale, administrators can head off trouble down the road by asking open-ended questions and by telling the employee at the outset that voicing personal concerns is all right. The administrator can suggest problem-specific uses of the financial assistance available, as it relates to stated problems or concerns. For example, an employee who voices concern about moving a valuable coin collection can be encouraged to look at special insurance or special shipping arrangements, all to be paid out of the policy-provided miscellaneous expense allowance. In other words, the administrator can promote the use of policy for individual needs without having to grant policy exceptions. In this way, employees see the policy as a potentially flexible plan to help them move. Without the administrator's time and direction, employees tend to see policy as a series of roadblocks instead of as a true assistance program. The administrator's counseling role, even in this simple example, is a valuable way of increasing the policy's usefulness to a relocating family.

2. The administrator can encourage the employee to regard the relocation policy as a program of assistance. This small adjustment portrays company-provided relocation reimbursements or services as counseling based versus financial assistance based. For example, home finding trips are usually offered to employees as a certain number of expense-paid days spread over a limited number of individual trips, restricted to the employee and usually the spouse. But most employees need assistance before their trip(s) to help them get the most out of the expense-paid time in the new location. Family needs assessment and itinerary preplanning offered by an experienced new-area counselor is often offered by relocation firms but is frequently overlooked or undervalued by companies. This orientation is what makes home finding trips worthwhile to employees, not the fact that the company picks up the tab for dinner. The relocation administrator can encourage the use of these services.

3. The administrator can go beyond encouraging employees to make use of available counseling, working closely with relocation service providers to ensure top-notch, counseling-centered assistance for relocating employees. This goes beyond just ensuring good service. It has more to do with selecting and directing relocation vendors to focus on the human side of relocation, with an underpinning of financial assistance rather than the reverse (finances first, human needs last).

Mastery of the human–financial equation will become increasingly important in determining the success or failure of relocation administration because of the constantly changing work force. Although no firm data show that employees are increasingly voicing personal relocation issues to human resources administrators, the changing social values of the baby boom generation indicate the importance of human values over financial considerations:

> With continued aging in the 1990's will come a trend toward resisting autocratic authority. . . . Workers [are] motivated more by opportunities for self-actualization and recognition than by basic needs for economic security. . . . Today's richer and better-educated workers are taking advantage of expanded opportunities in lifestyles. . . . Economic gain cannot realistically be the driving force. The real motivator is the psychological drive for self-actualization.[3]

In a climate of self-actualization, an administrator's talking through a list of financial assistance items with a relocating employee is not enough to get that employee to move, to help him or her forge a successful transition, or to help the family succeed in the new location. Relocation administration, often the hidden and underestimated element in a program of relocation assistance, can begin to capitalize on this social trend by moving the counseling issue to center stage early in the relocation process.

Home Finding: The First Step in Putting Down New Roots

Whether an employee's relocation is domestic or international, home finding assistance, in the form of good advice for finding a new and appropriate living situation, either falls to a local real estate representative or a haphazard assortment of well wishers: the boss's wife, new co-workers, or the friend of a friend.

In situations where employees are given a real estate contact in the new area through a referral network, the level of service and quality of counseling depend entirely on the person or real estate organization at the new location. With a referral system, where there is a small effort to precounsel, the employee will receive assistance from someone who wants to sell him or her something: a home, a condominium, or a lease on a rental residence.

Some cities have real estate companies with extremely sophisticated relocation counseling centers. So-called relocation counselors, expert at dealing with corporate transferees and their families, offer an overview of the residential area surrounding the new work location. This type of counseling is valuable because the transferee gets an overview of likely communities for resettling and meets handpicked real estate agents in the selected target towns in order to help the family shop.

The first step in counseling, even before selecting target communities, is a needs analysis, which gives the family an opportunity to raise issues that typically are invisible to the employee's supervisor or the corporate relocation administrator. Employees can discuss special educational needs, requirements for elder care or child care, commutation concerns, and the availability of recreational facilities or cultural events. The relocation counselor uses this information to identify the communities where the relocating family will most likely find what it is looking for.

Some of this type of assistance is top quality; moreover, help found through real estate company relocation centers is almost always free—a great benefit to the company. However, there are drawbacks. There is no way to guarantee the same level of service to employees relocating all over the country or globe; service consistency is a company-by-company consideration. Perhaps more important, this brand of relocation counseling is actually a sophisticated sales process targeted to corporate home buyers. Real estate companies know that relocation centers help them garner real estate commissions on home sales that typically are at the top of the market.

A good example of relocation counseling is found in group move situations, where a single division or the entire headquarters office is making a geographic move to a new facility. Some group moves take advantage of the destination-area real estate company relocation centers and counselors, but often companies see the added value in hiring independent contractors to act as relocation counselors and work independently or with relocation service firms. These relocation counselors offer services that are similar to those of their real estate company brethren plus others:

- Reviewing company group move relocation policy to help individual employees use the policy to suit their specific needs
- Planning home finding trips so that employees can use the time wisely and return home with the right questions answered
- Performing area research for the relocating employees
- Finding the most suitable agent or real estate firm for employees—and pulling the business away fom nonperforming real estate agents

Independent counselors are frequently used for very high-level moves or moves to international areas, where extra help is necessary. Occasionally, large companies, particularly ones with a preponderance of international moves, have a relocation counselor on staff.

Of course, the counseling bottom line is still the financial bottom line.

The vast majority of companies jump at the chance to take advantage of free services where they are available and typically cannot justify the cost of an independent or company staff counselor, except in special circumstances.

Home Purchase: Making the Financial Commitment to Move

Companies typically offer a financial package of benefits for employees who wish to purchase a home in the new location that includes the following assistance:

- ▲ Closing costs
- ▲ Subsidies for moves into high–cost-of-housing or -living areas
- ▲ Subsidies to protect employees from higher mortgage interest rates
- ▲ Mortgage rate buydown programs
- ▲ Mortgage fund availability through national mortgage vendors

But almost no counseling exists to help relocating employees sort through options, make good home buying decisions, and make responsible mortgage financing arrangements. Certainly there is some counseling through mortgage vendors that can be helpful in terms of shopping for the right mortgage product or learning about how different mortgage products measure up to one another. But this sort of advice only helps the employee take mortgage products into consideration, and there is more than the mortgage to consider when reviewing the range of home purchase financial options available to most employees in a standard relocation policy.

Whether the employee's company should be responsible for offering financial advice is clearly a tricky business. Yet the need to offer employees some guidance is becoming more profound with the economic complexity of the cost of housing from region to region in the United States and with employees stepping into home purchase arrangements overseas where tax implications alone can mystify even the most seasoned CPA. The only help on the horizon appears to be a financial remedy, but at least it is aimed at precounseling employees before they make a home purchase decision. Funds are increasingly being made available by some companies to pay for the services of an independent financial adviser. The intent is to help the employee explore all of the financial options regarding home buying that are offered by the employer, as well as weighing tax implications (capital gains, mortgage deductibility, financial assistance as an unintended salary booster, and so forth).

Another financial option, this one for the benefit of employee and company alike, is the prepurchase appraisal. Companies realize that the majority of employees who make one move make a subsequent move or moves as well. A prepurchase appraisal can hardly be considered counseling to the employee; however, it does get valuable information to the employee before making a hasty decision. The prepurchase appraisal can give the employee an opinion on the asking price of the home, any changes or improvements that ought to be made, and an estimate of the home's future resale potential. This type of assistance is not truly counseling, but it is indicative of the kind of half-measures companies are taking in order to provide good and timely information that has a long-term positive financial impact for both the company and the employee.

Home Sale: Leaving the Homestead for Good

Companies that use a home sale, third-party, or relocation firm offer home disposition counseling through the firm's customer contact person, called, for our purposes, the relocation coordinator. The relocation coordinator works with the employee on the transaction that is the most fraught with employee angst and worry: the sale of a home. It is also one area where grousing, complaining, and down-and-out yelling are not only socially acceptable within the corporation but is almost expected. Why is this the case?

Selling a home is by far the largest financial consideration in any employee move, a consideration that often overshadows the other relocation assistance offered. For the employee, much is riding on this transaction: the equity to purchase a home in the new location, a universal expectation that the home is worth much more than the market says it is, the sentimental attachment to the neighborhood, the lawn, or the wallpaper in the kitchen—a confusing amalgam of sentimental pain and financial strain.

On the company's side, there is much worry that the entire transaction be managed tightly. The sheer weight of financial assistance offered in a typical home sale program illustrates this point. For example, home sale assistance often includes a guaranteed offer to purchase the employee's home at an appraised value, equity advances and loans, company-paid inspections and appraisals, and protection against financial loss on the sale of a home, to name just a few categories of assistance.

To the company, the relocation coordinator is the friendly watchdog. For the relocation coordinator, keeping good relations with the relocating employee is challenging in the extreme. The coordinator must satisfy the employee in terms of friendly service, provide explanation and full management of the entire valuation and sale nightmare, and then pray that the employee gets a good value in the marketplace or that the employee does not feel robbed when he or she is forced to accept the guaranteed offer on the home. On the other hand, the relocation coordinator must also satisfy the company by laying down the law to the employee when disputes arise, denying special requests that are out of scope with company policy, breaking bad news to the employee (anyone who has ever bought or sold a home knows that there is plenty of this in every home sale transaction), all the while ensuring top-quality interpersonal service.

This person is also a counselor. The relocation coordinator is probably the best resource for home sale guidance and often home marketing assistance, other than the employee's listing real estate broker. Involved with the employee's home sale transaction from the start, the relocation coordinator is in an excellent position to address, assuage, and minister to the employee's worries about home sale and other relocation-related issues that arise in conversation.

The job is a difficult juggling act. The job burnout rate is high, and yet, as a career path start in the relocation industry, it continues to attract many ambitious real estate–backgrounded relocation professionals. There are a number of individual relocation coordinators who can balance the needs of the employee, the client company, and the relocation firm. The job they do on a daily basis is often the nearest any relocating employee comes to receiving true relocation counseling.

Home Marketing: Getting the Equity Out—Fast(er)

While some relocation firms combine home marketing assistance as an advance feature of the traditional buy-out program, other firms offer this as a separate service entity. Still other relocation companies offer home marketing services as their core business. Home marketing assistance is becoming a more central feature of most companies' home sale programs because of the astronomical cost of acquiring and then reselling employee homes in real estate markets that are slow, or worse.

Home marketing assistance is a counseling-intensive service. The type of counseling available tends to center on several points: selecting a marketing-savvy broker, reviewing the home's features and deciding on worthwhile reconditioning projects presale, and arriving at an attractive selling price for the home. Counseling is often provided by telephone with a centrally located manager at a relocation company; home inspection and information consolidation is provided by a local representative (often a real estate broker, who will use the opportunity to obtain the listing).

Behind the scenes, companies have several reasons for providing home marketing services to their relocating employees. In addition to keeping the home out of company inventory, home marketing assistance makes the employee an active partner in the home sale process. Rather than being merely processed through a buy-out program, placing home marketing at the forefront of the process gives employees several strong messages: they must play an active role in acquiring a fair price for the home; they must arrive at a reasonable asking price before the home is listed for sale (versus having the first valuation fixed through a contentious appraisal process); they must participate in (or at least hear about) a recommended fix-up plan. In short, the process of home marketing assistance sets employee expectations somewhere in the real world, whereas launching directly into a traditional buy-out program places a powerless employee on the fringes of an omnipotent relocation firm, which dictates the price of the home, how and when it will be sold, and other parameters.

Some companies have such belief in home marketing programs—their money-saving potential and reports of employee satisfaction—that employees are being allotted a special fund to use for reconditioning projects completed prior to listing the home for sale. The effect of the fix-up fund is to place financial importance, and company support, behind the employee's steps to attract a buyer.

The one error that companies make in offering home marketing programs is in not explaining exactly why the service is being offered. Introduction to the program through the relocation service firm virtually always centers on the benefit to the employee and on the steps involved in the service. The missing element is a message from the company explaining why participation in the program is so important to the employee in terms of overall satisfaction (self-determination, understanding the process, getting a true market price versus an appraised value) and to the company. If the employee does not understand why the company wishes to keep the home out of its inventory, the employee is not understanding the whole story. Some companies have instituted bonus programs for employees who participate and then achieve a sale in order to drive this point home. Clearly this approach must come from the company itself, not from a service provider.

Transportation: Getting There Is Not Half the Fun

Relocation firms and some large moving companies offer what could be considered a counseling option or feature that helps employees:

- ▲ Prepare for the packers to arrive.
- ▲ Anticipate needs for special shipping.
- ▲ Purchase additional insurance on valuable items.
- ▲ Arrange for the safe transport of family pets.
- ▲ Troubleshoot for the occasional employee who expects the company to move something unusual (say, an above-ground swimming pool or an outbuilding).

The transportation of household goods is highly problematic and a likely source of employee friction. Anyone who has ever moved, even across the street, has stories to tell: the fractured end table, the nicked baby grand piano, the broken crystal champagne glasses, and the lost motorboat. An employee who is carrying a load of personal, family, and career emotional baggage will not be soothed when told, "These things happen." For this reason, the counseling assistance provided by relocation firms and van lines stresses before-the-move planning. Setting expectations is the all-important objective.

The selected van line usually sends a representative to visit the relocating family and view the contents of the home, as well as run through a list of questions. The family is instructed to be prepared to meet the representative, to have questions ready, and to begin assessing their own needs. With a report from the local van line, the transportation counselor prepares the family for the steps they need to take and the services (and limits to services) offered by the company and the van line. This level of premove preparation helps give employees and their families some comfort with the services being offered and places the control of noncovered services back in their own hands. Transportation counseling properly done can serve to set the stage for a successful physical move—but transportation counseling normally does not stop there. The transportation counselor also helps with move scheduling and checks in with the family before the move as the important milestones approach and pass (acquiring additional insurance coverage, prepacking items that the family will move independently, checking in on the arrival of the packers). And after the move, the counselor follows up to inquire about any damage done to the family's belongings. Assistance with filing claims, managing the paperwork, and setting up proper documentation is critical to employee satisfaction. An employee can have a picture-perfect move, and yet, if just one item is damaged—and, worst, if restitution is not promptly made—that idyllic situation can be permanently and adversely changed.

As with the other categories of assistance, the company's relocation administrator can set the tone for the employee's relationship with the service provider (the transportation counselor). The transportation counselor can be positioned to advantage as the main feature of the transportation assistance program, not the assistance itself (packing, moving, unpacking, storage).

Spouse Career Assistance: The Two-Career Dilemma

No other category of relocation assistance gets more talk and less action than spouse career assistance, a pity because the two-person career is a major factor in relocation resistance. More has been written, studied, and proposed on this issue since the early 1970s than almost any other issue in employee relocation. But just as in other categories of assistance, corporations have elected to address the issue financially, and rarely through counseling. In addition, spouse career concerns may not always be raised by the relocating employee, especially when the trailing spouse is a man: "The career needs of a wife can handicap the career mobility of a man in exactly the same way that women traditionally have been handicapped by the presumption that they will always follow their husbands. . . . No one believe[s] that a competent man would quit to follow his wife."[4]

Most companies, in response to this intense challenge of changing social patterns, where ego is on the line and traditional sex roles are sometimes reversed or at odds, have simply backed away. Those that do make a passing effort typically offer résumé services, lists of prospective employers in the new area, workbooks, and reference materials (for example, the excellent but much overused *What Color Is Your Parachute?*). A book and a résumé do not amount to spouse career counseling by any standards. And occasionally in group move situations where a high rate of working spouses is a factor, companies offer additional funds to the home finding trips to allow a spouse time to interview for jobs.

Real spouse career counseling can be found among some major companies that have identified the durability of the two-person career problem and, most important, have the means to pay for top-notch assistance. It can be very expensive. When properly done, it involves most of the same features of traditional outplacement services: aptitude and skill testing, counselor interviews and consultations, group workshops, interview preparation classes, résumé writing and rewriting, networking skills coaching, career planning assistance, and information interview skills training. Spouses, employees, and companies on programs such as this uniformly view the service positively, yet there is no conclusive evidence that offering full financial support in a spouse assistance program, together with a full program of counseling, actually helps the spouse overcome objections to the move. At a minimum, it communicates to the employee and the spouse that the company recognizes the importance of two careers to the relocating family and that the company is willing to take steps to ease the transition. Companies that offer spouse career assistance of any stripe need to set employee and spouse expectations early. Regardless of the level of assistance, there is no guarantee of a job or of job satisfaction in the new area.

Cultural Assimilation and Reentry: Transferees Abroad

Moving overseas involves every bit of the stress already examined in this chapter and more. New languages and new customs can be an enormous challenge to the entire family. Even buying groceries and having the dry-cleaning done can seem insurmountable tasks to the uninitiated. Companies often do offer employees assistance for international transition, but the assistance tends to be compartmental, driven by a specific problem.

A good example of the compartmental approach is foreign language training. A crash course (or total immersion, as it is now called) in a foreign language is valuable for employees and relocating families, but not all companies see the need. There is an impression that English is the universal language of business. While this is increasingly so, it is far from being the total truth. Companies that offer only language training and none of the other programs discussed later in this section are accomplishing a great deal for their employees, and potentially for their business as well. Foreign language training helps the family feel secure on arrival; at least they can order a meal, say "hello," and ask for directions. In addition, language training gives a message to the employee that he or she should not arrive at the new job like a member of the colonial army. Learning the local language honors the integrity of the host country and its people. At first, trying to speak the language may be uncomfortable and possibly comical, but the initial gesture and the continued effort tend to benefit everyone. Assimilation of the family, the spouse, and the employee is hastened when language training is offered.

Cultural awareness and respect for local practices is becoming very important. Relocation service companies in both the United States and abroad offer what has become known as culture camp. They teach employees how things operate in the host country—for example, gift-giving customs; when to bow, shake hands, and smile; the patterns of business interaction; how neighbors typically begin and foster relationships with foreign nationals. The companies that resist using cultural training make a similar case to the argument against language training—that the world is becoming one culture, an international business culture. Nothing could be further from the truth. A true definition of global business and global culture is not necessarily American culture. Foreign nationals tolerate a certain amount of Americanization, but local customs and attitudes are cherished and fiercely guarded. The companies that can operate with global success will manage a crazy-quilt of cultures and languages with careful respect, all while keeping an eye on the company's core business.

One underestimated international relocation counseling option is both simple and economical: using a buddy system, a sponsor family (usually people who were relocated to that location by the same company) to help introduce the relocating family to the ways of the new area. This gives the relocating family an opportunity to ask questions in a nonthreatening environment and serves to create the first social link in the new area. The sponsoring family can open doors in simple but profound ways: helping the relocating family shop or get settled (telephone hookups, clothing, commuting); networking family members into different local and expatriate organizations or affiliation groups; giving the children in the family other children to recognize on their first day of school. Companies can help set up buddy systems by creating a central network of names and telephone numbers. In addition, the company can give a strong positive message and encourage potential sponsoring families to participate by allowing for a certain amount of time off to lend assistance and possibly approving limited meal or entertainment expenses.

Returning to the United States from abroad also poses problems. Most companies incorrectly assume that because an employee and family are returning to the home country, reassimilation should be a snap. But a quick return to American culture can be just as much a shock to a family as the original relocation abroad was. Reentry is a difficult counseling challenge because it is generally unrecognized as a problem. In addition to granting relatively frequent home leaves, companies have used a domestic buddy system to help returning families. The buddy system allows returning families a chance to share common experiences with other families that have experienced reentry shock. Simple matters—new products, new words or fads, new clothing styles—take on great meaning for families returning as strangers to their own country.

Returning families may have experienced subtle changes in their personal value systems while abroad. For example, using a string bag to buy groceries is common in Europe; the wastefulness of using disposable paper or plastic bags can hit returning Americans as an affront, an insult. There is a sense of loss of affiliation when the returning family has shifted its values offshore.

Whether the company sponsors an official buddy program for returning employees or simply makes available an opportunity to meet others in the same situation, it is clearly a positive and useful step to give the employee and his or her family a forum for voicing and working through their discomfort and disorientation.

Group Moves: Making the Group Experience Work for Company Goals

Group moves often contain more elaborate and more expensive relocation counseling features than any ongoing relocation program because these moves often put the entire company or division at risk. Potential attrition of key employees can be a major loss to the company in a group move situation. Ironically, the need for counseling becomes much more apparent to the company in this situation than in managing ongoing moves. Although some moves are planned to achieve personnel cuts, the majority of moves are made for cost savings, to be closer to customers or markets, or to achieve a more attractive life-style for the employees. Getting the employee at large to stay with the company and make the move is a normal objective.

Extensive orientation programs are offered, including family dinners, tours of the new area, resource materials, and special programs. In addition, relocation counseling is normally offered. Sometimes independent counselors are used, but often the services of a relocation center (part of a local real estate brokerage) are used when home finding alone is the key objective of counseling. Independent counselors are often brought on-site at the department location and occasionally set up shop at the destination location to assist the employees and families in settling in.

Another group move feature worth reviewing, although not directly related to counseling, is the group move survey. Often before a group move relocation policy is introduced, the relocating company polls its employees on any number of issues: intent to move, commutation patterns, family characteristics, special needs or desires, financial concerns. The survey provides an opportunity for the employee, or family, to sound off about the key sources of their aggravation and irritation surrounding the move. Simply doing a survey carries a powerful positive message ("The company is asking *my* opinion!") and a potential trap—or opportunity—for the company. A company that puts out a survey is implying that it will make a response or take an action as a result of the survey findings. If it takes no action, there can be a backlash of negative opinion. Most companies, however, use the survey findings to help them custom design the move and train and prepare counselors.

Relocation administrators also have an excellent opportunity to have their relocation service providers (home sale, home finding, mortgage) offer enhancements to their regular package of employee counseling or relocation transaction management features. For example, some relocation service providers move their services on-site during a group move, thereby giving employees an opportunity to receive counseling face to face versus over the telephone. Alternatively, service providers may be able to customize the content or flow of their counseling or services because of the efficiency of numbers. It is good business for relocation companies to listen to their client company's wishes and needs during a group move, because group move business is not always captured by the incumbent service providers. Service enhancement may mean business retention, a principle that can work to the benefit of the company and the relocating employee and family.

But if counseling or services cannot be enhanced, providers can offer alternative help in group moves. They can create or customize reference materials or participate in or sponsor special educational seminars (on topics like "How to Apply for a Mortgage," "Advice for First-time Home Buyers," "How Your Home's Value Will Be Determined," and "A Kid's-Eye View of the Destination Area"). In short, the human resources administrator's objective during a group move, other than being prepared by having a master plan in place, is to translate the extra relocation business generated by the group into improved service or counseling to the employee.

Relocation Counseling: What Is Next?

In the rest of the 1990s and beyond, relocation counseling increasingly will be provided by outside service providers as an integral part of the package of employee relocation assistance. Creating in-house positions in relocation counseling or using independent contractors will probably occur only in group moves or possibly in companies with an overwhelming business need (or the funds) to acquire this type of service.

One subtle change may occur in adapting certain categories of on-going employee counseling to relocation situations. For example, as elder care assistance becomes more commonplace in companies, employees will begin to request elder care assistance as a matter of course when a family is transferred to a new location. The same is true of child care and addiction-support programs.

While many relocation service providers claim to provide one-stop shopping or single point of contact to simplify the employee's move, the role of the specialist cannot be underestimated. Will the employee get better service from specialists or from one person who will counsel on everything from home purchase to home sale to spouse career assistance? Some companies are trying this approach, but experience thus far indicates that the employee gets the best help from counselors who are seasoned and know their specialty.

The ongoing challenge of the human resources administrator responsible for relocation is to listen closely to the grumblings of employees, read between the lines, and look for the hidden need because employees are not always direct about their personal needs. The administrator needs to communicate with transferring employees clearly, concentrate on the value of the counseling factor in each service being offered, and manage relocation service firms closely, examining the counseling aspect of their services on an equal footing with the financial considerations. The quality of counseling to the relocating employee can quickly translate to the corporate bottom line.

NOTES

1. Caroline Bird, *The Two-Paycheck Marriage* (New York: Rawson Wade Publishers, 1979), p. 193.
2. L. John Mason, *Stress Passages* (Berkeley, Calif.: Celestial Arts, 1988), p. 105.
3. Terence E. Deal and Allen A. Kennedy, *Corporate Cultures* (Reading, Mass.: Addison-Wesley, 1982), pp. 179–180.
4. Bird, *Two-Paycheck Marriage*.

SUGGESTED READING

Adler, N. J. *International Dimensions of Organizational Behavior.* Boston: Kent, 1986.

Bailyn, Lotte. "Career and Family Orientations of Husbands and Wives in Relation to Marital Happiness." *Human Relations* 23 (1970): 97–113.

Bird, Caroline. *The Two-Paycheck Marriage.* New York: Rawson Wade Publishers, 1979.

Brislin, R. W. *Cross-Cultural Encounters: Face to Face Interaction.* New York: Pergamon, 1981.

Burke, Ronald, and Tamara Weir. "Some Personality Differences between Members of One-Career and Two-Career Families." *Journal of Marriage and the Family* (August 1976).

Colin, J. "Helping the Repatriated Family." *Mobility* 3 (1982).

Deal, Terence E., and Allen A. Kennedy. *Corporate Cultures.* Reading, Mass.: Addison-Wesley, 1982.

Dooley, Thomas W. "Variety: The Spice of Activity in Relocation Benefits." *National Relocation and Real Estate Magazine* 3 (1988): 35–39.

Employee Relocation Council. *Employee Relocation and Relocation Policy Development.* Washington, D.C.: Employee Relocation Council, 1990.

———. *Impact of the Changing Family on Employee Relocation.* Washington, D.C.: Employee Relocation Council, 1987.

———. *Impact of Societal Shifts and Corporate Changes on Employee Relocation.* Washington, D.C.: Employee Relocation Council, 1990.

Erkut, S. "Coping with Teenagers' Resistance to Moving." *Mobility* 7 (1986): 39–43.

Fritz, Norma R. "Smoothing the Rocky Road to Relocation." *Personnel* 11 (1989): 27–35.

Gherman, E. M. *Stress and the Bottom Line: A Guide to Personal Well-Being and Corporate Health.* New York: AMACOM, 1981.

Harrison, Roger. "Understanding Your Organization's Character." *Harvard Business Review* 50 (May–June 1972): 119–128.

Holmes, W., and F. Piker. "Expatriate Failure—Prevention Rather Than Cure." *Personnel Management* 12 (1980): 30–32.

Kanter, Rosabeth. "Work and Family in the United States: A Critical Review and Agenda for Research and Policy." Russell Sage Foundation, 1977.

Kepler, J. Z. *Americans Abroad: A Handbook for Living and Working Overseas.* New York: Praeger, 1983.

Kiplinger, Austin A., and Knight A. Kiplinger. *America in the Global '90s.* Washington, D.C.: Kiplinger Books, 1989.

Kübler-Ross, Elisabeth. *Working It Through: An Elisabeth Kübler-Ross Workshop on Life, Death and Transition.* New York: Collier Books, 1982.

Lynch, Patricia N., and Glenna Salsbury. "Educating the Corporate Transferee." *Mobility* 2 (1989): 53–55.

Machan, Dyan. "Ici On Parle Bottom-Line Responsibility." *Forbes,* February 8, 1988.

McKenney, James L., and Peter G. W. Keen. "How Managers' Minds Work." *Harvard Business Review* 52 (May–June 1974): 79–90.

Mason, L. John. *Stress Passages*. Berkeley, Calif.: Celestial Arts, 1988.

Papanek, Hannah. "Men, Women and Work: Reflections on the Two-Person Career." *American Journal of Sociology* (1978): 852–872.

Peters, Thomas J. "Doing the Little Things Well." *Efficiencies, Effectiveness, Productivity* (September 1980).

Plumez, Jacqueline Hornor. *Divorcing a Corporation*. New York: Viking, 1985.

Savich, R. S., and W. Rodgers. "Assignment Overseas: Easing the Transition Before and After." *Personnel* 65 (1988): 44–48.

Schwamb, Karen. "The Reluctant Transferee." *National Relocation and Real Estate Magazine* (1988).

Toffler, Alvin. *The Third Wave*. New York: Morrow, 1980.

Vancil, Richard F. *Decentralization: Ambiguity by Design*. Homewood, Ill.: Dow Jones-Irwin, 1978.

Werkman, S. *Bringing Up Children Overseas: A Guide for Families*. New York: Basic Books, 1977.

RELOCATION COUNSELING RESOURCES

Employee Relocation Services

Associates Relocation
  Management Company
P.O. Box 650042
Dallas, TX 75265-0042
Fax: (214) 541-6227
(214) 541-6310

Boatmen's Relocation
  Management
510 Locust Street
St. Louis, MO 63101
Fax: (314) 982-4393
(314) 466-5900

Coldwell Banker Relocation
  Management Services, Inc.
27271 Las Ramblas
Mission Viejo, CA 92691
Fax: (714) 367-2550
(714) 367-2006

Genesis Relocation Management
8000 Midatlantic Drive
Mt. Laurel, NJ 08054
Fax: (609) 273-5750
(609) 273-5710

International Consulting

Black Horse Relocation Services
  Ltd.
Black Horse House
Thames Street
Windsor Berks SI4 1TX, England
Fax: 753 854940
44-753850581

Moran, Stahl & Boyer
  International
900 28th Street
Boulder, CO 80303
Fax: (303) 449-1064
(303) 449-8440

National Mortgage Lenders

GMAC Mortgage Corporation
8360 Old York Road
Elkins Park, PA 19117
Fax: (215) 881-3593
(215) 881-3351

Prudential Home Mortgage
274 Riverside Avenue, Second
  Floor
Westport, CT 06880
Fax: (203) 454-4321
(203) 221-3000

Premarketing Assistance

Premier Relocation Services, Inc.
2600 Michelson, Suite 200
Irvine, CA 92715
Fax: (714) 756-8225
(714) 553-1909

General Relocation Consulting

Moran, Stahl & Boyer
355 Lexington Avenue
New York, NY 10017
Fax: (212) 949-1693
(212) 661-4878

The Sequoia Group Inc.
54 Danbury Road
Suite 322
Ridgefield, CT 06877
Fax: (203) 438-4850
(203) 438-4948

Industry Groups

Employee Relocation Council
1720 N Street, NW
Washington, D.C. 20036
(202) 857-0857

Case Studies in Relocation Assistance

The Oldhams Move From St. Louis to Boston

The Oldhams are relocation veterans. Since Matt and Charlotte married in 1967, they have been corporate transferees eight times, an average of once every three years. Their two daughters have transplanted relatively well in each move—until this time. The younger daughter, Patty, who was just finishing up high school, resisted the move ferociously, because the company requested that the family move right away, in January. Making the move meant that Patty would have to miss the last semester of high school. But instead of having the entire family move right away, Matt and Charlotte made a difficult adjustment: Matt's company agreed to pay for his temporary living expenses in the new location from January through the end of May, thus allowing Patty to finish out the school year. This was a far longer period than company policy regularly allowed for, but because of Matt's senior position and the company's request to move on short notice, an exception was granted. Matt's home leave trips were limited to just twice monthly. While Patty was able to spend the spring finishing up high school, Matt sat alone in his hotel room, and Charlotte was left at home to manage the home sale process and prepare their outraged daughter for the imminent move.

As the months passed by, family tensions mounted. Finally, in April, it was time to do serious house hunting. Charlotte, who had personally designed the floor plan and decor of their current home, was not looking forward to picking out yet another new house (for the ninth time in her married life) and going through the redecorating, the resettling, the re-everything. In addition, Charlotte had spent the past seven years building a new career, master's degree and all, and she already had an excellent managerial job. Amazingly, Charlotte was able to find a great job in the new location: nice people, excellent pay, reasonable commute. Even more surprising was the lucky find of Charlotte's dream home.

Pronouncing their two home finding trips a complete success, Matt saw Charlotte off at the airport. Only four weeks to go until the move, what could go wrong? That same day, Matt received a call from his real estate agent who had "just a few more homes" to show him. After all, although Charlotte had found a house she liked, who knew what beauty was just around the corner? On that fateful home finding drive, Matt found the home of *his* dreams: old construction, beautifully crafted, an architectural gem. He bought it on the spot. When he called to tell his wife, she was speechless with fury. And when she made an extra trip out to see the new house, she was even less pleased. The house Charlotte had wanted had already been sold, and the new house, Matt's choice, was irrevocably theirs.

When Charlotte looked at the house, all she saw was a home with no air-conditioning, too close to the road (a busy one at that), with one fewer bedroom than she needed, and a Pepto-Bismol–colored dining room. The die was cast for the Oldhams. This was the home they would be in for awhile, at least for the next three years. Pity poor, well-meaning, but ill-advised, and "should have known better," Matt. Three years is a long time to live in the doghouse.

What could Matt Oldham's company have done to help?

▲ *Home finding.* Clearly, despite eight moves worth of experience, home finding remains an emotional experience for the Oldhams. Matt certainly should have known better than to buy a home without his wife's approval. But what about the real estate agent? Did he or she play a role in the snafu? A neutral relocation counselor might have helped in this case.

▲ *Temporary living arrangements.* Was it advisable for the company to allow Matt and Charlotte to be apart for so long? Is an extended temporary living arrangement healthy for a family and for marital relations? Would the Oldhams have been better at communicating with each other had they been able to see each other every weekend rather than every other weekend? This is a policy issue, a management issue, and probably a counseling issue too.

▲ *Relocating older children.* Patty was in an impossible situation. Agreeing to a move so late in her high school career would have been a devastating blow to her. Would counseling have helped her make the transition in January? It is doubtful. On the other hand, including Patty in the home finding process might have made Matt's faux pas more difficult to achieve. Companies rarely allow children to accompany parents on home finding trips because they are not the decision makers. Most families who have moved would dispute this opinion: Patty certainly was the only decision maker in this transaction. This is a policy decision. Over time perhaps companies will loosen the restrictions on home finding trips, thus acknowledging the fact that many families make decisions based on the needs of the group.

The Carettis Move From Indianapolis to Wilton, Connecticut

In the mid-1980s, real estate in the Northeast was appreciating rapidly. To duplicate their Indianapolis home in Fairfield County, Connecticut, David and Jayne Caretti needed to spend almost four times the sale price of their home. Luckily, David's company offered a high cost of housing subsidy that allowed the Carettis to qualify for a larger mortgage than David's salary alone could accomplish.

David and Jayne remember their home finding trips as tense and gloomy. Each time Jayne returned to Indianapolis to her 3,500-square-foot home, she wept and thought of the small house they would have to buy—and pay so dearly for. The Carettis finally settled on a home in a subdivision of similar homes. The kitchen was the main attraction in the home they chose; it was immense, almost as big as their kitchen in Indianapolis. The home's previous owner had spent quite a lot to renovate, installing special cabinets, a Mexican tile floor, and a huge solarium-style eating area. It was beautiful.

The Caretti children, Ken and Andrea, both junior high school age, were reticent to move. Their friends were in Indianapolis; would the kids in Connecticut consider them unsophisticated? David brought home photos and brochures about the new area to show the children, but nothing seemed to excite them about the move until David brought the family's video camera with him on his next business trip East to headquarters. Jayne, Ken, and Andrea still laugh at his directorial debut: filming Main Street through the front windshield of his rental car, a room-by-room tour of the house they would move to, and a stroll around a local park, complete with pool, pond, and tennis court. Now Ken and Andrea were interested because the move seemed real. Main Street looked quaint and interesting; the park was a short walk from their new front door.

Since the first showing of the video, four years have passed. The Caretti kids were right; the transition to the East was tough. Ken is going back to Indiana to college, and Andrea cannot wait to finish high school and follow in his footsteps back West. In addition, the real estate market deteriorated in the East; the Carettis have lost about $60,000 to $80,000 on the value of their home. This is only partly due to the bad market. They had bought a somewhat overimproved home. The kitchen they fell in love with was a better match for homes twice the value of the Caretti home. The added value of the special kitchen is negligible to the market value, especially in a neighborhood where most of the homes are virtually the same. If David's firm moves him again, the firm has a "loss on sale" policy to help him recover most of that loss. But the promise of that does not make his monthly mortgage payments any easier. Now, in the last year of their high cost of housing

(continues)

Case Studies in Relocation Assistance (continued)

subsidy, the Carettis are experiencing a real financial pinch in their monthly mortgage payment, although David has been given a raise and a promotion recently.

What could David Caretti's company have done to help?

▲ *Home finding and prepurchase appraisals.* David did a better job of providing his family with lively information on the new area than his real estate agent did. The video concept was a winner for the family and helped make the transition fun. But did the Carettis overbuy for their budget? Was it wise to buy an overimproved home? Did it make sense to buy a home that was above the means of his peers at work in order to approximate the home he had left behind? A prepurchase appraisal policy would clearly have helped the Carettis confront some of these issues earlier on. But without counseling, the appraisal alone would still not be enough to make a real difference in the long run. Corporate policy only helped the Carettis find a good real estate agent; they needed a good relocation counselor.

▲ *Relocating children.* Would counseling have helped the Caretti children? This is a debatable point. In retrospect, the Carettis felt they picked a town that suited their needs (convenience, social status, life-style), but it was likely a little too competitive for their children's tastes. A more rural town or a town with a lower-key social life might have been better, they all say now. But nobody ever asked the children's opinion. From the company's point of view, assistance (even recognition) was nonexistent. From the parents' point of view, the task was just to sell the children on the idea of moving. An experienced relocation counselor, particularly one with a strength in school district selection, would have been a great help for the Caretti family.

▲ *Financial assistance.* Did a high cost of housing subsidy enable the Carettis to move, or did it get them in trouble? Did they know what they were doing with the extra money, or was it offered as a matter of procedure? The problem with many of the housing-related subsidies available today (mortgage buy-downs, high cost of housing/living subsidies, mortgage interest rate differentials, loss on sale reimbursement) is that every relocation is different. Families have different personal and financial needs; the "to" and "from" locations vary wildly from a cost of living standpoint; and things change. Real estate markets rise and fall, just as family patterns and needs ricochet about. The answer perhaps is offering a more comprehensive counseling piece to go with all of the sophisticated financial remuneration schemes. The only policy being used in this area now is to help employees pay for financial advice before they accept an invitation to relocate.

The Alexanders Move From Philadelphia to Ankara, Turkey

Only a few months out of college, Perry Alexander landed his first big job, but it meant a year-and-a-half stint in Ankara, Turkey. The organization Perry worked for offered only the most rudimentary relocation assistance: limited household goods move, travel to the new location, plus a small fund for miscellaneous expenses. Because Perry and his wife, Joanne, were newlyweds, had no children, and were not home owners, their financial and family ties were fairly easy to suspend for eighteen months. But nothing prepared them for life in Ankara.

Perry's predecessor in his new position had suggested staying with another expatriate American family (total strangers to the Alexanders) for a few weeks to help with the initial adjustment and to pave the way for finding a place of their own. A few weeks' stay grew into almost two months. The host family was only too glad to help; the Alexanders feared they were imposing but feared moving out into Ankara even more. Eventually they moved into their own place, Perry got settled in his new job, and Joanne took lessons in Turkish at Perry's office. But soon Joanne gave up Turkish lessons because the demand for English lessons was so great. Joanne made the rounds at local embassies and began a burgeoning business as a private English tutor.

Ankara was sometimes frightening, sometimes enchanting, and always exasperating. Frequent power outages and water shortages made day-to-day life difficult. Household items and foodstuffs were sometimes hard to come by. An emergency trip to a Turkish hospital for Joanne and a telephone mysteriously ripped out of their wall added spice to their Ankara stay. Over time, Perry and Joanne felt comfortable in the camaraderie of the Ankara expatriate community. They enjoyed the lavish hospitality of new Turkish friends, and both of them prepared, served, and ate Turkish delicacies with abandon. After six or seven months they felt at home and could negotiate at the local bazaar with the most seasoned Turkish haggler.

As the assignment came to an end, Perry and Joanne looked forward to going home (they had made no home leave trips in eighteen months). Suddenly they found themselves in a rented condominium in the midst of rural Plainsboro, New Jersey, with no preparation or special arrangements made by the company. After all, they were coming "home." Perry was still employed, Joanne was newly employed, and they were back in their homeland feeling totally estranged. They recall feeling contempt for the Americans they met and were amazed at everyone's wastefulness, lack of tolerance, and emotional coolness. Homes, hearts, and dinner tables had opened for them in Turkey. They missed the challenge of life in Ankara. Here in a land of 150 brands of toothpaste, everything seemed sterile and lonesome. Reentry adjustment for the Alexanders took a long time. In fact, they returned over ten years ago, and they still have more than a little lingering reticence about having come back at all.

What could Perry Alexander's company have done to help?

▲ *Culture training.* Although Perry's company spent little on assistance, measures were taken to ensure that the Alexanders were taken care of. Language lessons helped and might have helped even more if they had begun prearrival, but this is perhaps a minor point. Counseling in local customs, and in the current norms of everyday life, would have helped the Alexanders more quickly overcome their initial shock upon arrival.

▲ *Living arrangements and acclimatization.* The family that took the Alexanders in is to be credited with helping them find a rental residence and with having made the living adjustment easier. If the Alexanders had begun their stay in a hotel or a furnished apartment, they never would have learned so much so fast. The host family played an informal but thorough role as counselors and area specialists.

▲ *Financial assistance.* The Alexanders had to use personal savings to help them through the first several months in Turkey. Because of the sparseness of company assistance, it took Perry quite awhile to be reimbursed for many of the basics of his relocation. While the financial stress of the move is really only a footnote to the Alexanders' story, a more comprehensive financial assistance plan (particularly one that prepaid expenses or provided funds in advance) would have helped the Alexanders measurably.

▲ *Reentry return transition assistance.* Because home leave time and funds were never available to the Alexanders, their immersion into Turkish life among the expatriate community was complete. Perry's company could have helped re-Americanize the family by providing regular trips home and by helping the Alexanders connect with company families that had also experienced reentry. Another step, beyond reentry assistance, would have been to relocate the Alexander family to a more stimulating U.S. locale. Their transition from urban Ankara to rural New Jersey was made more challenging because the cultural adjustment was accentuated by the marked life-style change. A move to a more bustling American city might have facilitated a quicker readjustment.

10

Literacy and Other Essential Skills

Linda Stoker and Rob Gunther-Mohr, Center for Essential
Workplace Skills

We are accustomed to assume that work and the training supporting it can
be defined in the context of output: whatever is reasonable to require in
order to produce the product in a reasonable amount of time and at a
reasonable cost is planned back from the desired outcome. One of the
dilemmas facing many human resources organizations is that the technological and human relations skills required in the new workplace depend
on foundations more extensive than what a large proportion of the work
force had the educational opportunity to develop during their school years.
The following scenario is illustrative:

> Harry MacDonald was conducting a turndown interview with
> Marlene Anderson, a middle-aged assembler who had applied
> for a technician's training position. "It's too bad you didn't
> study some electronics in high school," Harry said. "And you
> should have taken more math. Math is the key to the future."

> "Mr. MacDonald," Anderson replied, "I don't think they even
> had electronics when I was in high school, and I would have
> taken more math, but in those days they only allowed the boys
> to take things like algebra and trig in our town."

The old workplace called for a limited set of skills. Manufacturing
and, to a great extent, clerical, retail, and service sectors as well were
based on the mass production of similarly designed products that had a
relatively long product life. Skills, though potentially complex, changed
little over the course of the life of a product. What changes that did occur
created only a gradual demand for increased skills from employees, and
the skills themselves tended to be focused on a limited set of operations.
Both the time frame and the structure of the work made the acquisition of
skills a process that essentially took care of itself. Employees could learn
on the job and keep up.

Particularly between World War II and the mid-1980s, the staffing of
entry-level skilled labor jobs was completed largely by hiring from a

sizable population of high school graduates. This pool was supplemented by the immigration of potential workers coming from Western Europe where there were established apprentice traditions and by second career placements of workers.

The state of the workplace today, dictated by increased international competition and new technologies, is substantially different:

- New forms of organization have mandated pushing the level of decision making down as far as possible in the organization.
- New forms of working together, stressing teamwork and coopera-tion, are becoming the norm.
- Product life cycles are now shorter, and product lines customized to client needs and market niches are features of most industries.
- Turnaround on design and production to get a product to market has been dramatically reduced.
- Jobs change far more quickly as these other trends take hold.

All of these factors influence how companies design jobs and thus the skills employees need. Today, instead of hiring workers at the lowest skill level, teaching them a minimal set of skills, and setting them to work doing the same small set of tasks over and over for the least possible wage, a different pattern is becoming common. In the new global workplace, simple work is increasingly done by robotics or exported to other parts of the world where wages are lower (as are standards of living). The work that is left, the work that justifies high wages, calls for offering more flexibility, applying training in new and innovative ways, understanding the entire process and how a given set of tasks fits into it, and solving problems and applying critical thinking to work. In other words, the value brought by labor to this new workplace is brains, not brawn. If workers are not able to bring these skills to the workplace, jobs move offshore, where levels of skills may be competitive with lower wages. For American business to maintain or acquire a competitive edge or to keep domestic jobs, it needs employees who will be able to justify higher pay scales by bringing value added in the form of higher levels of skills and greater work flexibility.

Finding Employees

Formerly staff could expect to keep the new skills edge on a company's work force by hiring new workers, but the profile of the new job applicant is changing almost as fast as the work. Demographic trends show that the youth labor pool, relied on in the past for new workers, is drying up, and groups available for work include more women and members of minorities, who as groups have had less access to the standard schooling the workplace now requires. Typical entries to the labor pool in the future will have less education and will be more heterogeneous than the "old" American work force. Immigrants are coming from countries that typically have less-developed educational systems than that of the United States. Further, 75 percent of the work force that will be in the labor pool at the turn of the century is already at work. That group, long trained to the requirements in the ways of the old workplace, has a different set of skills than are called for by the "new." The hope of finding highly qualified workers who can do the more sophisticated jobs is not realistic in most cases.

If that were all, it would be challenge enough, but there is more to consider. Individuals currently in the work force or those in school are still learning ways of thinking and working that are difficult to transfer to the new corporate setting. Traditional methods of teaching and learning can be static and one-dimensional, particularly for students who "don't need more, because they're just going to work," as a candidate for public office in a southern state put it recently. In many places, the people who will become the blue-collar and technical work force are still being set tasks that will not qualify them for participation in the mainstream of the American work force. The ability to apply and integrate skills to solve problems in new settings is the key to future productivity and job security. The work force did not learn and is not yet learning these skills in school. Several federal and regional public and private agencies are working on revision of the public education system, but we cannot wait the five, ten, or fifteen years needed to educate a new generation of workers.

Workplace skills programs set within human resources development strategies are one major way that corporations can take the initiative and begin reframing the skills of its current work force. Integrating skills-upgrading programs with the routine part of doing business enables a company to continue to use its resources at an optimal level. An investment in enriching the skills and abilities of the work force is really no different from conscientious maintenance and upgrading of physical equipment, and it becomes a priority when the cost and competition to find new workers with new skills are high.

The Importance of an Essential Skills Program

There is only one valid reason for a corporation to include an essential skills program among the services and resources made available to its employees: its managers have confidence that the program will have a positive effect on the company's efforts to achieve its business goals. Ultimately a program must have a positive effect on quality, safety, and productivity to improve overall effectiveness and profitability.

Some advocates of essential skills programs propose that programs are justified by asserting that employers need to develop the whole person, improve the company's public image, or address illiteracy. Sometimes program rationales focus on the need for specific skills in order to produce specific new products. Although we do not disagree with any of these ends as goals, we recommend keeping the discussion focused on an organization's key business issues. Linking a program to quality, safety, and/or productivity as rationales for instituting a program will anchor the program in the organization in a way other rationales do not. This approach allows stakeholders from a variety of departments in the organization to see the way a program can pay off for them. For example, a manager who can see that an essential skills program is an investment in improved product quality is much more likely to support the program as part of his or her own strategy instead of as an ancillary program competing for resources in short supply.

There is no universal formula that will yield a valid measurement for all companies of the need for an essential skills program. Each company must decide what is of primary importance in relation to its business goals and evaluate whether an essential skills program is needed.

Figure 10-1 offers some ideas on outcomes that an essential skills program could effect. Among the human resources considerations for developing an essential skills program, safety, quality, and productivity are primary concerns. Indirect considerations include training, performance, career development, workplace culture, and communications. For each consideration, there can be possible positive and negative ways an essential skills program intervention might affect the organization—for example, increasing the understanding of safety regulation and materials, decreasing downtime, or reducing accidents.

The first step in seeing if there is a justification for an essential skills program intervention is to identify the priorities or particular issues in the company. A formal business plan or a survey of manager and supervisors are two appropriate methods of identifying a corporation's needs.

Once identified, these concerns must be associated with some cost-benefit measures. Cost-benefit analysis is often overlooked when training programs are launched. The process of connecting the values of a program to the organization's needs in order to decide whether the program is a worthwhile investment is another step in creating a program that will truly prosper by serving the organization's needs.

The usual approach human resources managers undertake for a cost-benefit analysis is the adoption of some type of accounting formula. Our view is that using a purely fiscal approach to this process is misleading. Although researchers have tried to develop effective cost analysis for human resources for many years, these algorithms tend to be complex and incomplete, and they invariably focus on economic costs alone. Many of these attempts are the result of managers bringing finance or engineering backgrounds to bear on the complex arena of human resources. The field

Figure 10-1. Rationales for developing workplace skills programs.

Human Resources Considerations	Reduce	Increase
Primary concerns		
Safety	Accidents	Understanding of safety signs and procedures
Quality	Error	Understanding of instrumentation
Productivity	Downtime	Ratio of production to worker
Contributing concerns		
Training issues	Training time	On-the-job application of concepts learned in training
Performance	Error rates	Speed of production
Career development	Unrealistic estimation of job potential opportunities	Worker's ability to meet the challenges of future work and plan for the future
Workplace culture	Misunderstanding of cultural mores and patterns	Begin to see learning as part of the job and part of the culture
Communications	Misunderstandings resulting from difficulty with written and or oral communications	Clear communications among all elements of the corporation

has much to gain from these perspectives but must not abrogate its responsibility to represent other kinds of costs and benefits that finance, return on investment or equity, or the time value of money offer by themselves. We must not reduce human resources to a simple dollar formula (although that is one very important element of the equation). On the other hand, too often human resources professionals allow the managers they support to swing to the other extreme and undertake costly interventions without accountability measures. Organizational approaches to cost-benefit rarely rely on value judgments informed by available cost data.

The Planning Approach

To address cost-benefit needs, as well as many other issues in program design, we advocate a participative planning approach, an effective method of developing program plans that is based on action research methods. It is particularly useful when the organization has or wants to develop a culture of participation, there are several stakeholder groups in the organization, or program relevance to business goals is a high priority. In this method the facilitator guides participants through a series of discussions exploring organizational issues, developing parameters for the proposed program, and reviewing and improving the resulting design. Participants are asked to contribute out of their areas of concern and expertise to consider the effect the proposed program might have on their area of the company and to make suggestions based on this reflection. The resulting process clarifies early on whether there is a need for the proposed program and builds strong support for the resulting strategy, program, or plan. (There are lists of books and organizations that provide relevant information at the end of this chapter.)

A participative needs analysis for essential skills programs must address a variety of issues:

1. *Identify company goals.* Recording and discussing company goals is the first step of the analysis of costs and benefits. Key goals and values need to be discussed and summarized because they will become the focus of the remaining steps of this process.

2. *Identify desirable program goals.* Table 10-1 can be used to generate ideas of how a potential skills program might support an organization in reaching those goals. Other possible program goals follow:

▲ Reduce turnover.
▲ Improve the advanced-training candidate.
▲ Support increased productivity.
▲ Reduce new product orientation time.
▲ Develop a stable work force.
▲ Prepare employees for change.
▲ Support work team effectiveness.
▲ Improve communications between employees and managers.
▲ Reduce spoilage.
▲ Improve promotability.
▲ Improve the productivity quotient.
▲ Increase the general educational level of the work force.

Once the group's goals have been ranked, members can generate conservative cost estimates for what effect an essential skills program could have on the goals. This step requires some research and estimation. The members bring their findings back to the group and discuss them.

At Consolidated Stores, for example, the turnover among stock clerks was 120 percent a year with 1,000 positions company-wide. Management estimated that the cost of bringing in each new employee, counting recruiting and staffing, the training and learning curve, and temporary overtime was just over $1,000 per new hiree. They figured that reducing turnover was one strong element in justifying an essential skills program. If they could reduce turnover by 10 percent, they would realize a substantial savings.

They projected that an essential skills program could affect this reduction by creating an incentive for employees to stay for a period of time to improve their skills. Additional intangible savings derived from having a more stable work force, contributing to increased productivity, and assisting employees in becoming more promotable in the long run. Retaining better-qualified candidates for promotion and training programs represented a potential savings to Consolidated Stores in the long term.

Walking systematically through the program goals exercise and identifying ways that the achievement of those goals specifically leads to savings will establish the foundation for the cost analysis. These goal-related savings statements are the first information element in the analysis.

3. *Identify potential program costs.* The third step is the analysis of costs. The following list contains typical costs associated with conducting an essential skills program. The list is not exhaustive, and not all items are carried as costs by every company, but it offers a starting place for identifying and evaluating potential program costs for a particular company:

- Classroom space
- Employee participant time
- Project/program coordination
- Needs assessment
- Program communications and recruiting
- Transportation
- Instruction
- Materials development, textbooks, hardware, software
- Program evaluation
- Instructor orientation and training
- Skills analysis and curriculum design

This list can serve as the basis for a discussion of potential program costs. After a reasonable program size and duration has been posed, the group can identify all the relevant costs that would be incurred by undertaking such a program.

Miller Machines had a small warehouse that was used primarily for equipment storage. The offices and reception area in the front of the building were temporarily unused. Since the equipment being stored required climate control, the building's heating, ventilation, and air-conditioning system had to be kept running. Miller's planning committee decided that if classes could be scheduled in that space, the company could reduce one aspect of cost substantially. Because the standing costs of keeping the building open were already a cost of doing business, the added expense of heat and light in using the front offices for classrooms was minimal.

Although such resources are not always available, this example gives a flavor of the kinds of information and resources that are useful to gather. This step may require research and investigation outside the meeting.

4. *Potential program benefits.* Once the potential costs and savings of the program are generated, the out-of-pocket cost of operating the program can be identified. But there are intangible elements of conducting an essential skills program that are critical and should not be undersold.

Employer benefits can take a variety of forms:
- Increased productivity
- Greater work force versatility
- Improved problem-solving skills
- Larger qualified applicant selection pool
- Team building
- Shorter learning curve for new assignments
- Greater participation in company culture
- Higher productivity quotient
- Business literacy
- More informed use of company programs such as quality, safety, and the performance evaluation system

There are two key questions to ask in focusing the discussion:
1. What does the company gain by these changes in employee attitude, ability, and performance?
2. Do these benefits add a sufficient advantage to overall operations when weighed against the net costs of the program?

When Amalgamated Industries was installing a new computer-integrated manufacturing (CIM) system, employees were required to cross-train and to work as a team. One year before training for the new CIM line was to begin, the company had initiated an essential skills program. When the training started, trainers noticed a perceptible difference between the employees who had participated in the essential skills program and those who had not. Program participants had better self-esteem and shorter learning curves, were better able to understand the new training concepts, and scored better on the post-tests than the others.

The planning group should rank its list of employer benefits to determine which ones seem most important. The short list is the third information element of the final analysis.

The process must be repeated with the employee benefits. In many cases this is a flip side of employee benefits; however, it is important to think through what value employees will accrue for themselves in this process. The following lists what research has shown to be benefits employees feel they get from participating in an essential skills program (if the program is not attractive to employees, they will not participate):

- Becoming better qualified for promotions
- Improved self-esteem
- Improved problem-solving skills
- Increased job security
- Improved communication and math skills
- Greater access to job-growth opportunities
- Becoming better team members
- Having more informed participation in benefits, and performance evaluation

5. *Analyze the data.* The final step is to review all the findings. By this time, a consensus should have emerged that there is (or is not) perceived value worth the net cost of integrating an essential skills program into the company's human resources development activities. If the data are not clear and participants reserve their commitment, the case is not proved. Participants can identify where the weaknesses lie and have the opportunity to conduct further research, or they may conclude that the need is not justifiable at this time. If the consensus is that a program would be a valuable addition, the sanction of key stakeholders in the company's operation advocating for and endorsing the program is secured.

Determining What Is Essential

An essential skills program's content and approach must be integrated into the culture of the business, aligned with the goals of the company, and clearly reflect the priorities of the corporation. These criteria appear obvious to human resources professionals accustomed to designing and delivering training. Yet basic skills programs often do not meet these basic criteria because they are often considered to be a fringe benefit or a social obligation rather than a business necessity. There are two areas to examine in finding what is essential in a workplace skills program: what skills should be taught and how the program delivers the skills.

Identifying the Skills

Essential skills can be divided into two sets: skills underlying work and skills used in work. These definitions are somewhat arbitrary slices of a natural continuum, but they are useful distinctions for thinking about skills and planning approaches to delivering support to workers who need skills.

Skills underlying work are those that a worker must be able to use in order to qualify for work at any point of entry into the work force. These skills include communications (reading, writing, and speaking standard English) and basic math. In terms of the skill taxonomy—the list of skills a reading or math instructor expects to teach—the skills underlying work are the closest to the usual body of basic skills.

Figure 10-2 summarizes the basic skills underlying work in the context of their application in the workplace. There are two groupings represented in the figure:

1. Application, showing the kinds of applications of the skill in the workplace. These compilations of applications represent the types of workplace applications found in nonexempt, blue-collar, and clerical applications of the basic skills of reading, writing, and speaking English, and basic math.
2. Skills, representing competencies in the domain. For example, "encode/decode words and phrases" represents a range or cluster of performance competencies in the content areas of reading and writing. Employees who are expected to use signs, panels, and keyboards in their work or to find their way around the work site will have to use skills in the clusters of sight/sound correspondence, encoding and decoding words and phrases, and entering information.

An instructor planning a course of study for a group of employees who use signs, panels, and keyboards should be able to delineate the specific skills that apply in each cluster and design work-related inventories and instruction to support them. This list of skills (taxonomy) serves as the core, the contract, and the map on which the program is built and allows all participants to understand the program's mission. It helps the curriculum designers know what skills must be covered in the curriculum and in what context they are used. Teachers know, by reviewing the list and visiting the workplace, what skills people need in order to complete work. Employees know what skills the company expects of them and what skills will be taught in a class. And program managers have a method of knowing what skills are taught and have a strategic document to which new skills can be added as new ones arise in the workplace.

These are the skills that an employee must be able to use in order to qualify for specific jobs, manage a career, and so forth. They are skills that employees will use to manage themselves and their relationships with

Figure 10-2. The skills underlying work.

Reading and Writing	Ability to Speak Standard English	Basic Math Skills
Application:	*Application:*	*Application:*
• panels, signs, and keyboards	• Gathering and sharing information	• Counting and measuring
Skills:	*Skills:*	*Skills:*
• Sight/sound correspondance • Encode/decode words and phrases. • Enter information.	• Develop key vocabulary. • Ask and answer questions. • Give and follow instructions.	• Whole numbers • Decimal fractions • Common fractions • Finding unknowns
Application:	*Application:*	*Application:*
• Forms, messages, and texts	• Engaging and interacting with others.	• Using formulas
Skills:	*Skills:*	*Skills:*
• Encode/decode words and phrases. • Enter and report information. • Gather and analyze information.	• Develop key vocabulary. • Ask and answer questions. • Give and follow instructions. • Explain point of view and discuss issues.	• Whole numbers • Decimal fractions • Common fractions • Finding unknowns
Application:	*Application:*	*Application:*
• Resource material, diagrams, matrices, and references	• Participating in groups and teams	• Using tables and graphs
Skills:	*Skills:*	*Skills:*
• Enter and report information. • Gather and analyze information.	• Develop key vocabulary. • Ask and answer questions. • Give and follow instructions. • Explain point of view and discuss ideas.	• Whole numbers • Decimal fractions • Common fractions • Finding Unknowns

others appropriately and under a variety of often changing circumstances. The three clusters of skills or competencies, as shown in Figure 10-3 are:

1. Developing a skill base for job readiness, such as problem solving, critical thinking skills, time management, sequencing and following directions, framing questions, and job content knowledge.
2. Managing relations, including understanding and using one's learning style, establishing appropriate work habits, personal development, career development, maintaining personal physical and emotional health, stress management, and team skills.

Figure 10-3. The skills used in work.

Developing a Skill Base for Job Readiness	Managing Relations: Personal and Group Boundaries	Working Within the Organization's Culture
Application:	*Application:*	*Application:*
• Managing one's work life	• Managing one's work life	• Managing one's work life
Skill set examples:	*Skill set examples:*	*Skill set examples:*
• Learning to learn,	• Work habits	• Business literacy,
• Following directions,	• Personal health	• Time management
• Organizing sequences,	• Emotional health	
• Basic job content,	• Job-keeping skills	
• Knowledge,		
Application:	*Application:*	*Application:*
• Working with others	• Working with others	• Working with others
Skill set examples:	*Skill set examples:*	*Skill set examples:*
• Framing questions,	• Team skills	• Social contracts
• Explaining/ demonstrating job tasks to others	• Interpersonal communication skills	• Negotiating skills
	• Listening skills	• Training the trainer
Application:	*Application:*	*Application:*
• Managing change	• Managing change	• Managing change
Skill set examples:	*Skill set examples:*	*Skill set examples:*
• Critical thinking	• Career development	• Meeting management
• Problem solving	• Stress management	
• Job-related learning	• Leadership skills	

3. Working within the organization's culture, such as social contracting, negotiating skills, and business literacy.

These skills are used in the workplace to manage one's work life, work with others, and manage change. Instruction for many of these skills can be found in management development programs. Their presence demonstrates that in the workplace today, responsibility and decision making are being passed further and further down into the lower echelons of the organization.

These skills represent the platform of competence on which a business will grow into the twenty-first century. By designing an essential skills program that supports employees' demonstrating the skills they have acquired and developing the skills they need, corporations take a major step necessary to establishing successful continuous-learning systems.

Delivering the Skills

Four questions are the keys to a manager's understanding of what to look for in an essential skills program proposal.

1. *Do the program manager and the instructors know what basic skills employees need on their jobs or in the jobs they will grow into?* Essential skills programs should focus on the skills employees need to perform their jobs. This focus can be achieved by interviewing key individuals, observing on the work floor and/or examining documents, conducting tests of employees' skills, or a combination approach. The first three approaches all have particular strengths and weaknesses. The fourth is best, since it produces the richest data. The issue, however, is not so much among choices of approach as between conducting a skills assessment or not. Any program proposal that sets program competencies or goals without some dialogue with the company is not as likely to yield success as one that does. In the Appendix is an example of a survey that can be used to collect information for deciding what needs to be taught and gathering the information about context needed to design effective instruction.

2. *Will everyone involved in the program—managers who support it, instructors who teach, employees who are taking classes—be able to understand why the program is being offered?* If there is not an overall sense of why the program is in operation, it will be viewed as yet another passing fad. Once a program is firmly anchored to the company's goals, the relationship between the program and the anticipated benefits of it must be explained, promoted, defended, and/or expanded to meet different constituencies' needs within the corporation. A plant manager or senior employee at a workplace is an important person to convince of the need for an essential skills program. This is a place to start but by no

means a place to finish. Students must see the connection between the essential skills program and company goals and personal career goals, for if this connection exists and is well communicated, they are the best source of publicity a program can cultivate.

One powerful method of building this sense of ownership is to include as many stakeholder groups as possible in the conduct of the needs assessment. Supervisors and quality control or process engineers must be in on the planning of the program so that they identify the program as their own. A convinced quality control engineer or supervisor is a powerful advocate for a program at budget time.

3. *Is the proposed program design based on adult learning theory?* Adults in general, and particularly those who have been out of school for a long period of time or those who had little schooling, often approach educational settings with the fear that "it will be like school used to be when I was a kid." This usually means that the curriculum is preset, that they have no expectations that what they learn will help meet their needs or help them solve their problems, that everyone covers the same material even if they already know it, and that the teacher will brook no insubordination. The more that adults encounter a class oriented to helping them solve problems in their work and conducted in a collaborative manner, the more likely it is that they will have a successful educational experience.

4. *Will all interested parties be able to get information about how the program is going?* In order to ensure its success, a program has to have a mechanism with which it can make adjustments in practices or policies. Attendance is one example of a problem that can arise with an essential skills program. Regardless of the type of difficulty, the program must respond to problems by asking questions and seeking accommodations or solutions if the program is to be successful. Suppose that five weeks into the program, attendance is running at 40 percent and has been steadily declining since the first day. One could easily draw the conclusion that the students are not interested and the program should be terminated. A successful program will have management mechanisms that allow the manager to go beyond this initial conclusion to discover why employees are not attending—for example:

- Supervisors are under extreme production pressure and are not letting employees off the line.
- Most employees car pool to and from work and have not been able to arrange alternate transportation to fit the class schedule, which is one hour on company time and one hour on employee time.
- The class location moves every week, and employees have difficulty finding the classroom.
- The employees forced to choose between being home when their children get out of school and taking a course that might lead to job growth at some later date chose to be with their children.

▲ A course was set up to conflict with scheduled overtime, and employees felt they could not afford to lose their places on the overtime schedule.

A program with a good program management system will have mechanisms for calling attention to problems before they grow out of proportion, identifying their underlying causes, and finding appropriate policy, procedure, personnel, and/or technological solutions for them.

Implementing Essential Skills Programs

After establishing that there is a compelling organizational need for an essential skills program, considering what skills are important, and determining that the business has appropriate strategies for the four key questions, it is time to develop and implement a program. Now is the time to identify the specific activities that will make up the program (what courses to offer, what instructional methods to employ, how to recruit participants, how to evaluate participants' progress) and the progress of the program itself. Each successful program will have its own unique form and specific approaches to these items; the best programs are sensitive to and adapt themselves to the company's climate and culture. These choices are governed by such factors as work culture, the existing and projected essential skills needs of the work force, the resources available to operate the program, and the qualifications of the instructors or providers. However programs may vary, there are four elements that must be included for the program to succeed:

1. *A skills audit to determine the skills needed.* A participative approach to the skills audit provides the richest data, triangulating informants with observation and skill sampling. Where this cannot be accomplished, at least two steps should be included.

First, the facilitator should convene a group of employees who have knowledge of the jobs and brainstorm the kinds of skills needed to complete the job or jobs being studied, using a taxonomy of skills for the content area (reading, math, etc.) under consideration as a guide. They should also assemble all the written documentation available for the job and setting. Next, a curriculum developer or an instructor trained in observation of the work context of skills should observe the employees doing the jobs and examine the written materials, using the brainstormed list as a guide. Then the products of these two exercises are combined and reduced to provide the working taxonomy or guide for the curriculum, as well as for designing recruitment, participant planning, and evaluation instruments.

2. *A delivery method and content for instruction.* There are many

possible choices for delivering instruction. Some of the factors that go into selecting a methodology are space and time available, availability of funds for capital investment for hardware and software, and availability of trained instructors. Generally as long as group instruction is feasible, an instructor who understands how to individualize instruction for a group of students with similar needs is the most cost-effective delivery method, since instructors are more flexible and adaptive than technology. In situations where economies of scale do not make group instruction an alternative, computers, videos, and interactive systems become more cost-effective.

As the costs of technology drop, interactive systems will begin to provide more attractive options. Computer-managed assessment, placement, and records systems are useful, but potential purchasers should be wary of promises about interactive computerized basic skills instruction systems. The instructional bases that have been developed are for youth markets and are not particularly suited to work context materials; they are only beginning to be redesigned for mature workers.

3. *A marketing and recruiting strategy.* Program success depends largely on the methods used to market it to supervisors, managers, and employees. Convincing the work force to buy into the program will require steps similar to advertising any other product or service.

Each organization has formal and informal information networks. In some companies, weekly staff meetings are used to update employees about new programs; in others, memos and brochures are used. Communications is critical to the success of a program and can include the following activities:

- Providing information through enrollment forms and brochures available in the company personnel office and any other official place (such as a company newsletter) and through any informal communications systems (pay envelope stuffers, notices posted in the lunchroom or locker rooms, etc.). Any information that is printed should also be available in spoken announcements for employees who are nonreaders or in the native languages of employees with limited English-speaking skills.
- Maintaining interest after an initial kickoff through a continuing communications program to keep the program current in the employees' minds.
- Monitoring employees' response in order to revise the communication strategies.
- Designing enrollment procedures to make application to the program easy.
- Sharing success to spread the news about the program by awarding certificates of completion and participation and encouraging managers to congratulate successful participants.

Employees often initially worry that stepping forward and stating that they need or want to improve their essential skills could result in the loss of their jobs—even when there is no evidence that this is a possibility. They can also be concerned about their reputations in the workplace and fear being stigmatized by either their peers or by the company. Many employees are anxious about whether they can do well in the company courses. Recruitment activities must be carried out with an awareness of these reactions, fears, and anxieties if they are to be effective.

4. *A management system for administering the program.* The management and administration may be assigned to one or more people, who may be employees of the company or of the provider (if an outside provider is used). An assigned person is needed to manage the program to ensure that activities are taking place on time and according to schedule. This role requires experience in managing programs and a willingness to learn how to direct and control the activities of the program. Information about the company's history, policies, procedures, work schedules, operations, and resources is needed in managing so that the program fits the company and its needs. The following activities are involved in managing and administering a program:

▲ Recruiting and developing program staff and instructors.
▲ Developing and monitoring program budget.
▲ Developing project standards, policies, and procedures.
▲ Exchanging information with supervisors and managers.
▲ Developing solutions to project problems.
▲ Acting as liaison with other organizations, both internal and external.
▲ Helping to develop and provide feedback on program evaluation.
▲ Integrating staff with varying schedules into a functional team.
▲ Monitoring program instruction and objectives.
▲ Evaluating instructional staff performance based on guidelines related to instructional techniques, experience working with adults, and achievement of program objectives.
▲ Selecting and scheduling program facilities and equipment.
▲ Securing summary attendance records from course instructors.
▲ Scheduling instructional staff.
▲ Ensuring that course material is prepared and available.
▲ Maintaining the physical environment.
▲ Establishing contingency plans for instructor backups and emergencies.

Research on basic skills programs and on employee participation in them shows that, regardless of industry, the best attendance, retention, and achievement occur when programs are job related and taught by well-trained instructors on company time. Although the last feature is not always feasible, particularly in small companies but even in large ones during busy seasons, these findings should be taken into serious consideration when planning a program schedule.

Every program manager has to decide on whose time the program will be scheduled: the employer's or the employee's? Possible arrangements are:

- 100 percent investment by the employer (employee attends during work hours; does homework on own time).
- 100 percent investment by employee (employee attends before or after work hours; does homework on own time).
- 50 percent investment by employer and 50 percent investment by employee (employee attends partly during work hours and partly on own time; homework is done on own time).

Whenever classes are scheduled, working adults are often under extraordinary pressures because of competing demands at home, in the community, and on the job. So even if thorough planning of every aspect of the program goes perfectly, if classes are not scheduled at times that allow employees to attend easily, some may be unable to stay in the program for long.

Judging the Program

The process of improving basic skills in the workplace needs to be thought out in an organizational context. Organizational learning is measured and evaluated on how skills and behaviors are integrated into jobs and into organizational practice. Success can be measured by how many participants learned how much in the classroom, but that is only the first step. The real job in evaluation is tracing how those new skills are integrated into the participant's daily work. It can be accomplished by:

- Gathering as much follow-up information about the original goals as possible
- Collecting anecdotal information and hard data from supervisors and others about participants' changes in work methods and habits
- Developing profiles of additional gains and benefits that may have become apparent since the beginning of the program
- Gathering profiles of participant skills gains in the classroom and of awards granted

The stakeholder group can use this information to determine whether the program is meeting its original goals. If it is not, additional program components might be needed to ensure that employees are supported in carrying the skills back to the job.

This is the key to success. If the program succeeds in supporting company business goals by improving quality, safety, and productivity, it will be because it has created a program intervention through which program participants, supported by their fellow workers and by supervisors and managers, have developed specific skills, have used them to change their work behavior, and have increased their margin of job security and growth.

SELECTED READING

How-To Guides

Workplace Basics Training Manual, by Anthony Carnevale, Leila Gainer, and Meltzer (Alexandria, Va.: American Society for Training and Development, 1990). Provides step-by-step guidelines for planning and implementing an effective workplace skills program, dealing with how to develop support for programs within and outside a company, as well as basic training methodology. A companion book, *Workplace Basics: Essential Skills Employers Want,* analyzes the skills employers need in the work force.

Job-Related Literacy Training: Teaching Reading on the Job, by Butruille, Philippi, and Petrini (Alexandria, Va.: American Society for Training and Development, 1989). Deals with how to assess job-related reading skills, conduct job task analysis, develop a lesson format, and assess an organization's reading needs and resources. Includes detailed information on the processes and competencies commonly needed for job literacy in some ninety-five different occupations.

Job-Related Basic Skills: A Guide for Planners of Employee Programs (New York: Business Council for Effective Literacy, 1987). Gives step-by-step guidelines for planning and implementing an effective job-related basic skills program for employees. Three major sections cover general principles to guide workplace efforts, specifics on developing and operating a program, and special issues to consider. To illustrate the application of procedures and principles, fourteen programs are profiled.

The Bottom Line: Basic Skills in the Workplace, by the Departments of Labor and Education (Washington, D.C.: U.S. Government Printing Office, 1988). Provides analysis and discussion of the workplace basic skills problem and gives detailed guidelines on how to develop a good workplace program. Contains charts on how to perform a literacy audit and evaluate workplace literacy programs and profiles numerous programs to illustrate the application of procedures and principles.

Worker-Centered Learning: A Union Guide to Workplace Literacy (Washington, D.C.: AFL-CIO, 1990). Examines definitions of literacy and the status and role of workplace literacy today and lays out a nine-step plan to follow in designing worker-centered basic skills programs, giving examples of union efforts.

Training Partnerships: Linking Employers and Providers, by Anthony Carnevale,

Leila Gainer, Janice Villet, and Shari Holland (Alexandria, Va.: American Society for Training and Development, 1984). Reports on a study conducted by the American Society for Training and Development and the U.S. Department of Labor on the use of outside providers of training. Identifies provider groups and systems, examines how employers interact with them, and gives guidance to employers on how to make informed decisions when buying outside training help.

The Work Education Project (Bloomington, Ind.: Indiana University, 1988), 2 vols. The first volume, *Bridging Education and Employment with Basic Academic Skills,* is a research synthesis of what is known about literacy, vocational education, math, science, and computer literacy and the implications for program and curriculum development. The companion volume, *How to Gather and Develop Job Specific Literacy Materials for Basic Skills Instruction,* gives guidance on how to build workplace programs geared to tasks workers encounter on the job and explains how to conduct literacy-related job task analysis and develop appropriate learning materials.

Policy and Research Reports

An Annotated Bibliography of Research on Basic Skills in the Workforce and Related Issues (Washington, D.C.: Southport Institute for Policy Analysis, 1990).

Workforce 2000: Work and Workers for the 21st Century, by William Johnston and Arnold Packer (Washington, D.C.: U.S. Government Printing Office, 1988). A groundbreaking report on the changing demographics of the American work force and implications for work force skills upgrading.

Worker Training: Competing in the New International Economy (Washington, D.C.: U.S. Government Printing Office, 1990). A comprehensive study for the Senate Labor and Human Resources Committee, the House Committee on Education and Labor, and the Senate Finance Committee, prepared under the guidance of a national advisory panel of corporate, union, government, research, and military leaders. Examines U.S. worker training and retraining needs in an international context and in terms of what is needed to maintain the American standard of living and remain globally competitive; analyzes the forces that shape training, the extent of U.S. employer-provided training compared to that of major competitors, and trends in instructional technology and its use in training programs; and offers sixteen policy options to Congress designed to broaden and deepen employer and employee commitments to training. The report's focus is on skills upgrading for already-employed workers because this will have the greatest competitive impact in the near and medium term.

America's Choice: High Skills or Low Wages, by the Commission on the Skills of the American Workforce (Rochester, N.Y.: National Center on Education and the Economy, 1990). Focuses on vestibule programs and action needed to address the skills and training needs of young people in transition from school to work.

From School to Work (Princeton, N.J.: Educational Testing Service). Focuses on the transition to work of non–college bound high school students. Notes that while other developed countries have institutional systems for helping young people make the school-to-work transition, the United States does not. Explores differences in skills and attitudes required for success in school and on the job and stresses the need for better communication between educators and employers to smooth the transition.

Training: The Competitive Edge, by Jerome Rosow and Robert Zager (San Francisco: Jossey-Bass, 1989). A report on a long-term national investigation of corporate training and development programs. Presents effective and innovative programs, with an emphasis on those for "mid-literate" workers. Filled with information on strategies and guidelines for redirecting corporate training programs to meet the changing requirements of jobs and new technology.

Training America: Strategies for the Nation, by Anthony Carnevale et al. (Alexandria, Va.: National Center on Education and the Economy and the American Society for Training and Development, 1989). An analysis of the role of business, education, and government in the United States in providing job-related training programs, as compared to Canada, Australia, Japan, and several European countries, with recommendations for improving public policy and developing new workplace program approaches.

Jump Start: The Federal Role in Adult Literacy, by Forrest Chisman (Washington, D.C.: Southport Institute for Policy Analysis, 1989). Concludes that the national literacy effort should have a major focus on basic skills for the currently employed.

Leadership for Literacy: The Agenda for the 1990s, by Forrest Chisman et al. (San Francisco: Jossey-Bass, 1990). A combination of background papers for *Jump Start* and new chapters that provides a detailed analysis of the current status of general and work force literacy in the nation, with reference to political, institutional, and intellectual forces. Sets forth a national agenda for overcoming barriers to skills upgrading in the work force, with recommendations for employers and other responsible groups.

Workforce/Workplace Literacy Packet (New York: Business Council for Effective Literacy). Includes a selection of national newsletters put out by the Business Council for Effective Literacy, collected newspaper and magazine articles on aspects of workplace–work force literacy, an annotated workplace–work force bibliography, and a reprint of the 1988 *Business Week* feature "Human Capital: The Decline of America's Workforce."

Recent Surveys

America's Work Force in the 1990s: Trends Affecting Manufacturers, by Jerry Jasinowsky (Washington, D.C.: National Association of Manufacturers. Examines trends identified in *Workforce 2000* in terms of their implications for manufacturers and recommends that manufacturers invest more in work force training and increase employee involvement in workplace decisions.

Literacy in the Work Force, by Leonard Lund and E. Patrick McGuire (New York: Conference Board). Finds, based on a mail survey of 1,600 manufacturing and service firms, that most companies do not test for literacy or math skills, most are concerned about illiteracy among their workers and expect the problem to get worse, and most have no in-house programs to address worker skills needs. Profiles a sampling of workplace programs and the particular features of each and sets forth several goals, constituting a literacy agenda for the business community.

1990 SHRM/CCH Survey: Workplace Literacy/Basic Skills, by Claire Anderson and Betty Ricks (Chicago: Commerce Clearing House and the Society for Human Resource Managers). Explores the extent of workplace illiteracy, the problems that arise from it, and what is being done to address it from questionnaires sent to a random sample of Society for Human Resource Managers members.

Workforce 2000: Competing in a Seller's Market: Is Corporate America Prepared? A Survey Report on Corporate Responses to Demographic and Labor Force Trends, by Towers Perrin and the Hudson Institute (Valhalla, N.Y.: Towers Perrin). Gives the results of a survey about how well positioned businesses are to address the issues identified in the Hudson Institute's *Workforce 2000,* based on questionnaires returned by 645 businesses representing a wide range of types. Contains a wealth of demographic information about the current and future work force and discusses the resulting work force problems that businesses will have to address.

NATIONAL TECHNICAL ASSISTANCE ORGANIZATIONS FOR WORK FORCE AND WORK PLACE LITERACY

Center for Essential Workplace Skills. The center has developed workplace programs for both big and small companies and for colleges and community agencies, has produced guides and other technical assistance material to aid others in the development of workplace literacy programs and the training of trainers, and is experienced in running workshops and seminars. Center for Essential Workplace Skills, P.O. Box 426, Cambridge, MA 02141. (617) 252-2426.

Center for Applied Linguistics (CAL). CAL has extensive experience in both large and small business settings. It specializes in programs for refugee and immigrant groups and operates the National (ESL) Clearinghouse on Literacy Education. CAL is a nonprofit organization and has worked broadly in the field of language and literacy for more than thirty years. Center for Applied Linguistics, 1118 22d Street, N.W., Washington, DC 20037. (202) 429-9292.

Center on Education and Training for Employment (CETE). CETE has developed workplace programs for schools, colleges, and government. It also offers workshops. Center on Education and Training for Employment, Ohio State University, 1900 Kenny Road, Columbus, OH 43210. (614) 292-4353.

Language Training Designs. The organization was established in April 1989 by Anne Lomperis, a specialist in workplace programs for limited English speakers. It is developing criteria that employers can use when selecting workplace education consultants. Language Training Designs, 16 Butterfield, Irvine, CA 92714. (714) 552-4601.

Center for Remediation Design. The center is a project of the U.S. Conference of Mayors, National Association of Private Industry Councils, National Association of Counties, and the Partnership for Training and Employment Careers. In addition to designing work force literacy programs, it has held regional training institutes for policymakers, program providers, and corporate managers focused on strategies for attacking basic skills deficiencies among at-risk youth and adults through Job Training Partnership Act programs and JOBS. Center for Remediation Design, c/o National Job Training Partnership, 1133 15th Street, N.W., Suite 1200, Washington, DC 20005. (202) 872-0776.

Matrices. Matrices offers a range of services, including workplace literacy planning and management seminars, training of trainers, and all aspects of designing and implementing workplace programs. Matrices, 4 Eversley Avenue, Norwalk, CT 06851. (203) 853-4163.

Performance Plus Literacy Consultants. Performance Plus has a special focus on small and medium-sized businesses but also works with larger companies and unions. It has developed job-specific curriculum and tests for the military, educationally disadvantaged young adults, business and industry, state and federal agencies, and private industry councils. Performance Plus, 7869 Godolphin Drive, Springfield, VA 22153. (703) 455-1735.

HRD Department, Inc. HRD specializes in the front-end activities of designing a program, such as job task analysis, employee skills assessment, and helping businesses clarify their training needs. It also works as a liaison between businesses and education providers at the local level, provides motivational services to get workers interested in skills training programs, and works with managers to help them examine logistical considerations. HRD has worked extensively with manufacturing but also with health care, utility, insurance, and other kinds of industry. HRD Department, Inc., P.O. Box 40035, St. Paul, MN 55104, (612) 642-1427 or (800) 642-1427.

Frontier College. Frontier College is a national literacy organization and Canada's oldest adult learning center. Among its services is the Learning in the Workplace project, which offers training, materials, and consultation. Learning in the Workplace, Frontier College, 35 Jackes Avenue, Toronto, Ontario, Canada, M4T 1E2. (415) 923-3591.

LIST OF NATIONAL RESOURCES

General

Division of Adult Education and
   Literacy
U.S. Department of Education
400 Maryland Avenue, S.W.
Washington, DC 20202-7240
(202) 732-2270

Office of Strategic Planning and
   Policy Development
U. S. Department of Labor
200 Constitution Avenue, N.W.,
   Room N5637
Washington, DC 20210
(202) 535-0662

Business Council for Effective
  Literacy
1221 Avenue of the Americas,
  35th Floor
New York, NY 10020
(212) 512-2415, (212) 512-2412

American Association for Adult
  and Continuing Education
1112 Sixteenth Street, N.W.
Washington, DC 20036
(202) 463-6333

International Reading Association
444 North Capitol Street, N.W.
Washington, DC 20001
(202) 347-3990

Southport Institute for Policy
  Analysis
440 First Street, N.W., Suite 415
Washington, DC 20001
(202) 783-7058

Community-Based Programs

Association for Community
  Based Education
1806 Vernon Street, N.W.
Washington, DC 20009
(202) 462-6333

Assault on Illiteracy Program
410 Central Park West
New York, NY 10025
(212) 967-4008

SER-Jobs for Progress, National
1355 River Bend Drive, Suite 240
Dallas, TX 75247
(214) 631-3999

United Way Programs

Literacy Initiatives
United Way of America
701 North Fairfax Street
Alexandria, VA 22314-2045
(703) 836-7100

Community Colleges

American Association of
  Community and Junior Colleges
One Dupont Circle, N.W., Suite
  410
Washington, DC 20036
(202) 293-7050

Voluntary Programs

Literacy Volunteers of America
Widewaters 1
5795 Widewaters Parkway
Syracuse, NY 13214
(315) 445-8000

Laubach Literacy Action
1320 Jamesville Avenue
Syracuse, NY 13210
(315) 422-9121

State Literacy Initiatives

Training and Employment
   Program
Center for Policy Research
National Governors' Association
444 North Capitol Street
Washington, DC 20001
(202) 624-5394

Literacy Network, Inc.
7505 Metro Boulevard
Minneapolis, MN 55439
(612) 893-7661

Union Literacy Programs

AFL-CIO Education Department
815 Sixteenth Street, N.W.
Washington, DC 20006
(202) 637-5141

Refugee and Immigrant Programs

Language and Communication
   Associates
1118 Twenty-Second Street, N.W.
Washington, DC 20037
(202) 223-6588

Federal Corrections

Correctional Education
   Association
8025 Laurel Lakes Court
Laurel, MD 20707
(301) 490-1440

American Correctional
   Association
4321 Hartwick Road, Suite L208
College Park, MD 20740
(301) 699-7650

Family Literacy Programs

National Center for Family
   Literacy
1 Riverfront Plaza, Suite 608
Louisville, KY 40202
(502) 584-1133

Barbara Bush Foundation for
   Family Literacy
1002 Wisconsin Avenue, N.W.
Washington, DC 20007
(202) 338-2006

Libraries

Office for Library Outreach
  Services
American Library Association
50 East Huron Street
Chicago, IL 60611
(312) 944-6780

National Literacy Hot Line

CONTACT Literacy Center
P.O. Box 81826
Lincoln, NE 68501
(800) 228-8813

(continues)

Reading Skills Survey for Managers

1. How Is Reading Used in the Workplace?

Job Studied: _____   Date: _____

Reporter: _____   Title: _____

This form is used to collect information that can be used to identify job-related reading skill needs in your operation and to develop functional context assessment and instruction materials.

▲ **Directions:**
Listed below are three distinct settings of **reading** in the workplace.
1. Please read this list to identify types of **reading** that are used for the job or set of jobs being analyzed.
2. Use two checks if, in your opinion, it is a critical skill.

▲ **Workplace Reading Includes:**

Signs, Labels, Panels, and Keyboards

Skill Application/Example   **Check**
▲ **Use letters** and numbers on a computer keyboard   ☐
▲ **Read alpha and numeric codes** (4NM67) like those used to find and replace files in a reprographics storage area; to distinguish among chemicals, medications, or types or quantities of supplies; to select stock or supplies from a supply catalog; or to identify error messages on a computer screen   ☐
▲ **Use alpha and numeric codes** to organize, store, and retrieve information   ☐
▲ **Read and follow directions** on signs like safety warnings, machine directions, and/or work area evacuation signs   ☐
▲ **Read and understand information** on labels like those found on medications, directions on the packaging for office supplies, or labels that are part of inventory systems   ☐
▲ **Follow instructions** like those found on the panel of a copier or fax machine or on the display board or control panel for an automated manufacturing process to start up or troubleshoot a piece of equipment   ☐

▲ **Forms, Messages, and Text**

Skill Application/Example   **Check**
▲ **Find relevant information** on forms that ask for standard information, like troubleshooting checklists, stock books and inventories, job applications, medical histories, or other standardized requests for information   ☐

Skill Application/Example   **Check**

▲ **Read and process information** in formats that include short narrative passages (short phrases of 3 to 5 words; reports of 5 or 6 sentences) like accident reports, critical incident reports, or the descriptive sections of production logs   ☐

▲ **Read** longer passages (up to 8–10 pages) of narrative text like articles about one's professional specialty, departmental memos, lab notes, or special reports   ☐

▲ **Read** technical text like the installation and start-up procedures for a personal computer printer, the operating procedures and change orders for an automated manufacturing process, or the manual or text for a training program   ☐

▲ **Resource Material:**

Diagrams, Matrices, and References

Skill Application/Example   **Check**

▲ **Find information** in a table like the Official Airline Guide, a shuttle schedule, or a spread-sheet   ☐

▲ **Find information** in a manual like the parts catalog, the table of contents or index to a book, or a dictionary or glossary of terms   ☐

▲ **Follow diagrams, schematics, and information maps** like evacuation plans, flow diagrams, charts and graphs, spread-sheets or system diagrams like the paper flow diagram in a copier, or the diagnostic check for an automated assembly machine   ☐

▲ **Directions:**
Please review your analysis and
   3. Add a star to any skill on which you think your employees need work.
   4. **Please attach an actual workplace example of each application you have checked.** Use a highlighter to mark any areas with which you would expect your employees to have trouble.

---

2. What Skills Do Employees Need to Use?

Job Studied: _____   Date: _____

Reporter: _____   Title: _____

This form is used to determine what *specific* reading skills are used in your operation so that an instructor can develop an appropriate instructional sequence.

(*continues*)

Reading Skills Survey for Managers (continued)

▲ **Directions:**
Listed below are four clusters of the reading skills used in the workplace.
1. Please read these lists and check each skill that is critical for your employees to use.
2. Use two checks for critical skill.

▲ **Levels of Skills:**
Not Needed: Your work can be done satisfactorily without calling for employees to use this skill.
Minimal: Employees must be able to use this skill at entry level or to qualify for job training.
Expected: Employees should be able to use the skill day to day in performing tasks with minimal supervision.
Optimal: Employees can use this skill to perform job tasks that exceed group norms.

▲ **Employees must be able to:**

	Levels of Performance			
	none	minimal	expected	optimal
1. Recognize English letters and numbers and understand the relationship between English letters and sounds				
▲ Copy short words or numbers accurately	☐	☐	☐	☐
▲ Find or replace records, documents, or inventoried material	☐	☐	☐	☐
▲ Enter records, documents, or material into inventory	☐	☐	☐	☐
2. Read and write commonly used words and phrases				
▲ Read/recognize a small set (less than 100) of simple words regularly used on the job	☐	☐	☐	☐
▲ Read/recognize a small set (less than 100) of technical words occasionally used on the job	☐	☐	☐	☐
▲ Read simple instructions of a few short sentences discussing familiar terms and concepts	☐	☐	☐	☐
▲ Read longer passages with familiar terms and concepts that are more complex, such as in a departmental memo discussing changes in procedures	☐	☐	☐	☐

	Levels of Performance			
	none	minimal	expected	optimal

3. Read to enter information and report data

▲ Find and respond appropriately to a set of regularly used screen cues and enter routine information ☐ ☐ ☐ ☐

▲ Respond appropriately to unexpected cues to select and input prepared information ☐ ☐ ☐ ☐

4. Read to gather and analyze information

▲ Find information needed to complete a presentation or report ☐ ☐ ☐ ☐

▲ Interpret data and develop findings ☐ ☐ ☐ ☐

▲ Check standard procedures, follow directions, identify exceptions to rules ☐ ☐ ☐ ☐

▲ Review and follow exceptions to rules, follow unfamiliar procedures, or practice new or unfamiliar operations ☐ ☐ ☐ ☐

▲ Troubleshoot a backup system ☐ ☐ ☐ ☐

▲ Develop a technical report or argue for a change in procedures or standards ☐ ☐ ☐ ☐

▲ Review drafted material and revise to strengthen an argument or approach ☐ ☐ ☐ ☐

▲ Review written material and find and correct errors of fact ☐ ☐ ☐ ☐

11

Outplacement

Frank P. Louchheim, Right Associates

A generation ago, there was no such service as outplacement counseling—or *consulting,* the term now preferred by the industry. The word *outplacement** itself had not yet been invented. And the concept of outplacement—that is, of an employer paying a consultant to assist separated employees in finding new employment in the shortest possible time with the least amount of emotional stress—was virtually nonexistent, even under other labels. Few employers felt a need or a responsibility to help displaced executives or other employees find new employment.

The change since the 1970s has been dramatic. From a group consisting of less than a handful of companies at the start of 1970, a new industry has emerged. The number of companies providing outplacement consulting services has grown to more than 200, producing more than $300 million a year in outplacement revenues, and the number continues to grow.[1] Not only do thousands of employers in the public and private sectors, large corporations as well as small businesses, provide outplacement counseling assistance to senior executives and middle managers, many have extended outplacement assistance—frequently under such euphemisms as *career options, new personal opportunities,* and *unlimited horizons*—to rank-and-file employees as well.

Another change has been the quality of the individuals being outplaced. Years ago, most outplaced employees were individuals being terminated because of poor performance in the workplace. Today, in large part because of economic pressures from consolidations and downsizings, many highly qualified people are being displaced, and outplaced candidates are no longer viewed negatively by prospective employers. Moreover, the concept of outplacement is no longer limited to terminated employees. Many employers now also use outplacement as a tool for downsizing their organizations by inducing employees to accept early retirement packages or to take voluntary separations from their jobs.

Changes in the workplace and in life-styles have given impetus to other new uses for outplacement. For example, longer life spans and

---

*Within the outplacement profession, Tom Hubbard is generally credited with inventing the word *outplacement.*

better health are causing many individuals to reassess the idea that retirement is their only option; outplacement enables these individuals to explore other options, such as second careers, becoming consultants, or establishing a business. Moreover, some people want to change career direction, rather common today, or need to change direction because of technological obsolescence. Outplacement helps point these individuals in the right direction.

The Growth of Outplacement

Initially altruism undoubtedly played a part in some early decisions to help terminated employees find new work. Certainly the development of a more humanistic attitude by a new breed of managers, particularly in the early 1970s, cannot be dismissed. It was during this decade that the term *outplacement* began to gain recognition, and more than a score of outplacement firms began operations. The real growth of outplacement came during the 1980s, when the number of outplacement firms approximately tripled in number.[2]

Outplacement grew primarily because it was perceived to save severance expense and unemployment compensation. Moreover, it allowed managers to deal with poor performance more quickly, saving months or even years of salary expense for the corporation. It also grew as middle managers were replaced as fact gatherers by computers.

The pressures for change can probably be attributed to three developments:

1. A new legal climate that permits terminated employees to sue their former employers for what they consider to be wrongful discharge
2. The erosion of the old employment-at-will doctrine, which allowed employers to fire workers for any reason—or no reason
3. The dramatic increase in the number of leveraged buy-outs and acquisitions and mergers during the 1980s, which led to the displacement of scores of thousands of individuals

A Changing Legal Climate

Prior to 1930, employers did not have to worry about any wrongful-discharge litigation. Employers had the absolute right to fire employees at will, even for reasons that by today's standards would be unconscionable, improper, arbitrary, or illegal. No cause was needed; it was what was known as the employment-at-will doctrine. Since that time, legislation, civil rights acts, health and safety laws, and similar enactments have placed restrictions on an employer's right to discharge employees.

In 1983, a federal appeals court in Philadelphia substantially changed the doctrine of employment-at-will, particularly for nonunion employers. It held that an employer's unilateral adoption of personnel policies and procedures that would give an employee reason to expect continued employment, except for unsatisfactory performance or other just cause for dismissal, may create for the employee a contractual and legally enforceable entitlement to continued employment.[3] In addition, the court threw wide open the range of potentially unlawful reasons for terminating an at-will employee.

By 1986, it had become apparent that high-level executives and middle managers were not the only ones taking their former employers to court; in fact, they were in the minority. In 1986, Los Angeles County reported that only 9 percent of the wrongful-discharge cases there were filed by upper-tier executives, while 40 percent were brought by mid-level managers. More significant, 51 percent of the wrongful-discharge cases had been brought by nonmanagement workers. Furthermore, 70 percent of those cases were won by the fired employees.[4]

As 1989 began, courts in forty-six states had issued rulings that erode the old employment-at-will doctrine.[5] In some states, discharges may violate public policy. In others, they may breach implied promises by employers to deal fairly with employees, or they may violate express agreements based on statements made to employees in handbooks and personnel policy manuals. A legal cause of action may even result from an employer's negligence in dealing with an employee. Because of these and other developments, an employer can no longer safely assume that an employee unprotected by a specific statute or collective bargaining agreement can be fired without risk of legal liability. In fact, with unions representing 12 percent of the private industry work force, down from 25 percent in 1973 and expected to fall to 5 percent by the end of the century, more and more nonunion employees are, and will be, looking to the courts for protection against arbitrary management decisions.[6]

Employers in a number of states have tried to bypass the contract theory of employment by adding or publishing at-will disclaimers in employee handbooks and manuals and/or employment applications stating that the employer retains the right to dismiss an employee without showing just cause. Not all states accept these. In California, some fifty workers at a company in Sausalito sued their employer when they were fired three weeks after signing an agreement that said they could be dismissed at any time for any reason.[7] New Jersey, on the other hand, is one of the few states in which the court has held that such disclaimers do allow an employer to discharge an employee without having to hold a hearing or show just cause.[8]

Because of the variety of theories adopted by the courts across the land, labor lawyers say it remains difficult to predict with any certainty the circumstances under which an employer will be found guilty of wrongful discharge. In addition, employers need to be aware of the potential for tort liability in connection with wrongful discharges other than the tort of wrongful discharge itself. Today employers can be sued not only for breach of contract and wrongful discharge but also for defamation in the form of libel or slander, intentional infliction of emotional distress, malicious prosecution, intentional interference with existing or prospective employment relations, or even negligence. In contract cases, damages usually are determined by the employee's actual loss in wages, moving expenses in locating new employment and so forth. Tort cases, on the other hand, may also involve damages for emotional distress, loss of consortium, and the award of punitive damages, which frequently can greatly exceed the actual damages, running into the hundreds of thousands of dollars. Nor are overseas employers exempt. The situation in Europe, where outplacement has also gained acceptance, is similar in regard to potential labor litigation. Europe's thick net of labor laws means that separation agreements frequently are conducted under the specter of lawsuits. In Belgium, an estimated 20 percent of termination disputes end up in court.[9]

The Effect of Mergers, Acquisitions, and Leveraged Buy-outs

To add to employer woes, changing economic circumstances, particularly as a result of mergers, acquisitions, and leveraged buy-outs (LBOs), increase the likelihood of such litigation. Many of these transactions often result in reorganizations and reductions in the work force, changes that increase the chances for litigation. Even when companies are not engaged in merger or buy-out activity, competition is exerting pressure on organizations to downsize their work force and otherwise streamline operations.[10]

The trend of the 1980s was toward increasing mergers, acquisitions, and LBOs. According to *Mergers and Acquisitions* magazine, more than 31,100 deals, a record number, representing more than $1.34 trillion, were completed between 1980 and 1989. As the decade ended, however, there were signs that merger and acquisition activity had passed its peak. Junk bond markets had tightened. A number of deals had soured as the new owners declared bankruptcy. In 1989 the total number of mergers and acquisitions dropped by 14.7 percent from 1988, and the dollar volume was down 2.4 percent.[11]

This trend continued into the 1990s. During the first half of 1990, the dollar volume of worldwide merger activity was down 39 percent to $188 billion from the same period in 1989, while U.S. merger volume dropped 54 percent to $88 billion, and the value of domestic LBOs plunged 83 percent to $7 billion.[12]

The Future Outlook

Increasingly the employment-at-will rule is being limited by the emergence of the judicially created doctrine of wrongful discharge, under which protection may be afforded in certain circumstances to workers who are not members of groups protected by any statute. The emergence and rapid growth of this doctrine eventually may lead to a broader public policy, possibly embodied in legislation, protecting all workers against any unfair treatment by employers. A model Employment Termination Act by the National Conference of Commissioners on Uniform State Laws on August 7, 1991.

Meanwhile, the risk for employers increases daily. Employees, encouraged by recent court decisions and imaginative lawyers, are finding enough legal ammunition to take their case before a jury and challenge an otherwise permissible personnel decision in court, and even obtain a favorable decision. This should not be surprising; it stands to reason that juries are usually more sympathetic to a fired employee than to an employer.

With so much increasing potential for litigation in prospect, it becomes increasingly incumbent on management to structure its employment relationships so that it minimizes the risk of being taken to court and becoming yet another statistic in the increasing series of wrongful-discharge cases that are becoming embodied in case law.

The Role of Outplacement

Although outplacement is not intended to reduce or eliminate suits against employers by discharged employees, there are indications that fewer employers using outplacement services end up in court. An understanding of what outplacement is and how it functions will explain the reason.

Outplacement consulting actually consists of two different and distinct, but complementary, programs: one geared toward the employer, the other toward the discharged employee (who in the parlance of the profession becomes "the candidate" or "the client"). The former guides the employer through the separation process, planning the termination in the correct way so as to minimize any legal risk and retain employee goodwill. The latter counsels and assists the terminated employee to further his or her career. By helping the employee to look forward to opportunity rather than backward toward individual rights, this helps cushion the blow to the employee and lessens the likelihood that a potentially disgruntled employee will turn his or her anger into a lawsuit. Seeking to minimize or eliminate litigation, is, however, only one benefit of outplacement. It offers a number of positive benefits as well.

▲ *It provides financial savings.* Because outplacement helps terminated employees find new jobs sooner, the company saves:

1. Severance expense. When employees must be terminated, professional reemployment services properly reduce the period of the job search and can reduce the severance.
2. Unemployment compensation. Utilizing outplacement often reduces the duration of unemployment, resulting in the reduction of unemployment payout.
3. Salary expense. When managers know the company will assist a terminated employee, they are quicker to dismiss a nonproductive employee, so lost salary through poor performance is alleviated.
4. Legal expenses. By minimizing legal risk, the company saves the cost of internal and external counsel.

▲ *It improves corporate performance.* When a company is considering a corporate reorganization, for whatever reason, outplacement allows the company to manage objectively for best corporate results, because it allows the resulting fallout to be handled compassionately and fairly and with the potential for better employment.

▲ *It improves community relations.* Because many former employees become employed in the same community or industry, many people believe that the former employee will remain loyal to the terminating employer and leave with a positive rather than negative feeling of the employee has not been harmed financially, personally, or otherwise from the termination.

▲ *It improves employee relations and internal morale.* When remaining employees recognize that their former colleagues do well with the outplacement assistance, productivity and internal morale are strengthened. The fact that the company provided assistance shows them the firm does care about its employees and their future. This is particularly important when terminations occur that are beyond the control of the employee.

▲ *It reduces executive and managerial turnover.* Often, during reductions caused by economic conditions, remaining employees begin looking elsewhere for employment. The use of outplacement signals that should the situation eventually affect them, they will be assisted by the company; therefore, it may be in their long-term interest to remain with the company. There is a second benefit as well: by reducing excessive job seeking, the company is better able to control its turnover, retaining high-quality personnel while easing the transition of poor performers.

▲ *It makes recruiting easier.* Managers and executives recruited by the company will be more likely to accept a new environment and challenge if they know they will receive considerate, fair treatment if the new position is not successful. In addition, managers and executives who recognize that their goals within the company might result in employee terminations are more likely to accept the challenge knowing that the company will assist those employees that they must terminate.

▴ *It increases productivity.* In raising the productivity level of an organization by replacing poor performers with better ones, the organization's productivity increases.

▴ *It forestalls negative publicity.* When a company takes a concerned approach during a termination based on any reason, adverse publicity concerning the termination is often avoided.

Other Uses for Outplacement

Outplacement has been expanded to provide management with an alternative to termination. The two most frequently used are early retirement and voluntary separation.

Early retirement is a frequently used method to achieve a major downsizing by persuading a number of redundant, retirement-eligible employees to leave the company early. The financial package offered for taking early retirement becomes more acceptable when, through outplacement counseling, the employees are able to see that future career opportunities are available and achievable elsewhere and that they can continue to earn money and remain productive even as they collect their pensions from their current employer. For many employees, particularly those in their fifties, this ability to continue working is as important as, and sometimes more so than, the financial package being offered.

Voluntary separation eliminates the termination dilemma for companies that have a paternalistic or family view of employees by providing the opportunity for the employee to separate voluntarily from the organization. Voluntary separation is particularly useful when an employer is faced with a situation in which an individual is no longer suitable for new work assignments as a result of technological changes, reorganization, or a relocation of a facility or function to another geographic area. It is also useful for a company that needs to separate an individual without proper documentation of performance reasons or to minimize the potential of legal actions by employees whom the company can no longer keep in their position.

In such instances, a manager discusses the situation with the employee and encourages him or her to make use of an available predecision process that will assist the person in considering which option is best in the light of long- and short-term career and family goals. This predecision process utilizes stages of the outplacement counseling process.

Frequently predecision counseling by an outplacement consultant helps employees to conclude that they may be better off leaving the company or accepting another position within the organization. The benefit of the process is that the employee feels it is his or her own decision and does not feel forced to accept a decision by management. In many instances, particularly where poor performance is involved, voluntary separation becomes a face-saving device whereby the individual can leave the organization and feel ownership in the decision.

The Outplacement Process

The outplacement process consists of two stages: the employer level and the employee level. At the employer level, the outplacement consultant prepares and assists the employer in the termination process. At the employee level, the consultant assists the individual in finding new employment in the shortest possible time with the least amount of emotional distress.

Preparing the Employer

The outplacement process begins with preparing the employer for the termination process through a six-step process designed to ensure that the employer has acquired proved methods for conducting effective separations.

1. *Review the termination factors.* In the initial step, the outplacement consultant seeks to determine the real reason the employee is being terminated. Experience has shown that half of all terminations are driven by the corporation and half by the individual. Those driven by the corporation are because of downsizing or a staff reduction based on economic conditions or a takeover in which a company is acquiring another or has been sold. Those effected by the individual employee may be the result of poor performance or wrong chemistry. Either way, it is essential that the real reason for the termination be determined and discussed with senior management.

Many companies that are downsizing remove persons who do not fit in with the firm's long-term plan, perhaps as a result of technological change or the need for new skills. Such dismissal is permissible if it is universally applied. Using different criteria for different personnel may not be illegal, but it does maximize the company's exposure to litigation. This is not to say that employees terminated in this manner may win in any suits, but they can expose the company to what they consider an unjust or malicious separation and tie up the company with considerable legal expenses and time.

In a uniform, across-the-board cutback, it is preferable to use the same standards for all employees. Whether the reductions are to take place, for example, in the marketing or accounting or public relations departments, it is essential that all department managers use identical criteria to help prevent legal problems. If, for example, each department has been told it must cut staff by 10 percent, each department manager uses the same basic criteria for separation. If accounting uses a last-in, first-out criterion while marketing makes its decision based on employee productivity, legal problems could arise. To ensure against this, the outplacement consultant will recommend that one senior manager be assigned the responsibility for coordinating the task, not four separate vice-presidents (each of whom might use a different criterion).

2. *Review the personnel selected for separation.* The objective of the outplacement consultant is to ascertain minimum legal risk by examining such factors as age, length of service, minority status, performance, and future skills applications of the candidates selected.

Compliance with requirements of the Equal Employment Opportunity Commission (EEOC) is of special concern. An older employee, for example, may exhibit poor performance skills or work habits, but his or her dismissal might be construed as age discrimination. Or if the criterion selected is last in, first out and all the last hirees were minorities, it could appear as though the planned downsizing was an attempt to reduce the number of minorities on the staff.

EEOC compliance is only one concern of the outplacement consultant. Another is the possible appearance of corporate revenge against an employee who, for example, has filed a discrimination or sexual harassment complaint or blown the whistle to an auditor. The outplacement consultant must review the candidates scheduled for termination to make certain the human resources manager has checked for these issues and called them to the attention of senior management in order to minimize legal risk.

Other issues that the outplacement consultant may review could include determining whether the individual is legally an employee or a contractor; what changes, if any, may be required in any restrictive covenants and how enforceable such covenants would be; unionization; and even matters of employee health. If an employee, for example, has a history of emotional trouble or a heart condition, the consultant will recommend that the company have medical personnel on alert at the time of the separation meeting, which is a stressful event.

3. *Review the separation benefits.* Most outplacement consultants can provide the company with a checklist to determine which benefits the employee may be entitled to—vacation time, accumulated paid leave, savings plans, vested retirement benefits, and the like—and which additional benefits might be offered, such as continuation of medical coverage and life and disability. In many instances, at the company's request, the outplacement consultant will recommend a benefits package appropriate to the situation and the status of the individual.

4. *Arrange for the return of company property and security clearance*

and provide counsel on what to do with the employee's personal belongings and how to allow the employee to remove them from the premises. These are important issues. If they are not handled properly, they can lead to future problems for both the company and the employee.

5. *Put it in writing.* Since it is advisable that all separation arrangements be spelled out in writing as well as delivered orally at the separation meeting, this is another area in which the outplacement consultant's guidance can be invaluable. The consultant can make certain that all pertinent points are covered in the formal letter of separation and can help with drafting that letter plus any announcements to other employees and the public that may be required.

For corporate continuity, employee morale, and good public relations, it is essential that all the facts regarding individuals and the reasons for the separation be properly communicated. This, too, is one of the important services provided by the outplacement consultant: preparing a statement with which both the company and employee can be comfortable and which explains why the individual has left the employ of the company. Such a statement ensures that everyone—company managers and employees talking to others, and the displaced employee talking to a prospective employer—speaks with one voice.

6. *Train the notifiers.* Training the individuals who will be responsible for delivering the separation notice to the affected employees is important to prevent having the separation meeting turn into a shouting match or a fighting match. The manner in which the separation interview is conducted affects the success of the separation process.

Clearly outplacement consultation begins well before the actual separation takes place. Preparing the corporation for the separation issues to be considered, reviewing any necessary documentation, and assisting with any packaging and communications are as important an outplacement function as counseling candidates on how to find new employment.

Handling the Actual Separation

Many corporate executives have a deep-seated fear of firing a subordinate and will put it off as long as possible. Inevitably, they must break the bad news to the individual, and it is imperative, especially considering any potential legal consequences, that the separation interview be conducted properly.

Firing a person should never be done by letter or telephone. It is always better done in person and in a way that helps to preserve the employee's dignity. One of the principal functions of the outplacement consultant is to help prepare for the separation meeting in advance and to train the notifier, the supervisor of the employee about to be separated, in how to handle the separation interview and what types of employee reactions to expect and how best to deal with them.

Most outplacement consultants agree that a well-handled separation interview generally takes about 10 minutes and goes through eight distinct stages:

1. Putting the person at ease
2. Setting the stage in general terms
3. Defining the separation clearly and succinctly
4. Explaining the separation benefits and reemployment assistance
5. Listening and being understanding
6. Offering support
7. Discussing details of the work transition
8. Introducing the person to a reemployment specialist or designated personnel contact

Being able to fire an employee who is underproductive or whose job is being eliminated is a tough but necessary job. The outplacement consultant can train and rehearse the manager on what to say, how to say it, and how to manage the separation interview in a professional manner for the benefit of both the company and the employee.

Once the outplacement consultant has prepared and guided the employer through the separation process and the employer has notified the employee of separation, the next step is to assist the outplaced candidate through the career transition.

Types of Programs

Like automobiles, there are a wide variety of outplacement counseling services available to fit every personal need and every budget, from a basic, bare-bones model to top of the line with every luxury option available. Counseling programs are usually custom tailored to the specific client's needs. They can range from economical half-day group seminars for large numbers of nonexempt employees to fully supported, extensive one-on-one sessions with executive perquisites for senior executives that may last for months. The majority of organizations prefer to use outside firms for outplacement consulting.

The outplacement consulting firm, working closely with the firing organization prior to termination, will seek to get some sense of the people being terminated, their interests, and whether their need will be strictly finding reemployment or whether these might be individuals who would be interested in career reassessment and the possibility of making a directional change. After gathering and analyzing this information, the consultant advises the client which type of program it believes is most appropriate, but the final decision will be the client's.

Among the basic outplacement offerings available are the following:

▴ *Group workshops,* the most economical programs because they can serve large numbers of employees over a short period of time at minimum cost. Group workshops can vary by number of individuals and number of days. The optimum number in a group depends on the employment level of the participants. As a rule, the higher the level of employees in the organization, the fewer who can be successfully accommodated in a group workshop. Conversely, the lower the level, the more employees can be accommodated. In addition, for the workshop to be most effective, the group should be as homogeneous as possible. Workshops can be tailored to the needs of blue collar, clerical, managerial, technical, or any other group.

Group workshops are usually conducted in a lecture format, where participants are taught about job searching and given instruction on how to use detailed work manuals that are provided. In smaller groups, the outplacement consultant may also give participants individual exercises to help them get started in résumé preparation.

Workshops can range from a half-day to five days. The time required depends on the extent of hands-on assistance versus lectures that is offered. That, in turn, will vary with the participants' rank in the organization.

▴ *Group workshop/individual counseling combinations,* an effective compromise for companies seeking a high-quality, moderate-cost outplacement program designed specifically to assist separated employees whose needs cannot be effectively met in group workshops. They are also used by organizations whose budget constraints do not allow full one-on-one outplacement. These programs provide both individual and group career consulting. Consultants assist candidates in the preparation of their résumés, and there are weekly group job search strategy sessions, as well as self-marketing seminars.

▴ *Individual counseling,* the most effective choice, provided by many companies for middle- and upper-level managers and executives. There are a number of reasons that these persons are given individualized counseling. Their position within the organization sometimes may make it more difficult to find similar high-level employment because there are fewer such positions in the marketplace. Many of these individuals tend to be older and therefore may need more emotional support. Or because of their age and experience, they may be more receptive to other options, such as establishing consultancies, setting up a business, turning to public service, teaching, or early retirement. Interestingly, a large number of executives frequently discover during this process that they prefer early retirement or a career in public service.

Outplacement consultants work with these managers and executives on a personal basis to ensure that they make the right choice. The consulting firm also provides support services, such as secretarial assistance, résumé preparation, and a message center. It may provide a private office, research facilities, and an opportunity for the candidate to interact with peers, who may become a support group for each other.

Services for Key Executives

There has been a growing recognition of the need for specialized outplacement services for key corporate executives, typically individuals whose annual compensation is in six figures, who are probably between 42 and 62 years of age, whose impact on the organization is substantial, and whose separation package could contain income from deferred compensation, stock options, and other executive perquisites.

Outplacing such individuals involves special considerations, not the least of which is retaining the executive's goodwill and not creating a life-long corporate foe. Executives called on to replace senior management people need to consider:

- The impact of this decision on the company's own board
- The result it may have on company morale
- The way it may be interpreted in the financial community
- The manner in which it may be treated in the press
- The public reaction it may cause
- The importance of avoiding potential litigation
- The cost of overly generous severance packages
- The consequences of having created a corporate foe
- The effect it may have on recruiting

Obviously the organization's needs in outplacing a key executive differ from those involved in outplacing other executives, managers, and employees.

For the company, the specialized outplacement consultant can assist in planning the separation arrangements, developing the separation benefits, establishing a credible rationale for departure, and developing the proper climate for notifying the executive. With such assistance, the organization can arrange for a parting with minimal detrimental impact on the executive's peers, other employees, the board of directors, press, shareholders, and the executive and his or her family.

For the key executive, the specialized consultant brings together a team of advisers and staff support to evaluate, target, and reach a goal as rapidly and professionally as possible while retaining a balanced concern for the career and the financial, physical, and emotional well-being of the executive. Consulting services may include:

- Financial planning consulting and advice
- Investment banking advice
- Strategic planning and business planning advice
- Image and communications consulting
- Physical fitness and wellness planning
- Psychological and psychiatric medical advisory services
- Mortgage origination assistance
- Private office and secretarial assistance
- Research assistance
- Five-year follow-up to provide informal counseling to the now "new" employee concerning career management issues

The time span for the provisions of these services varies with the outplacement contract. Normally, at this level, consulting and office support services continue until the executive achieves his or her personally defined objectives.

As a result of this specialized program, in addition to what one would normally expect in a successful career transition, many key executives move into new opportunities, such as a partnership in a new business, a top management position in a start-up company, directorship on a number of boards, an independent consultancy, a senior management position in a corporation, or a top administrative position in a nonprofit organization, foundation management, or philanthropy.

The Employee Counseling Process

The employee counseling process consists of two phases: the initial meeting and the career transition process. These two phases, which have their own specific objectives, form the basis of all outplacement counseling programs, from group workshops and seminars to individualized one-on-one programs.

THE INITIAL MEETING

The first moments following the announcement of termination are critical. Individuals react differently to the news: some may need to vent their anger; others may be so devastated that they need immediate emotional support. The initial meeting provides these corrective measures and helps bridge the candidate from loss to optimism. It is at this time that the consultant explains to the candidate that the employer is providing outplacement assistance, what that assistance will consist of, and how the outplacement guidance will benefit the individual. In most instances, the outplacement consultant will be on-site at the time of the separation interview so that he or she can meet with the candidate immediately to help the employee view the departure as a positive step for the future and to reestablish individual self-worth.

This is an important first step because many people initially feel victimized. The task of the outplacement consultant is to work with the candidate to make him or her realize that this represents an unusual opportunity to take charge of his or her career—to change from an external locus of control to an internal locus of control, to be active rather than reactive. The consultant then usually outlines the kind of career transition assistance that will be provided. (Candidates in group workshops usually meet initially with the outplacement consultant at a group session where they are told about the help being provided.)

To help shift the candidate's focus from a negative to positive outlook, as well as quickly begin the career transition process, the outplacement consultant may give the candidate a homework assignment and set the appointment for the next career counseling session. The "homework" serves three purposes: it gets the candidate to focus on successes rather than the current "failure," it prepares the candidate to think about what he or she will say in a future job interview, and it begins to form the basis for a résumé.

THE CAREER TRANSITION PROCESS

Because the outplacement consultant files reports on the candidate's career transition progress during outplacement, some consulting firms use separate consultants for the initial meeting and for the counseling process as their way of ensuring candidates of confidentiality, especially if the candidate said something negative about the employer in the heat of the moment following the separation interview. In general, career transition consists of four stages.

1. *Setting campaign objectives.* A recent Gallup survey found that 75 percent of workers between the ages of 18 and 49 felt some discontent with their jobs. More than half of those aged 50 years and above also were less than completely satisfied with their jobs.[13] In addition, many young people, often not knowing what type of work they would really like to do, make choices they later regret.[14] Other individuals sometimes stumble by accident into their careers. In other words, many people spend years in the wrong job fit, unable to break out. For these individuals, outplacement can represent a significant turning point in their lives. As a result of their unemployed situation, these individuals, through outplacement counseling, now have an opportunity to make career adjustments designed to bring them lasting satisfaction.

During this first phase, the consultant counsels the candidate not to try to make any career judgments for the future but instead to explore the options. (It should be emphasized that this type of career analysis is best conducted in individual one-on-one programs where there is time for in-depth consultation.) Thus, the first step in the counseling process is to prepare the candidate to determine his or her job objective.

The process starts with achievement analysis, which gives the candidate an opportunity to review all achievements and contributions over a lifetime—school, avocations, hobbies, clubs and organization, and sports, for instance, and especially in the workplace, because this will become an important part of the résumé. From this, the consultant is able to draw a reliable measure of the individual's specific skills and talents and develop a skills pattern that will tell the consultant and the candidate where he or she functions well and where not.

Some consultants also conduct psychological tests. Others use psychological testing only if they believe a need exists.

By measuring skills and combining them with the candidate's interests to see where they overlap, it becomes possible to develop a list of options for consideration:

- Employment in a similar situation
- Self-employment
- Consulting
- Entrepreneurship
- Significant volunteerism
- Retirement

After the consultant and the candidate have narrowed the list of options to the one or two that appear most promising, the next step is for the consultant to assist the candidate in converting the information into a résumé geared to achieving the target career move. Although résumé preparation appears to be rather basic, there is more to a résumé than a chronological listing of jobs, positions, and achievements. For example, in one outplacement situation, a counselor discovered that the candidate had hated his previous job and wanted to move to another career in a different field; however, the candidate's résumé concentrated on his last jobs and accomplishments and was thus geared to obtaining a similar position to the one he hated. With the consultant's guidance, the candidate learned to prepare a functional résumé that showed he had skills adaptable to the new career field he sought.

While the résumé is being prepared, other objectives are prioritized: geographic location, financial requirements, travel, compliance with personal values (e.g., not working for a company that contaminates environment), spouse's career, and others.

During this period, it is not uncommon for the outplacement specialist to meet with the candidate's spouse to build up the spouse's confidence with regard to the change about to take place. Spousal support is vital for success during the transition process, especially if the possibility of relocation or reduced financial expectations must be considered.

At this stage of the process, the main objective of the outplacement consultant is not only to make the candidate aware of his or her demonstrated (and latent) skills but also to be able to speak about them with confidence to prospective employers or clients. The next step is to learn what the market is like—campaign preparation.

2. *Preparing for the campaign.* This step might also be called the research phase, because it is here that the candidate makes an assessment of what information he or she knows and needs to know in order to be able to make an informed decision about a particular segment or job. A basic part of the outplacement consultant's function is to make certain that when the candidate goes out to talk with prospective employers, he or she will have focused on specific skills and interests and how they will fit in solving the prospective employer's problems. That requires good information.

The best information comes from people intimately involved in the area of work the candidate wants to get into. The consultant's job at this stage is to teach the candidate how to gather that good information and, in the process, build a resource network that will provide information, referrals, and support during the job search. The idea is to help the candidate develop a network not of one-time contacts but of individuals who can be helpful in personal career management from then on. Often the contact network will contain the candidate's next job, although neither the candidate nor the contact will know it at that time.

Many candidates initially conclude that they do not have time to go through what appears to be a lengthy process; they insist they need a job immediately. Another function of the consultant is to explain why this step-by-step approach is actually the shortest route to the right job and then show the candidate how to do it.

Suppose the candidate's expertise is in the financial area. There are a number of different market segments such a candidate could consider: banks, investment counselors, financial services, and real estate investment companies, for instance. Which should the candidate choose? Which would be a direct match in terms of abilities, opportunities, and working conditions? By researching—that is, meeting with people working in those fields and asking the right questions (under the consultant's guidance)—the candidate is able to narrow the search, build a resource network, save time, and be certain the job is a good match for his or her abilities and needs.

In the first stage, the candidate makes a career choice. The second stage validates that choice.

3. *Conducting the campaign.* Although information gathering is the principal purpose of the previous stage, in actuality it also serves as the

beginning of the actual campaign the candidate will conduct. This is important because it has been said that 80 percent of all jobs, the so-called hidden job market, are never advertised. After focusing the campaign and identifying the most desirable industry segment, the candidate revisits the people most relevant to that segment for the purpose of validating the candidate's focusing decision and his or her understanding of the industry segment to be targeted.

By this time, the key members of the candidate's contact network have become partners in the campaign, and the candidate is no longer fighting alone. He or she has created a validation and support structure, which energizes and propels his or her campaign forward.

Naturally, not every contact made will be suitable for becoming a productive member of such an elite career contact network. The consultant's job is to help the candidate identify the best people among actual or potential contacts and develop and maintain relationships with these people. The consultant may use a number of tools to help the candidate accomplish this, including written reports of meetings and interviews, workshops, and research summaries. But the most important asset is the consultant's understanding of the professional process and the professional creativity in applying it.

4. *Successfully concluding the campaign.* When the job offer comes, the consultant helps the candidate consider and refine the offer, turning it to his or her best advantage. This includes pinning down the details of the offer and formally confirming the job acceptance in a way that eliminates any possibility of misunderstanding. With some consultants, the outplacement process ends here; with others, the process continues for a time after the candidate has begun his or her new assignment. This follow-up may be used to help ease the candidate's transition into the new situation or provide additional consulting for the candidate to find new employment or another option if the first new position does not work out satisfactorily. (The extent of follow-up assistance available will vary according to the outplacement program selected.)

The chapter ends with a brief outplacement case history.

Outplacement Costs

Outplacement fees vary widely by consulting firms and the type of program selected—group workshop versus individualized executive placement. Individualized outplacement is usually based on a percentage of the counseled candidate's salary, most commonly 15 percent, although the range extends from 6 to 20 percent of salary. In addition, approximately three of four firms have a minimum fee, which ranges from $450 to $12,000, with the most common minimum being about $5,000.[15] Many firms, however, tailor a program to the specific needs of the candidates and the budgetary requirements of the sponsoring organizations.

Summary

Outplacement helps both the employer and the employee; it is both humanitarian and practical.

Employee benefits are obvious. The individual is helped through a traumatic experience and assisted in finding a new (often better) position or in making a new and better career move in minimal time.

Employer benefits are sometimes less obvious. Nonetheless, they include:

- Improved employee relations and internal morale
- Improved productivity
- Reduced executive and managerial turnover
- Improved community relations
- Easier recruiting of new personnel
- Reduced severance expenses, unemployment compensation, and salary expenses
- Enhancement of early retirement windows
- An alternative to termination
- Improved corporate image
- Savings in potential legal expenses

For many employers, the last may be the most important reason to consider outplacement, especially in view of the changing legal climate in which the employment-at-will doctrine has been eroded in many states and where new court interpretations of wrongful discharge are leading to an increasing number of successful employee suits and damage awards. However, even without the stimulus of a desire to minimize or avoid litigation, outplacement offers employers sufficient other benefits to make its use worthy of consideration.

NOTES

1. James H. Kennedy and Kathleen Kennedy Burke, *An Analysis of The Outplacement Consulting Business in the U.S. Today,* based on forms submitted by firms for listing in the 1988–1989 edition of *The Directory of Outplacement Firms* (Fitzwilliam, N.H.: Kennedy Publications).
2. Ibid., p. 5.
3. *Novasel v. Nationwide Insurance Co.,* 721 F.2d 894 (3d Cir. 1983).
4. Robert F. Stewart, Jr., Bruce J. Kasten, and Virginia M. Lord, *Management*

Rights or Employee Rights . . . Who's Running the Show? (Philadelphia, 1988).

5. "Firing Policy: There Is No Middle Ground," *Business Week,* October 17, 1988, p. 122.
6. Selwyn Feinstein, "Labor Letter," *Wall Street Journal,* April 17, 1990, p. 1.
7. Aaron Bernstein, "More Dismissed Workers Are Telling It to the Judge," *Business Week,* October 17, 1988, pp. 68–69.
8. *Wooley v. Hoffman-LaRoche, Inc.,* 99 N.J. 284, 491 A.2d 1257, modified, 101 N.J. 10, 499 A.2d 515 (1985).
9. Barbara Lau, "Translating Employee Outplacement into 'European,' " *Wall Street Journal*, March 22, 1988, p. 9.
10. A 1989 research study of members of American Management Association conducted by Right Associates. See "Managing Change in the 90s," *The Right Research*, Report No. 2 (Right Management Consultants).
11. Ibid.
12. "Less Urge to Merge," *Philadelphia Inquirer*, July 9, 1990, p. C1.
13. Andrew Kohut and Linda DeStefano, "Jobs for Older Americans Are 'Twice as Nice,' " *Boston Herald*, September 4, 1989, pp. 29–30.
14. Andrew Kohut and Linda DeStefano, "Workers 'Doing Time,' " *Boston Herald*, September 4, 1989, pp. 29–30.
15. Kennedy and Burke, *An Analysis.*

(continues)

An Outplacement Case History

When two of America's largest corporations merged in 1986, the inevitable displacement of employees that followed was greatly cushioned by the use of outplacement. At the one division studied, the consultant provided all of the steps described in this chapter, from preparing the employer, including the training of separation notifiers, to developing a voluntary separation program, to outplacement employee counseling.

Four career transition programs were provided, each designed to meet the specific needs of executives, managers, professionals and exempt employees, and nonexempt personnel.

Career transition assistance for executives was custom-tailored to their special interests, needs, and career objectives. It included one-on-one counseling by a trained, certified consultant and explored career options such as finding new employment, setting up a consultancy, becoming an entrepreneur, or purchasing and developing business ventures. Executive counseling began immediately following the separation interview and continued until the executive was placed. In addition, each executive received financial counseling and six months of ancillary support, such as office support services, stationery, work space and a message center, plus one year of follow-up after placement.

The managers' transition program, which also began immediately following the separation interview, consisted of three one-on-one sessions, six months of group workshops and ancillary support, such as assistance with résumé preparation and a message center.

Exempt personnel and professionals attended a three-day group workshop and received six months of individual telephone follow-up.

Nonexempt personnel attended a two-day group workshop.

A follow-up study conducted two years later found:

- ▲ All employees displaced by the merger who wished to be employed after leaving the company found employment before the expiration of their severance pay. Of those, 76 percent were still employed at the time of the follow-up study.
- ▲ 68 percent were earning more money than when they worked for the company, 7 percent were earning the same salary, and 23 percent (mostly part-timers and retirees) were earning less than before.
- ▲ 55 percent were in positions of greater responsibility than when they worked for the company.
- ▲ 77 percent reported they were very happy with their new position.
- ▲ 87 percent were confident in both their career and their future.

12

Cultural Diversity Counseling

Muriel Gray, School of Social Work, University of Maryland

Human resources management for the 1990s and beyond will require an integrated, open, and flexible approach that reflects the realities of the work force and the needs of the work organization.[1] According to *Workforce 2000*, the realities of the American work force over the 1990s will reflect the following:

- ▲ The number of workers will decrease.
- ▲ The average worker will be older.
- ▲ More women will be on the job.
- ▲ One-third of new workers will be people of color.
- ▲ There will be more immigrants entering the work force than in any other period since World War I.
- ▲ Most new jobs will be in the service and information industries.
- ▲ The new jobs will require higher skills.

These facts will result in a change not only in the way the work force will look but in the relationship between employer and employee.[2] The new work force will primarily consist of people of color (African-Americans, Hispanic-Americans, Asian-Americans), immigrants from Asia, Latin and Central America, and the Eastern bloc countries, and women. In order for any company to compete, it will be necessary to manage a culturally diverse work force.

Human resources managers will have the dual challenge of creating a workplace that is receptive to these changing demographics while preparing workers to be productive in a changing workplace.[3]

Addressing the needs of a diverse work force requires interventions on institutional, organizational, and individual levels. Typically, institutional interventions refer to policies; organizational interventions refer to programs, practices, and procedures; and individual interventions address attitudes and behaviors. All levels are equally important, but each requires addressing in a different way. For instance, institutional and organizational interventions require policies and programs that respond to the needs or issues of the diverse workplace; interventions on the individual level typically focus on education, training, and counseling.

Managing and Affirming Diversity

Many U.S. businesses have experience in attempting to assimilate ethnic, racial, and gender differences into their work culture, but few have experience in valuing cultural differences and adapting the workplace so that managers learn to value and manage this diversity.[4] Workplace diversity programs are designed for this purpose.

The philosophy and principles guiding workplace diversity programs are that diversity among workers is a source of richness and a strength for the workplace. It can bring a wide range of ideas and benefits if the business manages the diversity by helping its employees to accept a multicultural workplace instead of trying to assimilate workers to a traditional homogeneous work force that has become obsolete.[5]

Diversity programs are also based on the assumptions that proper management of cultural differences will result in greater worker productivity and worker satisfaction, while poor management will create divisiveness and tension. Cross-culturally appropriate management can improve job performance by presenting an opportunity to understand and identify the potential capabilities of all workers.[6] Diversity management thus becomes an economic issue.

Programs that value diversity must reflect the intergroup behavior and dynamics in society at large.[7] For instance, several social-psychological researchers have shown that the principle of racial tolerance does not extend to all situations and that even whites with liberal views on race are not willing to make sacrifices so that minorities can achieve equity.[8] Diversity programs must understand this reality and develop mechanisms by which such problems can be overcome for the economic good of the organization and its workers.[9]

Another assumption underlying the development of workplace diversity programs is that most U.S. businesses do not know how to value and manage a work force of employees of differing cultures, languages, customs, and values. Diversity management acknowledges different value systems but does not imply that each cultural group will operate independent of the organization. Rather, behavior is viewed from a cultural perspective, and problem solving involves relating to workers from their own cultural/ethnic point of reference.[10] Thus, the most important assumption is that there needs to be a comprehensive, well-developed plan to help the employer and workers learn to appreciate and accommodate differences. This plan must be deliberate and skillful, and it should focus on the workplace culture as a whole, affirming diversity.

Affirming diversity does not mean affirmative action, although affirmative action may be an appropriate mechanism.[11] The affirmative action issue is one of social justice that carries legal implications; the diversity issue is one of employer survival and is based on social, economic, and political world realities.[12] U.S. businesses already have experience in dealing with racism and sexism, and some of these resources can be used in the development and implementation of diversity programs. Formal affirmative action plans, Equal Employment Opportunity (EEO) programs, employee relations, and employee assistance program (EAP) specialists are invaluable resources in the development of diversity programs. Moreover, in order to develop an effective diversity program, it is necessary to determine how existing resources can be adapted to contribute to the overall goals and objectives of the program. For example, Digital Corporation's diversity program, Valuing Differences, has several facets: EEO focusing primarily on legal issues; affirmative action, which focuses on structural issues and systemic change; and personal and group development.[13]

In general, the development of a program to affirm and manage diversity stems from a philosophy of valuing differences that must be endorsed by and have the commitment of top management.

Policy Considerations

To ensure program success, policies must be designed to reduce barriers to valuing diversity. The policies should address both institutional and interpersonal barriers to fostering diversity—for example:

- ▲ Which existing policies are directed toward the needs of women, older workers, lesbians and gays, racial or ethnic minorities, and other groups?
- ▲ Do these policies foster the valuing of diversity, or do they foster resentment of these groups?
- ▲ What kind of policies could change informal, subjective, and interpersonal interactions among the diverse groups in the workplace?[14]

In addition to analyzing existing policy, it is also necessary to develop new policies. Pettigrew and Martin, for example, have suggested policies designed to restructure the work organization for the inclusion of black Americans:[15]

- ▲ Train white supervisors and co-workers in positive multicultural communication.
- ▲ Create interdependence in interracial work teams.
- ▲ Modify supervisors' reward systems to link compensation to the quality of interracial interactions and minority employees' performance.[16]

These suggestions regarding the social-psychological process of inclusion are also appropriate for other workers who have been historically excluded from the mainstream of U.S. workplaces. Some of them may be difficult to apply, but surely the spirit of these concepts is worth implementing. Diversity programs, for instance, need to address stereotypic assumptions—that minorities are less qualified for employment than white workers and that they are hired only because of affirmative action—because they perpetuate a prejudicial myth and foster resentment, intergroup tensions, and lower performance expectations.

Practice Considerations

Often there is a gap between policy, which informs of what and how things should be done, and practice, which informs of what and how things are done. Moreover, policy typically addresses formal operations, while practice also includes the informal. Therefore, in order to develop a program that manages to affirm diversity, it is important to analyze organizational practice:

- ▲ Are there any practices that exclude women, older workers, people of color, or lesbians and gays?
- ▲ How can specific practices be changed to foster diversity appreciation?
- ▲ Are there any practices that foster intercultural resentments?

It is important to be specific. For example, the practice of conducting business at a country club or while playing golf may inadvertently exclude some people of color and women. Conversely, a company that includes a variety of ethnic foods when it caters office functions is showing that it values diversity.

Program Development

The development of a diversity program occurs in phases, each with major tasks.

The Exploratory Phase

This phase usually begins with an awareness within the organization that in the future, the nature and composition of U.S. businesses will be drastically different from that of U.S. businesses of the past, and that many of the traditional management approaches will not be effective with a diverse work force. Many businesses explore the concept of managing diversity in order to become or to remain economically competitive; usually, however, it occurs because managers are trying to minimize interpersonal conflicts and communication problems between peoples of varied experiences, values, and expectations. In either instance, it is important to understand that creating a work force that values diversity has implications for the entire organization, so a successful approach should have top management and labor commitment.[17] Although there are many strategies for soliciting this support, emphasizing that affirming diversity is an economic issue is usually very effective.

The second step of this phase is to put together an internal advisory team familiar with the latest approaches to management. The team needs to consider program policies and practices that balance traditional management approaches, which address the personal growth and career needs of individual workers and of organizational needs and structures, with nontraditional approaches.[18]

From the beginning, the organization should consult with people in other workplaces where these issues are being addressed. This consultation should elicit an overview of the program possibilities and provide an opportunity to gain knowledge about approaches to avoid and those to consider based on other businesses' experiences. A number of corporations have implemented diversity programs. They include Aetna, Apple, AT&T, Avon, Corning, Digital, Hewlett-Packard, IBM, Pacific Bell, Procter & Gamble, and Xerox.

The Information-Gathering Phase

The information-gathering phase encompasses first the assessment of the current workplace culture and workers' attitudes and then the hiring of an outside consultant. The assessment will determine what existing philosophies, policies, and practices present barriers to fostering diversity.

ASSESSING THE WORKPLACE

This assessment of workers' attitudes can be conducted through an anonymous survey questionnaire that explores the prejudices and resistance that present barriers to fostering workplace diversity. It also determines aspects of the workplace that foster diversity.

From the organizational perspective, the assessment identifies the organizational factors that impede or that foster the valuing of diversity and the extent to which other existing organizational efforts may complement the success of the program—for instance:

- How will the attainment of affirmative action goals affect the goals of the diversity program?
- How can the EAP be used to help achieve the goals of the diversity program?
- What other programs or departments should be directly and/or indirectly involved and/or consulted?

CONSULTATION

The services of an outside consultant are critical because this type of assessment requires in-depth data gathering about the organization.[19] The outside consultant is likely to render a more objective interpretation of the data than an internal consultant who is a part of the workplace culture. An outside consultant also has experience and knowledge regarding other workplace cultures and other diversity programming efforts. He or she should be part of an advisory team that consists of employees from all levels of the work organization. (See the list of selected technical assistance resources at the end of this chapter.)

The Planning Phase

Once the workplace culture has been assessed and the information analyzed, it is time to use this knowledge to answer such questions as:

- What does the assessment say about where the organization is?
- Is this where the organization wants to be?
- What are the organizational goals for a multicultural work force?
- What type of program will be most effective in meeting the goals?
- How will the program operate?
- What policies need to be implemented?
- How will program success be measured?

The planning phase consists of three steps.

1. *Set goals.* While goals are unique to each workplace, a generally acceptable goal in the management of a diverse work force is to have diverse representation at all levels of the organization[20]—a concept that is very different from the "melting pot" concept, which encourages the assimilation of minorities and women into the dominant culture. In this case, the goal is to create a culture that does not assume that there is something wrong with individual differentness or that differentness is a problem to be overcome.[21] Examples of goals are the achievement of a specific average retention or promotion rate in order to achieve cultural diversity or the ability of supervisors and co-workers to see a situation from another culture's perspective.

2. *Select the program model.* There are as many diversity models and programs as there are work organizations. The following human resources management development approaches are prototypes from which many diversity programs are modeled.

The *personal growth model* focuses on the concept that workers who traditionally have not been in the U.S. work force need special training to ease their integration into the workplace. This model also focuses on individual managers and supervisors who have new job responsibilities or who have difficulties in performing their jobs. Programs stemming from this model typically involve personal development training such as assertiveness training, leadership skill seminars, and performance evaluation training.

The problem with this model is that it focuses on individual deficits and may reinforce stereotypes of "minorities" as being unqualified. Moreover, singling out any group of people based on their differences may reinforce the idea that something is wrong with them.[22] On the other hand, it may signal the organization's commitment to the retention and advancement of minorities. It should be emphasized that all workers can grow personally and professionally by increasing their knowledge of many cultures.

The *organizational reform model* focuses on the concept that the organization itself presents barriers to the expression and appreciation of differentness. Historically, these barriers have resulted in discrimination against women and minority workers. Affirmative action strategies and the threat of legal liability have been instrumental in helping organizations remove some of the formal barriers to a multicultural workplace, but informal barriers resulting in work units that are either overrepresented with people of color and women or underrepresented—with token or no representation of people of color and women—may still exist. Informal approaches stemming from this model typically involve changing traditional practices geared toward people who have been in the work force. These approaches include informal practices that present opportunities for increasing job skills through cross training by sanctioning temporary transfers to other work units; recruitment and hiring practices based on perceived potential rather than on demonstrated ability; and developing ways for workers who are already in the work force to apply and compete for positions with a career path.

The model used by companies most experienced with managing diversity includes aspects of both models—personal growth and organizational reform—and moves beyond them. The *organizational growth model* operates on the premise that a comprehensive program evolves over time, addresses the relationship between organization and worker, and incorporates components to help the organization address the workplace from a systems perspective. It recognizes the interdependent relationship of work force and workplace—that is, each is affected by the other. It also assumes that both the organization and the worker need help in developing a bias-free, multicultural workplace. It helps to empower workers to address barriers to their own personal and professional development and helps the workplace remain competitive by tapping all of its resources.

The model recognizes and addresses the need for skills development and professional growth while addressing the individual worker perspective and the organizational perspective. For instance, if employees are expected to work together in a different manner, the organization may have to change its view of how work is structured. An organization that has a goal of promoting good relations among its workers may need to provide cultural education to its employees and develop work teams whose members reflect the organization's diversity. Organizations adopting this model need to answer the following key questions:

▲ How does a particular organizational change affect individuals and groups of workers?
▲ How do the specific diverse needs of the individuals and groups of workers affect the organization?
▲ How will both benefit?
▲ How can this approach be cost-effective?
▲ In what ways will this approach affirm diversity?
▲ What barriers to diversity appreciation are created?

3. *Determine program components.* The basic program components are usually education, training, and counseling; the way these components are used varies according to organizational goals, work environment, available resources, and the nature of the diversity. (See the example of a comprehensive multicultural education and training course at the end of this chapter.)

Education focuses on attitudes and personal awareness, usually taking place within a discussion group format in order to facilitate self-exploration and personal sensitivity. This component of the program addresses such things as:

▲ Culturally specific awareness facts
▲ Diversity education
▲ Cultural biases and stereotypes
▲ Cultural pluralism
▲ Personal ethnic identity
▲ Multicultural awareness
▲ Goals and philosophies of the program
▲ Organizational attitudes and barriers as well as cultural awareness
▲ Historical and social aspects of diversity

Training teaches the skills and behaviors needed for the program to succeed. When a diversity program is first developed and implemented, the primary goal is usually behavioral change, with the assumption that attitudinal change will follow.[23] Training usually includes:

▲ General interpersonal communication skills
▲ Intercultural and sensitivity training
▲ Multicultural training for managers, supervisors, and trainers (already employed by the organization or hired from outside)

One of the goals of the program is to teach managers and supervisors how to counsel workers in a culturally sensitive manner. Multicultural counseling assumes that the worker and the supervisor differ on some significant dimension—age, ethnicity, culture, gender, or sexual orientation—and that the greater the cultural difference, the more likely the potential for misunderstanding. Thus, in multicultural counseling, the focus is on the meaning of a worker's behavior instead of the importance of the behavior, understanding the complexity of the worker's cultural development, and recognizing that counseling occurs in both formal and informal ways.[24] The training program should include simulations of situations managers and supervisors are likely to experience on the job. This is important in helping the supervisor begin to understand and emphasize the complexity and nuances that make multicultural counseling different from counseling from a homogeneous perspective.

After defining and conceptualizing the program models and components, the next phase is implementation.

The Implementation Phase

This is the phase in which the diversity program becomes operational. Many large organizations begin by running top management and labor officials through the program in order to secure commitment from these levels; this process also serves as a trial run. Any program components can be refined before the program is introduced to the entire workplace.

The evaluation process begins during the planning phase and should be based on evaluative research methodology. Therefore, the services of a research consultant are important. (See the list of selected assistance resources available to provide program evaluation services at the end of this chapter.)

The Evaluation Phase

The evaluation is important because the success of the diversity program depends on how the program is implemented and whether it accomplishes its objectives. Therefore, the researcher needs to be involved during the program planning phase.

The evaluation process consists of a process evaluation and an outcome evaluation. In general, the process evaluation addresses information related to the development and operation of the program:

- How does the diversity program operate?
- What are the components?
- How do the components relate to each other?
- Who or what departments are involved?
- Which departments are collaborating?
- Which departments are not involved?
- What factors facilitate or impede coordination and collaboration?
- What do staff do?

- What are personal and career demographic characteristics of the staff?
- Who has received training?

The outcome evaluation focuses on whether the program activities make a difference. It requires that goals and objectives be stated and that data on the work force be collected before program implementation. Outcome evaluation, therefore, examines the outcome of the program to determine if the program resulted in a workplace that values diversity and is truly multicultural. In order to determine this, the goals, objectives, and data collected must be specific and measurable. For example, a goal of having at least a 40/60 male/female worker ratio in all departments at all levels of the organization is measurable. Research can provide evidence of whether this goal has been met. For a goal that is to change worker attitudes toward other workers who are culturally different, it is necessary to specify behaviors that can be observed as reflecting attitudinal changes. Research may help determine effectiveness by measuring worker attitudes before and after program implementation.

Corporate Diversity Counseling: A Conceptual Framework

Counseling programs need to be able to help the work force acquire the degree of sensitivity necessary to manage and/or resolve conflict. They need to focus on active counseling interventions rather than the traditional reactive interventions.

Counseling Approaches

The traditional counseling model, which focuses on individual worker problems, is not particularly effective in working with people of color.[25] Instead, counselors must use pro-active approaches to promote team building. These programs must focus on the relationship between the individual workers and workplace practices. Further, diversity counseling may occur on several levels, and therefore anyone who performs any type of counseling should use a multicultural perspective.

Counseling Issues

Historically, workplace counseling is not a process that has been embraced by minority workers, although it has been embraced by women.[26] Similarly, employee assistance counseling programs have also been underutilized as a management resource. Like other counseling programs, diversity counseling programs and counselors need to overcome several barriers—barriers brought by individual minority workers and their supervisors as well as those brought or created by the workplace. These barriers have implications for the design of specific counseling program components, counseling models, and skills.

BARRIERS TO THE COUNSELING CONCEPT

Many people of color, especially African-Americans, tend not to trust the counseling process in general because it has often ignored their racially based sociopolitical experiences,[27] and they do not trust workplace counseling programs in particular because the focus has often been on casting individual blame and firing the employee.[28] Thus, a counseling model that takes into account the importance of different experiences and backgrounds and includes all of the individuals who are affected by the situation being addressed is likely to be far more acceptable to minority workers.

INDIVIDUAL BARRIERS TO THE COUNSELING PROCESS

Overcoming obstacles to counseling is just the beginning. The actual process of counseling also has barriers to overcome, most of them indigenous to cultural differences, such as language, values, stereotyping, and expectations.[29] These are not only barriers to the actual counseling process but may also be the basis of misunderstandings that prompted the need for counseling. For instance, if a supervisor believes that African-American workers are hostile and difficult to get along with and begins to document problems involving only African-American workers, such stereotyping will result in a self-fulfilling prophecy and a hostile working relationship. Similarly, if that same supervisor is referred to a traditional counselor who initially focuses on the worker's reactions (attitude) without considering it in the context of the supervisor's stereotypic beliefs and interprets the worker's resistance to the approach as confirmation of the supervisor's beliefs, that counselor is also insensitive to the possibility that the worker's reaction could be a normal one in light of an unfamiliar process or the perception of unfair treatment.

A preferred approach initially defines the problem as a relationship problem instead of an attitude problem and thus includes both the worker and the supervisor in the counseling process. A counselor who is sensitive to issues of diversity will be alert to certain words or phrases that indicate stereotyping is a problem—for example, *they, them, us, we, those people*.

P. Pederson has offered the following group exercise for stereotype awareness:

> Distribute one or more note cards to each participant. Write an incomplete sentence stem on the blackboard relevant to the group such as, "Most refugees will say that Americans are. . . ."

Ask participants to complete the sentence with one or two words
on their note card. Gather the note cards and code the responses
and discuss stereotypes and generalizations.[30]

Although there are many customs, values, and beliefs that help to
distinguish groups, that does not mean that all members of the same sex
or the same cultural, racial, or ethnic group are homogeneous. For
instance, not all Japanese-Americans are alike, although there are some
generalizations that could be made about their culture. The culturally
sensitive supervisor and counselor must be able to assess the individual
worker's primary group identification instead of assuming that because a
person is, say, Japanese-American he or she primarily values those things
associated with the Japanese culture. Making such an assumption is
another way of stereotyping.

Language differences may also present barriers because they interfere
with establishing rapport and therefore can result in misunderstanding.
Furthermore, an intolerance of the use of any language other than standard English often results from a belief of ethnic and cultural superiority,
concerns about not being included, and a fear of not knowing how to
interpret interactions. When language barriers do occur there is a tendency
to rely on nonverbal gestures, postures, and verbal inflections.[31] For
instance, differences in nonverbal responses are seen in the frequent
comparisons of blacks and whites: "When speaking to another person,
Anglos tend to look away from the person [avoid eye contact] more often
than do black individuals. When listening to another person speak, however, blacks tend to avoid eye contact while Anglos make eye contact."[32]
If these aspects of culture are not understood, it would be easy to
misinterpret the avoidance of eye contact by African-Americans as not
paying attention or to misinterpret the avoidance of eye contact when
speaking by whites as degrading.

Values that are class and culture bound may also present barriers to
the counseling process for both supervisor and counselor—for instance,
regarding the significance and meaning of time. For cultures of people of
color, as compared to mainstream culture, time typically is divided into
broader, estimated segments rather than into tiny, finite segments. At the
workplace, this difference could be the basis of many problems, since
much of the workday revolves around time. For instance, individual
workers of color may not make a distinction between arriving at work
between 9:00 and 9:15, whereas the Anglo supervisor may make a distinction between 9:00 and 9:01. In such a case, the culturally illiterate
supervisor or counselor may interpret the worker's behavior as not being
conscientious, while the worker may interpret the supervisor's concern as
"picky." A culturally sensitive supervisor will be able to see that these
value differences may be the source of the problem. Again, this situation
requires that the supervisor be culturally knowledgeable and sensitive.

WORKPLACE BARRIERS TO THE COUNSELING PROCESS

Most of the workplace barriers to the counseling process are found in organizational policies and procedures. Sometimes these organizational constraints may dictate behaviors and influence attitudes that we know are inequitable or inflexible—for example, strict reporting and/or counseling relationships. In large organizations, workers typically communicate primarily with their immediate supervisors, even if they have communication problems with that person and prefer another supervisor.

Another barrier may be found in the way the counseling service is offered and by whom. Too often supervisory counseling occurs when there is a problem—typically between the worker and the supervisor or between the worker and the counselor, who may be perceived as acting as the supervisor's agent. Therefore, seeing the worker in a private meeting with a supervisor carries a stigma. In the past, this has been the counseling context. To be effective in working with many people of color, a more balanced, casual counseling approach helps to overcome this stigma.[33]

When the supervisor or counselor is culturally or racially different from most of the workers, another barrier is created because the workers assume that the counselor does not understand them. Having a multicultural perspective will help the supervisor or counselor overcome this particular barrier.

Above all, all supervisor and diversity counselors must be skilled in working with a diverse work force. The skills that made them effective in working with a more homogeneous work force are inadequate in working with the culturally, racially, and sexually diverse workplace of the 1990s.

Small Businesses

Small businesses have had more experience with a culturally and racially diverse work force; historically, more minorities have been employed in small businesses than in large businesses. Businesses that have dealt with this diversity in a positive manner already know the benefits that accrue— for example, a more cohesive and harmonious work force. Those that have not yet learned how to address some of the realities of a diverse work force probably are characterized by frequent worker turnovers and worker disputes.

The needs of the small business are the same as those of the large corporation: to develop mechanisms that let employees know that many of their cultural differences will be valued and to help the organization understand and learn how to address differences. The major difference between small and large businesses is in their availability of resources, especially time and money.

Small businesses usually do not have time to address issues that seem peripheral to their primary business. Often, they probably will not have a separate human resources unit to handle personnel issues. The result is less tolerance for differences. Ironically, intolerance or insensitivity is particularly disruptive because the work groups are much smaller and need to work as teams. Similarly, many small businesses may not have written policies that can guide supervisors in managing diversity issues in a thoughtful way; in the absence of such policies, decisions may appear arbitrary and could be perceived as unfair, thus allowing for misunderstanding and distrust.

Small businesses usually do not have money to hire a specialist to help develop programs to educate, train, and/or counsel the workplace on matters of diversity and team-building.

Another facet unique to small businesses is that there are mostly generalist employees and few specialists; therefore, the supervisor or manager may perform many roles but not have special training, even when he or she has had experience in diversity counseling, sensitivity training, and multicultural education.

Nevertheless, small businesses have some of the same needs as big businesses in affirming diversity. The following suggestions can help them in this regard:

1. Small businesses should join together to discuss issues of diversity and consider hiring a consultant to work with the group. Sharing the fee cuts the economic burden.

2. Local universities and colleges have professors and students who need to work on special projects, such as training, group work, and counseling. They can be hired as consultants. In some instances there may not be a fee.

3. Videotapes can help in training. (See the list of selected technical assistance resources at the end of this chapter.)

The 1990s will be a time of many cooperative joint ventures as the business community and educational institutions join forces in addressing many commonly shared interests. Therefore, it will be an environment favorable to the needs of the small-business environment.

The needs of a multicultural workplace—large or small—reflect the needs of a multicultural society. Society, workplaces, and workers must develop innovative and creative equitable policies and practices to ensure that diverse values and customs are appreciated and affirmed.

NOTES

1. B. Mandell and S. Kobler-Gray, "Management Development That Values Diversity," *Personnel* (March 1990): 41–47.
2. U.S. Department of Labor, *Workforce 2000* (Washington, D.C.: Government Printing Office, 1987).

3. U.S. Department of Labor, *Opportunity 2000* (Washington, D.C.: Government Printing Office, 1988).
4. R. Thomas, Jr., "From Affirmative Action to Affirming Diversity," *Harvard Business Review* (March–April 1990): 107–117.
5. L. Copeland, "Making the Most of Cultural Differences at the Workplace," *Personnel* (June 1988): 52–50.
6. Thomas, "From Affirmative Action," pp. 107–117.
7. T. Smith and P. Sheatsley, "American Attitude toward Race Relations," *Public Opinion* 8 (October–November 1985): 7, 14–15, 50–53.
8. J. Kluegel and E. Smith, *Beliefs about Inequality: Americans' Views or What Is and What Ought to Be* (New York: Aldine de Gruyter, 1986); H. Schuman, C. Steeh, and L. Bobo, *Racial Attitudes in America: Trends and Interpretations* (Cambridge: Harvard University Press, 1985), pp. 14–15.
9. A. Smith, "Racial Trends and Countertrends in American Organizational Behavior," *Journal of Social Science Issues,* 43, no. 1 (1987): 92; J. Cox-Burton, "Leadership in the Future—A Quality Issue," *SAM Advanced Management Journal* (Autumn 1988): 39–43.
10. M. Tanke, "Course Design for Multicultural Management," *The Cornell Quarterly* (August 1988): 67–68.
11. R. Jones, "How Do You Manage a Diverse Workforce?" *Training and Development Journal* (February 1989): 13; Thomas, "From Affirmative Action."
12. Jones, "How Do You Manage a Diverse Workforce?" p. 15.
13. Thomas, "From Affirmative Action."
14. W. Bielby, "Modern Prejudice and Institutional Barriers to Equal Employment Opportunity for Minorities," *Journal of Social Issues* 43, no. 1 (1987): 79–84.
15. I. Pettigrew and J. Martin, Jr., "Shaping the Organizational Context for Black American Inclusion," *Journal of Social Issues* 43, no. 1 (1987): 44–78.
16. Bielby, "Modern Prejudice."
17. Cox-Burton, "Leadership in the Future," p. 43.
18. Mandell and Kobler-Gray, "Management Development That Values Diversity."
19. Thomas, "From Affirmative Action."
20. Jones, "How Do You Manage a Diverse Workforce?"
21. Thomas, "From Affirmative Action"; Mandel and Kobler-Gray, "Management Development That Values Diversity," p. 42.
22. Mandel and Kobler-Gray, "Management Development That Values Diversity," p. 42.
23. Copeland, "Making the Most of Cultural Differences at the Workplace."
24. P. Pederson, *A Handbook for Developing Multicultural Awareness* (Alexandria, Va.: American Association for Counseling and Development, 1988), pp. 109–112.
25. D. Atkinson et al., *Counseling American Minorities,* (Dubuque, Iowa: Brown, 1989), p. 13.
26. M. Gray, "Designing Employee Assistance Programs to Meet the Needs of Black Clients," in F. Brisbane and M. Womble, eds., *Treatment of Black Alcoholics* (New York: Haworth Press, 1985), p. 88.

27. W. Smith et al., *Minority Issues in Mental Health.* (Menlo Park, Calif.: Addison-Wesley, 1978), p. 187.
28. Gray, "Designing Employee Assistance Programs," p. 87.
29. Atkinson et al., *Counseling American Minorities,* p. 24.
30. Pederson, *Handbook,* p. 27.
31. Atkinson, *Counseling American Minorities,* p. 20.
32. Ibid., p. 21.
33. Gray, "Designing Employee Assistance Programs," p. 95.

SELECTED TECHNICAL ASSISTANCE RESOURCES

Professional Associations and Educational Foundations

American Association for
  Counseling and Development
5999 Stevenson Avenue
Alexandria, VA 22304
(703) 823-9800

American Management
  Association
135 West Fiftieth Street
New York, NY 10020
(212) 586-8100

American Psychological
  Association
University of Georgia
Division 17, Ethnic and Cultural
  Diversity
Department of Counseling
402 Aderhold Hall
Athens, GA 30602
(404) 542-1812

American Society for Training
  and Development
4227 Forty-sixth Street, N.W.
Washington, DC 20016
(202) 362-1498

Employee Assistance
  Professionals Association
4601 North Fairfax Drive, Suite
  1001
Arlington, VA 22203
(703) 522-6272

Institute for Policy Studies
1601 Connecticut Avenue, N.W.
Washington, DC 20009
(202) 234-9382

Society for Intercultural
  Education, Training, and
  Research
733 Fifteenth Street, N.W., Suite
  900
Washington, DC 22314
(201) 737-5000

Society for Human Resource
  Management
606 North Washington Street
Alexandria, VA 22314
(703) 548-3440

National Education Association
1201 Sixteenth Street, N.W.
Washington, DC 20036
(202) 833-4000

National Foundation for the Study
  of Employment Policy
1015 Fifteenth Street, N.W., Suite
  1200
Washington, DC 20005
(202) 789-8685

Training Aids

BNA Communications
9439 Key West Avenue
Rockville, MD 20850
(301) 948-0540

Dartnell Productions
4660 Rabenswood Avenue
Chicago, IL 60640
(312) 561-4000

Copeland Griggs Productions
302 Twenty-third Avenue
San Francisco, CA 94121
(415) 668-4200

Selected Videotape Titles

"A Costly Proposition" (sexual
  harassment-video)
"Bridges: Skills to Manage a
  Diverse Work Force" (eight
  video-based modules)
"Choices" (EEO, twelve video-
  based modules)
"Dealing with Discrimination"

"Fair Employment Practices"
  (five video-based modules)
"Going International" (seven
  video-based modules)
"Simile 11" (simulation games)
"Valuing Diversity" (seven video-
  based modules)

University-Based Resources

American Graduate School of
  International Management
15249 North Fifty-Ninth Avenue
Glendale, AZ 85306
(602) 978-7011

American Institute for Managing
  Diversity
830 Westview Drive, Suite 315
Morehouse College
Atlanta, GA 30314
(404) 524-7316

Brigham Young University Center
for International and Area
Studies
216 HRCB
Provo, UT 84602
(801) 378-5459

Business Council for International
Understanding
American University
3301 New Mexico Avenue, N.W.,
Suite 244
Washington, DC 20016
(202) 686-2771

Florida International University
School of Hospitality
Management
15101 Bisbayne Boulevard
North Miami, FL 33181
(305) 948-4500

School for International Training
P.O. Box 676
Brattleboro, VT 05302
(802) 257-7751

Stanford Institute for Intercultural
Communications
8835 Southwest Canyon Lane
Portland, OR 97225
(503) 297-4622

University of Maryland
College of Business and
Management
Center for International Business
and Research
Tydings Hall
College Park, MD 20742
(301) 405-2259

Example of a Multicultural Management Training Course

The following graduate-level course, designed by Mary L. Tanke, Ph.D., Assistant Professor in the School of Hospitality Management at Florida International University, is an example of a comprehensive course design dealing with ethnic diversity and various related issues found in the U.S. work force. This semester-long course has a prospectus that states its objectives, main topics, and course design. In her article, "Course Design for Multicultural Management" (*The Cornell Quarterly,* August 1988, page 67), Dr. Tanke provides helpful suggestions for others wishing to teach such a course.*

Course Prospectus for Multicultural Human Resource Management

Course Description
A study of both personnel and consumer relations in the hospitality industry within a multiracial, multi-ethnic, and multicultural society that will provide the students with a cross-cultural perspective on management styles and skills.

Course Objectives
1. To provide an environment in which students can analyze selected aspects of dominant cultures and social structures.
2. To develop a cross-cultural awareness and understanding of ethnic identity on the part of students.
3. To improve students' understanding of the lifestyles and contributions of selected ethnic groups in world society.
4. To improve students' ability to communicate, motivate, manage, and interact positively in a multicultural environment.
5. To provide students with an understanding of the power of cultural biases and sociocultural influences within the vast array of food-service and lodging establishments.
6. To identify training techniques and styles that are appropriate for the cross-cultural environment found in the hospitality industry.

Course Design
The course is broken into seven topics, starting with an introduction to the language of multicultural management. Second, the students discuss major beliefs and premises about American society regarding ethnic diversity and cultural pluralism, and they redefine assimilation and the "melting pot" as they apply to a workplace setting. During this section of the course, the students establish goals for cultural pluralism and uncover assumptions that must be recognized before these goals can be realized.

The third topic is the competencies necessary for learning about different ethnic groups. Knowing how to learn about and study the heritages, lifestyles, and contributions of ethnic and racial groups is necessary for manager self-improvement. Ethnic diversity and the self-discovery that occurs in the classroom contribute greatly to the learning process. Before the students can be expected to understand cultures, they need a realization of their own ethnic orientation and biases. This realization can be gained through

*Reprinted with permission of *The Cornell H.R.A. Quarterly.*

(continues)

Example of a Multicultural Management Training Course (continued)

self-awareness exercises, which constitute a part of the fourth topic of discussion—namely, cultural awareness and ethnic identification and formation of oneself and others. For students who have never examined their own ethnicity or come to terms with who they are as individuals, this can be both a painful and joyful process.

Next, the students develop an awareness of the cultural values and behavior patterns of different ethnic groups. This section of the course begins with an overview of oppression, stereotyping, and prejudicial behavior. I [Tanke] did not originally intend to delve into these topics, believing them to be beyond the scope of the course. The first semester that the course was taught, however, these topics were constantly arising in class discussions. Instead of dancing around this subject matter, therefore, I allocated time for the discussion of these behavior patterns. In subsequent sessions, these topics have generated some of the most thought-provoking classroom discussions, as well as showing the students the source of some of their own prejudices. During the course of the discussion, the students identify points of cultural conflict in ethnically pluralistic work environments and consider the implications of these conflicts for training and managing ethnically different employees.

The last two topics center around ethnic learning and communication styles. I teach ways to recognize different learning styles and explore ways to use these styles advantageously in the management process. At the conclusion of the course, the students have learned how to recognize the effects of ethnicity in their management of employees. They should have the tools to view cultural diversity as a valuable, not detrimental, resource and see the need for positive functional involvement of ethnic groups in the workplace as an asset to management.

13

AIDS Counseling

Dale A. Masi, School of Social Work, University of Maryland

The potential that AIDS has of damaging the workplace can no longer be avoided. Predictions of the numbers of those afflicted with the HIV virus bring the potential for work disruption, a decrease in employee morale, discrimination suits, and incredible monetary costs for health care. Yet a recent survey of over 2,000 firms indicated that only 10 percent of U.S. companies have a written policy on AIDS.[1]

If AIDS continues to be ignored in the workplace, business organizations will end up in economic straits. Perhaps unknowingly, the workplace is already picking up the tab for caring for AIDS patients because 90 percent of AIDS patients are between the ages of 20 and 49, the age of most working adults. Estimates of the costs of AIDS-related medical care were greater than $8.5 billion by 1991.[2]

Finally, information about AIDS constantly needs updating. New facts, revised legal decisions, and new medical findings have important implications for the workplace. The decision not to address AIDS in the workplace can (and has) put employers into economic, legal, moral, and ethical turmoil.

Medical Facets

AIDS is an acronym for acquired immune deficiency syndrome. When individuals are diagnosed with cases of full-blown AIDS, they are in the final stages of a series of health problems caused by the human immunodeficiency virus. This virus primarily infects certain cells of the immune system. People who are infected with the virus but do not exhibit symptoms of AIDS are described as HIV positive.

Prevalence of the Disease

Virtually every country on every continent except Antarctica has reported cases of AIDS to the World Health Organization (WHO). As of October 1991, 418,403 cases had been reported by 158 countries to WHO. This figure, however, represents only a fraction of those afflicted. Experts say that close to 1.5 million people are infected. Jonathan Mann of WHO estimated that in the 1990s there would be 5 million new infections with HIV, 600,000 cases of AIDS, and 300,000 deaths. He said that the cumulative total of AIDS cases might reach 6 million by the year 2000.[3] As of 1990, continental Africa and Brazil lead the world in AIDS infection. The Caribbean, particularly Bermuda, and Mexico are the regions with the fastest growing number of AIDS cases.

AIDS in the United States

As of September, 1991, 195,718 cases of full-blown AIDS had been reported in the United States—192,406 of them in adults and adolescents. Fifty-nine percent of those with AIDS are male homosexuals, 22 percent are intravenous drug abusers, about 7 percent are both male homosexuals and intravenous drug abusers, 5 percent are people infected by heterosexual transmission, 2 percent are people infected by blood transfusions, 1 percent are hemophiliacs, and the remaining 4 percent are undetermined.[4]

In the District of Columbia, which has a substantial minority and transient population and a high incidence of drug abuse, the infection rate is the highest in the nation. San Francisco, which led the nation in the number of AIDS cases for several years, reported in 1988 less than a 1 percent increase in cases. This was due to the fact that male homosexuals—the first identified high-risk group—recognized the threat of the disease and began to practice "safer sex" techniques to halt the spread of the virus. Currently, the infection and disease rates of the predominantly infected groups in other parts of the United States are shifting considerably. The infection rate appears to have reached a plateau in the white homosexual male population, largely as a result of changes in behavioral patterns, but the disease rate among other populations is still climbing; there is a marked increase in the needle-using population, of concern to public health experts because intravenous (IV) drug users, through their sexual contact, are viewed as a bridge to the general heterosexual population.[5]

The fastest-growing infected portions of the population are women and IV drug users. Over 40 percent of women with AIDS were infected through heterosexual contacts with men who were principally bisexual or IV drug users. Children, too, are at risk of AIDS infection—over 90 percent of them contracting the disease from their mother in utero.

Finally, teenagers are also at risk. At least three of every 1,000 military recruits (usually persons in their late teens or early twenties) are testing HIV positive.[6]

Stages of the Disease

The course of AIDS has been divided into six stages by Robert A. Redfield of the Walter Reed Army Institute of Research. After the initial infection with the virus, a person may appear to be healthy for up to eight to ten years. In the first stage, an unknown proportion of infected people do experience an early, brief, mononucleosislike illness with fever, malaise, and possibly a skin rash. Such symptoms, when they are present, develop at about the time antibodies produced by the body against HIV can first be detected. This usually occurs between two weeks and three months after infection. The second stage occurs with a condition called lymphadenopathy, a chronic lymph node disease, which may last several years without any other signs of the disease. After these two stages, the virus can remain dormant for many years. The third and fourth stages are defined by a marked decrease in the body's immune system, which is shown by measuring levels of immune system cells called T4 cells. At stage five, symptoms of immune collapse, typically chronic infections of the skin and mucous membranes, develop. During the sixth and final stage, life-threatening infections may strike a wide variety of organs. Most patients die within two years after entering stage six.[7]

Transmission

One of the most important pieces of information about AIDS in the workplace is transmission. Misconceptions about transmission have led to lawsuits, strikes, work stoppages, and employee tension due to fear caused by ignorance of the facts. The workplace must take responsibility for educating all employees about the transmission of the virus; subsequently, employee fear will be decreased.

The transmission of the AIDS virus occurs in only a few ways: through sexual contact, through the sharing of needles and syringes when injecting drugs, through the transfusion of blood or its components, from a pregnant woman to the fetus she is carrying, and from mother to child through breast-feeding. The risk of infection with the AIDS virus is increased by having multiple sexual partners (either homosexual or heterosexual).

As former Surgeon General C. Everett Koop stated:

> Everyday living does not present any risk of infection. One CANNOT get AIDS from casual social contact. Casual social contact should not be confused with casual sexual contact which is a major cause of the spread of the AIDS virus. Casual social contact such as shaking hands, hugging, social kissing, crying,

coughing, or sneezing, will not transmit the AIDS virus. Nor has AIDS been contracted from swimming in pools or bathing in hot tubs or from eating in restaurants (even if a restaurant worker has AIDS or carries the AIDS virus). AIDS is not contracted from sharing bed linens, towels, cups, straws, dishes, or any other eating utensils. You cannot get AIDS from toilets, doorknobs, telephones, office machinery, or household furniture. You cannot get AIDS from body massages, masturbation, or any nonsexual contact.[8]

Companies need to keep employees informed of accurate medical information about the AIDS virus. Periodic discussions addressing prevention, transmission, and realistic interpretations of such data will help assuage employee fear, as well as alleviate discrimination of employees carrying the HIV.

Legal Issues

There are three areas of the law that apply to AIDS issues: federal, state, and common law. The most commonly addressed issues related to AIDS resulting in legal action are HIV testing, discrimination, torts (resulting from a claim of injury or wrong done), insurance and benefits, and co-workers' concerns related to occupational and health safety.

HIV Testing

Although no federal law expressly bars employers from testing applicants or employees for HIV infection, government employees at federal, state, and local levels may be protected by constitutional limitations. It was determined in one case that mandatory HIV testing for workers in a state-run facility who had intensive contact with clients was an infringement on their Fourth Amendment right to be free from unreasonable searches and seizures, particularly in the light of medical evidence that the virus is not transmitted by casual contact.[9] States that prohibit such testings are Wisconsin, Massachusetts (as a condition of employment), Florida, the District of Columbia, and California (as a condition of employment). Localities include Austin, Texas, and San Francisco, Los Angeles, and Berkeley in California. Some states, such as New Jersey, have administrative interpretations under equal employment opportunity laws, and in New York, the state insurance department prohibits testing of applicants for health insurance but not for life or disability insurance policies. The legal issues that affect HIV testing are invasion of privacy claims under state laws, as well as defamation claims arising from dissemination of test results, and claims based on confidentiality concerns and/or intentional infliction of emotional distress claims.

The issue of confidentiality is important. According to Willis Gold-beck, President of the Washington Business Group on Health:

> Employers have no right to know what an employee's diagnosis is for any illness. That is privileged information between patient and medical professionals. Precedents exist in law to handle the management of information where rights of the individual's confidentiality must be balanced against the need to protect the rest of society. Should this become the case for AIDS, the decision should be based on science, not fear, and should be promulgated by national public health policy rather than by local employers facing uninformed pressures.[10]

Discrimination

The federal Rehabilitation Act of 1973 prohibits government contractors, subcontractors, or entities receiving any type of federal financial assistance from discriminating against an employee or applicant who is otherwise qualified to perform the work because of any physical or mental impairing condition.[11] Employment in this instance is viewed as a major life ability, and this law protects persons who currently have impairments, have a history of impairment, and are perceived to be impaired by an employer. This last group is very important in cases of AIDS because it protects high-risk groups, such as homosexuals or certain minorities, against potential discrimination.

In March 1988, the Office of Federal Contract Compliance Programs (OFCCP) provided that all employees testing HIV positive are to be included under the discrimination interpretation of physically impaired. Further, these cases will have the highest priority in expediting claims because of the life expectancy of the claimant. OFCCP, which is within the Department of Labor, has regional offices across the country that process AIDS-based claims. All local OFCCP officers must notify the national office of any claims immediately.

The guidelines additionally empower the OFCCP to take corrective action if discrimination is found; it can rescind the federal contract, order the employee to be rehired, order promotion, order back pay, and bar the company from receiving any other federal contract until compliance is achieved. These actions may be taken only after a hearing before an administrative law judge.

A number of recent federal cases have extended the rights of employees with infectious diseases.[12] As long as a person is otherwise qualified to perform, in the absence of any evidence that the disease will spread or is a safety or health threat to others, the employee has the right to work. The trend among states in developing statutory provisions has been in accordance with the federal guidelines and law.

In 1989, Congress passed the Americans with Disabilities Act. Under the act, the Civil Rights Act of 1964, which outlaws discrimination on the basis of race, religion, sex, and national origin, has been extended to AIDS patients. AIDS is considered a disability because it interferes with carrying out ordinary activities. Employers cannot discharge AIDS carriers unless they can no longer perform their job or risk infecting co-workers.

Torts

Tort claims are increasing in employment suits, with punitive damages awarded by juries. The areas most involved are breach of employment contracts, emotional distress claims, good faith and fair dealing contract claims, and defamation of character.

Insurance and Benefits

The Employee Retirement Income Security Act of 1974, section 510, makes it unlawful to discriminate against a person by obstructing or preventing pursuit of an employee benefit or right. This provision has been strengthened through some state and district laws (Massachusetts, Washington, D.C., Wisconsin), court cases (e.g., *National Gay Rights v. Alvida* [Fla.]), and administrative opinions.[13]

Co-workers' Concerns

Some legal issues raised by co-workers' concerns have been addressed through the federal Occupational Safety and Health Act (OSHA) and the National Labor Relations Act. In terms of health and safety, the requirement is that precautionary measures must be taken and safety procedures implemented in special occupational settings where there may be a heightened risk of employee exposure (e.g., laboratory work on body fluids from AIDS patients or handling of hospital waste products against blood-borne diseases).

Policy

A company-wide AIDS policy sends an important message to employees, customers, and the community that the organization values its employees, will provide human resources management of an important issue, and will help to ensure employees of a fair, legally sound, and equitable legal response. Moreover, a clear company position helps to reduce employee fear and uncertainty.

An AIDS policy in the workplace should communicate to all employees that the employer:

▲ Will treat AIDS like any other chronic or life-threatening disease.

▲ Will give support to enable employees with AIDS to continue working as long as possible.

▲ Will emphasize to all employees that there is no danger of transmission through normal workplace contact.

▲ Will provide education for all employees about the disease, methods of transmission, and prevention.

The policy enables the employer to set a standard of fair management, justice, and compassion.

Planning and Goals of the Company AIDS Policy

Before developing its AIDS policy, a company should take the following actions:

1. Define the company's goals and develop a plan for reaching the goals. The following elements should be considered for inclusion:[14]

▲ Comply with the law to steer a safe, clear course through sometimes conflicting demands.

▲ Maintain productivity.

▲ Manage costs, particularly those involving expensive medical care.

▲ Retain the trust of employees, customers, and the public in the company's commitment to the health and safety of those whose lives the company or its products touch.

▲ Show the company's caring for an employee who experiences the personal catastrophe imposed by the illness.

▲ Demonstrate management competence and integrity in the handling of a sensitive issue.

▲ Facilitate informed behavior on the part of all employees, especially those most directly associated with an afflicted fellow worker.

▲ Anticipate avoidable mistakes so that the potential for generalized catastrophic effects is contained.

▲ Learn valuable lessons applicable to future experiences.

2. Decide how, for whom, and under what circumstances there will be education about AIDS. Everyone should be educated; however, managers and supervisors are trained with more depth than the average employee population.

3. Determine how the organization will respond to an AIDS crisis—for example, who will be involved, what they will do, and how they will make and carry out decisions.[15]

4. Decide on the approach to AIDS. Certain employees need to be responsible for updating and disseminating the medical facts about AIDS.

Typically they are based in the human resources department and work directly with the employee assistance program (EAP).

Policy Strategy

Important ingredients of strategy development and implementation of the company AIDS policy include the following:

1. Establish a task force of key personnel—members of such departments as human resources, legal, medical, employee assistance, public relations, training, employee communications, unions, and senior management.

2. Identify community medical and legal experts, and maintain a resource list in the office of human resources for any employees with questions and referral needs. This list should be updated and personally checked out by the human resources department in conjunction with the company's EAP. Many mental health professionals are not trained specifically in the issues surrounding the AIDS virus and its specialized needs. Therefore, all medical, psychological, and professional experts should specify their training and expertise in relation to the field of AIDS.

3. Analyze employee demographics by considering the risks of the particular type of workplace and the geographic location of the work site.

4. Ascertain the appropriate level of complexity of the educational package; for example, a company with fewer than 100 employees has needs that are much different from those of a company with 30 regional offices and 10,000 employees. The AIDS policies of these companies should be similar, however; regardless of the size of the company, every employer shares the same AIDS issues and risks.

5. Educate and gain senior management support. In all stages of policy development and implementation, senior management support is crucial. If top management is not aware of policy decisions and development, then the policy is written and presented without the endorsement of its key management role models. This could lead to mixed messages and a diffused impact of the educational package and company AIDS policy.

6. Develop and implement a company educational standard. This is the responsibility of the human resources and EAP departments. The AIDS policy should be made clear to employees before a known AIDs case or problem arises. This information will minimize crises and reduce employee fear, mistrust, and uncertainty. Possible dissemination methods include special announcements, inclusion in employee and supervisor guides, inclusion in company newsletters and health columns, special meetings, and inclusion as part of new-employee orientation.

7. Evaluate the educational impact. As with any other policy and educational effort, the company needs outside evaluation to ensure that

its efforts are in line with the company philosophy and that the program accomplishes its objectives.

Elements of the Company AIDS Policy

The company AIDS policy should include the following elements:[16]

- The commitment of the company to act responsibly in the face of this major public health crisis.
- The commitment of the company to protect the health of all its employees.
- The commitment to provide a safe work environment.
- The commitment to treat AIDS like any other life-threatening illness; an employee who is medically fit and able to perform job duties will be permitted to work.
- The provision of reasonable accommodation and job modification for AIDS victims when appropriate.
- An outline of the company position on AIDS testing, if any.
- Procedures for supervisors to handle AIDS fairly, with compassion, and with understanding.
- The commitment to keep policy medically updated and provide employee education on AIDS and policy.
- The commitment to keep medical information confidential.
- A declaration stating that special transfer requests [from co-workers] will not be accepted, unless medically indicated.
- The commitment to consider benefit plans that provide case management, hospice or home care, and experimental treatment when applicable.
- The commitment to provide referrals through the company's EAP or other departments to community resources and experts for consultation and treatment.
- A statement of the role of the company in contributing to the community's efforts for development of treatment and support of research. This includes availability of company resources when appropriate.

Small Businesses and the Employee AIDS Policy

Employers with fewer than 100 employees will bear a heavy burden when dealing with AIDS. They cannot afford the increased health care benefits cost for employees with AIDS or the loss of productivity of employees with AIDS.[17] Therefore, they too must institute an AIDS policy and educational program. These programs are more likely to be developed with off-site EAP providers and external educators such as the Red Cross, as well as other resources listed at the end of this chapter.

Other Employees Affected by AIDS

It is necessary for companies to develop policies for employees with full-blown AIDS, but it is equally important for the policy to include employees in the other stages of the disease. Individuals who test HIV positive or show minimal symptoms may not develop full-blown AIDS for many years. During these years, the individuals will remain in the workplace, and as they live with the disease, they will need medical and psychological support. Because the workplace is such an important element in these individuals' lives, it has been demonstrated to be life lengthening for an employee to remain in familiar, supportive, and productive surroundings.

Companies should also have a policy for employees whose family members or other loved ones have been diagnosed as HIV positive, who show symptoms, or who have full-blown AIDS. These employees are typically distressed, depressed, and anxious. They must often sort through an overwhelming amount of changing medical and scientific information in order to make the best decisions about health care and life planning.[18]

Role of the EAP

In respect to dealing with AIDS in the workplace, the EAP staff can:

- ▴ Counsel the employee who has AIDS or is HIV/positive.
- ▴ Counsel the employee who is a family member of a person who has AIDS or is HIV positive.
- ▴ Counsel family members of employees who are HIV positive or have AIDS.
- ▴ Train managers and supervisors about AIDS issues as they relate to the workplace.
- ▴ Assist employees and the company on specific issues, such as what to do when an employee dies of AIDS or when workers learn that an employee has AIDS.
- ▴ Serve on the company's task force on AIDS issues.
- ▴ Keep management informed of current developments.
- ▴ Work with community resources for employees with AIDS and develop health care resources and alternatives.

In many companies, the role of the EAP has broadened to become a professional counseling service for employees with a variety of emotional and personal problems. Because many are staffed, either in-house or by contract, by professionally trained mental health persons (psychologists and social workers), these counselors can become valuable resources to companies in dealing with issues surrounding AIDS. Companies should call upon their EAPs for assistance in designing AIDS policy, in allaying employees' fears as company philosophy and policy is being developed, and in calming the workplace environment as reactions and overreactions set in when the first AIDS-affected employee is identified.

A significant role of the EAP, often in collaboration with the medical department, is to educate employees about the disease and lay the foundation for co-worker support of an employee with AIDS. The most prudent approach is to develop a fact sheet on AIDS that can be important in prevention, case finding, and diagnosis.[19]

EAP counselors are particularly well suited to work with employees with AIDS and their families. Their professional objectivity enables them to operate as an advocate for the person with AIDS while remaining sensitive to the anxieties of co-workers. In addition, EAP personnel have experience in working with community resources and are knowledgeable regarding services. They will be able to assist in making contact with the appropriate community programs that employees with AIDS and their families may require just as the EAP has developed community resources to treat alcoholism, drug addiction, and mental illness, so must it become familiar with referral sources for AIDS.

EAPs have become institutionalized in work organizations in increasing numbers as a result of their ability to respond to the personal problems of employees. EAP personnel's counseling about AIDS often gives employees the help they need to deal with co-workers, supervisors, and the workplace in general. Family members, as well as the infected person, experience denial, bewilderment, and shame; they need assistance as they face their own loss and try to cope with the disease.

The EAP can also assist companies in the interpretation and implementation of legislation pertinent to AIDS-infected employees. Already familiar with the Rehabilitation Act of 1973 and the Developmental Disabilities Act as it pertains to other handicapping conditions, EAP staff will be invaluable in understanding the ramifications of this legislation for employees who have AIDS concerning disability benefits and other issues.

Education

AIDS information and education programs are most effective if they begin before a crisis arises relative to AIDS and employee concerns. Experience has demonstrated that employees' level of receptivity to accurate information is higher when management has a policy of open communication and when educational efforts are initiated before an incident.

An employee educational program for AIDS in the workplace can be developed by following these steps:

1. *Inform and gain the support of top management.* Without their knowledge and approval, any education program will be ineffective. This support should be communicated to all employees when the program is announced.

2. *Establish a resource education committee made up of supervisors and employees.* The committee should include representatives from human resources, legal, medical, labor, communications, EAP, and special interest groups. This group first needs to be educated about the issues surrounding AIDS, the company's policies, and the availability of community resources. Then its task is to design the company's AIDS educational program and respond to employee questions and concerns.

3. *Decide on the time frame of the AIDS education program.* Companies that already have an AIDS education awareness program state that employees' awareness of AIDS is increased over time with repeated approaches through a variety of dissemination methods. Consequently, an AIDS program must be long enough to promote behavioral change and alleviate fear.

4. *Present educational material.* As new information becomes available, it must be disseminated through brochures, videos, posters, and seminars. (At the end of this chapter is a listing of national organizations with free publications and material available for a variety of populations covering all aspects of AIDS.) AIDS education should be consistent with other employee education programs and consider the special needs of particular employee populations (for example, non-English speakers).

5. *Appoint an AIDS resource person within the company.* This individual should be responsible for answering questions about the company's AIDS policy, benefits, and other personnel issues related to AIDS. By designating one person, a company can be assured of confidentiality for individual employees, as well as dissemination of correct information to the employees at large.

6. *Conduct in-house educational workshops.* Employees may feel more comfortable and trusting of an in-house workshop rather than outside resource organizations, and they are relatively easy to conduct and are effective. Members of the resource/education committee, the human resources department, and the EAP should contribute to the meeting. The Red Cross and state department of health can provide extensive information about and guidelines for conducting an in-house AIDS education seminar.

7. *Consider the information to be presented in the educational program.* One of the most controversial areas in AIDS education is the subject of safer sex. It would be hypocritical not to include this as a major area of education. Prevention is the only weapon to fight the spread of the disease. The basics of AIDS prevention should be incorporated in the employee educational package. Distribution to and discussion of the information to family and friends should be emphasized.

In addition, the program should address the following issues:

▴ All employees should be educated. Mandatory or required attendance for all managers and supervisors and all employees is important in order for the educational program to complete its goal of comprehension, clarity, and consistency.

▴ The number of employees per education group should not exceed thirty, to ensure an effective presentation.

▴ The educational program should be conducted in such a way as to protect any persons with AIDS in the company.

In addition, education provided on company time is more likely to be favorably received and increases management's credibility.

EDUCATION AND MANAGERS AND SUPERVISORS

When managers and supervisors are trained to deal with AIDS, issues such as confidentiality, legal obligations, and co-worker stress come into focus. Some common concerns of managers and supervisors who have had to deal with AIDS in their department include the following:

▴ What should I do if someone in my department is suspected of having AIDS?

▴ How do I handle a rumor that someone in my work group has AIDS?

▴ Can I insist that an employee be tested for AIDS?

▴ How do I handle the issue of confidentiality if an employee who has AIDS wishes to remain anonymous?

▴ What are my legal obligations to an employee with AIDS?

▴ What are my obligations to co-workers who must work with an employee who has AIDS?

▴ What benefits are employees with AIDS entitled to?

▴ What should I do if employees react with a sudden outburst of panic because of a co-worker who has AIDS?

▴ Is there counseling available for employees with AIDS or any other life-threatening illnesses?[20]

Managers and supervisors must be trained and prepared to deal with AIDS-related issues in the workplace. Ongoing training seminars and education programs on AIDS can be used to provide information on the latest medical developments, to provide advice on how to recognize and handle situations that arise in organizations, and to convey the importance of maintaining the confidentiality of any medical and other information about employees' health status. In addition, managers and supervisors should be given someone in the company to call to obtain further information or to discuss problems in their departments. Companies should provide training and guidance activities *before* problems arise.

EVALUATION OF THE EDUCATION PROGRAM

A confidential evaluation by employees on presentation of material and policy, videotapes, the educator, and written material is necessary after the initial educational effort is complete. Another way to evaluate the success of an AIDS education program is to note what has *not* occurred since the program's inception. Companies that have implemented a policy note such nonevents as the following:

- People no longer refuse to work with employees who are diagnosed with AIDS.
- Companies are not criticized about the uncertainty of their stand on AIDS.
- There are no outbreaks of panic. (A company AIDS educational program, however, is not a guarantee that there will not be any work disruption.)

Employee Reactions to AIDS in the Workplace

Dr. David M. Herold of the Georgia Institute of Technology has conducted the only research concerning employee attitudes and behavior about AIDS in the workplace.[21] Details on the survey and its results follow, printed with Dr. Herold's permission.

(*text continues on page 339*)

Background

In order to better understand the nature of workers' beliefs and attitudes about AIDS, a national probability sample of American households was used to conduct telephone interviews with over 2,000 workers who were at least 18 years old, worked full-time, were civilian employees, and were not self-employed. Interviewees were assured that their responses will be treated with complete confidentiality and reported only as part of a nationwide sample. For a sample of this size, the chances are 95 in 100 (0.95 confidence level) that survey results differ by no more than $+/-3\%$ from the similarly defined U.S. worker population.

The survey focused on four areas of particular interest: (1) the extent and types of fears people have concerning contact with AIDS patients, (2) people's willingness to accommodate workers who have AIDS, (3) people's beliefs about issues thought to be central to their attitudes towards AIDS, and (4) the extent to which people in the workforce have personal knowledge of people with AIDS. The questions and results are reported below.

Findings

Fears Concerning Contact With Employees Known to Have AIDS

If a person were known to have AIDS:

	Yes	No
1. Would you be concerned about using the same bathroom?	66%	34%
2. Would you be concerned about eating in the same cafeteria?	40%	60%
3. Would you be willing to share tools or equipment with the individual?	63%	37%

Comments: As can be seen here, substantial portions of the work population expressed concerns or fears about sharing facilities and/or tools with people who have AIDS. The percentages of people fearful of using bathrooms and cafeterias suggest possible disruptions of day-to-day activities in organizations. The fact that over one third of the sample would be unwilling to share tools or equipment could have severe implications for those jobs where such contact or sharing is essential. . . .

Willingness to Accommodate

If a person were known to have AIDS:

	Yes	No
1. Would you favor making special work arrangements for the individual if his or her health deteriorated?	75%	25%
2. Would you be willing to help the individual perform aspects of the job with which he or she was having difficulty?	81%	19%

Comments: In contrast to the rather negative views expressed in the last set of items, this set indicates a strong degree of sympathy for the AIDS-afflicted co-worker. A strong majority of workers favor making special arrangements to accommodate the AIDS patients, with an overwhelming proportion offering to provide assistance. . . .

Associated Beliefs

	Unlikely	Unsure	Likely
1. What are the chances that people who are thought to have various illnesses are really covering up the fact that they have AIDS?	22%	36%	42%

(continued)

	Yes	No
2. Do you believe the reported evidence that AIDS can only be transmitted by sexual contact or blood contamination?	65%	35%

Comments: This set of items offers interesting insights into the fears and concerns expressed in the first set of items. Namely, over one-third of the workers in the sample do not believe the bulk of the information which has been offered by government agencies such as the C.D.C. [Center for Disease Control], and the medical profession, concerning how AIDS is transmitted. If the alternative personal hypothesis is that casual contact may lead to the transmittal of the disease, then it is easy to see why such contact would be feared. The finding concerning beliefs that people are covering up the fact that they have AIDS is a potentially important issue, since it suggests a certain level of hysteria, as illnesses which have similar symptoms (e.g. pneumonia, leukemia, skin cancer) are rumored by workers to be AIDS. This would probably be especially true if the affected worker belongs to one of the so-called "high risk" groups.

Personal Knowledge

	Yes	No
1. Do you personally know anyone who has the disease AIDS or who has died from it?	14%	86%

Comments: This last item was intended to assess the penetration of AIDS into the lives of the general population. . . .

Recommendations

The data suggest two general areas in which considerable work needs to be done by organizations. First, major educational agendas need to be addressed if the workplace is to impact those workers' beliefs and attitudes which may form the basis for future problematical behaviors. Second, organizations need to realize that corporate denial, or pat answers and solutions are not likely to address the problems which are likely to be encountered. A proactive and integrated approach must be taken.

Education: There is no question but that any corporate response to AIDS in the workplace will need to have a strong educational component. The data from the present survey reveal a strong need for education. Furthermore, the data point out that different messages may be needed for different audiences, and, perhaps more importantly, that some messages may be heard but not believed.

AIDS education for all segments of society is vital. The workplace cannot rely on the media, schools, or churches to provide the necessary education about AIDS to its employees. It is too vast and complex an issue and demands that all institutions work together to educate the entire population. It is in the workplace's best interest to take responsibility for educating employees.

Other Populations Affected by HIV

A comprehensive policy and educational package must contain components that focus on special work populations that might be at risk, such as health care workers, emergency personnel, police and firefighters, and personal service workers, and special work populations, such as women, children, minorities, and drug-addicted employees.

Special Work Populations

People do not contract AIDS by doing the tasks they are paid to do in the workplace. No evidence suggests that organizations need to take special precautions or establish procedures designed to prevent the spread of AIDS in the workplace. Nevertheless, certain workers (such as food handlers, personal service workers, police and firefighters, other rescue personnel, and medical and dental personnel) may be at increased risk.[22] It is now federal law that U.S. workplaces must comply with regulations and guidelines for a safe working environment for all their employees. Although most applicable to health care workplaces, these guidelines provide a set of regulations and guidelines designed to prevent the transmission of the AIDS virus in any workplace.

With advice from health care professionals, the Occupational Safety and Health Administration (OSHA) has made recommendations to protect workers from HIV and HBV (the virus that causes hepatitis B). These precautions should be practiced routinely; they are aimed at preventing the transmission of these viruses and other blood-borne–type infections. These guidelines are for *all* workplaces, not just those at increased risk for HIV transmission. The following recommendations are from OSHA's guidelines:[23]

Personal Protective Equipment

- Use gloves where blood, blood products, or body fluids will be handled.
- Use gowns, masks, and eye protectors for procedures that could involve more extensive splashing of blood or body fluids.
- Use pocket masks, resuscitation bags, or other ventilation devices to resuscitate a patient to minimize exposure that may occur during

emergency mouth-to-mouth resuscitation. Employers should place these devices where the need for resuscitation is likely.

Workplace Practices

- Wash hands thoroughly after removing gloves, and immediately after contact with blood or body fluids.
- Use disposable needles and syringes whenever possible. Do not recap, bend, or cut needles. Place sharp instruments in a specially designated puncture-resistant container located as close as practical to the area where they are used. Handle and dispose of them with extraordinary care to prevent accidental injury.
- Follow general guidelines for sterilization, disinfection, housekeeping, and waste disposal. Use appropriate protective equipment. Place potentially infective waste in impervious bags and dispose of them as local regulations require.
- Clean up blood spills immediately with detergent and water. Use a solution of 5.25 percent sodium hypochlorite (household bleach) diluted at 2–10 parts water for disinfection, or other suitable disinfectant.
- Treat all blood and body fluids as potentially infectious.

Education

- Know the modes of transmission and prevention of these infections.

Enforcement of OSHA standards

- Various OSHA standards apply to exposure to both HIV and HBV. These standards cover personal protective equipment, sanitation, and waste disposal.

The other side of the question of the health care worker and AIDS is the HIV-infected health care worker still performing his or her duties. A superior court judge had ruled in New Jersey that a surgeon infected with the AIDS virus must inform patients before operating on them:

> In what is believed to be the first court ruling in the nation to weigh the protection of a health-care worker's confidentiality against a patient's right to know, the judge said, "If there is to be an ultimate arbiter of whether the patient is to be treated invasively by an AIDS-positive surgeon, the arbiter will be the fully informed patient."[24]

This decision is more severe than the CDC's guidelines, which recommend that infected physicians voluntarily suspend performing procedures that carry a risk of transmission or seek the approval of local committees.

Women and HIV Infection

The rate of HIV infection in women has risen steadily. As of October 31, 1991, of the 192,406 cases of adult and adolescent cases of AIDS reported in the United States, 10 percent were women. Women are becoming dramatically affected by AIDS. Whether they are at direct risk for infection or are caretaking AIDS-infected family or friends, AIDS-related issues have a profound effect on their relationships to their loved ones and their partners. The workplace offers an efficient and powerful setting for reaching the largest number of women possible.

Minorities and HIV Infection

Although blacks comprise 11.5 percent of the U.S. population, they make up a much larger proportion of persons with AIDS: 29 percent. The same is true for Hispanics, who constitute 7 percent of the nation's population but make up 16 percent of people with AIDS. Other minorities have lesser rates of infection. Asian/Pacific Islanders make up 1.6 percent of the U.S. population, but AIDS cases among this group constitute 0.6 percent of all AIDS cases. And the percentage of all AIDS cases among American Indians and Alaskan natives is 0.1 percent, although they represent somewhat less than 1 percent of the population.

The issues surrounding minorities and HIV infection involve more than statistical communication and precautionary measures necessary for preventing the spread of the virus. When educating minorities about the spread of the disease, businesses must be sensitive to the issue of discrimination and its repercussions. They need a full understanding of all the issues surrounding minorities and AIDS to provide a comprehensive, effective, and accurate AIDS education program.

Children and AIDS

As of October 31, 1991, the CDC had received reports of 3,312 cases of AIDS reported in children (under 13) and 751 in adolescents (ages 13–19). This is an important workplace issue not only because of the emotional impact on affected employees but also because the workplace pays the health bills for children of employees. Parents and other loved ones of children with AIDS need support and information; this should be offered through the EAP and human resources departments.

Teenagers and AIDS

A workplace education program should provide employees with access to information that can help them educate the young people in their lives about AIDS. The program should address the issue of educating the employees as well as their children. Employers know that teenage substance abuse is costing them the largest share of their escalating mental health budget. What they have not yet perceived is that this population is also vulnerable to AIDS and may even now be carrying the virus. Additionally, employers will be faced with the financial cost of AIDS treatment for these teenagers unless the behavior of substance-abusing adolescents is changed. AIDS education at the work site must address employees who are parents of teenagers.

AIDS and Drugs

The Rehabilitation Act of 1973, as interpreted in 1978 by the attorney general at the request of the U.S. Department of Health and Human Services secretary, Joseph Califano, as well as subsequent Supreme Court decisions supporting it, have defined drug abuse clearly as a disease. It is important for executives, managers, and employees to understand that they must set aside their own biases toward drug abusers and approach these individuals as people who have a disease and need to be treated accordingly. On the other hand, it is not impossible to understand the mixed feelings experienced by the employer who often has to pay the medical bills for such employees. These are exceedingly difficult issues and must be handled with thoughtfulness and sensitivity.

Since the stereotype of needle-using addicts is usually thought to be minority members and poor, employers tend to assume that these individuals are unemployed or unemployable and therefore not in the work force. This is not the case. In fact, many addicts hold jobs and often cannot be distinguished from any other employee. In addition, many professionals and paraprofessionals use drugs (alcohol, sedatives, and stimulants like amphetamines) recreationally. Mood-altering substances often reduce inhibitions, and the likelihood that users will practice safer sex decreases dramatically.[25]

Conclusion

The workplace represents a key part of society. Not only must companies manage the issue of AIDS within their organizations, but they also must take responsibility to join the fight against AIDS in society at large. In many ways, AIDS has become society's biggest social challenge.

NOTES

1. Kathleen C. Brown and Joan G. Turner, *AIDS, Policies and Programs for the Workplace* (New York: Van Nostrand Reinhold, 1989), p. 39.
2. Presidential Commission on the Human Immunodeficiency Virus Epidemic, "Chairman's Recommendations" (Washington, D.C.: February 29, 1988) p. 23.

3. Anthony R. Measham, "Subject: World Health Organization/Global Programme on AIDS (WHO/GPA) Management Committee Meeting, Geneva, December 6–8, 1989," World Bank/International Finance Corp./Multilateral Investment Guarantee Agency Office memorandum, p. 1.

4. The Centers for Disease Control AIDS hotlines (404-330-3020; 3021; 3022) provide statistics that are updated monthly.

5. Patricia Gadsby, "AIDS Watch," *Discover* (April 1988): 31.

6. U.S. Department of Health and Human Services, "Human Immunodeficiency Virus in the United States: A Review of Current Knowledge," *Morbidity and Mortality Weekly Report* 36, No. 5–6 (Dec. 18, 1987): 10.

7. Richard Golob and Eric Brus, eds., *The Almanac of Science and Technology: What's New and What's Known*, (New York: Harcourt Brace Jovanovich, 1990), p. 387.

8. *Surgeon General's Report on Acquired Immune Deficiency Syndrome*, (Washington, D.C.: U.S. Department of Health and Human Services and the American Red Cross, 1987), p. 21.

9. Glover v. Eastern Nebraska Community Office of Retardation, 686 *Fed. Suppl.* 243 (1988).

10. D. Masi and R. Maiden, "AIDS in the Workplace, Part II," *ALMACAN* (February 1986): 30.

11. Rehabilitation Act of 1973, Public Law 93-112:87 Stat. 355, September 26, 1973.

12. School Board of Nassau County v. Arline (U.S.S. Ct. 1987); Chalk v. Orange County (9th Cir. 1988); Shuttleworth v. Broward County (S.D. Fla. 1986).

13. Oregon Administrative Opinion (1/9/88). State and district laws in Washington, D.C., Massachusetts, and Wisconsin. *National Gay Rights v. Alvida* (Florida). Illinois Administrative Opinion (1/1/88).

14. Maryland Center for Business Management, "AIDS in the Workplace and Other Catastrophic Diseases," joint presentation by the Maryland Center for Business Management and M. Rosenberg and Co., Johns Hopkins University School of Hygiene and Public Health, and Educational Center of Sheppard Pratt, Division of Employee Assistance Programs, October 22, 1987, p. 4.

15. Sam B. Puckett and Alan R. Emery, *Managing AIDS in the Workplace*, (Reading, Mass.: Addison-Wesley, 1988), p. 65.

16. Allstate Forum on Public Issues, "Corporate America Responds" (Allstate, 1987), pp. 6–7.

17. Bryan Lawton, Ph.D., notes from a speech presented at NIDA Meeting: HIV/AIDS in the Workplace.

18. Presidential Commission on the Human Immunodeficiency Virus Epidemic, *Chairman's Recommendations*, p. 28.

19. Masi and Maiden, "AIDS in the Workplace," p. 29.

20. Allstate Forum, "Corporate America Responds," p. 9.

21. David M. Herold, "Employees' Reactions to AIDS in the Workplace" (Atlanta: Center for Work Performance Problems, College of Management, Georgia Institute of Technology, February 1988), pp. 4–9.

22. Mark A. Katz, "Understanding AIDS: A Personal Handbook for Employees and Managers," *Employee Benefits Review* 1 (1988): 28.

23. Katz, "Understanding AIDS," p. 29.

24. Joseph F. Sullivan, "Judge Rules Surgeons Infected with AIDS Must Tell Patients," *New York Times*, April 26, 1991, p. B-1.
25. Edith Springer, "Drug Dependency: A Conduit for AIDS," *Executive Briefing* 2, no. 6 (June 1989): 2.

NATIONAL AND INTERNATIONAL RESOURCE LIST FOR AIDS

There are many resources that provide information about AIDS and the workplace. Those available at the local level can be found through the local chapter of the American Red Cross, and city, state, or county health departments. Accurate information pertaining to AIDS, state and local health policies, and HIV testing sites may be obtained through local resources and in the resources that follow. Larger cities have AIDS service agencies that can provide speakers and literature, in addition to direct services for people with AIDS.

National AIDS Organizations

Centers for Disease Control
Office of Public Inquiries
1600 Clifton Road, N.W.
Building 1, Room B63
Atlanta, GA 30333
(404) 639-3534

American Red Cross National
   Headquarters
AIDS Education Program
Seventeenth and D Streets, N.W.
Washington, DC 20006
(202) 639-3223

National Institutes of Health
Building 1, Room 307
Bethesda, MD 20892
(301) 496-5787

U.S. Public Health Service
Public Affairs Office
Hubert H. Humphrey Building,
   Room 725-H
200 Independence Avenue, S.W.
Washington, DC 20201
(202) 245-6867

Pan American Health
   Organization
World Health Organization
525 Twenty-third Street, N.W.,
   Room A108
Washington, DC 20037
(202) 861-3457

U.S. Conference of Mayors
1620 Eye Street, N.W.
Washington, DC 20001
(202) 293-7330

Planned Parenthood Federation of
   America
2010 Massachusetts Avenue,
   N.W., Suite 500
Washington, DC 20036
(202) 785-3351

People with AIDS Coalition
263A West Nineteenth Street
New York, NY 10011
(212) 532-0290

National Lesbian and Gay Health
  Foundation
P.O. Box 65472
Washington, DC 20035
(202) 797-3708

Gay Men's Health Crisis
Box 274, 132 West Twenty-fourth
  Street
New York, NY 10011
(212) 807-7517

San Francisco AIDS Foundation
25 Van Ness Avenue
San Francisco, CA 94102
(415) 864-4376

AIDS Project Los Angeles
7362 Santa Monica Boulevard
Los Angeles, CA 90046
(213) 876-AIDS

AIDS Action Committee
661 Boylston Street
Boston, MA 02116
(617) 437-6200

Minnesota AIDS Project
2025 Nicollett Avenue
  South #200
Minneapolis, MN 55404
(612) 870-7773

AIDS and the Workplace Resources

OSHA Information Office
200 Constitution Ave., S.W.,
  Room N3647
Washington, DC 20210
(202) 523-8148

National Leadership Coalition on
  AIDS
1150 Seventeenth Street, N.W.,
  Suite 202
Washington, DC 20036
(202) 429-0930

Service Employees International
  Union
A.F.L.-C.I.O.
1313 L Street, N.W.
Washington, DC 20005
(202) 898-2300

Workplace Health
  Communications Corporation/
  Institute for Disease Prevention
  in the Workplace
4 Madison Place
Albany, NY 12202
(518) 456-1854

Minority and Women's Organizations

National Minority AIDS Council
714 G Street, S.E.
Washington, DC 20003
(202) 544-1076

Minority Task Force on AIDS
New York City Council of
  Churches
475 Riverside Drive
New York, NY 10015
(212) 749-1214

National Coalition of Hispanic
  Health and Human Service
  Organizations
1030 Fifteenth Street, N.W., Suite
  1053
Washington, DC 20005
(202) 371-2100

National Jewish AIDS Project
1082 Columbia Road, Suite 32
Washington, DC 20009
(202) 387-3097

Hispanic AIDS Forum
c/o APRED
853 Broadway, Suite 2007
New York, NY 10003
(212) 870-1902, (212) 870-1864

Haitian Coalition
50 Court Street
Brooklyn, NY 11201
(718) 855-0972

Mothers of AIDS Patients
c/o Barbara Peabody
3403 E Street
San Diego, CA 92102
(619) 544-0430

AWARE (Women and AIDS)
Ward 84
San Francisco General Hospital
995 Potrero Avenue
San Francisco, CA 94110
(415) 476-4091

Stuyvesant Polyclinic
Women and AIDS Counseling
  Group
137 Second Avenue
New York, NY 10003
(212) 674-0267

Women and AIDS Project
1209 Decater Street, N.W.
Washington, DC 20011
(202) 387-4898

Women's AIDS Resource
  Network
P.O. Box 020525
New York, NY 11202
(718) 596-6007

Hemophiliac AIDS Organizations

World Hemophilia AIDS Center
2400 South Flower Street
Los Angeles, CA 90007
(213) 742-1357

National Hemophilia Foundation
Resource and Consultation Center
  for AIDS/HIV Infection
110 Greene Street
New York, NY 10012
(212) 219-8180

Hot Lines

National Hot Lines

National Gay and Lesbian Crisis Line	800-767-4297
National STD Hotline/American Social Health Association	800-227-8922
Public Health Service AIDS Hotline	800-342-AIDS
	800-342-2437

Hot Lines

Alabama	800-455-3741	Nevada	
Alaska	800-478-2437	Reno	702-329-AIDS
Arizona	800-334-1540	Las Ve-	
Arkansas	800-445-7720	gas	702-383-1393
California		New Jersey	800-624-2377
Northern	800-FOR-AIDS	New Mex-	
Southern	800-922-AIDS	ico	505-827-0006
Colorado	303-331-8305	New York	800-462-1884
Connect-		North	
icut	203-566-1157	Carolina	919-733-7301
Delaware	302-995-8422	North Da-	
District of		kota	800-592-1861
Colum-		Ohio	800-332-AIDS
bia	202-332-AIDS	Oklahoma	405-271-6434
Florida	800-FLA-AIDS	Oregon	503-229-5792
Georgia	800-551-2728	Pennsyl-	
Hawaii	808-922-1313	vania	800-692-7254
Idaho	208-334-5944	Rhode Is-	
Illinois	800-AID-AIDS	land	402-227-6502
Indiana	317-633-8406	South	
Iowa	800-532-3301	Carolina	800-332-AIDS
Kansas	800-232-0400	South Da-	
Kentucky	800-654-AIDS	kota	800-472-2180
Louisiana	800-992-4379	Tennessee	800-342-AIDS
Maine	800-551-AIDS	Texas	
Maryland	800-638-6252	Dallas	214-559-AIDS
Massa-		Houston	713-524-AIDS
chusetts	800-235-2331	Utah	800-843-9388
Minnesota	800-248-AIDS	Vermont	800-882-AIDS
Mississippi	800-826-2961	West	
Montana	406-252-1212	Virginia	800-642-8244
Nebraska	800-782-2437	Wisconsin	800-334-AIDS
		Wyoming	307-777-7953

National Resource Service Directories

Educational and informational material regarding HIV and full-blown AIDS may be obtained through these services. The procedure calls for an interested party to receive a summary of their available information, and then relevant materials will be forwarded.

American Foundation for AIDS
  Research
1515 Broadway, Thirty-sixth
  Floor
New York, NY 10036
(212) 719-0033

National AIDS Information
  Clearinghouse
U.S. Department of Health and
  Human Services
P.O. Box 6003
Rockville, MD 20850
(800) 458-5231 (multiple copies);
  (800) 342-AIDS (single copies);
  (800) 344-SIDA (Spanish
  speaking); (800) AIDS-TTY
  (TDD/TTY) (deaf and hard of
  hearing)

International Resources

Australia/New Zealand

National AIDS Coordinating
  Committee
Commonwealth Department of
  Health
P.O. Box 100
Woden, 06, Australia

Victorian AIDS Council
P.O. Box 174 Richmond
Melbourne 3121, Australia

New Zealand AIDS Foundation
Auckland Hospital
Auckland, New Zealand

Canada

AIDS Vancouver
1033 Davie Street
Vancouver, B.C.

AIDS Committee of Toronto
556 Church Street
Toronto, Ontario

Centretown Community
  Resources
100 Argyle Avenue
Ottawa, Ontario

Comité SIDA du Quebec
3757 rue Prud'homme
Montreal, Quebec

Europe

Terrence Higgins Trust
BM AIDS
London, WCIN, England

AIDS Policy Coordination
Burgo GVO
Prins Hendricklaan 12
1075 BB Amsterdam, Holland

Deutsch AIDS-Hilfe
Neibuhrstrasse 71
1000 Berlin 12, Germany

SIDA STUDI
Bruc, 26, prol
08010 Barcelona, Spain

Mexico

Puerto Rico

CONA SIDA
Ministry of Health
Mexico, D.F.

Fundación AIDS de Puerto Rico
Call Box AIDS
Louisa Street Station
San Juan, P.R. 00914

Videotaped Material on AIDS for the Workplace

Videotapes are available through local AIDS agencies and the Red Cross.

"Bill: A Special Story"
Council on Foundations
1828 L Street, N.W.
Washington, DC 20036
(202) 466-6512

"A Letter from Brian"
American Foundation for AIDS
    Research
Ambrosia Home Video
    Publishing, Department 1087
381 Park Avenue, Suite 1601
New York, NY 10016
(800) 526-4663

"Beyond Fear," produced by the
    American Red Cross

"Don't Forget Sherrie" (provides
    information for blacks and
    urban youth), produced by the
    American Red Cross

Index

[Page references to illustrations are printed in *italics*.]

About the Editor

Dale A. Masi is professor at the University of Maryland School of Social Work and an adjunct professor at the College of Business and Management. She is also president of Masi Research Consultants, Inc., which specializes in employee assistance programs and managed mental health design and evaluation. Dr. Masi is the recipient of many awards and has published widely. Her most recent book is *AIDS Issues in the Workplace*. Dr. Masi holds a doctorate from Catholic University of America. She was a Fulbright scholar and held a postdoctoral research grant from the American Association of University Women.

About the Contributors

Lee I. Dogoloff is executive director of the American Council for Drug Education and maintains a private clinical practice specializing in the treatment of drug and alcohol problems. The author of numerous articles, he frequently provides expert commentary to the media. He has received the Distinguished Service Award for his work with the White House Special Action Office for Drug Abuse Prevention.

Muriel Gray is an assistant professor at the University of Maryland at Baltimore School of Social Work and director of EAP Healthcare Institute, a training and consultation firm for workplace issues. She has written numerous publications on employee assistance, substance abuse, counseling, and workplace program development.

Rob Gunther-Mohr is associate director of and consultant to the Center for Essential Workplace Skills. His professional interests focus on workplace skills program management and supervision, course and curriculum design, and training and education issues for adults with learning deficits.

Denise F. Loftus is manager of work force education at the American Association of Retired Persons. In this capacity, she provides retirement planning programs through employers, agencies, and community organizations, directs career development and job search programs for older workers, and develops training programs on issues affecting the recruitment, management, and training of older workers.

Frank P. Louchheim is chairman and chief executive officer of Right Associates. He has also served as the head of an outplacement firm and has been a consultant.

Ethel W. McConaghy, a child care advocate and planner, is vice-president and director of the Midwest office of Work/Family Directions, Inc., a national firm providing dependent care programs and consultation. She frequently presents papers at conferences and is a founding member of the National Association of Resource and Referral Agencies.

Diane S. Piktialis is vice-president for elder care at Work/Farmily Directions, Inc., where she heads development and management of elder care services for corporate clients. She has extensive experience in gerontology and aging services and is an expert on corporate elder care. She frequently presents papers at professional meetings.

Stirling Rasmussen is the manager of organization development and training for *The Washington Post*, where he and his staff have created a performance review and counseling process. He has done graduate work at George Washington University's business school, specializing in organizational behavior, and has worked in the public sector.

Deborah Jaffe Sandroff is executive director of the Worksite Wellness Council of Greater Chicago, which assists member organizations in all phases of health promotion programming. She has also worked at AT&T as a regional manager for its Total Life Concept Program, implementing on-site health promotion at large and small locations for a variety of employee populations.

Linda Stoker is director of the Center for Essential Workplace Skills, where she assists organizations with training and education program planning, problem solving, design and development of programs and courses, and staff training. A pioneer in the development of applications of basic skills programs in the workplace, she has written several articles on workplace education programs.

Gerald M. Sturman is chairman and chief executive officer of The Career Development Team, Inc., a national corporate training firm that designs, develops, and delivers a wide variety of programs in career management. He is the author of *If You Knew Who You Were . . . You Could Be Who You Are!* and *Managing Your Career with "POWER."*

Christine Z. Tafe is an assistant vice-president of Merrill Lynch & Co., Inc., where she manages employee relocations. In the past, she has done home finding and group move counseling. Her first experience with the relocation process was as a "trailing spouse."